IFIP Advances in Information and Communication Technology

433

IFIP – The International Federation for Information Processing

IFIP was founded in 1960 under the auspices of UNESCO, following the First World Computer Congress held in Paris the previous year. An umbrella organization for societies working in information processing, IFIP's aim is two-fold: to support information processing within its member countries and to encourage technology transfer to developing nations. As its mission statement clearly states,

> *IFIP's mission is to be the leading, truly international, apolitical organization which encourages and assists in the development, exploitation and application of information technology for the bene t of all people.*

IFIP is a non-profitmaking organization, run almost solely by 2500 volunteers. It operates through a number of technical committees, which organize events and publications. IFIP's events range from an international congress to local seminars, but the most important are:

- The IFIP World Computer Congress, held every second year;
- Open conferences;
- Working conferences.

The flagship event is the IFIP World Computer Congress, at which both invited and contributed papers are presented. Contributed papers are rigorously refereed and the rejection rate is high.

As with the Congress, participation in the open conferences is open to all and papers may be invited or submitted. Again, submitted papers are stringently refereed.

The working conferences are structured differently. They are usually run by a working group and attendance is small and by invitation only. Their purpose is to create an atmosphere conducive to innovation and development. Refereeing is also rigorous and papers are subjected to extensive group discussion.

Publications arising from IFIP events vary. The papers presented at the IFIP World Computer Congress and at open conferences are published as conference proceedings, while the results of the working conferences are often published as collections of selected and edited papers.

Any national society whose primary activity is about information processing may apply to become a full member of IFIP, although full membership is restricted to one society per country. Full members are entitled to vote at the annual General Assembly, National societies preferring a less committed involvement may apply for associate or corresponding membership. Associate members enjoy the same benefits as full members, but without voting rights. Corresponding members are not represented in IFIP bodies. Affiliated membership is open to non-national societies, and individual and honorary membership schemes are also offered.

Gilbert Peterson   Sujeet Shenoi (Eds.)

Advances in Digital Forensics X

10th IFIP WG 11.9 International Conference
Vienna, Austria, January 8-10, 2014
Revised Selected Papers

 Springer

Volume Editors

Gilbert Peterson
Air Force Institute of Technology
Wright-Patterson Air Force Base, OH 45433-7765, USA
E-mail: gilbert.peterson@afit.edu

Sujeet Shenoi
University of Tulsa
Tulsa, OK 74104-3189, USA
E-mail: sujeet@utulsa.edu

ISSN 1868-4238   e-ISSN 1868-422X
ISBN 978-3-662-52608-8   e-ISBN 978-3-662-44952-3
DOI 10.1007/978-3-662-44952-3
Springer Heidelberg New York Dordrecht London

Typesetting: Camera-ready by author, data conversion by Scientific Publishing Services, Chennai, India

Printed on acid-free paper

Springer is part of Springer Science+Business Media (www.springer.com)

Contents

PART II   FORENSIC TECHNIQUES

PART III   MOBILE DEVICE FORENSICS

Contents

Contributing Authors

Oluwasola Mary Adedayo is a Lecturer and Ph.D. student in Computer Science at the University of Pretoria, Pretoria, South Africa. Her research interests include digital forensics and database security.

Sadia Afroz is a Postdoctoral Researcher in the Computer Science Division at the University of California at Berkeley, Berkeley, California. Her research interests include security, privacy and machine learning.

Waqas Ali is an M.S./M.Phil. student in Information Security at the National University of Sciences and Technology, Islamabad, Pakistan. His research interests include vulnerability discovery, penetration testing and digital forensics.

Panagiotis Andriotis is a Ph.D. student in Computer Science at the University of Bristol, Bristol, United Kingdom. His research interests include digital forensics, content analysis and systems security.

Ibrahim Baggili is an Assistant Professor of Computer Science at the University of New Haven, West Haven, Connecticut. His research interests include digital forensics and cyber crime.

Harald Baier is a Professor of Internet Security at the Darmstadt University of Applied Sciences, Darmstadt, Germany; and a Principal Investigator at the Center for Advanced Security Research Darmstadt, Darmstadt, Germany. His research areas include digital forensics, network-based anomaly detection and security protocols.

Stefanie Beyer received her M.Sc. degree in Computer Science from the Vienna University of Technology, Vienna, Austria. Her research interests are in the area of digital forensics, with a focus on the reliability of digital alibis.

Clive Blackwell is a Research Fellow in Digital Forensics at Oxford Brookes University, Oxford, United Kingdom. His research interests include cyber security and digital forensics, with a focus on developing a scientific basis for digital forensics.

Frank Breitinger is a Ph.D. student in Computer Science at the Darmstadt University of Applied Sciences, Darmstadt, Germany; and a Researcher at the Center for Advanced Security Research Darmstadt, Darmstadt, Germany. His research interests include digital forensics, file analysis and approximate matching.

Patrick Brennan is the Chief Executive Officer of Juola and Associates, Pittsburgh, Pennsylvania. His research interests include digital forensics and stylometry.

Vivien Chan is a Research Project Manager at the University of Hong Kong, Hong Kong, China. Her research interests include cyber criminal profiling and digital forensics.

Ahmad Raza Cheema is an Assistant Professor of Information Security at the National University of Sciences and Technology, Islamabad, Pakistan. His research interests include network security and digital forensics.

Kim-Kwang Choo is a Senior Lecturer of Cyber Security at the University of South Australia, Adelaide, Australia. His research interests include anti-money laundering, cyber crime, digital forensics and information security.

Kam-Pui Chow is an Associate Professor of Computer Science at the University of Hong Kong, Hong Kong, China. His research interests include information security, digital forensics, live system forensics and digital surveillance.

Philip Craiger is an Associate Professor of Engineering Technology at Daytona State College, Daytona Beach, Florida. His research interests include the technical and behavioral aspects of information security and digital forensics.

Quang Do is a Ph.D. student in Computer and Information Science at the University of South Australia, Adelaide, Australia. His research interests include user privacy preservation and mobile device security.

Xiao-Xi Fan is a Ph.D. student in Computer Science at the University of Hong Kong, Hong Kong, China. Her research interests include digital forensics, digital profiling and data mining.

Tobias Fink is an M.Sc. student in Computer Science at the Darmstadt University of Applied Sciences, Darmstadt, Germany. His research interests include embedded systems and cryptography.

Guy Fong is a Senior Official with the Hong Kong Customs and Excise Department, Hong Kong, China. His research interests include intellectual property rights protection and intellectual property rights infringement in cyber platforms.

Alex Fridman is a Ph.D. student in Electrical and Computer Engineering at Drexel University, Philadelphia, Pennsylvania. His research interests include machine learning, numerical optimization, robotics and communications networks.

Simson Garfinkel is an Associate Professor of Computer Science at the Naval Postgraduate School (National Capital Region Office) in Arlington, Virginia. His research interests include security and privacy.

Kyle Gorak is a Cadet majoring in Computer Science at the U.S. Military Academy, West Point, New York. His research interests include security exploitation and encryption techniques.

Jayaprakash Govindaraj is a Senior Technology Architect at Infosys Labs, Bangalore, India; and a Ph.D. student in Computer Science and Engineering at Indraprastha Institute of Information Technology, New Delhi, India. His research interests include anti-forensic and anti-anti-forensic techniques for mobile devices.

Lukas Graner is a B.S. student in Computer Science at the Technical University of Darmstadt, Darmstadt, Germany. His research interests include digital forensic tool testing using synthetic test data.

Rachel Greenstadt is an Assistant Professor of Computer Science at Drexel University, Philadelphia, Pennsylvania. Her research centers on the privacy and security properties of intelligent systems and the economics of electronic privacy and information security.

Gaurav Gupta is an Assistant Professor of Computer Science at Indraprastha Institute of Information Technology, New Delhi, India. His research interests include digital forensics, digitized document fraud detection and mobile device forensics.

Aubin Heffernan is a Cadet majoring in Computer Science at the U.S. Military Academy, West Point, New York. His research interests include cyber security and digital forensics.

Scott Horras is a Cadet majoring in Computer Science at the U.S. Military Academy, West Point, New York. His research interests include artificial intelligence and data processing.

Markus Huber is a Computer Security Researcher at SBA Research, Vienna, Austria. His research focuses on security and privacy issues in social networks.

Aleksandar Hudic is a Researcher at the Austrian Institute of Technology, Vienna, Austria. His research interests are in the area of autonomic security management systems for distributed environments.

Michael Hui is a Senior Inspector with the Hong Kong Customs and Excise Department, Hong Kong, China. His research interests are in the area of intellectual property rights protection.

Ricci Ieong is the Director of eWalker Consulting, a digital forensics consultancy in Hong Kong, China; and a Researcher in Computer Science at the University of Hong Kong, Hong Kong, China. His research interests include live forensics, peer-to-peer forensics, cloud forensics and time correlation analysis.

Mian Muhammad Waseem Iqbal is a Lecturer of Information Security at the National University of Sciences and Technology, Islamabad, Pakistan. His research interests include network security and digital forensics.

Yasser Jafar received an M.S. degree in Information Technology (Cyber Security Specialization) from Zayed University, Abu Dhabi, United Arab Emirates. His research interests include digital forensics and information security.

Patrick Juola is a Co-Founder of Juola and Associates, Pittsburgh, Pennsylvania; and a Professor of Computer Science at Duquesne University, Pittsburgh, Pennsylvania. His research interests include humanities computing, computational psycholinguistics, and digital and linguistic forensics.

Tahar Kechadi is a Professor of Computer Science and Informatics at University College Dublin, Dublin, Ireland. His research interests include data extraction and analysis, and data mining in digital forensics and cyber crime investigations.

Katharina Krombholz is a Computer Security Researcher at SBA Research, Vienna, Austria; and a Ph.D. student in Computer Science at the Vienna University of Technology, Vienna, Austria. Her research interests include usable security and digital forensics.

Michael Kwan is an Honorary Assistant Professor of Computer Science at the University of Hong Kong, Hong Kong, China. His research interests include digital forensics, digital evidence evaluation and the application of probabilistic models in digital forensics.

Steffen Lange is a Professor of Theoretical Computer Science at the Darmstadt University of Applied Sciences, Darmstadt, Germany. His research interests include algorithmic learning theory, formal language theory and information technology security.

Nhien-An Le-Khac is a Lecturer of Computer Science and Informatics at University College Dublin, Dublin, Ireland. His research interests include data mining in criminal investigations, cloud security and privacy, and grid and high-performance computing.

Wee-Yong Lim is a Researcher in the Cybercrime and Security Intelligence Department at the Institute for Infocomm Research, Singapore. His research interests include predictive intelligence, text analysis, object recognition and machine learning.

Jonathan Looi received his Bachelor's degree in Information Technology from the University of South Australia, Adelaide, Australia. His research interests are in the area of digital forensics.

Andrew Marrington is an Assistant Professor of Information Technology at Zayed University, Dubai, United Arab Emirates. His research interests include digital forensics and information security.

Ben Martini is the Digital Forensics Research Administrator and a Ph.D. student in Computer and Information Science at the University of South Australia, Adelaide, Australia. His research interests include cyber security and digital forensics.

Martin Mulazzani is a Postdoctoral Researcher at SBA Research, Vienna, Austria. His research interests include digital forensics, privacy and applied security.

Martin Olivier is a Professor of Computer Science at the University of Pretoria, Pretoria, South Africa. His research interests include digital forensics and privacy.

Thomas Otterbein is a Researcher in the Secure Systems Laboratory at the Vienna University of Technology, Vienna, Austria. His research interests are in the area of digital forensics.

Rebekah Overdorf is a Ph.D. student in Computer Science at Drexel University, Philadelphia, Pennsylvania. Her research interests include security and privacy, machine learning and stylometry.

Heloise Pieterse is an M.Sc. student in Computer Science at the University of Pretoria, Pretoria South Africa. Her research interests include information security, digital forensics and mobile botnets.

Christian Platzer is a Senior Researcher and Head of the Secure Systems Laboratory at the Vienna University of Technology, Vienna, Austria. His research areas include malware analysis, digital forensics and network security.

Mark Pollitt recently retired from his position as an Associate Professor of Engineering Technology at Daytona State College, Daytona Beach, Florida. His research interests include digital forensics, textual and narrative theory, and knowledge management.

Mark Roeloffs is a Forensic Examiner at the Netherlands Forensic Institute, The Hague, The Netherlands. His research interests include digital forensics of mobile phones, navigation systems and other embedded systems.

Amit Sachan is a Researcher in the Cybercrime and Security Intelligence Department at the Institute for Infocomm Research, Singapore. His research interests include information security, digital forensics and digital rights management.

Sebastian Schrittwieser is a Lecturer of Information Security at the St. Polten University of Applied Sciences, St. Polten, Austria; and a Ph.D. candidate in Computer Science at the Vienna University of Technology, Vienna, Austria. His research interests include digital forensics, software protection and code obfuscation.

Michael Seefried is an M.Sc. student in Computer Science at the Darmstadt University of Applied Sciences, Darmstadt, Germany. His research interests include digital forensics and information security.

Martin Steinebach is the Head of Media Security and IT Forensics at the Fraunhofer Institute for Secure Information Technology, Darmstadt, Germany. His research interests include digital watermarking and robust hashing.

Ariel Stolerman is a Ph.D. student in Computer Science at Drexel University, Philadelphia, Pennsylvania. His research interests include security and privacy, applied machine learning and text analysis.

Atsuhiro Takasu is a Professor in the Digital Content and Media Services Research Division at the National Institute of Informatics, Tokyo, Japan. His research interests include symbol sequence and time series analysis based on statistical models and their application to information integration.

Jemy Tang is a Training Officer at the Electronic Crime Investigation Centre of the Hong Kong Customs and Excise Department, Hong Kong, China. His research interests include digital forensics and the analysis of cyber crime investigations.

Vrizlynn Thing leads the Cybercrime and Security Intelligence Department at the Institute for Infocomm Research, Singapore. Her research interests include network security, systems security, mobile device security, digital forensics and security analytics.

Theo Tryfonas is a Senior Lecturer in Systems Engineering at the University of Bristol, Bristol, United Kingdom. His research interests are in the areas of defense and security systems, and technologies for sustainable development.

Robin Verma is a Ph.D. student in Computer Science and Engineering at Indraprastha Institute of Information Technology, New Delhi, India. His research interests include digitized document fraud detection, mobile device forensics and cloud forensics.

Yu Wang received his Bachelor's degree in Information Technology from the University of South Australia, Adelaide, Australia. His research interests are in the area of digital forensics.

Edgar Weippl is the Research Director at SBA Research, Vienna, Austria; and an Associate Professor of Computer Science at the Vienna University of Technology, Vienna, Austria. His research focuses on information security and e-learning.

Christian Winter is a Research Associate in IT Forensics at the Fraunhofer Institute for Secure Information Technology, Darmstadt, Germany. His research interests include statistical forensics and fuzzy hashing.

Fei Xu is an Assistant Professor of Computer Science at the Institute of Information Engineering, Chinese Academy of Sciences, Beijing, China. Her research interests include information security and digital forensics.

York Yannikos is a Research Associate in IT Forensics at the Fraunhofer Institute for Secure Information Technology, Darmstadt, Germany. His research interests include digital forensic tool testing, synthetic test data generation and multimedia file carving.

Carolina Zarate is an undergraduate student in Computer Science at Carnegie Mellon University, Pittsburgh, Pennsylvania. Her research interests include cyber security and digital forensics.

Georg Ziroff received his B.Sc. degree in Computer Science from the Darmstadt University of Applied Sciences, Darmstadt, Germany. His research interests include approximate string matching and similarity hashing, and their applications in malware detection.

Preface

Digital forensics deals with the acquisition, preservation, examination, analysis and presentation of electronic evidence. Networked computing, wireless communications and portable electronic devices have expanded the role of digital forensics beyond traditional computer crime investigations. Practically every type of crime now involves some aspect of digital evidence; digital forensics provides the techniques and tools to articulate this evidence in legal proceedings. Digital forensics also has myriad intelligence applications; furthermore, it has a vital role in information assurance – investigations of security breaches yield valuable information that can be used to design more secure and resilient systems.

This book, *Advances in Digital Forensics X*, is the tenth volume in the annual series produced by IFIP Working Group 11.9 on Digital Forensics, an international community of scientists, engineers and practitioners dedicated to advancing the state of the art of research and practice in digital forensics. The book presents original research results and innovative applications in digital forensics. Also, it highlights some of the major technical and legal issues related to digital evidence and electronic crime investigations.

This volume contains twenty-two edited papers from the Tenth IFIP WG 11.9 International Conference on Digital Forensics, held at the Vienna University of Technology in Vienna, Austria on January 8–10, 2014. The papers were refereed by members of IFIP Working Group 11.9 and other internationally-recognized experts in digital forensics.

The chapters are organized into four sections: Internet crime investigations, forensic techniques, mobile device forensics, and forensic tools and training. The coverage of topics highlights the richness and vitality of the discipline, and offers promising avenues for future research in digital forensics.

This book is the result of the combined efforts of several individuals. In particular, we thank Martin Mulazzani and Yvonne Poul for their tireless work on behalf of IFIP Working Group 11.9. We also acknowledge the support provided by the National Science Foundation, National

Security Agency, Immigration and Customs Enforcement, Internal Revenue Service and U.S. Secret Service.

GILBERT PETERSON AND SUJEET SHENOI

I

INTERNET CRIME
INVESTIGATIONS

Chapter 1

CONDITIONAL WEIGHTED TRANSACTION AGGREGATION FOR CREDIT CARD FRAUD DETECTION

Wee-Yong Lim, Amit Sachan, and Vrizlynn Thing

Abstract   Credit card fraud causes substantial losses to credit card companies and consumers. Consequently, it is important to develop sophisticated and robust fraud detection techniques that can recognize the subtle differences between fraudulent and legitimate transactions. Current fraud detection techniques mainly operate at the transaction level or account level. However, neither strategy is foolproof against fraud, leaving room for alternative techniques and improvements to existing techniques. Transaction-level approaches typically involve the analysis and aggregation of previous transaction data to detect credit card fraud. However, these approaches usually consider all the transaction attributes to be equally important. The conditional weighted transaction aggregation technique described in this paper addresses this issue by leveraging supervised machine learning techniques to identify fraudulent transactions. Empirical comparisons with existing transaction level methods and other transaction aggregation based methods demonstrate the effectiveness of the proposed technique.

Keywords: Credit card fraud, transaction analysis, aggregation, machine learning

1.   Introduction

Credit card fraud causes significant losses to credit card companies and consumers. Security upgrades are constantly thwarted by fraudsters intent on stealing credit card data dumps. Given the prevalence of credit card theft, it is important to develop fraud detection techniques that can recognize the subtle differences between fraudulent and legitimate transactions.

Most credit card fraud detection techniques work at the transaction level and/or account level. Transaction-level fraud detection systems

G. Peterson and S. Shenoi (Eds.): Advances in Digital Forensics X, IFIP AICT 433, pp. 3–16, 2014.

classify individual transactions based on characteristics such as transaction amount and payment mode. A transaction-level model is limited because it does not consider previous transactions that could help identify fraudulent activities.

Account-level fraud detection systems model the normal behavior of consumers; a substantial deviation from normal behavior is an indicator of possible fraudulent activity. A typical example is an unexpected large online transaction from an account for which the vast majority of previous transactions were retail purchases at supermarkets. The account-level model can take into account the previous transactions of consumers, but it is limited by the impracticality of creating a global model based on all consumers.

Previous transactions are not considered in a transaction-level model because of the possibly large number of features that come into play. To address this drawback, Whitrow, *et al.* [9] proposed a transaction aggregation strategy that only aggregates transactions of the previous few days to boost fraud detection performance. The method works well compared with single transaction based methods. However, the primary limitation is that it treats all previous transactions as equal, ignoring the sequential nature of credit card transactions.

This paper describes the conditional aggregated transaction aggregation method, which leverages supervised machine learning techniques to determine fraudulent credit card transactions. It addresses the limitation of the transaction aggregation strategy of Whitrow, *et al.* [9] by performing aggregation in a weighted manner. In particular, the method modifies the weight of a previous transaction based on its distance from the current transaction.

2.   Related Work

Fraud detection methods involving transaction data are generally divided into two categories. The first category includes methods for detecting outliers in transaction data. These methods generally use clustering algorithms to group transactions and identify outlier transactions from the known clusters. Predefined rules are typically used to classify transactions as fraudulent or legitimate.

The second category of methods analyze individual transactions using models trained by classifiers such as artificial neural networks [1, 5] and support vector machines [3]. This section reviews some of these methods before focusing on the transaction aggregation strategy. Interested readers are referred to Bhattacharyya, *et al.* [2] for a comprehensive survey of the various methods.

Panigrahi, *et al.* [6] have proposed a hybrid approach for credit card fraud detection. Their approach involves three steps. The first step is rule-based filtering in which rules are applied to filter fraudulent transactions based the deviations of transactions from normal user profiles. The rules, which focus on address mismatch and outlier detection, are based on characteristics such as transaction amount, inter-transaction time gap, billing address and shipping address. DBSCAN (density-based spatial clustering of applications with noise) [4] is used to detect outliers. In the second step, a data fusion technique (i.e., a Dempster-Shafer adder) is applied to combine evidence from the address mismatch and outlier detection rules. In the third step, Bayesian learning is employed to assess the suspicion score of a transaction. Another approach [8], which focuses on fraudulent insurance claim detection, uses superior boosted naive Bayes classification.

Yu and Wang [10] have proposed an outlier detection method that computes the distance of each transaction from every other transaction. A transaction whose sum of distances is greater than a threshold distance is considered to be an outlier. The method exhibits good accuracy, but incurs high overhead to compute and compare the distances for all the transactions.

A two-stage approach for credit card fraud detection, involving anomaly checking and comparisons against known fraud history, has been proposed by Sherly and Nedunchezhian [7]. K-means clustering of training data and special rules are used to discretize transaction attributes into categories to accommodate transaction variability. However, aside from the discretization, no multi-transaction behavioral information is extracted from the training transaction records to construct the training model.

Most of the work described in the literature uses credit card transaction data for fraud detection purposes. However, Chen, *et al.* [3] also incorporate questionnaire data collected from consumers to create user profiles. A major drawback of this method is that new questionnaires have to be created and analyzed when user behavior changes.

Whitrow, *et al.* [9] have proposed a novel approach using transaction aggregation as an alternative strategy to employing single transaction or behavioral models. They argue that transaction aggregation is a better fraud predictor than individual transaction and behavioral models (behavioral models do not consider global patterns). Experimental results using real-world data demonstrate the effectiveness of the method over different aggregation periods for several classification techniques (random forests, logistic regression, support vector machines, naive Bayes, quadratic discriminant analysis, classification and regression trees, and k-nearest neighbors; the best results were obtained with random forests).

3.   Fraud Detection Methodology

This section describes the proposed conditional weighted transaction aggregation method.

3.1   Data Attributes

The datasets used in this work comprised several transaction entries. Each entry had the attributes: consumer ID, credit card limit, transaction time, transaction amount, transaction mode ("online" or "pos" for point of sale) and address match result ("match," "mismatch" or "NA" for not applicable). Each transaction was labeled as "fraudulent" or "legitimate." The objective of credit card fraud detection is to predict the label of a new transaction given its attribute values and the relevant accumulated attribute values from previous transactions.

3.2   Transaction Aggregation Method

This section outlines the transaction aggregation method of Whitrow, *et al.* [9] and proceeds to describe the enhanced conditional weighted transaction aggregation method.

Transaction Aggregation Method. The method of Whitrow, *et al.* [9] computes the aggregate of the transaction amounts associated with different attribute values over the previous d days. The aggregate and the individual transaction attributes are used as features in fraud detection.

Let N be the total number of transactions during the previous d days and let $Amount(i)$ be the monetary amount of the ith transaction. Assume that an attribute A considered for aggregation has m possible values (e.g., attribute "transaction mode" has two possible values "online" and "pos") with A_j denoting the jth ($1 \leq j \leq m$) value. The aggregation involves a summation over all transactions over the previous d days that have similar values for attribute A; this helps capture the relevant behavioral characteristics over the aggregation period.

The aggregation of an attribute value A_j is given by:

$$Aggregation(A_j) = \sum_{i=1}^{N} Amount_i : A(i) = A_j \qquad (1)$$

where $A(i)$ is the value of attribute A in the ith transaction. The aggregation values obtained from Equation (1) are used as features in addition to the attributes listed in Section 3.1.

Conditional Weighted Transaction Aggregation Method. The method of Whitrow, *et al.* [9] considers all transactions during the previous d days to be equal, ignoring the sequence of transactions and examining only the state of the credit card account at a given point in time. Whitrow and colleagues acknowledge that excessive aggregation over a long time span could negatively affect the prediction model.

To address these concerns, we designed the conditional weighted transaction aggregation method to capture the sequential nature of credit card transactions. Weights are assigned to all previous transactions. The weights are inversely proportional to the distance between current and previous transactions. That is, for a set of N previous transactions, the ith ($1 \leq i \leq N$) transaction in the history (from the first transaction to the current transaction) is assigned a weight w_i that increases with increasing i. This gives more weight to recent transactions compared with older transactions that have lower correlations with the current transaction. Details about the weighting function are provided below.

As in the method of Whitrow, *et al.* [9], aggregation is only performed for attributes that are relevant to the current transaction. The idea is that these attributes, when aggregated, define a behavior characteristic of the consumer. For example, a card holder's transaction mode is regarded as a behavioral attribute while the address match indicator is not. This is because the former provides insight into the shopping habits of the consumer; the latter is dependent only on the merchant or transaction mode. In this work, previous transactions with the "pos" payment mode are not considered in the aggregation if the current transaction is performed "online." This helps reduce false predictions by filtering transactions with irrelevant attributes. The conditional selection of previous transactions is reflected in Equation (2) below using a binary multiplication factor C_j that is dependent on the relevance of the jth attribute.

Finally, a factor is associated with each aggregated attribute based on the probability of the attribute value. Given a consumer c and probability $p_c(A_j)$ of an attribute value, the factor for its aggregated feature is $1 - p_c(A_j)$ (see Equation (2)). In other words, the higher the probability of an attribute value for the consumer, the lower the weight for each of its occurrences. Thus, if Consumer A engages in "online" transactions less frequently than Consumer B, the factor for the aggregation value for "online" transactions would be higher for Consumer A than for Consumer B. In the experiments discussed in this paper, the probability of the payment mode was calculated based on all the transactions during the first four months in the training and test datasets.

Based on the preceding discussion, the aggregation for attribute value A_j is computed as:

$$Aggregation(A_j) = C_j * (1 - p_c(A_j)) * \sum_{i=1}^{N} w_i * Amount_i : A(i) = \dot{A_j} \quad (2)$$

Weighting Function. Two weighting functions, the transaction gap function and the time gap function, are used to give more weight to recent transactions during aggregation. In the case of the transaction gap function, the weight w_i simply corresponds to the number of transactions between the ith transaction and the current transaction. Specifically, the weight w_i is given by:

$$w_i = N - i \quad (3)$$

where N is the total number of transactions in the period under consideration.

The time gap function assigns weights based on the time difference between the current and latest transaction. For an aggregation period of d days with N previous transactions, the ith transaction is given a weight of:

$$w_i = d - (time_N - time_i) \quad (4)$$

where $time_N - time_i$ is the time gap between the Nth and i^{th} transactions.

Experiments were performed using the two weighting functions, with the results favoring the time gap function under most conditions. This implies that closeness in time is a better indicator of fraudulent behavior than closeness based on transaction gap.

4.   Experiments

This section describes the experimental setup and the experimental results.

4.1   Experimental Setup

Experiments were performed using datasets with simulated credit card transactions. Specifically, three datasets corresponding to low-dominant, middle-dominant and egalitarian distributions of spending profiles in the

Table 1. Distribution of spending profiles in simulated datasets.

	Spending Profiles		
Dataset	Low	Medium	High
1: Low-Dominant	0.80	0.15	0.05
2: Middle-Dominant	0.20	0.60	0.20
3: Egalitarian	0.33	0.33	0.33

population were generated. Table 1 shows that the distributions differ in the ratios of low, medium and high spending profiles in the population. Each dataset contained 200 credit card accounts, 100 of which were used for training and 100 for testing.

Table 2. Parameters for legitimate spending profiles.

Profile	Transaction (tx)	Prob.	Mean	Std. Dev.	Min.
	Low	0.90	30	10	10
Low	Medium	0.08	150	50	50
	High	0.02	500	200	200
	Low	0.80	30	10	10
Medium	Medium	0.15	150	50	50
	High	0.05	500	200	200
	Low	0.60	30	10	10
High	Medium	0.25	150	50	50
	High	0.12	700	300	200
	V. High	0.03	2,000	500	1,000

Each spending profile models the monetary amounts involved in low, medium or high transaction amounts using a Gaussian distribution. Table 2 presents the parameters for Gaussian simulated transaction (tx) amounts for legitimate spending profiles.

In addition to the legitimate transaction profiles, two fraudster profiles of equal probability were created. The first profile assumes that fraud is committed via infrequent, but large, transaction amounts. The second profile assumes smaller transaction amounts (possibly larger than legitimate transactions) with a wider spread over time. Table 3 presents the parameters for Gaussian simulated transaction (tx) amounts for fraudulent spending profiles.

The arrival rates of transactions were simulated as Poisson processes. Different arrival rates were used for legitimate and fraudulent transactions based on the following equation:

$$T_n = T_{n-1} - \log(U)/\lambda \qquad (5)$$

Table 3.   Parameters for fraudulent spending profiles.

Profile	Transaction (tx)	Prob.	Mean	Std. Dev.	Min.
	Low	0.1	700	300	200
Active	Medium	0.1	1,300	400	400
	High	0.8	2,200	600	500
	Low	0.1	150	50	50
Passive	Medium	0.8	500	100	200
	High	0.1	1,500	300	500

where T_n is the occurrence time of the nth transaction, T_{n-1} is the occurrence time of the $n-1^{th}$ transaction, U is a random value from $[0,1]$ and λ is the arrival rate.

The training and testing data simulations were executed for periods of ten months, with fraudulent transactions occurring with a 15% probability during each of the previous five months. This reflects a likely real-world scenario where the number of legitimate transactions is generally much larger than the number of fraudulent transactions. Since most machine learning algorithms work best on balanced datasets, subsets of the legitimate samples were used during the training process. These subsets were chosen randomly and the performance values of the resulting classifiers were aggregated and averaged to assess the overall performance. Note that this sub-sampling process overcomes dataset imbalance and it is, arguably, necessary when dealing with large real-world datasets.

4.2   Performance Measurement

The misclassification rate, which measures the number of misclassified instances from among all the instances, is commonly used to assess classification performance. However, using the ratio of legitimate to fraudulent transactions is not recommended because it is highly imbalanced; also, different costs are associated with the misclassification of legitimate and fraudulent transactions. Whitrow, *et al.* [9] have suggested that, except for the case of a correctly classified legitimate transaction, costs are involved in all the other classification scenarios. Legitimate and fraudulent transactions that are classified as fraudulent incur costs of $C_{l/f}$ and $C_{f/f}$, respectively; the costs represent the work required to conduct further investigations. Likewise, a fraudulent transaction that is wrongly classified as legitimate incurs a cost of $C_{f/l}$, which corresponds to the amount of money lost in the transaction.

Due to the different costs associated with different classifications, we used a loss function to measure classification performance instead of the typical misclassification rate. In particular, we used the same costs and cost function as Whitrow, *et al.* [9]. Based on an analysis of real credit card data, the cost values $C_{l/f} = 1$, $C_{f/f} = 1$, $C_{f/l} = 100$ and $C_{l/l} = 0$ were employed.

Given n_f fraudulent transactions and n_l legitimate transactions, let $n_{l/f}$ be the number of legitimate transactions classified as fraudulent, $n_{f/f}$ be the number of fraudulent transactions classified as fraudulent and $n_{f/l}$ be the number of fraudulent transactions classified as legitimate. Then, the total cost function for the classification is given by:

$$C = \frac{C_{l/f} * n_{l/f} + C_{f/f} * n_{f/f} + C_{f/l} * n_{f/l}}{C_{f/l} * n_f + C(l/f) * n_l} \tag{6}$$

where the numerator is the cost of the current classification and the denominator is the maximum cost that can be incurred. Thus, the cost associated with a transaction is bounded between 0 and 1, and a method with a lower cost is considered to be better than a method with a higher cost.

4.3   Comparison of Methods

Four methods were compared based on their costs. The methods were: (i) transaction based (Tx) (i.e., without any aggregation information); (ii) simple aggregation (SA); (iii) weighted aggregation with transaction gap as the weighting function (TxG); and (iv) weighted aggregation with time gap as the weighting function (TG). The simple aggregation method is a minor adaptation of the method of Whitrow and colleagues [9] for the (simpler) simulated dataset used in this work. Note that all the methods, except for the transaction based method, require the aggregation of features over some time period.

The performance of a method clearly depends on the aggregation period. Experimentation with aggregations ranging from one day to seven days indicated that the best performance is achieved with aggregations of three to five days for all three datasets. Thus, the results reported for all the methods involving aggregated features are based on the average performance over aggregation periods of three to five days.

Several common classification techniques were used in the experiments: random forests, naive Bayes, AdaBoost, logistic regression and k-nearest neighbors (kNN). To obtain a balanced dataset, a random subset of the legitimate transaction was selected before training and testing each classifier. The selection, training and testing process was iterated

Table 4. Costs ($\times 10^3$) of methods with different classifiers (Dataset 1).

Classifier	TG	TxG	SA	Tx
Random Forests	14.897	**13.765**	14.309	17.404
Naive Bayes	**32.396**	41.776	37.878	35.252
AdaBoost	**24.741**	25.785	25.283	32.034
Logistic Regression	**18.304**	20.468	18.909	24.527
kNN	**33.307**	37.052	36.049	40.641
Average	**24.729**	27.769	26.486	29.972

Table 5. Costs ($\times 10^3$) of methods with different classifiers (Dataset 2).

Classifier	TG	TxG	SA	Tx
Random Forests	23.946	23.897	**23.599**	28.375
Naive Bayes	61.065	78.934	79.131	**53.992**
AdaBoost	34.858	35.692	**34.108**	51.293
Logistic Regression	**25.999**	27.582	26.018	34.993
kNN	**43.174**	48.318	46.054	48.241
Average	**37.808**	42.885	41.782	43.379

Table 6. Costs ($\times 10^3$) of methods with different classifiers (Dataset 3).

Classifier	TG	TxG	SA	Tx
Random Forests	**21.128**	21.547	21.383	27.275
Naive Bayes	81.688	106.843	102.699	**70.959**
AdaBoost	**33.199**	33.578	33.459	43.613
Logistic Regression	**33.210**	35.449	36.256	40.239
kNN	47.808	51.832	50.810	**46.000**
Average	**43.407**	49.850	48.921	45.617

ten times to obtain the average performance for each classification technique.

Tables 4, 5 and 6 show the performance of different methods and classification techniques for Datasets 1, 2 and 3, respectively. The cost function defined by Equation (6) is used as the performance measure. For purposes of clarity, the actual costs are multiplied by a factor of 10^3 to produce the table values. Note that the costs for the datasets can be very different due to the different transaction amounts in each dataset. Therefore, the costs of different classifiers should be compared only for the same dataset.

The performance of weighted aggregation with transaction gap weighting is poor compared with the other aggregation methods. In fact, it is the worst aggregation method based on its average cost over all the classification techniques. Moreover, its performance is mixed when compared with that of the basic transaction based method.

On the other hand, the time gap weighted aggregation method performed significantly better than the other methods. Although it was not the best performing method for some classification techniques in the case of Datasets 2 and 3, the costs incurred by the time gap weighted aggregation method are consistently the second lowest among the tested methods, and its average cost is the lowest for all methods. This provides empirical evidence of performance stability of the time gap weighted aggregation method across the various classification techniques and datasets.

4.4   Transaction vs. Time Gap Weighting

As discussed above, the weights used during the aggregation process are meant to emphasize the relative importance of newer transactions over older transactions. The results obtained for the datasets clearly show that weighted aggregation helps improve the classification performance when an appropriate weighting function is used. However, it is also apparent that a poor weighting function such as the transaction gap weighting function results in performance that is poorer than the simple aggregation method. This could be because the transaction gap weighting function is unable to capture the different arrival rates between legitimate and fraudulent (passive and active) transactions. Although transaction gap weighting assigns an adjusted weight to each previous transaction during aggregation, the weights are independent of the transaction time and merely capture the transaction sequence.

To conduct a "fairer" analysis of the two weighted aggregation methods, the same experiments were conducted on (additional) Datasets 4, 5 and 6 with the same parameters as Datasets 1, 2 and 3, respectively, except that adjustments were made for equal arrival rates for all legitimate, passive and active fraudulent profiles. This restricted the differences between legitimate and fraudulent transactions to their different spending profiles. Table 7 through 9 show the results of the second set of experiments.

In the original experiments (Tables 4, 5 and 6), the average cost incurred by the transaction gap weighted aggregation method is 13.52% higher than the cost incurred by the time gap weighted aggregation method. However, when the arrival rates are similar, the results in Tables 7, 8 and 9 show that the difference in the average cost between the

Table 7.   Costs ($\times 10^3$) of methods with different classifiers (Dataset 4).

Classifier	*TG*	*TxG*	*SA*	*Tx*
Random Forests	19.265	**18.835**	19.377	24.711
Naive Bayes	**42.817**	49.484	49.851	60.221
AdaBoost	32.747	28.289	29.656	**27.747**
Logistic Regression	24.912	**23.887**	24.881	33.418
kNN	45.010	47.160	46.353	**43.030**
Average	**32.950**	33.531	34.024	37.825

Table 8.   Costs ($\times 10^3$) of methods with different classifiers (Dataset 5).

Classifier	*TG*	*TxG*	*SA*	*Tx*
Random Forests	**19.873**	21.47	19.926	24.711
Naive Bayes	**58.403**	68.359	77.104	60.221
AdaBoost	39.052	37.552	**36.675**	46.642
Logistic Regression	**26.915**	28.563	27.053	38.776
kNN	**40.704**	42.788	43.025	40.776
Average	**36.990**	39.747	40.757	42.225

Table 9.   Costs ($\times 10^3$) of methods with different classifiers (Dataset 6).

Classifier	*TG*	*TxG*	*SA*	*Tx*
Random forests	24.375	**21.864**	23.248	27.520
Naive Bayes	99.868	103.931	113.325	**87.364**
AdaBoost	**42.552**	46.730	44.579	53.542
Logistic regression	38.179	39.184	**36.683**	45.936
kNN	46.925	49.983	47.888	**40.776**
Average	**50.380**	52.338	53.145	51.028

two weighted aggregation methods drops to just 4.37%. This confirms that capturing the arrival rates of transactions can significantly improve classification performance. Nevertheless, the superior performance of the time gap weighted aggregation method over the transaction gap weighted aggregation method suggests that weights assigned based on the temporal differences between previous transactions are better than the assignments based on the sequence of previous transactions.

5. Conclusions

Transaction aggregation is a promising strategy for detecting fraudulent credit card transactions. The experimental results in this paper (as well as previous work in the area) demonstrate that aggregation based methods work better than transaction based methods. This is mainly due to the ability of aggregation based methods to capture additional evidence from previous transactions.

The main contribution of this paper is an enhanced aggregation based method that incorporates weights for all the previous transactions in an aggregated period. Transaction gap weighting considers the number of transactions between current and previous transactions while time gap weighting considers the temporal difference between current and previous transactions. The experimental results demonstrate that time gap weighting intensifies the importance of recent transactions over older transactions, thereby enhancing credit fraud detection. However, care should be taken when choosing weighting functions because weights that are directly dependent on transaction time result in better classification performance compared with weights that are based on the sequence of previous transactions.

References

[1] E. Aleskerov, B. Freisleben and B. Rao, Cardwatch: A neural network based database mining system for credit card fraud detection, *Proceedings of the IEEE/IAFE Conference on Computational Intelligence for Financial Engineering*, pp. 220–226, 1997.

[2] S. Bhattacharyya, J. Sanjeev, K. Tharakunnel and J. Westland, Data mining for credit card fraud: A comparative study, *Decision Support Systems*, vol. 50(3), pp. 602–613, 2011.

[3] R. Chen, S. Luo, X. Liang and V. Lee, Personalized approach based on SVM and ANN for detecting credit card fraud, *Proceedings of the International Conference on Neural Networks and the Brain*, vol. 2, pp. 810–815, 2005.

[4] M. Ester, H. Kriegel, J. Sander and X. Xu, A density-based algorithm for discovering clusters in large spatial databases with noise, *Proceedings of the Second International Conference on Knowledge Discovery and Data Mining*, pp. 226–231, 1996.

[5] S. Ghosh and D. Reilly, Credit card fraud detection with a neural network, *Proceedings of the Twenty-Seventh Hawaii International Conference on System Sciences*, vol. 3, pp. 621–630, 1994.

[6] S. Panigrahi, A. Kundu, S. Sural and A. Majumdar, Credit card fraud detection: A fusion approach using Dempster-Shafer theory and Bayesian learning, *Information Fusion*, vol. 10(4), pp. 354–363, 2009.

[7] K. Sherly and R. Nedunchezhian, BOAT adaptive credit card fraud detection system, *Proceedings of the IEEE International Conference on Computational Intelligence and Computing Research*, 2010.

[8] S. Viaene, R. Derrig and G. Dedene, A case study of applying boosting naive Bayes to claim fraud diagnosis, *IEEE Transactions on Knowledge and Data Engineering*, vol. 16(5), pp. 612–620, 2004.

[9] C. Whitrow, D. Hand, P. Juszczak, D. Weston and N. Adams, Transaction aggregation as a strategy for credit card fraud detection, *Data Mining and Knowledge Discovery*, vol. 18(1), pp. 30–55, 2009.

[10] W. Yu and N. Wang, Research on credit card fraud detection model based on distance sum, *Proceedings of the International Joint Conference on Artificial Intelligence*, pp. 353–356, 2009.

Chapter 2

USING FRAUD TREES TO ANALYZE INTERNET CREDIT CARD FRAUD

Clive Blackwell

Abstract   Because of the difficulties inherent in accurately identifying individuals on the Internet, online merchants reduce the risk of credit card fraud by increasing restrictions on consumers. The restrictions are often overly burdensome on consumers and may result in lost sales. This paper uses the concept of a fraud tree, an extension of an attack tree, to comprehensively model online fraud techniques and to suggest defensive obstacles for merchants to counter threats. The fraud tree model can advise merchants about the checks to be performed to reduce risk even in the presence of incomplete knowledge of the circumstances of the transactions. Since fraud cannot be completely avoided, the paper also describes auditing that can be performed to assist merchants in identifying the responsible parties and potentially limiting, if not avoiding, liability due to fraud.

Keywords: Credit card fraud, fraud tree, obstacles, card-not-present transactions

1.   Introduction

As more people make purchases online, criminals take advantage of weak authentication checks to commit credit card fraud. The amount of remote fraud, technically called "card-not-present fraud," is estimated to be about £250 million in the United Kingdom – more than all the other types of payment card fraud put together [5].

Merchants are in a difficult position to reduce their liability in a system set up by credit card issuers that emphasizes legal protection for consumers. The fraud tree model presented in this paper is designed to assist merchants. The model uses the concept of a fraud tree, an extension of an attack tree, to comprehensively model online fraud techniques and suggest defensive obstacles for merchants to counter threats. The model can advise merchants about additional checks that can be per-

G. Peterson and S. Shenoi (Eds.): Advances in Digital Forensics X, IFIP AICT 433, pp. 17–29, 2014.
© IFIP International Federation for Information Processing 2014

formed to limit their risk in various transaction scenarios while taking
into account the fact that merchants have partial and imperfect knowledge of transactions.

The fraud tree model adapts the anti-goal model provided by the
KAOS requirements engineering framework. Following the KAOS requirements, possible fraudulent transactions are determined and appropriate obstacles are proposed. The approach can potentially be applied
to other distributed systems where attackers exploit the partial knowledge possessed by system participants, but for which sufficient information can be collected for subsequent attribution.

2.   Related Work

Schneier's attack trees [13] provide the foundation for implementing
several computer security attack assessment tools. One of the scenarios investigated by Schneier involved attacks against a payment system. However, his work focused on protocol weaknesses instead of the
wider perspective taken in this paper. Attack trees have also been used
to identify forensic goals [2] and to support investigations of document
forgery [3, 4].

The original KAOS framework [16] incorporated a goal model to help
determine system requirements and obstacles for analyzing hazards to
the goals. An anti-goal model was later included in KAOS to model security threats. The initial work also examined threats to online banking,
but the scenario was limited to a single threat involving the compromise
of account numbers and PINs [15, 17].

Attack-defense trees [9] are a recent parallel development to the KAOS
framework. These trees extend attack trees by allowing nodes representing defensive measures to appear within a tree. Attack-defense trees are
supported by a detailed theoretical model, but they do not have the tool
support offered by KAOS.

Edge, al. [7] have employed a protection tree in an investigation of an
online banking system to defeat various fraudulent methods modeled in
the corresponding attack tree. The approach is extended in this paper
by placing fraud methods and the corresponding protection measures
in the same tree to clarify the relationship between fraud methods and
fraud protection.

2.1   Goal Trees

The specification language of the KAOS framework has four domains:
goal, operation, object and responsibility. This paper analyzes credit

card fraud in the goal domain. However, the other domains are also relevant to fraud analysis and will be the subject of future research.

A goal is an objective that a system is designed to achieve. An AND-refinement decomposes or refines a goal into a set of subgoals such that the satisfaction of all the elementary subgoals in the refinement is a sufficient condition for satisfying the composite goal. An OR-refinement relates a goal to an alternative set of subgoals such that that the satisfaction of one of the refined goals is a sufficient condition for satisfying the overall goal. Goal decomposition terminates when atomic goals called requirements are reached that can be directly executed (or "operational-ized" in the KAOS terminology) by individual agents.

An obstacle [11] is a dual notion to a goal; it captures the possible undesirable conditions that frustrate a goal. Obstacles are a fundamental aspect of goal trees that facilitate detailed and practical analyses of how system goals may be breached. Obstacles can also be decomposed into finer and finer obstacles until they can be directly implemented at the level of anti-requirements, just like positive goal requirements. Finally, the resolution stage provides ways to counter the discovered obstacles so that the overall goals are satisfied even if undesirable issues occur.

An attack tree [13], like a goal tree, is also an AND-OR tree, except that an attack tree examines a system from an adversarial perspective instead of a defensive perspective. Goal trees are more functional and systematic than attack trees because the concept of obstacle is included directly with a tree along with the explicit linkage to the object, operation and responsibility domains.

Obstacle trees are sufficient for modeling and resolving inherent and inadvertent problems, but they are too limited for modeling and resolving malicious interference. The goal-oriented framework for generating and resolving obstacles was extended to address malicious obstacles called anti-goals [17], which could be executed by attackers to defeat security objectives.

3.   Credit Card Transactions

A merchant's primary goal is to receive payment for the goods that are supplied. A scenario involving a remote payment is more difficult than when a customer purchases goods in person. This is because a credit card transaction relies on other system participants such as the card issuer, cardholder and courier to act correctly, and the evidence that is relied upon is often weak and open to challenge.

A merchant who accepts credit cards is committed to the rules of the card issuer such as Visa or MasterCard. If the transaction goes wrong,

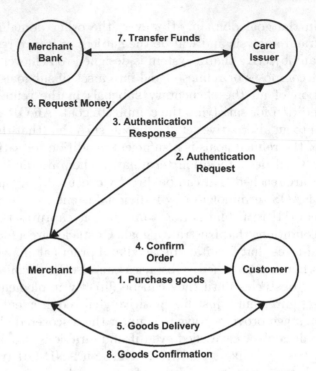

Figure 1.   Card-not-present transaction.

the customer may receive a chargeback, which leads to the reversal of
the payment. This situation can result in a loss for the merchant if weak
authorization is used (e.g., provision of the card details alone), especially
if the merchant cannot prove who initiated the transaction.

Internet credit card payments have complex security issues because
the customer and merchant never meet and they rely on evidence communicated through potentially insecure channels using weak authentication measures that may be exploited by fraudsters. A remote credit card
transaction over the Internet (using email or a website), or by phone, fax
or regular mail is known as a "card-not-present" (CNP) transaction [14].

The EMV specification [8, 12] formally describes the process. The
main parties to a payment card transaction are the merchant, the merchant's bank, the customer and the card issuer. There may be other
participants, including a payment processor who performs transactions
on behalf of the card issuer or merchant, and a courier who delivers the
goods.

Figure 1 shows the EMV specification of a CNP transaction as a
protocol exchange between the four main participants. The protocol
involves several related flows of goods, information and money from one

participant to another in a temporal order, which is modeled later in this paper using goal trees.

A crucial issue is that the merchant may act on incomplete or incorrect information, because he/she may not be notified of fraud-related events if they occur (e.g., credit card theft or forgery). However, the merchant may be able to avoid liability for fraudulent transactions even with inadequate knowledge by passing the responsibility for fraud detection to another participant such as the cardholder or card issuer. In addition, the merchant can endeavor to collect sufficient auditing information to avoid liability when the merchant is responsible in the credit card system.

4. Fraud Analysis

Analysis of around 150 cases of fraud targeting banking systems has revealed that defective procedural controls and implementation flaws were exploited in nearly all the cases; only two cases involved the exploitation of weaknesses in cryptographic protocols, which received the most attention during system design [1]. A pragmatic and detailed fraud model can help merchants avoid or mitigate threats by imposing adequate obstacles.

The construction of a fraud tree involves building a KAOS goal tree from the attacker's perspective as in the case of an attack tree. It is useful to incorporate the attacker's perspective because the attacker's goals, motivation and activities could be missed when the focus is only on system goals.

In KAOS, the main obstacle corresponds to the logical negation of the goal that it is intended to defeat. An attacker goal that cannot be satisfactorily overcome indicates a failure of requirements engineering and the need to restructure the goal model. However, the credit card system is already in operation, so the obstacles under the attack goal may only be partially effective. In addition, some obstacles, such as the determination of card theft by the merchant, may be impossible to implement directly. We call these abstract obstacles, and they are forwarded to the later stages of a transaction for resolution.

Obstacles may be imperfect and incomplete, and can be overcome by further adversarial counter-goals unless additional obstacles are proposed. This is still useful because the merchant can take on transactions that might otherwise be rejected (an imperfect obstacle may be effective in the particular transaction context). In another context where the customer's identity cannot be established adequately, the definitive obstacle is to abandon the transaction after all the attempted checks fail.

4.1   Transaction Modeling

Building a fraud tree analyzes the threats to CNP from the fraudster's perspective. This is easier than decomposing the merchant goals and ensures that all plausible threats are recognized and addressed. It also provides an effective counterbalance against the idealized threat models that are produced when the focus is on the merchant's goals.

The model progressively decomposes the fraudster's goals into actionable steps as in the case of an attack tree. However, a fraud tree also contains defensive goals in the form of obstacles that can potentially defeat the adversarial goals. Because the defensive obstacles possibly offer imperfect and incomplete remedies, the process iterates through the fraudster's additional counter-goals and defensive obstacles for the counter-goals.

In requirements engineering, system threats are typically analyzed from all the stakeholders' points of view in order to formulate a collective system goal model. However, the participants in a transaction have their own goals, do not have complete visibility or control of the entire transaction system and may potentially be in an adversarial situation because a legitimate participant has to bear the cost of fraud.

At this stage, the fraud tree represents both perspectives – the merchant's and fraudster's – and must be transformed into a merchant-only view before use. Transforming the fraud tree converts abstract obstacles against adversarial activities that are invisible to the merchant to realizable obstacles that obstruct fraud in a different way. For example, although the merchant cannot detect the initial card compromise, the authenticity of the transaction can be confirmed when the goods are delivered by changing the payment to a local card-present transaction or by verifying the identity of the customer.

The transformation process begins with the initial fraud tree and imposes obstacles under each adversarial goal. The obstacle is purely abstract if it cannot be implemented, partial if it can be realized successfully under certain conditions, or total if it provides effective mitigation. In Figure 2, a total obstacle is represented using a rounded white square underneath the obstacle indicating success. Forwarded abstract obstacles (gray) and partial obstacles (lighter gray) extend into later steps in the transaction together with an annotation that indicates the circumstances causing the unresolved issue. All transaction flows should ideally end with resolved obstacles (white), but some light gray obstacles remain, indicating that, although fraud is significantly reduced, it is still possible.

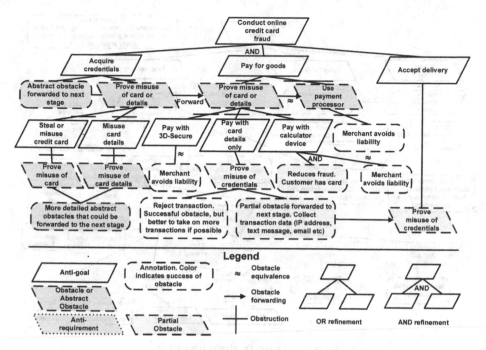

Figure 2. Fraud tree for the first two fraud stages.

Forwarded obstacles may be implemented directly to avoid fraud or they may be transformed to equivalent or weaker obstacles in order to avoid liability if fraud does occur. Realizable forwarded obstacles include avoiding fraud by aborting a suspicious transaction (Figure 2), reducing the probability of fraud by making additional identity checks during the delivery stage, avoiding liability by using the 3D-Secure payment mechanism (Figure 3) and collecting additional evidence to transfer accountability to the responsible party during the purchase and delivery stages.

The analysis is limited to the unauthorized use of a credit card to purchase tangible goods on the Internet as shown in the fraud tree in Figure 2. CNP fraud is the most common type of fraud. It is also the most challenging because the merchant does not see the card but, instead, uses a password for authentication. Card security codes along with PIN numbers can also be considered to be weak passwords, along with passwords used with 3D-Secure and for accessing merchant sites.

The obstacles for the first stage are negations of the fraudulent goals, which cannot be directly implemented by the merchant; thus, they are abstract obstacles that are forwarded to the second stage. A forwarded abstract or partial obstacle has an arrow between the parent and child that is annotated with the conditions for successful resolution. Because

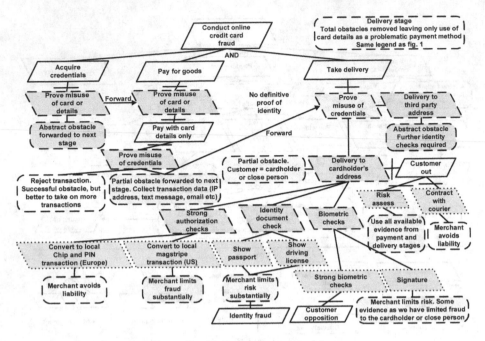

Figure 3. Delivery stage fraud tree.

the obstacle for the first stage is abstract, there is no annotation as no limitations are imposed on the transaction.

4.2   Fraud Tree

The resulting fraud tree shown in Figure 2 has three branches from the root AND-node that represent the three essential stages of fraud: (i) acquiring the card or card details; (ii) using them to purchase goods; and (iii) accepting delivery of the goods. Figure 2 shows the first two stages and Figure 3 presents the final delivery stage with the only unobstructed fraud path from the first two stages. The child nodes representing the three stages are subdivided into branches, recursively, until the decomposition terminates at unexpanded attack steps in the leaves that can be directly executed or that are deemed outside the scope of analysis.

The two possibilities for the first branch are to obtain the card or just the card details, which are equivalent in online transactions because the card is never seen and is not directly used for authorization, except for the relatively rare case when a calculator-like device is used to compute a one-time password for each transaction. However, having the card or just the card details can be distinguished by later checks, so they can be forwarded as different obstacles to the delivery stage. It is far easier for a fraudster to discover card details than to acquire a card because the card details are provided to a merchant or proxy (e.g., payment processor) in every transaction.

Card details can be compromised in multiple ways, but this analysis limits it to someone close to the cardholder or an unknown third party. Finally, the transaction could be carried out and subsequently denied by the cardholder, which is impossible to demonstrate under the current transaction system, and is a reason why additional forensic evidence should be collected to establish the identity of the customer.

The second branch is to select and pay for the goods, where the different payment methods are the different anti-goals that can be satisfied by the adversary. The obstacle for "Acquire credentials" is also the child of the "Pay for goods" node in the second branch.

3D-Secure is a good payment method when the cardholder is deemed responsible or negligent for fraud (e.g., for revealing the card details and password). The card issuer typically provides the purchaser with a popup window in which a password is entered [10]. The obstacle for avoiding fraud forwarded from the first stage is transformed from discovering the identity of the customer to the alternative acceptable obstacle of avoiding liability (shown by the white annotation indicating success and the ≈ symbol for transformation to an equivalent obstacle).

Another possibility is to use a calculator-like device to compute a one-time password that restricts fraud to the less common case of having access to the card. This could have been shown as a total obstacle for the compromise of card details (stops the fraud) and partial obstacle for card theft (fraud is still possible) if both classes had been forwarded separately. However, by forwarding the two fraud methods as a single class, the measure is only a partial obstacle for the entire class (shown as light gray in Figure 2). The method also avoids merchant liability because the card issuer assumes the responsibility, indicated by the satisfied obstacle under the calculator payment node (colored white).

For the situation where only the card details are supplied, a complete obstacle is to reject any weakly authorized transaction using only the card details and card security code. However, merchants often allow weak authentication to take on more business, because their goal is to increase profits instead of avoiding fraud entirely.

An additional way to resolve the obstacle is to engage a payment processor who decides on the legitimacy of transactions; this transfers merchant liability for a fee. The transformation of the forwarded obstacle "Prove misuse of card or details" to "Use payment processor" for a fixed cost is usually a good option because it also avoids administrative effort and further security issues outside the scope of the scenario (e.g., disclosure of sensitive cardholder details). Thus, the obstacle at the root of the payment branch is resolved if the merchant chooses to use a payment processor.

The outcome of the first two transaction stages leads to one unsatisfied obstacle that is forwarded to the delivery stage. Figure 3 presents the fraud tree for the delivery stage. When the merchant insists on delivery to the cardholder's address, the analysis can extend to establishing additional checks that the merchant can perform when the goods are delivered elsewhere.

Fraud in the case of home delivery is only possible when the customer is the cardholder or is in close proximity to the cardholder and can take delivery of the goods. After the partial obstacle provided by the address check, the significant issue of remote fraud is avoided and the customer's identity is narrowed down to the cardholder or someone close.

It is necessary to collect further evidence to show that the cardholder is responsible because it is not adequate to claim that, since all the other possibilities are ruled out, the cardholder or someone close to the cardholder must have executed the transaction. For example, fraud is not ruled out on the part of the merchant, the courier and their employees.

Most fraud checks are ineffective against insiders, such as cardholders who act legitimately until they claim that they did not carry out certain transactions. Alternatively, it is entirely possible for a friend, colleague or family member to carry out fraud successfully without detection, so it is imperative that the merchant can establish attribution by collecting additional evidence outside the transaction system.

We summarize the situation if the third stage is reached without establishing the identity of the customer or avoiding liability. The first point is that it is not known if the transaction is legitimate or fraudulent; therefore, it is important not to execute clumsy and ill-directed checks when the vast majority of transactions are legitimate. A reasonable assumption is that the cardholder or someone close to the cardholder executed the transaction if the goods were delivered to the cardholder's address.

The merchant needs to augment the system when weak payment authentication is used by conducting additional verification checks to limit fraud or collect additional evidence to avoid liability. Note that, when a transaction is fraudulent, it is not known if the card or card details were misused. It is sensible to assume the worst that the card was stolen, but the two cases can be distinguished and different checks can be conducted to avoid them.

If the transaction circumstances suggest that a person close to the cardholder might have misused the card details, then it is reasonable to insist on a local card transaction. However, if the cardholder is implicated, then it would be more reasonable to ask for stronger identity checks and to use both types of checks if the identity of the recipient is unclear. The different types of control systematically provide obstacles to each type of fraud proactively, before the fraud method is known and even before it is known that the fraud has occurred. The controls have to be lightweight enough not to discourage the vast majority of legitimate purchasers. Therefore, onerous verification checks should only be applied to high value or suspicious transactions.

The major issues with physical delivery are practical concerns such as the need to provide fallback checks if the safest methods are unavailable. These practical issues are often inadequately analyzed using attack trees and other approaches. A crucial issue, modeled by an additional adversarial goal that defeats the obstacle of requiring strong authentication, is that the customer may not be at home and a neighbor or someone else at the address accepts the goods.

The possibility of fraud cannot be eliminated easily, but liability can be avoided by specifying a contract with the courier that transfers the fraud detection responsibility to the courier. This passes the risk assessment decision to the courier who decides whether to deliver the goods to a third party or to return when the customer is at home. This transformed obstacle of avoiding liability is a sufficient obstacle for the merchant, who also avoids all the logistical and security issues regarding delivery while passing the risk assessment decision to the courier, to whom it most sensibly belongs.

5. Conclusions

The use of fraud trees to analyze Internet credit card fraud can systematically provide an obstacle to each type of fraud proactively before the fraud method is known. By including obstacle formation and transformation, fraud trees are more refined than attack trees and adopt a different perspective compared with goal trees. An interesting aspect is that *a priori* knowledge of the branches of the fraud tree occupied by a transaction is required because the tree includes countermeasures to deal with each type of fraud. Fraud trees have applications to other types of investigation where wrongdoing is discovered after the fact, as in the case of the insider threat. Many insider threat incidents cannot be stopped, but it is possible to collect sufficient evidence to hold the perpetrators responsible.

Other benefits of the fraud tree framework include completeness (all known fraud techniques can be analyzed), scope (while the focus is on the logical transaction, incorporating physical and social checks helps reduce fraud and liability), participant perspective (participants do not share the same goals and can be in an adversarial position when there is a successful fraud, so it is useful to consider what each participant knows and can control), adversarial perspective, and narrative structure (the security measures used by the merchant are incorporated in the fraud tree and help explain the fraud).

Our future research will attempt to develop a firm theoretical foundation using temporal logic and model checking. Also, the use of binary yes/no measures is less than satisfactory; incorporating probabilistic measures of fraud and the costs of countermeasures will enhance risk assessment. Another related topic is to combine probabilities and other numerical measures as in the case of KAOS goal trees [6]. Other research topics involve the examination of partially satisfied obstacles that incorporate weaknesses that could be targeted by fraudsters, and the estimation of the intangible costs of performing checks.

References

[1] R. Anderson, Why cryptosystems fail, *Proceedings of the First ACM Conference on Computer and Communications Security*, pp. 215–227, 1993.

[2] B. Aziz, Towards goal-driven digital forensic investigations, *Proceedings of the Second International Conference on Cyber Crime, Security and Digital Forensics*, 2012.

[3] B. Aziz, C. Blackwell and S. Islam, A framework for digital forensics and investigations: The goal-driven approach, *International Journal of Digital Crime and Forensics*, vol. 5(2), pp. 1–22, 2013.

[4] C. Blackwell, B. Aziz and S. Islam, Using a goal-driven approach in the investigation of a questioned contract, in *Advances in Digital Forensics IX*, G. Peterson and S. Shenoi (Eds.), Springer, Heidelberg, Germany, pp. 153–167, 2013.

[5] M. Bond, O. Choudary, S. Murdoch, S. Skorobogatov and R. Anderson, Chip and skim: Cloning EMV cards with the pre-play attack (arxiv.org/pdf/1209.2531.pdf), 2012.

[6] A. Cailliau and A. van Lamsweerde, Assessing requirements-related risks through probabilistic goals and obstacles, *Requirements Engineering*, vol. 18(2), pp. 129–146, 2013.

[7] K. Edge, R. Raines, M. Grimaila, R. Baldwin, R. Bennington and C. Reuter, The use of attack and protection trees to analyze security for an online banking system, *Proceedings of the Fortieth Annual Hawaii International Conference on System Sciences*, p. 144b, 2007.

[8] EMVCo, EMV 4.3, Otley, United Kingdom (`www.emvco.com/speci fications.aspx?id=223`), 2011.

[9] B. Kordy, S. Mauw, S. Radomirovic and P. Schweitzer, Attack-defense trees, *Journal of Logic and Computation*, 2012.

[10] S. Murdoch and R. Anderson, Verified by Visa and MasterCard SecureCode: Or, how not to design authentication, in *Financial Cryptography and Data Security*, Springer-Verlag, R. Sion (Ed.), Berlin Heidelberg, Germany, pp. 336–342, 2010.

[11] C. Potts, Using schematic scenarios to understand user needs, *Proceedings of the First Conference on Designing Interactive Systems: Processes, Practices, Methods and Techniques*, pp. 247–256, 1995.

[12] C. Radu, *Implementing Electronic Card Payment Systems*, Artech House, Norwood, Massachusetts, 2002.

[13] B. Schneier, Attack trees, *Dr. Dobbs Journal*, vol. 24(12), pp. 21–29, 1999.

[14] The U.K. Cards Association, Card-not-present transactions, London, United Kingdon (`www.theukcardsassociation.org.uk/car ds-transactions/card-not-present.asp`).

[15] A. van Lamsweerde, Elaborating security requirements by construction of intentional anti-models, *Proceedings of the Twenty-Sixth International Conference on Software Engineering*, pp. 148–157, 2004.

[16] A. van Lamsweerde, *Requirements Engineering: From System Goals to UML Models to Software Specifications*, Wiley, Chichester, United Kingdom, 2009.

[17] A. van Lamsweerde, S. Brohez, R. De Landtsheer and D. Janssens, From system goals to intruder anti-goals: Attack generation and resolution for security requirements engineering, *Proceedings of the Workshop on Requirements for High Assurance Systems*, pp. 49–56, 2003.

Chapter 3

AUTOMATED ANALYSIS OF UNDERGROUND MARKETPLACES

Aleksandar Hudic, Katharina Krombholz, Thomas Otterbein, Christian Platzer, and Edgar Weippl

Abstract   Cyber criminals congregate and operate in crowded online underground marketplaces. Because forensic investigators lack efficient and reliable tools, they are forced to analyze the marketplace channels manually to locate criminals – a complex, time-consuming and expensive task. This paper demonstrates how machine learning algorithms can be used to automatically determine if a communication channel is used as an underground marketplace. Experimental results demonstrate that the classification system, which uses features related to the cyber crime domain, correctly classifies 51.3 million messages. The automation can significantly reduce the manual effort and the costs involved in investigating online underground marketplaces.

Keywords: Underground marketplaces, automated analysis, machine learning

1.   Introduction

Cyber criminals routinely use online underground marketplaces to communicate and trade stolen or illegal goods and services. Typically, publicly-accessible chatrooms and web forums are used as marketplaces by criminals who openly hawk their goods and initiate contractual agreements. Recent research has shown that underground marketplaces are a significant security risk because they provide venues for buying and selling stolen credentials, credit card numbers and other sensitive data [6]. Detecting these marketplaces and investigating the criminal activities being conducted are tedious and time-consuming tasks. Automating this process could significantly enhance the ability of forensic analysts to investigate criminal activities conducted in underground marketplaces. Unfortunately, the large number of online marketplaces and their ad

G. Peterson and S. Shenoi (Eds.): Advances in Digital Forensics X, IFIP AICT 433, pp. 31–42, 2014.
© IFIP International Federation for Information Processing 2014

hoc nature and volatility prevent naive detection approaches such as web crawling systems from being effective. Furthermore, criminals often "hijack" benign websites (e.g., websites containing classified ads and abandoned forums) instead of using dedicated underground websites.

This paper demonstrates how machine learning can be used to automatically detect underground marketplaces. An experimental evaluation is presented based on eleven months of real-world Internet Relay Chat (IRC) and web forum communications. The results show that the classification system can successfully locate and monitor communication channels used by cyber criminals, significantly reducing the manual effort and the costs involved in investigating online underground marketplaces.

2.   Background

While any type of communication channel could be used as an underground marketplace, the two most common types of channels are IRC chatrooms and web forums. IRC chatrooms and web forums are very popular communication channels and have multitudes of legitimate users.

A large number of publicly-accessible IRC networks are accessible over the Internet (e.g., QuakeNet, IRCnet, Undernet, EFnet, Rizon, Ustream and IRC-Hispano). In most cases, they do not have user authentication mechanisms, which unfortunately means that there is no straightforward means of attribution. Cyber criminals exploit IRC networks to advertise their goods and services. While some IRC networks appear to be specifically designated for criminal activities, benign networks are abused as well. The organizers simply create channels with names that are known to insiders. For example, channel names with the prefix #cc (short for credit card) are often used by criminals involved in credit card fraud.

Cyber criminals also operate underground marketplaces on websites that contain forums and message boards. The forums organize individual messages (i.e., posts) in the form of "threads" (i.e., lists of messages belonging to the same topic). Unlike IRC networks, the contents of these forums are persistent and users can communicate in a more organized manner, e.g., by replying to specific posts or to groups of users. Forums generally have stricter admission procedures than IRC networks (e.g., users have to sign-up to receive login credentials). Also, they offer "convenience" services to their members such as escrow and private messaging.

3.   Related Work

Research related to underground marketplaces has focused on the evaluation of message content [9] and the acquisition of reliable data from underground marketplaces [6, 16].

Franklin, *et al.* [3] conducted a systematic study of IRC channels exploited as underground marketplaces. They evaluated the content using machine learning techniques and demonstrated that underground marketplaces have considerable security implications; they also presented approaches for disrupting underground marketplaces. A Symantec report [13] on the underground economy provides useful analysis based on a significant amount of data collected from IRC networks and web forums over a period of one year; however, detailed information is not provided about the methodologies used to collect and analyze the data. Thomas and Martin [14] have studied the structure and players of the underground economy by examining IRC-based marketplaces. They describe the infrastructure established by criminals along with their activities, alliances and advertising methods.

Zhuge, *et al.* [16] have presented an overview of the underground market and malicious activities on Chinese websites based on a black market bulletin board and an online business platform. Holz, *et al.* [6] have studied "dropzones" that trade stolen digital credentials; they also evaluated a method that enables the automated analysis of impersonation attacks.

In contrast, Herley and Florencio [5] argue that marketplaces such as IRC channels and web forums do not have a significant impact. Instead, they describe them as standard markets for lemons where the goods are hard to monetize and the only people who derive benefits from the markets are the rippers.

Fallmann, *et al.* [2] have presented a novel system for automatically monitoring IRC channels and web forums. Furthermore, they extracted information and performed an experimental evaluation of the monitored environments.

4.   Locating Underground Marketplaces

Finding underground marketplaces is a manual task that is complex and time-consuming. We present a novel classification system for automatically discovering and monitoring underground marketplaces, even when they are hidden in benign information channels.

Figure 1 presents an overview of the training process. The learning algorithm of the classifier approximates the optimal function $f : D \to C$ that maps document vectors $d \in D$ to a specific class $c \in C$ based on the training set, where class c is either benign or criminal.

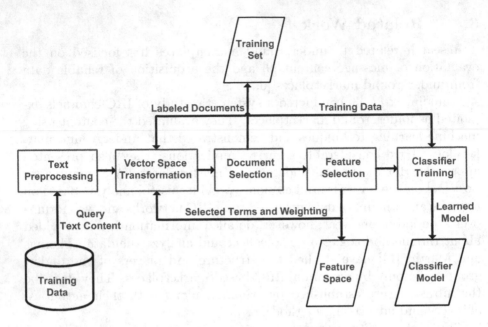

Figure 1. Training process.

In the classification process, a "document" is assumed to be an IRC chatroom or a web forum (thread), and "terms" are the words in IRC messages or web forum posts. The terms are mapped from each document to a numeric vector via the bag of words (BoW) model [4]. This model is agnostic to the exact ordering of terms within a document and interprets the terms as a set for each document. The resulting vector space model allows different weightings of the frequencies of individual terms.

4.1   Text Preprocessing

The raw training data contained noise and content that was not relevant to classification. The first step involved the extraction of the plaintext content. During this step, HTML elements and specific character encodings were eliminated.

4.2   Vector Space Transformation

The second step involved the generation of the vector space using tokenization [8]. Tokenization separates chunks of text with specific semantic values. A word-based model was employed because it has been shown to have the best performance [1, 11].

The next step in vector space transformation was to tag semantically-meaningful units that carry domain-relevant information. Various labels were attached to uniform resource identifiers (URIs), domain names, IP addresses, e-mail addresses, and numbers and dates to help identify the content. The tagging process helps reduce the feature space, e.g., by substituting frequently-changing values such as dates with a single date label.

The terms in the vector space model were weighted using *tf-idf* (term frequency – inverse document frequency) [10]. The term frequency $tf_{t,d}$ is the frequency of term t in document d and the inverse document frequency idf_t indicates the importance of term t to the document corpus. The *tf-idf* weighting scheme reduces the impact of common words (i.e., words that appear with high frequencies in the document). Since the documents had different lengths, the vectors were normalized using cosine normalization [12].

4.3   Document Selection

The third step involved the selection of appropriate documents according to their relevance. The document selection was based on hierarchical agglomerative clustering (HAC), a commonly-used deterministic bottom-up clustering algorithm that does not require a pre-specified number of clusters as input. HAC merges documents with the highest similarity into a cluster. The similarity of a merged cluster is called the combination similarity. Our HAC prototype implementation supports single-link and complete-link clustering. Single-link clustering defines the combination similarity in terms of the most similar members; the merge criterion is, therefore, local in nature. Complete-link clustering, on the other hand, defines the similarity of two merged clusters in terms of the similarity of the most dissimilar members and merges clusters using a non-local criterion. The algorithm merges documents into clusters until a predefined cutoff similarity value is reached.

The document selection process currently supports two methods for choosing a representative for each cluster. The first selects the document that represents the centroid based on the Euclidean distance, while the second is based on a definable score function.

Similarity. The cosine similarity measure is commonly used to compute the similarity between two documents in vector space:

$$sim(d_1, d_2) = \cos \theta = \frac{\vec{V}(d_1) * \vec{V}(d_2)}{|\vec{V}(d_1)||\vec{V}(d_2)|}.$$

Cosine similarity measures the similarity of the relative distribution of the terms by finding the cosine of the angle between the two document vectors $\vec{V}(d_1)$ and $\vec{V}(d_2)$. The cosine of the angle θ between the two document vectors ranges from zero to one, where zero indicates that the documents are independent and one means that the two document vectors are identical.

Distance. The Euclidean distance is another measure for comparing two vectors. This distance is more appropriate when the lengths of the documents are considered. For example, the Euclidean distance measure can be used to compute the nearest neighbors or, in our case, to determine the centroid of the cluster during the document selection process.

4.4   Feature Selection

Feature selection involves the selection of a subset of terms from the training set that is used for the vector space model. This process decreases the cardinality of the vector space and reduces the computation time.

In our case, features that occurred less than three times in the training set of the document corpus were removed (as proposed by Joachims [7]). Each term t was also ranked according to its information gain (IG) with regard to class c using the equation:

$$IG(c, t) = H(c) - H(c|t)$$

where H is the entropy. Selecting terms based on their information gain produces more accurate results. In this case, IG-based feature selection retained the top 10,000 terms from the IRC data collection.

4.5   Classification

The SVM-Light classifier [7] from the Weka toolkit [15] was used as the classifier. SVM-Light with a linear kernel function was chosen as the classifier because it performed better than Naive Bayes (NB), IBk (a k-nearest neighbor classifier), SMO (which implements the sequential minimal optimization algorithm) and the J48 algorithm (which is based on a pruned C4.5 decision tree).

Figure 2 presents an overview of the classification process. The initial stage involved the preprocessing of text as in the training phase. Following this, the data was transformed to a vector space model. Finally, the corresponding features were weighted according to the feature space

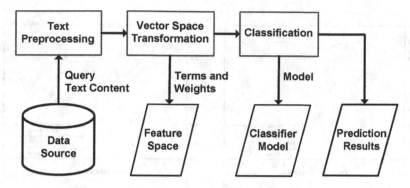

Figure 2. Classification process.

model and classified using the classifier constructed during the training phase.

5. Performance Evaluation

The IRC data corpus was collected over a period of eleven months using an observation framework [2]; the corpus contains 51.3 million IRC messages transmitted over 2,693 channels on 246 networks. The web forum data corpus was collected by crawling through more than 203,000 threads in ten forums. This section evaluates the performance of the classification system and the effectiveness of various vector space models and document selection methods.

5.1 IRC Channels

To evaluate the performance of the classification system on IRC channels, we manually labeled all 2,693 IRC channels based on their relationship to the underground economy and performed k-fold cross-validation. Figure 3 shows the cross-validation results for the various vector space models.

Figure 3(a) shows that the SVM classifier maintains a consistently high precision, which means that the predicted results do not contain many false positives. The drop in the recall rate in Figure 3(b) is mostly due to channels in which the underground-economy-related content accounts for a fraction of the exchanged messages and are mistakenly classified as false negatives. In general, removing terms with $tf < 3$ combined with the English stop word list and the Porter stemmer produced an average precision of 99.43% and increased the recall from the initial 85.76% to an average of 88.09%. The feature selection based on the top 10,000 terms ranked by the IG reduced the vector space to 4% of the

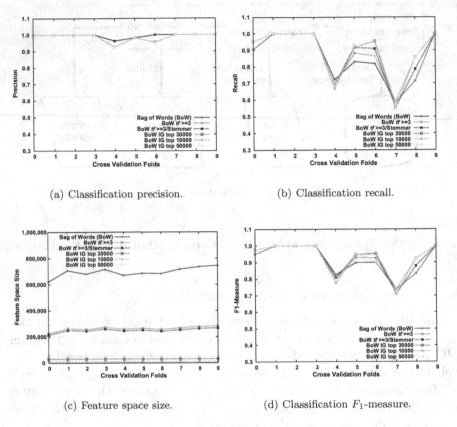

(a) Classification precision.   (b) Classification recall.

(c) Feature space size.   (d) Classification F_1-measure.

Figure 3.   Underground marketplace detection in IRC channels.

noise-filtered space and yielded the best score with an average precision of 98.59% and recall of 89.32%. This results in an average F_1-measure of 93.14% and an average accuracy of 97.84%. Thus, the classification system performs very well despite the noisy content of IRC channels.

Additionally, we evaluated the performance of document selection for different similarity values. To this end, the IRC channels were merged into clusters determined by the combination similarity cutoff value. The document selection evaluation also analyzed the selection methods for the cluster representative and compared the centroid-based method against the score function approach, which is defined as the ratio of unique textual content to the number of messages in the channel.

A k-fold cross-validation was also performed based on the training sets generated by document selection. Figure 4 shows the average performance results.

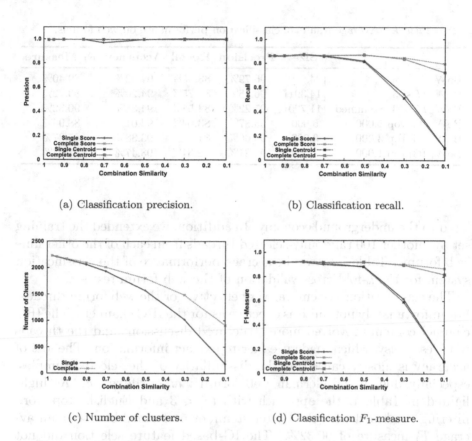

(a) Classification precision.

(b) Classification recall.

(c) Number of clusters.

(d) Classification F_1-measure.

Figure 4.   Classification performance of document selection IRC channels.

While single-link clustering reduces the number of clusters for the given similarity values more rapidly, it produces a significant accuracy loss. In contrast, complete-link clustering can reduce the number of needed training samples to less than 40% with minimal loss of recall. As shown in Figure 4(d), the selection methods for the cluster representative, which would be added to the training set, performed equally well for the upper interval of the combination similarity. Ultimately, the deviation between the two methods is only visible for very low combination similarity, where the score function based on the content information performed slightly better.

5.2   Web Forums

To evaluate the performance of the classification system on web forums, we manually labeled 300 randomly selected threads from the web forum `www.clicks.ws` depending on whether or not the posts were re-

Table 1. Average results of classification performance on web forums.

	Size	Precision	Recall	Accuracy	F_1-Measure
BoW	$\lfloor 34{,}890 \rfloor$	96.79%	83.55%	94.02%	89.40%
BoW, $tf < 3$	$\lfloor 14{,}391 \rfloor$	96.95%	83.75%	94.20%	89.72%
BoW, $tf < 3$, Stemmed	$\lfloor 11{,}720 \rfloor$	97.22%	84.58%	94.38%	90.32%
BoW, IG Top 5,000	5,000	95.87%	83.04%	94.01%	88.90%
BoW, IG Top 3,000	3,000	94.66%	81.60%	93.38%	87.37%
BoW, IG Top 1,000	1,000	94.81%	82.31%	93.47%	87.93%

lated to the underground economy. In addition, we extended the training set by another 100 randomly-selected threads from each of the other nine web forums. Table 1 shows the average performance of the classification system for the k-fold cross-validation of the web forum test set.

The classification system was very effective for the web forum threads, but unfortunately not quite as effective as for the IRC channels. The IRC channel contents involved more structured discussions and the threads were less noisy, which made it easier to extract information. The loss of accuracy is mostly caused by the dissimilarity of the selected samples, especially due to the German web forum www.carders.cc. As highlighted in Table 1, the approach with $tf < 3$ and English stop word filtering combined with the Porter stemmer performed best with an average F_1-measure of 90.32%. The IG-based feature selection did not show its advantages, but it is clearly not necessary in this case because of the dimensionality of the vector space. In conclusion, the vector space models show similar behavior as in the case of the IRC channel evaluation, demonstrating that the system is effective at detecting web forums used by cyber criminals.

6.   Conclusions

A machine-learning-based classification system can be very effective at detecting underground marketplaces that use venues such as IRC chatrooms and web forums. Indeed, automatically identifying and monitoring these marketplaces can greatly enhance investigations of online criminal activities. The classification system described in this paper detected underground marketplaces in a collection of 51.3 million IRC messages with an average accuracy of 97%. Furthermore, the system classified a subset of threads from ten web forums, ranging from underground economy discussion forums to hijacked benign web forums, with an average accuracy of 94%.

Acknowledgement

This research was funded by the Austrian Research Promotion Agency (FFG) under COMET K1.

References

[1] L. Baker and A. McCallum, Distributional clustering of words for text classification, *Proceedings of the Twenty-First International ACM SIGIR Conference on Research and Development in Information Retrieval*, pp. 96–103, 1998.

[2] H. Fallmann, G. Wondracek and C. Platzer, Covertly probing underground economy marketplaces, *Proceedings of the Seventh International Conference on the Detection of Intrusions and Malware and Vulnerability Assessment*, pp. 101–110, 2010.

[3] J. Franklin, A. Perrig, V. Paxson and S. Savage, An inquiry into the nature and causes of the wealth of Internet miscreants, *Proceedings of the Fourteenth ACM Conference on Computer and Communications Security*, pp. 375–388, 2007.

[4] Z. Harris, Distributional structure, *Word*, vol. 10(23), pp. 146–162, 1954.

[5] C. Herley and D. Florencio, Nobody sells gold for the price of silver: Dishonesty, uncertainty and the underground economy, *Proceedings of the Eighth Annual Workshop on the Economics of Information Security*, pp. 33–53, 2009.

[6] T. Holz, M. Engelberth and F. Freiling, Learning more about the underground economy: A case-study of keyloggers and dropzones, *Proceedings of the Fourteenth European Conference on Research in Computer Security*, pp. 1–18, 2009.

[7] T. Joachims, Text categorization with support vector machines: Learning with many relevant features, *Proceedings of the Tenth European Conference on Machine Learning*, pp. 137–142, 1998.

[8] P. McNamee and J. Mayfield, Character n-gram tokenization for European language text retrieval, *Information Retrieval*, vol. 7(1-2), pp. 73–97, 2004.

[9] J. Radianti, E. Rich and J. Gonzalez, Using a mixed data collection strategy to uncover vulnerability black markets, presented at the *Second Pre-ICIS Workshop on Information Security and Privacy*, 2007.

[10] G. Salton and C. Buckley, Term-weighting approaches in automatic text retrieval, *Information Processing and Management*, vol. 24(5), pp. 513–523, 1988.

[11] F. Sebastiani, Machine learning in automated text categorization, *ACM Computing Surveys*, vol. 34(1), pp. 1–47, 2002.

[12] A. Singhal, C. Buckley and M. Mitra, Pivoted document length normalization, *Proceedings of the Nineteenth International ACM SIGIR Conference on Research and Development in Information Retrieval*, pp. 21–29, 1996.

[13] Symantec, Symantec Report on the Underground Economy, July 07–June 08, Technical Report, Mountain View, California, 2008.

[14] R. Thomas and J. Martin, The underground economy: Priceless, *;login*, vol. 31(6), pp. 7–16, 2006.

[15] I. Witten, E. Frank and M. Hall, *Data Mining: Practical Machine Learning Tools and Techniques*, Elsevier, Amsterdam, The Netherlands, 2011.

[16] J. Zhuge, T. Holz, C. Song, J. Guo, X. Han and W. Zou, Studying malicious websites and the underground economy on the Chinese web, *Proceedings of the Seventh Annual Workshop on the Economics of Information Security*, pp. 225–244, 2008.

Chapter 4

AN EXPLORATORY PROFILING STUDY OF ONLINE AUCTION FRAUDSTERS

Vivien Chan, Kam-Pui Chow, Michael Kwan, Guy Fong, Michael Hui, and Jemy Tang

Abstract   Online auctions are one of the most popular e-commerce applications. With the growth of online auctions, the amount of online auction fraud has increased significantly. Little work has focused on the criminal profiling of online auction fraudsters. This exploratory study uses multivariate behavioral analysis to profile 61 online auction fraud offenders based on their behavior. The relationships between offender behavior and personal characteristics are also examined. The results yield a taxonomy of online auction fraud offenders: (i) novice-moderately-active; (ii) intermediate-inactive; and (iii) experienced-active. Discriminant analysis of the personal characteristics of offenders yields 78.6% accurate identification of the offender type. The results demonstrate that (intrinsic) personal motivation, education level and age are the most significant characteristics of experienced-active offenders.

Keywords: Online auctions, criminal profiling, multivariate behavioral analysis

1.   Introduction

The growth of online shopping has been phenomenal. Online auctions are one of the most popular online shopping platforms as evidenced by eBay's 19% increase in profits (totaling $677 million) during the first quarter of 2013 alone [11]. The increased popularity of online auction sites has seen a related growth in online auction fraud. According to the U.S. Federal Bureau of Investigation (FBI) Internet Crime Complaint Center (IC3), online auction fraud is consistently among the top complaints, with a high of 71.2% in 2004 [1].

Research on online auction fraud by Dong, et al. [4] and Trevathan and Read [15] has focused on the typology of online auction frauds. Pandit, et al. [10] have identified online auction fraudsters by analyzing

G. Peterson and S. Shenoi (Eds.): Advances in Digital Forensics X, IFIP AICT 433, pp. 43–56, 2014.

interactions between buyers and sellers. Meanwhile, researchers have ascertained that traditional criminal profiling techniques can be very useful in dealing with different types of cybercrimes [12]. However, empirical studies that apply criminal profiling techniques to real online auction offender data are practically nonexistent.

This paper uses multivariate behavioral analysis to profile 61 online auction fraud offenders. The relationships between offender behavior and personal characteristics identify three types of online auction fraud offenders: (i) novice-moderately-active; (ii) intermediate-inactive; and (iii) experienced-active. The results also demonstrate that (intrinsic) personal motivation, education level and age are the most significant characteristics of experienced-active offenders.

2.   Profiling Fraudsters

Casey [3] states that criminal profiling is very useful when little is known about the offenders, which is particularly important because criminals often use the Internet to conceal their identities and activities. Rogers [12] emphasizes the importance of using criminal profiling in cybercrime investigations, but there is no general theoretical model or approach for profiling cybercrime offenders.

Rogers [12] notes that two major criminal profiling approaches are employed by forensic scientists and practitioners: inductive and deductive profiling. An inductive approach is commonly employed by the FBI in profiling traditional crimes; many forensic scientists also adopt an inductive approach in profiling cybercrimes. However, other forensic scientists (e.g., [16]) argue that a deductive approach should be employed in investigating cybercrimes. In particular, they recommend the use of behavioral evidence analysis for cybercrime offender profiling because it is more objective, i.e., it relies more on facts than statistical inferences.

The application of traditional criminal profiling models to cybercrime investigations is an interesting concept. Goodwill, *et al.* [6] have compared three models of offender profiling on a group of (stranger) rapists to help predict the characteristics of offenders. The three models include the power and anger model of Hazelwood [7], the behavioral thematic model of Canter, *et al.* [2], and the MTC:R3 typology [9] with a multivariate approach adapted from [2]. Goodwill, *et al.* [6] recommend a fourth model, multivariate behavioral analysis, which combines clusters of behavior over simple bivariate relationships between individual behavior and background characteristics. In fact, their study concluded that multivariate behavioral analysis yields results that greatly surpass those obtained with the other three models.

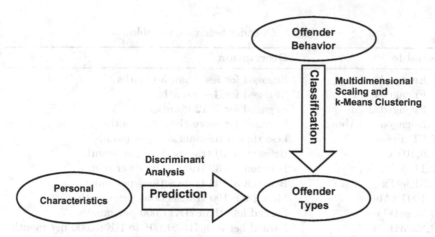

Figure 1. Multivariate profiling approach.

The multivariate profiling approach [6] illustrated in Figure 1 helps understand the underlying factors that can be used to classify offenders, and how personal characteristics may be used to predict the types of offenders. Multivariate analysis has proved to be effective at profiling cybercrimes. Stabek, *et al.* [14] have applied the technique to understand the incidence of scams. Their content analysis technique is similar to that used by Goodwill, *et al.* [6], who leverage hierarchical clustering and discriminant function analysis. Kjaerland [8] has applied multivariate profiling to account for the multitude of features that appear simultaneously in cyber incidents.

This exploratory study applies the multivariate profiling methodology to analyze offender behavior. The relationships between the behavior and personal characteristics of offenders are also examined. The results provide insights into the use of multivariate profiling to create profiles of online auction fraudsters.

3.   Profiling Methodology

Aleem and Antwi-Boasiako [1] have developed a taxonomy of eBay auction frauds based on the *modus operandi* of cyber criminals. The frauds include non-delivery of merchandise, failure to pay, counterfeits and reproductions, bid shilling, bid shielding, misrepresentation, fee stacking, shell auctions and phishing, triangulations and fencing, buying and switching, and loss/damage claims. This exploratory study focuses on one type of online auction fraud – counterfeits and reproductions. The reason is that the study is based on the online auction offender database of the Hong Kong Customs and Excise Department, which maintains data pertaining exclusively to counterfeit goods.

Table 1. Offender behavior variables.

Variable	Description
S1_Engaged3mLess	Engaged for less than 3 months
S1_Engaged4_6m	Engaged for 4–6 months
S1_Engaged7_12m	Engaged for 7–12 months
S1_Engaged13mAbove	Engaged for more than 13 months
S2_5TxBelow	Less than 5 transactions per month
S2_6_10Tx	Between 6–10 transactions per month
S2_11_30Tx	Between 11–30 transactions per month
S2_31_99Tx	Between 31–99 transactions per month
S2_100TxAbove	More than 100 transactions per month
S3_Earn1kLess	Earned less than HK$1,000 per month
S3_Earn1k_5k	Earned between HK$1,001 to HK$5,000 per month
S3_Earn5kMore	Earned more than HK$5,001 per month
S4_BoughtFromWebsite	Items bought from online websites (e.g., Taobao)
S4_BoughtFromHK_China	Items bought from shops/factories in China/HK
S4_BoughtFromFriends	Items bought from friends or other sources
S5_SeizureValueBelow10k	Total seizure value was less than HK$10,000
S5_SeizureValue10k_50k	Total seizure value was HK$10,001 to HK$50,000
S5_SeizureValueAbove50k	Total seizure value was more than HK$50,001

The online auction offender database contained case reports from 2012 to the middle of 2013. In the study, we assumed that each offender was responsible for his/her offenses, although not all the offenders were convicted of their alleged crimes at the time of the study. The database had 121 cases. Cases with missing data were eliminated, yielding a total of 61 online auction offender cases that were considered in the study. Seven offenders were accused of copyright infringements while 54 were accused of trademark infringements.

3.1 Preparation of Variables

The variables collected from the offender database were divided into two categories: (i) offender behavior variables; and (ii) personal characteristics variables.

All the offender behavior variables were recoded as dichotomous variables to facilitate analysis and interpretation. Variables with multiple categories were dummy coded as multiple dichotomous variables (e.g., variables for the engagement period and source of auction items) and a pool of eighteen variables was created. The eighteen variables and their descriptions are presented in Table 1. Note that all currency values are expressed in Hong Kong dollars (HK$).

The personal characteristics variables are categorized into two conceptual groups: demographic variables (e.g., sex, age and education level) and intrinsic motivation (e.g., reason for engaging in online auction activities and why [the offender was] not afraid of being caught). The personal characteristics variables, their descriptions and other key information are presented in Table 2.

3.2 Analytical Process

The data analysis process involved three steps. First, multidimensional scaling analysis was applied to the eighteen dichotomous offender behavior variables. This technique identified the underlying structure of the offender behavior variables: similar variables formed clusters when the variables were plotted as points in two-dimensional space. The second step performed k-means clustering to classify the offender cases into offender types based on the clusters of offender behavior variables. The final step performed discriminant analysis to check if the offender types could be predicted from the personal characteristics variables.

4. Results

This section describes the multidimensional scaling results and the discriminant analysis results.

4.1 Offender Behavior Variables

Nearly 50% (30 of the offenders were engaged in online auction fraud for periods ranging from four months to twelve months, while 28% (17) and 23% (14) were engaged in online auction fraud for less than three months and more than one year, respectively. The total seizure value was about HK$1 million, but only 5% (3) of the offenders were involved in seizures valued at more than HK$50,000. Most of the offenders (52%) earned less than HK$1,000 per month from online auction fraud activities, with about 16% (10) earning more than HK$5,000 per month. Only 18% of the offenders were actively involved with more than 30 transactions per month; the majority of the offenders were less active with fewer than eleven transactions per month (48%) or moderately active with 11–30 transactions per month (31%). About 80% of the counterfeit goods were sourced from other online websites while the remaining 20% of the goods were bought from factories in Hong Kong or China or bought from other sources.

Table 2.　Personal characteristics variables.

Variable	Description	Value	Frequency
Sex	Gender of offender	Female	32.80%
		Male	67.20%
Age	Age of offender	–	Mean = 30
			Min = 18
			Max = 54
Education Level	Education level of offender	Primary or lower	3.30%
		Secondary	63.90%
		Tertiary	13.10%
		University or higher	19.70%
Occupation	Occupation of offender	Unemployed	24.60%
		Student	14.80%
		Employed	55.70%
		Housewife	4.90%
Income Level	Income level of offender	No stable income	14.80%
		Income of HK$9,999 or lower	21.20%
		Income of HK$10,000 to HK$19,999	27.90%
		Income of HK$20,000 or higher	8.20%
		Missing data	27.90%
Economic Status	Economic status of offender	Poor	63.90%
		Average	32.80%
		Rich	3.30%
Marital Status	Marital status of offender	Single	63.90%
		Married	27.90%
		Divorced	8.20%
Living Status	Living arrangement of offender	Lived alone	4.80%
		Lived with parents	63.90%
		Lived with spouse or friend	31.30%
Arrest History	Previous arrests of offender	No arrest history	90.20%
		Related fraud arrest history	4.20%
		Non-related arrest history	5.60%
Objective	Reason for engaging in online auction activities	Monetary	78.90%
		Thrill	21.10%
Why not afraid of being caught	Why the offender was not afraid of being caught by the Customs and Excise Department	Believed would not get caught easily	42.60%
		Did not know it was an offense	49.20%
		Did not disclose	8.20%

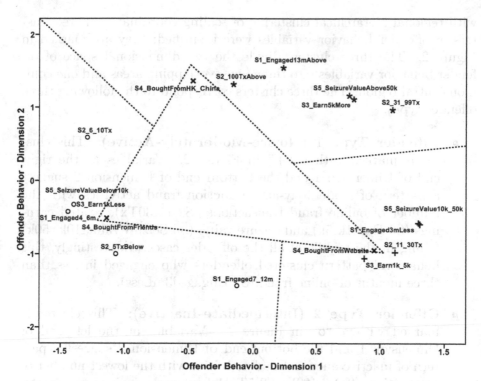

Figure 2. Multdimensional scaling plot of the offender behavior variables.

4.2 Personal Characteristics Variables

Table 2 provides detailed information about the personal characteristics variables. The personal characteristics variables reveal that most of the offenders were male (67%), single or divorced (72%), lived with their parents (64%) and were between the ages of 22 and 39 (68%). Most of the offenders had secondary school education (64%) and were employed (56%), but were relatively poor (64%) with only 8% (5) of them earning more than HK$20,000. Nearly all the offenders (90%) did not have a previous arrest history. Most of them (79%) were engaged in online auctions for monetary reasons (e.g., to improve their living standards). About half the offenders (49%) said that they did not know that the goods they sold were counterfeit.

4.3 Multidimensional Scaling Results

The two-dimensional coordinates for the 18 offender behavior variables were hierarchically clustered using Ward's Method with the squared Euclidean distance and standardized Z-score. Figure 2 shows the results with regional hierarchical clustering of scaling coordinates. Three clusters of offender behavior variables were identified; they are marked in Figure 2. The three clusters divide the two-dimensional space of offender behavior variables into three non-overlapping areas and one common central region. The three clusters correspond to the following three offender types:

- **Offender Type 1 (Novice-Moderately-Active):** This cluster is marked with a "+" in Figure 2. Variables at the right end of Dimension 1 and the bottom end of Dimension 2 suggest a pattern of moderately-active auction fraud activities with the number of online fraud transactions (S2_11_30Tx), related earnings (S3_Earn1k_5k) and seizure value (S5_SeizureValue_10k_ 50k) falling in the middle of all the offender cases. Interestingly, this behavioral pattern clustered offenders who engaged in less than three months of online fraud (S1_Engaged3mLess).

- **Offender Type 2 (Intermediate-Inactive):** This cluster is marked with a "o" in Figure 2. Variables at the left end of Dimension 1 and the bottom end of Dimension 2 suggest a pattern of inactive auction fraud activities with the lowest number of transactions (S2_6_10Tx, S2_5TxBelow) and earnings per month (S3_Earn1kLess). In addition, these variables are also clustered with the lowest seizure value (S5_SeizureValue10kBelow) and the offenders who engaged in online fraud for a moderate period of time (S1_Engaged4_6m, S1_Engaged7_12m).

- **Offender Type 3 (Experienced-Active):** This cluster is marked with a "-" in Figure 2. Variables at the right end of Dimension 1 and the top end of Dimension 2 suggest a pattern of very active auction fraud activities with the largest number of transactions (S2_31_99Tx, S2_100TxAbove) and earnings per month (S3_Earn5kMore). In addition, these variables are also clustered with the highest seizure value (S5_SeizureValueAbove50k) and the offenders who engaged in online fraud for the longest period of time (S1_Engaged13mAbove).

The central region of the two-dimensional scaling plot (marked with three "x" symbols in Figure 2) shows an absence of variables related to online fraud offender behavior. Careful examination reveals that this common region shared by the three clusters is the source of goods bought, which means that all the offender types bought goods from similar sources. In addition, Dimension 1 suggests a measure of the activity level of offender behavior while Dimension 2 suggests a measure of the period of engagement in online fraud activities.

4.4 Discriminant Analysis Results

The k-means clustering technique (with $k = 3$ clusters) was used to group the offender cases. The data was analyzed using a non-parametric mean test with k-independent samples on the set of offender behavior variables. A Kruskal-Wallis test indicated significant effects of the grouping on engagement period ($\chi^2(2)=17.189$, p<0.01), transactions ($\chi^2(2)=14.304$, $p < 0.01$), earnings ($\chi^2(2)=10.011$, $p < 0.01$) and seizure value ($\chi^2(2)=23.587$, $p < 0.01$), but no significant effect on the source ($\chi^2(2)=0.905$, $p > 0.05$). These results are consistent with the results of the multidimensional scaling analysis described in the previous section, where the three types of offenders had distinct behavior, but no difference with regard to the sources of their auction items.

Further analysis indicated that the effects of the grouping on age ($\chi^2(2)=7.08$, $p < 0.05$), education level ($\chi^2(2)=8.21$, $p < 0.054$) and why not afraid of being caught ($\chi^2(2)=10.22$, $p < 0.01$) are significant. However, the effect on motive is marginally insignificant ($\chi^2(2)=4.69$, $p = 0.096$) and the effects on the other personal characteristics variables are not significant.

Upon closer examination of the three offenders types using the three significant personal characteristics variables, we noticed that the novice-moderately-active offender group is the youngest of the three groups (mean = 28), with half the offenders (50%) having tertiary or university or higher education levels (50%) and most of them (61.5%) believing that they would not get caught. On the other hand, the experienced-active offenders is the oldest group (mean = 36), with the vast majority of them (81.8%) having primary or secondary education levels and almost all of them (90.9%) claiming that they did not know that their activities were illegal. The mean age of the intermediate-inactive offender group is 29, most of them (79.2%) having a secondary school education level, about half of them (45.8%) claiming that they did not know that their activities were illegal and 41.7% believing that they would not get caught.

Discriminant function analysis was applied to differentiate the three offender types: novice-moderately-active, intermediate-inactive, and experienced-active. The independent variables corresponded to the personal characteristics, which included demographic characteristics (e.g., sex, age, education level and income level) and intrinsic motivation (e.g., objective and why the offenders were not afraid of being caught).

Table 3. Wilks' lambda and canonical correlations for the three offender types.

Function	Wilks' Lambda	χ^2	df	p	R_c	R_c^2
1–2	0.327	37.8	22	0.019	0.771	59.40%

Table 3 presents the Wilks' lambda and canonical correlations for the three offender types. The canonical discriminant functions show a high correlation (0.771) with an effect of $R_c^2 = 59.4\%$. The first and second functions significantly differentiate the three groups (Wilks' Lambda = 0.327, $\chi^2(22) = 37.8$, $p < 0.05$). The results obtained for the second function alone were not significant ($p = 0.713$).

Table 4. Standardized discriminant function and structure coefficients.

Scale	Coefficient	r_s	r_s^2
Function 1			
Sex (x_1)	−0.09	−0.20	3.96%
Age (x_2)	0.62	0.33	10.69%
Education Level (x_3)	−0.84	−0.28	8.07%
Occupation (x_4)	0.20	0.03	0.07%
Income Level (x_5)	−0.20	0.07	0.53%
Economic Status (x_6)	−0.04	0.04	0.14%
Marital Status (x_7)	−1.05	0.08	0.69%
Living Status (x_8)	0.52	0.18	3.13%
Arrest History (x_9)	−0.43	−0.21	4.20%
Objective (x_{10})	0.69	0.29	8.24%
Why no fear of being caught (x_{11})	0.75	0.35	12.11%

Table 4 presents the structure matrix and structure coefficients for the three offender types corresponding to the first function (Function 1). Note that age, education level and intrinsic motivation (objective and why [an offender was] not afraid of being caught) are primarily responsible for differentiating between the offender types. On the other hand, education level is negatively correlated with the other three variables, which are positively correlated in Function 1.

Table 5 shows the centroids of the three offender groups for Function 1. The group centroids suggest that intrinsic motivation and age (i.e., Function 1) tend to be most elevated for experienced-active offenders and least evident in novice-moderately-active offenders. This suggests that the offender type differences observed in Function 1 pertaining to the personal characteristics variables (age, education level, objective and

Table 5. Group centroids resulting from discriminant function analysis.

Offender Type	Function 1
Novice-moderately-active	−1.314
Intermediate-inactive	0.124
Experienced-active	1.761

why not afraid of being caught) can be attributed to experienced-active offenders.

Based on the data presented in Table 4, the following equation can be used to determine the offender type based on personal characteristics information:

$$Offender\ Type\ (Function\ 1) = -0.09x_1 + 0.62x_2 - 0.84x_3 + 0.20x_4$$
$$-0.20x_5 - 0.04x_6 - 1.05x_7 + 0.52x_8$$
$$-0.43x_9 + 0.69x_{10} + 0.75x_{11}.$$

Tests of this equation with the available data revealed that 78.6% of the original cases were classified correctly.

5. Discussion

The results of the study show that a multivariate approach [6] is useful for profiling online auction offenders. Three distinct types of offenders, novice-moderately-active, intermediate-inactive and experienced-active, were identified using multidimensional scaling and hierarchical clustering, and these three types of offenders are statistically different.

Discriminant analysis applied to the personal characteristics variables yielded an equation (model) for offender type determination that is 78.6% accurate when used with the available data. In addition, certain personal characteristics variables (i.e., age, education level, objective and why not afraid of being caught) have higher predictive values in discriminating online auction fraud offenders. These variables are most elevated in the case of experienced-active offenders, which is consistent with the k-independent sample test results (i.e., a group of older offenders with lower education levels who mostly believed that the online auction activities they were conducting were not illegal). At the other end are the novice-moderately-active offenders, typically young with high education levels who did not believe that they would get caught, which is also consistent with the k-independent sample test results. Additionally, although the experienced-active offenders said that they were unaware

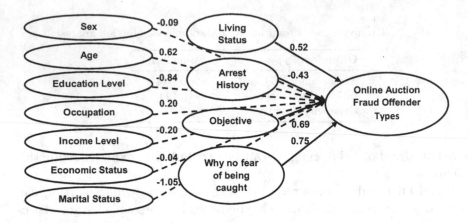

Figure 3.   Predictive model of offender types based on Function 1.

that their online auction activities were illegal, there is the possibility that they were lying to law enforcement investigators.

Figure 3 shows the predictive model constructed based on the results of this study. This model could assist investigators in narrowing their search for offenders after the online auction activities and behavior of the subjects are known.

The two personal characteristics variables, objective and why not afraid of being caught, correspond to the intrinsic motivation of offenders. Interestingly, the results of the study reveal that this psychological factor may play an important role in predicting the offender type. As Rogers, *et al.* [13] note, like any other crime, people are also involved in cybercrimes, so it is necessary to include psychological traits and personal characteristics when profiling cyber criminals. Therefore, it would be useful if future research on online auction fraud (and other cybercrimes) could also study how psychological factors could be used to predict offender behavior.

The current study only considered online auction fraudsters who were apprehended. It is possible that undetected offenders may have certain personal characteristics that could enhance prediction. Although the inclusion of undetected offenders is difficult in empirical research, it is, nevertheless, important to acknowledge the fact that this group was not considered in the study.

In addition, the use of law enforcement records as research data is not ideal. The data was not collected for the purpose of empirical research and, therefore, may be biased towards criminal investigations [2]. In fact, Farrington and Lambert [5] note that law enforcement data has limited utility with regard to offender profiling.

The results of this exploratory study show how a taxonomy of online auction fraud offenders can be created and that certain personal characteristics could predict the offender type. A good topic for future research is to collect data pertaining to additional personal characteristics and examine if the profiling of online auction fraudsters could be improved. In particular, the motivations of offenders could be explored more deeply to discern new offender behaviors. Additionally, the multivariate profiling approach employed in this study could be applied to other types of cybercrimes.

6. Conclusions

Multivariate behavioral analysis is a promising approach for profiling online auction fraud offenders. Multidimensional scaling and hierarchical clustering of the various offender behavior variables yielded a taxonomy of three distinct types of auction fraud offenders: (i) novice-moderately-active; (ii) intermediate-inactive; and (iii) experienced-active. Personal characteristics were also found to be predictive of the offender types; discriminant analysis of the personal characteristics of offenders resulted in 78.6% accurate identification of the offender type.

Acknowledgement

The authors wish to thank Dr. Kenneth Yuen for his valuable advice during the data analysis phase.

References

[1] A. Aleem and A. Antwi-Boasiako, Internet auction fraud: The evolving nature of online auction criminality and the mitigating framework to address the threat, *International Journal of Law, Crime and Justice*, vol. 39(3), pp. 140–160, 2011.

[2] D. Canter, C. Bennell, L. Alison and S. Reddy, Differentiating sex offenses: A behaviorally based thematic classification of stranger rapes, *Behavioral Sciences and the Law*, vol. 21(2), pp. 157–174, 2003.

[3] E. Casey, Cyberpatterns: Criminal behavior on the Internet, in *Criminal Profiling: An Introduction to Behavioral Evidence Analysis*, B. Turvey (Ed.), Academic Press, San Diego, California, pp. 547–573, 2003.

[4] F. Dong, S. Shatz and H. Xu, Combating online in-auction fraud: Clues, techniques and challenges, *Computer Science Review*, vol. 3(4), pp. 245–258, 2009.

[5] D. Farrington and S. Lambert, The Feasibility of a Statistical Approach to Offender Profiling: Burglary and Violence in Nottinghamshire, Home Office, London, United Kingdom, 1992.

[6] A. Goodwill, L. Alison and A. Beech, What works in offender profiling? A comparison of typological, thematic and multivariate models, *Behavioral Sciences and the Law*, vol. 27(4), pp. 507–529, 2009.

[7] R. Hazelwood, Analyzing the rape and profiling the offender, in *Practical Aspects of Rape Investigation: A Multidisciplinary Approach*, R. Hazelwood and A. Burgess (Eds.), Elsevier, New York, pp. 169–199, 1987.

[8] M. Kjaerland, A taxonomy and comparison of computer security incidents from the commercial and government sectors, *Computers and Security*, vol. 25(7), pp. 522–538, 2006.

[9] R. Knight and R. Prentky, Classifying sexual offenders: The development and corroboration of taxonomic models, in *Handbook of Sexual Assault: Issues, Theories and Treatment of the Offender*, W. Marshall, D. Laws and H. Barbaree (Eds.), Plenum, New York, pp. 23–52, 1990.

[10] S. Pandit, D. Chau, S. Wang and C. Faloutsos, NetProbe: A fast and scalable system for fraud detection in online auction networks, *Proceedings of the Sixteenth International Conference on the World Wide Web*, pp. 201–210, 2007.

[11] F. Richter, eBay's profit rises 19 percent, *Statista.com* (`www.stat ista.com/topics/871/online-shopping/chart/1053/ebays-fi rst-quarter-results`), April 18, 2013.

[12] M. Rogers, The role of criminal profiling in the computer forensics process, *Computers and Security*, vol. 22(4), pp. 292–298, 2003.

[13] M. Rogers, K. Seigfried and K. Tidke, Self-reported computer criminal behavior: A psychological analysis, *Digital Investigation*, vol. 3(S), pp. S116–S120, 2006.

[14] A. Stabek, P. Watters and R. Layton, The seven scam types: Mapping the terrain of cybercrime, *Proceedings of the Second Cybercrime and Trustworthy Computing Workshop*, pp. 41–51, 2010.

[15] J. Trevathan and W. Read, Undesirable and fraudulent behavior in online auctions, *Proceedings of the International Conference on Security and Cryptography*, pp. 450–458, 2006.

[16] B. Turvey (Ed.), *Criminal Profiling: An Introduction to Behavioral Evidence Analysis*, Academic Press, Oxford, United Kingdom, 2012.

Chapter 5

WEB USER PROFILING BASED ON BROWSING BEHAVIOR ANALYSIS

Xiao-Xi Fan, Kam-Pui Chow, and Fei Xu

Abstract   Determining the source of criminal activity requires a reliable means to estimate a criminal's identity. One way to do this is to use web browsing history to build a profile of an anonymous user. Since an individual's web use is unique, matching the web use profile to known samples provides a means to identify an unknown user. This paper describes a model for web user profiling and identification. Two aspects of browsing behavior are examined to construct a user profile, the user's page view number and page view time for each domain. Four weighting models, based on the term frequency and term frequency – inverse document frequency weighting schemes, are proposed and compared. Experiments involving 51 personal computers demonstrate that the profiling model is very effective at identifying web users.

Keywords: Web user profiling, browsing behavior, term frequency

1.   Introduction

Due to the widespread use of computers and networks, digital evidence plays an important role in criminal investigations. The large amount of digital evidence that resides on computer systems can help investigate and prosecute criminal actions [3]. The evidentiary artifacts are varied and include chat logs, agendas, email, application information, Internet history and cache files. In many cases, investigative leads are found in a criminal's web browser history [8].

Investigators often face situations where a computer associated with a cybercrime has been found, but the suspect is unknown. In such a scenario, the investigator can create the suspect's profile from the digital evidence residing on the computer, and match the profile with the profiles of other individuals to identify the suspect.

G. Peterson and S. Shenoi (Eds.): Advances in Digital Forensics X, IFIP AICT 433, pp. 57–71, 2014.
© IFIP International Federation for Information Processing 2014

Identifying a user from his/her web browsing history requires an efficient model that associates individuals with their web activities. This paper proposes a web user identification model that creates a user profile based on web browsing activities and identifies relationships between different users. The model provides web user identity information based on the assumption that a given user has consistent preferences. Experiments involving 51 computers demonstrate that the profiling model can be used to identify web users.

2. Related Work

User profiling has been used in the context of e-commerce and personalization systems, the two primary applications being content-based filtering and collaborative filtering. Grcar, *et al.* [6] have developed a topic-ontology-based system that creates dynamic profiles of users from their browsed web pages. The viewed pages are represented as word vectors and hierarchical clustering is performed to construct a topic ontology. A similarity comparison maps users' current interests to the topic ontology based on their browsing histories.

Fathy, *et al.* [4] have proposed a personalized search that uses an individual's click-history data to model search preferences in an ontological user profile. The profile is then incorporated to re-rank the search results to provide personalized views.

Some research has been conducted in the area of behavioral profiling. Bucklin, *et al.* [2] have modeled the within-site browsing behavior of users at a commercial website. Their model focuses on two browsing behaviors: a user's decision to continue browsing the site or to exit, and how long a user views each page during a website visit.

Forte, *et al.* [5] conducted a web-based experiment to observe how people with different backgrounds and levels of experience make decisions. The experiments analyzed the types of actions, sequences of actions and times between actions using significance testing, regression modeling and evidence weighting. The results suggest that recording the actions taken and the time spent on each decision can help create statistical models that can discern demographic information.

Similarly, Hu, *et al.* [7] have presented an approach that predicts user gender and age from web browsing behavior. Gender and age are predicted by training a supervised regression model based on users' self-reported gender, age and browsing history. Then, based on the age and gender tendency of the web pages that a user has browsed, a Bayesian framework is used to predict the user's gender and age.

Research in the areas of user profiling and behavior analysis have not explicitly targeted digital forensic investigations. Indeed, criminology profiling techniques have primarily focused on violent criminal activities.

One area in which criminal profiling has been applied to computer crimes is the insider threat. McKinney, *et al.* [10] have proposed a masquerade detection method, which creates a user profile using a naive Bayesian classifier that analyzes running computer processes. Bhukya and Banothu [1] engage GUI-based behavior to construct user profiles; a support vector machine learning algorithm is used to train the system to classify users. To our knowledge, there is little, if any, research that has explicitly focused on identifying web users based on their browsing history.

3. Methodology

Figure 1 presents a schematic diagram of the proposed web user profiling and identification model. The investigator uses evidence from the target computer to identify the user. The suspect computers are the candidate computers that are compared with the target computer. The candidate computer with the highest similarity score is assumed to have been used by the same user as the target computer.

Browsing activity data is extracted from all the browsers installed on the target and candidate computers. After preprocessing the data, the user's domains of interest are extracted and the page view number (PVN) and page view time (PVT) are calculated for each domain. Each computer is then represented as a weighted vector of the domains, where each weight is the term frequency (TF) or term frequency – inverse document frequency (TFIDF) of the PVN or PVT. Finally, a cosine similarity measure is applied to calculate the similarity scores between the target computer profile and the candidate computer profiles to identify the candidate computer with the highest similarity score.

3.1 Data Extraction

Web browsers can be classified based on their web browser engines, as shown in Table 1 [15]. Different browsers record browsing history in different ways. Table 1 shows that most browsers are based on the Trident engine (IE core). Every web page visited by a Trident engine browser is stored in the `index.dat` file, along with the access time, Windows user name, etc. Analyzing the `index.dat` file can help understand a user's browsing behavior. Some browser forensic tools can automatically parse the `index.dat` file; example tools are Index.dat Viewer, Pasco, IE History View, Web Historian and NetAnalysis. We used IE History View

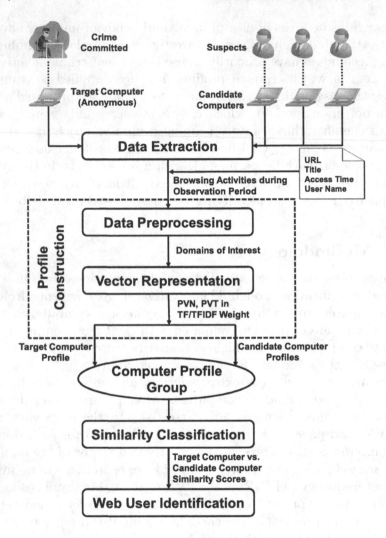

Figure 1. Proposed web user profiling and identification model.

v1.70 [12] to extract Internet history records from `index.dat` files in this research. Also, Chrome History View v1.16 [13] and Mozilla History View v1.51 [14] were used to extract history records from Google Chrome and Mozilla Firefox browsers, respectively.

For each computer, the history records from all the installed browsers were extracted and combined together. Each record contained a URL, title, access time and Windows user name. When a computer had multiple users, a separate profile was created for each user.

Table 1. Web browser categories.

Engine	Corresponding Browsers
Trident (IE Core)	Internet Explorer, MyIE9, The World, Maxthon, Tencent Traveler, 360 Secure Browser, Sougou Explorer, 360chrome, MenuBox, GreenBrowser
Gecko	Mozilla Firefox
Webkit	Google Chrome, Safari
Presto	Opera

History records from the target and candidate computers were extracted for the last 40 days. The reason for using a 40-day observation period is that users can easily change their browsing topics over short periods of time, but it is much harder for users to change their browsing interests over the long term.

3.2   Data Preprocessing

Several preprocessing steps were applied to the history data that was collected. For Trident engine browsers, duplicate records may exist in the primary `index.dat` history file as well as the daily/weekly `index.dat` file. Duplicate records with the same URLs and access times were deleted. Also, pop-up desktop news notices were removed because, if the users did not actively click on the pop-ups, they were likely not of interest.

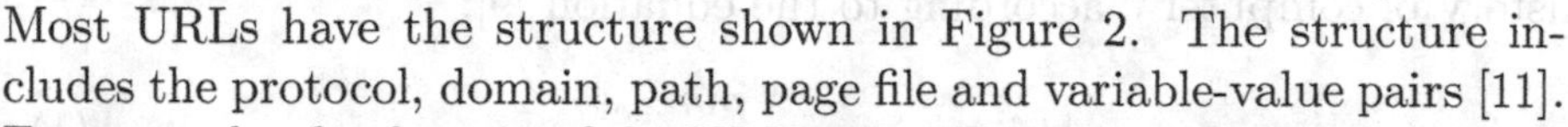

Protocol://	Domain	/	Path(/../../)	Page File	?	Variable-Value	...

Figure 2. URL structure.

Next, the domain information was extracted from each history record. Most URLs have the structure shown in Figure 2. The structure includes the protocol, domain, path, page file and variable-value pairs [11]. For example, the domain of the URL `http://en.wikipedia.org/wiki/Domain` is `en.wikipedia.org`. Every domain name is a hierarchical series of character strings, with the different levels separated by dots proceeding from the top-level domain at the right end to specific host names on the left (Table 2).. The top-level domain is expressed using a generic code (e.g., `.com`, `.edu` or `.gov`) or a country code (e.g., `.cn` or `.uk`). The second label from the right denotes the second-level domain. Labels to the left of the second-level domain correspond to sub-domains of

Table 2.   Examples of domain names.

Domain Example	Host Name	Sub- Domain	Second- Level Domain	Top- Level Domain	Extracted Domain Part
www.hku.hk	www	–	hku	hk	hku.hk
www.cs.hku.hk	www	cs	hku	hk	hku.hk
www.discuss.com.hk	www	–	discuss	com.hk	discuss.com.hk

the second-level domain. The top-level and second-level domains (ref-erenced as domain in later sections) were extracted from every history record.

Note that an extracted domain visited only once during the observa-tion period was not included in a profile. This is because one-page visits were assumed to be primarily due to user input errors.

3.3   Vector Representation

A vector space model was used to build computer profiles. Each computer (c_j) was represented as a vector $c_j = (w_1, w_2, ..., w_N)$, where N is the number of domains. Each weight domain pair (w_i) corresponds to a domain extracted from the history records of the target computer. The weight was calculated using TF and TFIDF over the PVN or PVT of the domain. Domains were ranked according to their weighting values. The top N domains from the target computer were chosen to form the profile vectors of the target and candidate computers. This resulted in four web user profile models: TF-PVN, TF-PVT, TFIDF-PVN and TFIDF-PVT.

TF-PVN Model.   Term frequency (TF) is the number of times that a term occurs in a document. In this study, the TF-PVN model assigns a weight to the page view frequency $tf\_pvn_{d,c}$ of domain d in the browser history of computer c according to the equation [9]:

$$tf\_pvn_{d,c} = \frac{pvn_{d,c}}{\sum_k pvn_{k,c}} \qquad (1)$$

where $pvn_{d,c}$ is the number of page views of domain d from computer c during the observation period and $\sum_k pvn_{k,c}$ is the total number of page views from computer c during the observation period.

For a given computer c, the set of weights determined by TF-PVN may be viewed as a quantitative digest of the computer. Table 3 shows the top seven domains from a target computer sorted by their TF-PVN

Table 3. TF-PVN weighting results.

Domain	pvn	tf_pvn (3,067 Visits)
google.com	535	0.174
hku.hk	366	0.119
taobao.com	235	0.077
chinamac.com	202	0.066
hsbc.com.hk	102	0.033
hkst.com	68	0.022
youtube.com	60	0.020

values. The exact ordering of domains can be ignored, but the number of occurrences of each domain is material. However, certain domains such as google.com are visited very frequently by users. These domains have high TF-PVN values for most users and, therefore, have little or no user discriminating power.

TFIDF-PVN Model. TFIDF-PVN attenuates the effect that frequently visited domains have on domain weighting by giving high weights to domains that occur frequently for one computer but rarely for the other computers.

Computing the TFIDF-PVN of a domain for a given computer involves two sub-calculations: how often the domain is visited by the computer (TF) and how many computers in the collection visit the domain (DF). The DF is inverted to yield the IDF, which is then combined with the TF. IDF is calculated as the logarithm (base 2) of the quotient of the total number of computers ($|C|$) and the number of computers containing the domain ($|\{c \in C | d \in c\}|$) in order to scale the values [9]:

$$tfidf\_pvn_{d,c} = tf\_pvn_{d,c} \times \log_2 \frac{|C|}{|\{c \in C | d \in c\}|}. \tag{2}$$

Table 4 shows the same seven domains from the target computer as in Table 3 sorted by their TFIDF-PVN values. Note that some new domains have emerged among the top seven domains. Also, the weight of chinamac.com has increased substantially because only two out of fifteen computers shared this domain (high IDF). Furthermore, the weight of google.com has decreased because it appeared in almost all the computers (low IDF). The reason for these differences is that TFIDF-PVN assigns a high value to a domain when it occurs many times in a small number of computers (high discriminating power for the computers).

Table 4.   TFIDF-PVN weighting example.

Domain	pvn	tf_pvn (3,067 Visits)	idf (15 Computers)	tfidf_pvn
chinamac.com	202	0.066	2.907	0.191
taobao.com	235	0.077	1.100	0.084
hku.hk	366	0.119	0.447	0.053
hkst.com	68	0.022	1.585	0.035
hsbc.com.hk	102	0.033	0.907	0.030
youtube.com	60	0.020	0.907	0.018
google.com	535	0.174	0.100	0.017

The value is lower when a domain occurs few times on a computer or occurs on many computers (low discriminating power for the computers). The value is the lowest when a domain appears on virtually all the computers.

TF-PVT Model. The PVN indicates a user's preferred (i.e., frequently visited) websites, but the same weight is assigned to each visit and the weight does not reflect the amount of time the user spent viewing the website. For example, a user who watches videos on a website would spend more time on the website, but the click frequency would be low. The page view time (PVT) is used to capture this important aspect of a user's browsing behavior.

The PVT calculation is based on a view session [2]. A view session starts when a website is requested and ends after an idle period of at least 30 minutes or when a new domain is requested. The idle period accounts for the fact that a browser does not record when a user leaves a page. The PVT is computed as the difference in access times between two consecutive page views based on the assumption that a user browses the new page after clicking a link. Thus, the TF-PVT weight is the time spent on domain d based on the browser history of computer c:

$$tf\_pvt_{d,c} = \frac{pvt_{d,c}}{\sum_k pvt_{k,c}} \qquad (3)$$

where $pvt_{d,c}$ is the total page view time for all the pages corresponding to domain d for computer c during the observation period, and $\sum_k pvt_{k,c}$ is the total page view time for computer c during the observation period.

Table 5 shows the same seven domains and their weights. Note that TF-PVT gives different results than TF-PVN. For example, the weights of youtube.com and taobao.com are high because the user watches

Domain	pvt (sec.)	tf_pvt (207,021 sec.)
google.com	42,506	0.205
youtube.com	16,805	0.081
taobao.com	14,474	0.070
hku.hk	14,112	0.068
chinamac.com	11,343	0.055
hkst.com	3,815	0.018
hsbc.com.hk	859	0.004

videos and shops online. Like TF-PVN, this weighting scheme does not abandon non-discriminating domains such as google.com that may lead to incorrect user identification.

TFIDF-PVT Model. Like TFIDF-PVN, TFIDF-PVT attempts to provide more meaningful weights. If a domain is viewed for a long time from most of the computers, the discriminating ability of this domain is weaker. Consequently, TFIDF-PVT ranks the website lower than TF-PVT. The TFIDF-PVT weight is computed as:

$$tfidf\_pvt_{d,c} = tf\_pvt_{d,c} \times \log_2 \frac{|C|}{|\{c \in C | d \in c\}|}. \qquad (4)$$

Table 6. TFIDF-PVT weighting example.

Domain	pvt (sec.)	tf_pvt (207,021 sec.)	idf (15 Computers)	tfidf_pvt
chinamac.com	11,343	0.054	2.907	0.159
taobao.com	14,474	0.070	1.100	0.077
youtube.com	16,805	0.081	0.907	0.074
hku.hk	14,112	0.068	0.447	0.031
hkst.com	3,815	0.018	1.585	0.029
google.com	42,506	0.205	0.100	0.020
hsbc.com.hk	859	0.004	0.907	0.004

Table 6 shows the same trend as TFIDF-PVN (Table 4) in that TFIDF-PVT enhances the domain weight due to a high IDF. Specifically, TFIDF-PVT assigns a high weight to a domain when it consumes a lot of browsing time on a few computers (high discriminating power).

A low weight is assigned when the page view duration for the domain was short or the domain was browsed by many computers (low discriminating power). The lowest weight is assigned when a domain was browsed by all the computers.

3.4   Web User Identification

The cosine similarity measure is commonly used to assess the similarity of two documents. We use this measure to assess the similarity of two browsing histories:

$$Similarity_{cos} = \frac{c_1 \cdot c_2}{||c_1||||c_2||} = \frac{\sum\limits_{i=1}^{N} c_{1,i} \times c_{2,i}}{\sqrt{\sum\limits_{i=1}^{N} (c_{1,i})^2} \times \sqrt{\sum\limits_{i=1}^{N} (c_{2,i})^2}}. \qquad (5)$$

In the cosine similarity calculation, $c_1 \cdot c_2$ denotes the intersection of computers c_1 and c_2, and $||c_i||$ is the norm of vector c_i. Candidate computers that share domains with the top N domains of the target computer have higher similarity scores, while candidate computers that share no domains are assigned similarity scores of zero. The candidate computer with the highest similarity score has the highest probability that it was used by same web user as the target computer.

4.   Experimental Design and Results

The web user profiling model was tested using 34 participants from the University of Hong Kong. The participants, all of whom were students between the ages of 20 to 31, provided their personal computers for model testing. All the computers had been in use for at least two months.

A total of 51 computers were collected from the 34 participants; seventeen of the participants had two computers. Thirty four computers, one from each participant, were assigned to Group I (i.e., computers that can be used as the target computer or candidate computers). The seventeen remaining computers were placed in Group II (i.e., computers that can only be used as candidate computers).

Browsing history records from July 1, 2013 through August 9, 2013 (40 days) were extracted from each computer. The time settings and time change logs were reviewed before data extraction. Table 7 presents the browsing history statistics of the collection of 51 computers.

Table 7. Browsing history statistics.

July 1, 2013 to August 9, 2013 (40 days)	
Number of computers	51
Number of sessions	36,801
Total page views	131,709
Total page view time (seconds)	8,822,703
Mean sessions per computer	721.588
Mean page views per computer	2,582.529
Mean page view time per computer (seconds)	172,994.177
Mean extracted domain per computer	63.980
Mean page views per session	3.579
Mean page view time per session (seconds)	239.741
Mean page view time (seconds)	66.986
Mean sessions per domain	11.278
Mean page views per domain	40.364
Mean page view time per domain (seconds)	2,703.862

4.1   Evaluation Metric

The performance of the profiling model was evaluated using an accuracy metric, which is defined as the proportion of the correctly identified examples out of all the examples to be identified. The accuracy was calculated using the equation:

$$accuracy = \frac{\sum_j^J tp_j}{K} \tag{6}$$

where tp_j is the number of true positives for participant j chosen in Group I, J is the number of different participants chosen in Group I and K is the total number of computers chosen in Group I.

4.2   Experimental Design

Two evaluations of the web user profile model were performed. The first evaluation compared the impact of TF-PVN, TFIDF-PVN, TF-PVT and TFIDF-PVT. The second examined the impact of the size of the profile group (M) on model accuracy.

The target and candidate computers were selected from the pool of $M = 51$ computers. Computers from Group I were successively selected as the target. Three samplings of candidate computers were used ($M = 15, 33, 51$). The samplings included ten computers from Group I and five computers from Group II ($M = 15$); 22 computers from Group I and eleven computers from Group II ($M = 33$); and all the computers from

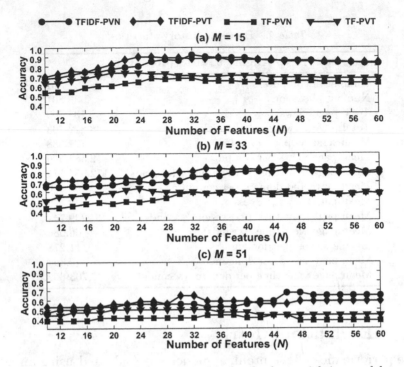

Figure 3. Influence of feature number for the four weighting models.

the two groups ($M = 51$). When $M < 51$, ten repeated experiments were performed for each M and the average accuracy was computed.

After the weight of each domain was computed for the target computer, the top N domains were chosen. When $N < 10$, the possibility existed that these domains could not be found on any of the candidate computers if the domains were too special. Therefore, we decided to choose more than ten domains on the target computer as features.

4.3   Feature Influence

Since the average number of extracted domains per computer was 63, we tuned the parameter N from 10 to 60 to observe the influence on web user identification accuracy for the four weighting models: TF-PVN, TFIDF-PVN, TF-PVT and TFIDF-PVT.

Figure 3 presents the results obtained for the three computer group profile sizes ($M = 15, 33, 51$). For all four weighting models, when user identification was performed on a small group ($M = 15$), the performance improves and then flattens as N increases. In the case of the TF-PVN model, the best user identification result occurred for $N = 26$ (67%). For TFIDF-PVN, the best user identification result was 92%

Table 8. Web user identification accuracy for the four weighting models.

M		TFIDF-PVN	TFIDF-PVT	TF-PVN	TF-PVT
15	Min	0.670 (N=10)	0.690 (N=10)	0.520 (N=10)	0.62 (N=10)
	Max	0.920 (N=32)	0.900 (N=24)	0.670 (N=26)	0.730 (N=20)
33	Min	0.650 (N=12)	0.677 (N=10)	0.427 (N=10)	0.505 (N=10)
	Max	0.873 (N=46)	0.845 (N=34)	0.595 (N=32)	0.636 (N=24)
51	Min	0.471 (N=10)	0.529 (N=10)	0.382 (N=10)	0.441 (N=10)
	Max	0.676 (N=46)	0.647 (N=30)	0.441 (N=34)	0.500 (N=20)

when $N = 32$, which indicates that TFIDF is more effective than TF. The best accuracy for TFIDF-PVT was 90% when $N = 24$, which is a slightly lower than TFIDF-PVN, but this result was obtained with fewer domains. Also, TF-PVT yielded better results (73%, $N = 20$) than TF-PVN, but worse results than TFIDF-PVT.

The trends for each feature remain consistent as M increases. However, Table 8, which presents the complete results, shows that better performance was obtained for smaller computer profile groups.

4.4   Profile Group Size Influence

Figure 4 presents the analysis of the influence of the computer profile group size M. For all the features, as the size of computer profile group increases, the web user identification accuracy gradually decreases. Also, when the number of domains (N) is 20 and 30, the performance relation TFIDF-PVT > TFIDF-PVN > TF-PVT > TF-PVN holds for all M. However, when $N = 40$, TFIDF-PVN and TFIDF-PVT have about the same accuracy. When $N = 50$, TFIDF-PVN has better performance than TFIDF-PVT for all M, which implies that if high accuracy is required, TFIDF-PVN should be used, but more domains would be required; otherwise TFIDF-PVT is a good choice.

5.   Conclusions

The model proposed for web user profiling and identification is based on the web browsing behavior of users. Experiments involving 51 computers show that the profiling model can be applied to identify web users. Evaluation of the performance of the four weighting models, TF-PVN, TFIDF-PVN, TF-PVT and TFIDF-PVT, demonstrates that TFIDF-PVN is the most accurate at identifying web users.

Our future research will attempt to combine PVN and PVT to create a more accurate identification model. Additionally, the dataset will be

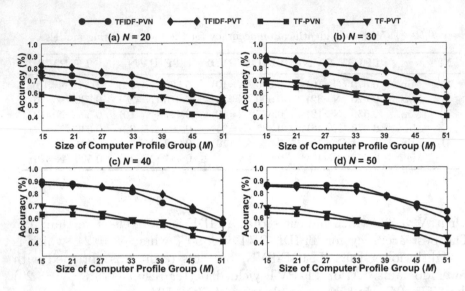

Figure 4. Influence of computer profile group size using the four weighting models.

expanded by collecting computers from a broader population in a real-world scenario. Our research will also focus on more complex scenarios, such as identifying all the users who have used a public computer.

Acknowledgement

This research was supported by the University of Hong Kong and by a Conference Grant.

References

[1] W. Bhukya and S. Banothu, Investigative behavior profiling with one class SVM for computer forensics, *Proceedings of the Fifth International Conference on Multi-Disciplinary Trends in Artificial Intelligence*, pp. 373–383, 2011.

[2] R. Bucklin and C. Sismeiro, A model of website browsing behavior estimated on clickstream data, *Journal of Marketing Research*, vol. 40(3), pp. 249–267, 2003.

[3] C. Colombini and A. Colella, Digital profiling: A computer forensics approach, *Proceedings of the IFIP WG 8.4/8.9 International Cross Domain Conference on Availability, Reliability and Security for Business, Enterprise and Health Information Systems*, pp. 330–343, 2011.

[4] N. Fathy, N. Badr, M. Hashem and T. Gharib, Enhancing web search with semantic identification of user preferences, *International Journal of Computer Science Issues*, vol. 8(6), pp. 62–69, 2011.

[5] M. Forte, C. Hummel, N. Morris, E. Pratsch, R. Shi, J. Bao and P. Beling, Learning human behavioral profiles in a cyber environment, *Proceedings of the IEEE Systems and Information Engineering Design Symposium*, pp. 181–186, 2010.

[6] M. Grcar, D. Mladenic and M. Grobelnik, User profiling for the web, *Computer Science and Information Systems*, vol. 3(2), pp. 1–29, 2006.

[7] J. Hu, H. Zeng, H. Li, C. Niu and Z. Chen, Demographic prediction based on user's browsing behavior, *Proceedings of the Sixteenth International Conference on the World Wide Web*, pp. 151–160, 2007.

[8] K. Jones and R. Belani, Web Browser Forensics, Part 1, Symantec, Mountain View, California (www.symantec.com/connect/art icles/web-browser-forensics-part-1), 2010.

[9] C. Manning, P. Raghavan and H. Schutze, *Introduction to Information Retrieval*, Cambridge University Press, Cambridge, United Kingdom, 2008.

[10] S. McKinney and D. Reeves, User identification via process profiling: Extended abstract, *Proceedings of the Fifth Annual Workshop on Cyber Security and Information Intelligence Research: Cyber Security and Information Intelligence Challenges and Strategies*, art. no. 51, 2009.

[11] J. Oh, N. Son, S. Lee and K. Lee, A study for classification of web browser logs and timeline visualization, *Proceedings of the Thirteenth International Workshop on Information Security Applications*, pp. 192–207, 2012.

[12] N. Sofer, IE History View v1.70 – View Visited Web Sites of Internet Explorer, NirSoft (www.nirsoft.net/utils/iehv.html), 2011.

[13] N. Sofer, Chrome History View v1.16, NirSoft (www.nirsoft.net/utils/chrome_history_view.html), 2012.

[14] N. Sofer, Mozilla History View v1.52 – Mozilla/Firefox Browsers History Viewer, NirSoft (www.nirsoft.net/utils/mozilla_hist ory_view.html), 2013.

[15] Wikipedia, List of web browsers (en.wikipedia.org/wiki/List_of_web_browsers), 2014.

Chapter 6

VALIDATION RULES FOR ENHANCED FOXY P2P NETWORK INVESTIGATIONS

Ricci Ieong and Kam-Pui Chow

Abstract   Experiments with the Foxy P2P network have demonstrated that the first uploader of a file can be identified when search queries are submitted to all the network nodes during initial file sharing. However, in real Foxy networks, file search queries are not transmitted to the entire Foxy network and this process may not identify the first uploader. This paper presents a set of validation rules that validate the observed first uploader. The validation rules define the seeder curve that consistently describes the number of uploaders over time. Analysis of four scenarios shows improved accuracy at detecting the first uploader and that, in situations with insufficient competition for file content, the first uploader may not be identified precisely.

Keywords: Peer-to-peer networks, Foxy, first seeder, network simulation

1.   Introduction

The Foxy peer-to-peer (P2P) network, which employs the Gnutella 2 protocol, has for several years been a popular file-sharing P2P application in Chinese communities. When the Government of Taiwan shut down the Foxy client publisher in 2009, the use of the Foxy network dramatically decreased and leakage of files through the network dropped temporarily. However, recent incidents have brought considerable media attention. In August and September 2013, sensitive Hong Kong government documents were leaked using the Foxy network [1, 6]. In such situations, if the appropriate legal entities can identify the first uploader of the sensitive files, then they can reduce or even eliminate the leaks at an early stage.

Ieong, *et al.* [5] have shown that the seeder curve – a plot of the number of uploaders (seeders) over time – provides information about

G. Peterson and S. Shenoi (Eds.): Advances in Digital Forensics X, IFIP AICT 433, pp. 73–83, 2014.

the number of seeders as well as the stage of P2P file sharing. However, monitoring rules derived for detecting the first uploader using the seeder curve have high error rates as the number of hub nodes increases [4]. A second monitoring strategy used three rules to monitor search queries in the Foxy P2P network to identify the first uploader [3]. The rules leverage the fact that, in search-based P2P networks, a user locates files by executing a search query in the network. Hub nodes relay and filter search queries from the leaf nodes in the Foxy network. Thus, it is possible to identify the first uploader by monitoring queries at hub nodes.

This paper examines the effects of large numbers of hub nodes on monitoring accuracy. Increasing the number of hubs from one to 1,000 indicates that the number of hubs affects the overall accuracy of the monitoring rules by introducing delays in the appearance of the first uploader without affecting the shape of the seeder curve. To counteract this behavior, supplementary rules are proposed to enhance the accuracy of validation if the first uploader is identified during the slow-rising or rapid-rising periods of the seeder curve. If the first uploader is not identified before the rapid-rising period, then the identified individual is unlikely to be the first uploader.

2.   Foxy P2P Query Monitoring

The rules utilized to monitor the Foxy network were presented in a previous study [3]. When file-sharing activities are observed, the monitoring rules initiate file content requests to the nodes that possess the targeted file and then determine if the observed file contains the entire file content. The first uploader returned in the uploader lists that have been verified to possess the entire file content is considered to be first seeder. This rule is referred to as the file existence verification function.

Figure 1 shows a simplified diagram of a Foxy P2P network with four hubs. The solid lines denote the connections between the hubs and leaf nodes. The black and white leaf nodes represent the uploader and downloaders, respectively. The dashed line indicates the direction of file download.

Previous experiments have tested the effect of a small number of hubs on the accuracy of first seeder identification [4]. When a small number of hubs is introduced to the Foxy network, the probability of identifying the first seeder remains the same. To evaluate the functionality of the monitoring rule, it is assumed that the hub node broadcasts all the search queries to all the leaf nodes in the network in a simulated environment. Therefore, all the hubs share the same list of seeders, such that all the leaf

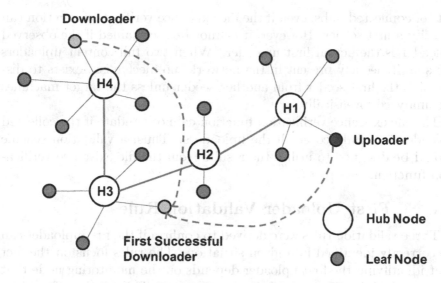

Figure 1. Foxy P2P network with four hubs.

nodes can identify the uploaders. If the search query reaches the entire Foxy network, the identified first uploader should be the first uploader of the file.

However, in a real Foxy network, a hub node does not broadcast a search query message to all the nodes; only a limited set of nodes receive the search query [3]. Thus, a file search request may only be observed by leaf nodes that are connected to a hub where the search query can be accessed. Additionally, since the hub nodes serve as the repository for the list of available uploaders close to the downloader, when a downloader is connected to the hub with the uploader (H3 in Figure 1), its download requests are accepted first. In contrast, although the initial search queries of downloaders located at hubs not connected to the uploader were submitted earlier (e.g., H4 in Figure 1), these downloaders can initiate downloads only after the nodes connected to the hub because uploaders have initiated and completed their file downloads (e.g., leaf node H3 in Figure 1).

The hub node connectivity in a search-based P2P file-sharing network means that, as the number of hub nodes increases, the probability of identifying the first seeder through the investigation algorithm is only affected by the probability of the first uploader and the monitoring node connected to the same hub.

With this implicit nature of the partial uploader list, the investigation algorithm can only confirm if the identified uploader is the first observable full content file holder among the uploaders in the localized lists of connected hubs, even if the file existence verification function can identify a first seeder. However, it cannot be ascertained if the observed uploader is the actual first uploader. When two full content uploaders are simultaneously present in the network, no mechanism exists to distinguish the first seeder from another seeder unless the target machines are analyzed forensically.

The file existence verification function cannot validate if the collected uploader lists fully cover all the uploaders. Thus, a validation scheme should be designed to utilize the results from the file existence verification function.

2.1   First Uploader Validation Rules

Three validation rules were derived to confirm if the first uploader can be correctly identified in a given situation. The rules focus on the fact that identifying the first uploader depends on the monitoring node that receives the initiation time of the search query. This can be affected by the distance from the query and the size of the file being shared. The first two rules are concerned with the issue of the shared file being small and, therefore, being replicated quickly. The two rules are:

- **Rule 1:** If the time required to download the file is short, then the probability of confirming the observed first uploader is very small. Therefore, the observed uploader should be rejected.

- **Rule 2:** If the entire file existence verification test is completed by the queried uploader in a short time, then the observed first uploader is less likely to be the actual first uploader. Therefore, the observed uploader should be rejected.

Although numerous downloaders are present in a P2P network, only one uploader has the full file content when the monitoring node initiates the search during the slow-rising period. Many detected uploaders from the list should be confirmed as partial file-content uploaders only, especially during the slow-rising period. A third rule then confirms that there is only one individual with the full version of the file. This rule is given by:

- **Rule 3:** In the list of returned uploaders, if all the detected uploaders are full file-content uploaders with no partial file-content uploaders detected by the file existence verification test during the initial stage, then the observed uploader should be rejected.

3.   Experimental Design

Simulations were performed in a Foxy ns-3 simulation environment [4] using the monitoring and validation rules. All the parameters other than the number of hub nodes and the size of the files being shared were the same as specified in [3]. The request broadcast cascade level (defined by the time-to-live (TTL) value in the query) was set to three and the maximum number of connected hubs for a leaf node was set to three according to the GnucDNA implementation [2]. The number of leaf nodes was set to 200, number of downloaders to 100, search time to approximately 500 seconds and transfer bandwidth to 1,024 KB.

Four experiments were performed to determine the effect of hub nodes and file size on identifying the first uploader. In each experiment (set), an average was obtained from five simulations using the same parameters.

- **Set 1:** This set of simulation experiments focused on the random search time with ten hub nodes. Two hundred of the 500 leaf nodes were downloaders. The transferred file size was 13 MB. The mean data rate was approximately 1 Mbps.

- **Set 2:** This set of simulation experiments was performed to analyze the effect of the number of hub nodes on the accuracy of the validation rules. The parameters were the same as those used in Set 1, except that the number of hubs was increased to 1,000 nodes.

- **Set 3:** This set of simulation experiments was derived from the monitoring record of a popular television episode. The file size was set to 100 MB. One hundred and thirty-five of the 200 leaf nodes were downloaders; the leaf nodes were connected to 1,000 hub nodes. The mean data transfer rate was approximately 10 Mbps.

- **Set 4:** This set of simulation experiments was derived from the monitoring record in which a small, popular file was shared over the network. Files of size 512 KB were used in the simulation. One hundred thirty-five of the 200 leaf nodes were downloaders; the leaf nodes were connected to one hub node. The hub node was reduced to one to focus on the validation rules in the simulation experiments. The mean data transfer rate was approximately 1 Mbps.

The simulation results for the four experiment sets were evaluated using four criteria:

Table 1.   Simulation experiment results.

Experiment	Correct Identification	Correct Reject	False Reject (Type I)	False Accept (Type II)
Set 1	60%	40%	0%	0%
Set 2	0%	100%	0%	0%
Set 3	0%	20%	80%	0%
Set 4	0%	80%	20%	0%

- **Criterion 1:** A correct identification occurs when the first seeder is identified correctly and is validated correctly by the validation rules.

- **Criterion 2:** A correct rejection occurs when a first seeder is identified incorrectly and is rejected correctly by a validation rule.

- **Criterion 3:** A false rejection or Type I error occurs when the first seeder is identified correctly but is rejected incorrectly by a validation rule.

- **Criterion 4:** A false acceptance or Type II error occurs when a first seeder is identified incorrectly but is validated correctly by the validation rules.

4.   Experimental Results

Table 1 shows the results of the simulation experiments. When the P2P investigation algorithm and validation rules were applied to the four experiment sets, more than half of the experiments correctly rejected or confirmed the uploader. However, in two experiment sets, most of the actual seeders were rejected by the validation rules.

4.1   Set 1 Results

Figure 2 shows the seeder curve for Set 1. The two indicators show the times of the initial search query responses of the monitoring node for the two correct rejections. The results show that 40% of the simulations did not locate an uploader in the network. The rejections are correct because the monitoring node submitted the first search query after the rapid-rising period. When the number of available uploaders exceeded the response limit, uploader responses were filtered from the monitoring node list, and the validation rules correctly rejected these first uploaders. The result also demonstrates that, in the case of search-based P2P file-

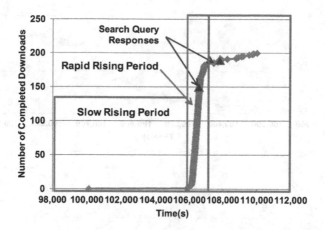

Figure 2. Seeder curve for Set 1.

sharing networks, accurate results can only be obtained if the search is initiated during the slow-rising period.

4.2   Set 2 Results

Set 2 modified Set 1 by increasing the number of hubs and reducing the file size. Two changes are expected in the output. First, with more hubs involved, the probability of correctly identifying the first uploader should be reduced. This is because detection depends on the probability that the monitoring node and the uploader are connected to the same hub node. Second, with a small file size, the download duration decreases and the file should propagate rapidly across the network.

Figure 3 shows the results from a Set 2 simulation. The upper graph shows the seeder curve for the network while the lower graph shows the seeder curve created by the monitoring node. However, the two validation tests failed. The file existence verification was extremely short (rejected by Rule 2). Also, only one partial uploader was identified throughout the verification period (rejected by Rule 3). Since the monitoring node did not see the uploaded file until there were 20 uploaders, the validation rule correctly rejected the incorrectly-identified first uploader.

4.3   Set 3 Results

Figure 4 shows the results from a Set 3 simulation. The upper graph shows the seeder curve created by the monitoring node while the lower graph shows the seeder curve for the first 60 uploaders.

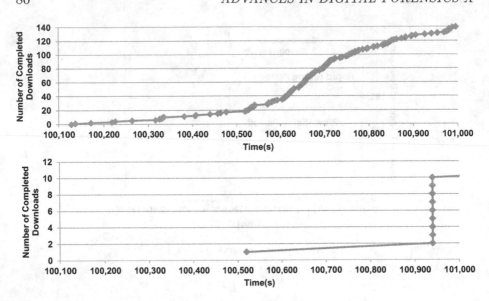

Figure 3. Summary of results from a Set 2 simulation.

Four simulations in Set 3 had a Type I error because the observed seeders were rejected by the validation rules. In this set, the uploader list collected by the monitoring node included the actual first uploader. The file existence verification function also returned the first uploader as the detected first uploader. However, the returned results did not pass the validation rules.

In most of the Set 3 simulations, the file existence verification function completed in a very short time. Therefore, the observed uploader was rejected by Rule 2. As a result, the first uploader in Set 3 was incorrectly rejected by the validation rules.

A review of the overall seeder curve in Figure 4 shows that the competition among downloaders might not have been sufficiently demanding. Thus, the download activities had a very short slow-rising period and quickly entered the rapid-rising period. This behavior is similar to that observed when sharing a small file.

The file existence verification function also executed at an early stage of the slow-rising period. The result is that the uploader may not be sharing the file requested by the other downloaders. Without competition for file content, a delay in the file request might not be observed.

Further analysis of the overall seeder curve and the corresponding download duration time shows that shortly after the appearance of three uploaders in the P2P file-sharing network, the download activities proceeded to the rapid-rising period. Therefore, the actual slow-rising pe-

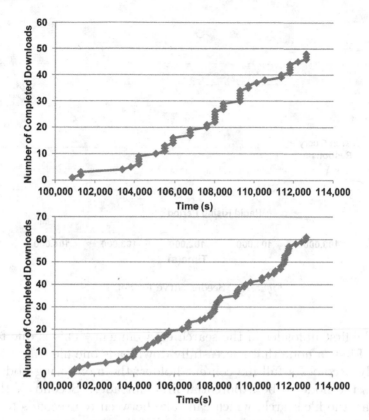

Figure 4. Summary of results from a Set 3 simulation.

riod in Experiment Set 3 was rather short. Even with the complete hub information, the probability of rejecting the first seeder was relatively high.

4.4   Set 4 Results

The Set 4 file size was small, which resulted in short file transfer times. Although the hub node serviced all the uploaders and downloaders, the time available for the monitoring node to submit the initial search query was insufficient. Figure 5 shows the seeder curve for Set 4. The query occurred after the slow-rising period and the search query response occurred at 100,400 seconds during the rapid-rising period. The observed first uploader was rejected by all three validation rules.

When the file size is smaller than 512 KB, the Gnutella2 protocol transmits the file in one fragment. Since the transfer time was so short, confirming that a file was originally from a particular uploader was impossible for the monitoring node even if the file locating function in-

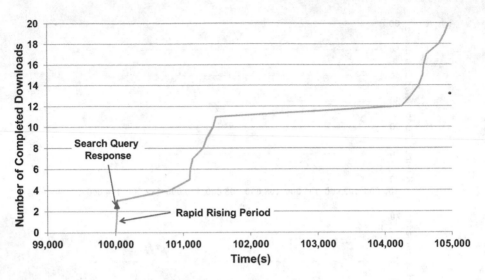

Figure 5.   Seeder curve for Set 4.

cluded the first uploader in the search environment. This is due to two
reasons. First, a node that successfully downloads one file fragment immediately becomes a full file content holder; the monitoring node then
considers the node to be a potential first uploader. Second, if the file
is popular, the file search, which can take between ten seconds to a few
minutes, may not complete before the end of the slow-rising period. The
result is that multiple file uploaders are identified in the network.

Based on these simulation results, it can be concluded that, when
a small file is shared, a forensic investigator is unlikely to distinguish
the first uploader even if the monitoring node was enabled since the
beginning of the file download. However, the investigator can identify
the participants, including the potential uploaders and downloaders.

5.   Conclusions

The research presented in this paper enhances the first uploader detection strategy in Gnutella networks. The three proposed validation
rules validated and correctly rejected all the incorrectly-identified first
uploaders in the simulation experiments. However, the validation rules
incorrectly rejected 80% of the actual first uploaders in Set 3 and 20% in
Set 4, resulting in a Type I error of 25% over all the experiments. The
error is due to the short slow-rising periods and the competition among
downloaders.

The overall analysis suggests that, if the seeder curve has an extremely
short slow-rising period or if the seeder is identified after the slow-rising

period, then the observed first seeder cannot be accurately validated. The validation rules can verify an observed seeder, but they eventually result in an incorrect rejection of the seeder.

Future research will investigate P2P network scenarios with short slow-rising periods to enhance the monitoring rules. Also, the research will analyze the characteristics of file-sharing activities and extract attributes that can accurately determine the slow-rising period.

References

[1] ckseol, More personal data identified by Foxy King (in Chinese), HKHeadline.com, Hong Kong, China (`blogcity.me/blog/reply_blog_express.asp?f=C6T2E3Z19P239366&id=566836`), August 18, 2013.

[2] Gnucleus, GnucDNA – Free P2P Core Component (`www.gnucleus.org/GnucDNA`).

[3] R. Ieong and K. Chow, Enhanced monitoring rule through direct node query for Foxy network investigation, presented at the *First International Conference on Digital Forensics and Investigation*, 2012.

[4] R. Ieong, K. Chow and P. Lai, Validation of rules used in Foxy peer-to-peer network investigations, in *Advances in Digital Forensics VIII*, G. Peterson and S. Shenoi (Eds.), Springer, Heidelberg, Germany, pp. 231–245, 2012.

[5] R. Ieong, P. Lai, K. Chow, M. Kwan, F. Law, H. Tse and K. Tse, Forensic investigation and analysis of peer-to-peer networks, in *Handbook of Research on Computational Forensics, Digital Crime and Investigation: Methods and Solutions*, C. Li (Ed.), IGI Global, Hershey, Pennsylvania, pp. 355–378, 2010.

[6] Sing Tao, Another personal data leak from HK Police Force identified by Foxy King (in Chinese), Toronto, Canada (`news.singtao.ca/toronto/2013-09-25/hongkong1380094959d4714768.html`), September 25, 2013.

II

FORENSIC TECHNIQUES

Chapter 7

WINDOWS EVENT FORENSIC PROCESS

Quang Do, Ben Martini, Jonathan Looi, Yu Wang,
and Kim-Kwang Choo

Abstract   Event logs provide an audit trail that records user events and activities
on a computer and are a potential source of evidence in digital forensic
investigations. This paper presents a Windows event forensic process
(WinEFP) for analyzing Windows operating system event log files. The
WinEFP covers a number of relevant events that are encountered in
Windows forensics. As such, it provides practitioners with guidance on
the use of Windows event logs in digital forensic investigations.

Keywords: Windows event forensic process, Windows event logs

1.   Introduction

Microsoft Windows has been the most popular personal computer operating system for many years – as of August 2013, it had more than
90% of the personal computer market share [11]. This suggests that the
majority of the personal computers seized in digital forensic investigations run Windows. To fully extract and interpret the wealth of data
contained in a Windows environment requires an in-depth understanding
of the operating system and, in the context of this work, event logs.

A key step in digital forensics is to gather evidence about an incident
involving computer systems and their associated networks. In such circumstances, the expectation is that there has been some accumulation
or retention of data on various system components that has to be identified, preserved and analyzed. This process can be documented, defined
and used to obtain evidence of a crime or cyber incident [7].

Event log files provide digital forensic practitioners with a wealth of
data describing the operations of computer systems. As such, they often
contain valuable information that could connect particular user events
or activities to specific times.

G. Peterson and S. Shenoi (Eds.): Advances in Digital Forensics X, IFIP AICT 433, pp. 87–100, 2014.
© IFIP International Federation for Information Processing 2014

Windows event logs provide a range of descriptors to allow for the compilation of events into categories such as "informational" and "critical." Individual event IDs indicate specific types of events and recent Windows versions have separate event log files for various applications and services. Despite these filtering options, it can be difficult for digital forensic practitioners to locate events pertinent to their investigations from among the large volume of stored events. The problem is even more acute for practitioners with limited expertise related to event logs. This paper attempts to address this gap by providing a summary of key events that are useful in Windows forensic investigations. The key events summary is used to derive a process that digital forensic practitioners can adapt and follow to obtain useful evidentiary data from Windows event logs.

2. Related Work

Several researchers have noted that Windows event logs contain a large amount of digital evidence. Kent, *et al.* [5] have shown that various types of logs pertaining to the operating system and applications are useful in post-incident response. While Kent and colleagues provide high-level guidance on the use of event logs in digital forensics across a range of operating systems, other researchers focus specifically on Windows event logs. For example, Ibrahim, *et al.* [4] discuss the potential use of Windows event logs as sources of evidence in cyber crime investigations. They found a number of useful data items in their simulated attack, which they assert could be used as evidence in court. In particular, they analyzed login events and network data contained in event logs. Event logs are often a valuable source of data that can link an individual or remote device to a specific event. For example, if a login event is recorded and the system time is changed shortly after the login, this can indicate that the individual who logged in changed the time on the personal computer.

Marrington, *et al.* [6] describe a system for profiling computers to detect activities that are of interest to forensic investigators. While their profiling system uses a number of data sources, event logs feature significantly in their proof-of-concept system. Their study also demonstrates the effectiveness of event logs in augmenting other digital evidence to demonstrate clear usage patterns.

Hashim and Sutherland [3] focus on event logs in their discussion of Windows artifacts. They cover a range of logs with potential forensic value, such as application, security and system event log files, including login, application usage and policy audit logs.

Table 1.   Source computer specifications.

Computer	Operating System	CPU (Intel)	Primary Memory	Secondary Memory
1. Desktop	Win 7	Core i7 2600k	8 GB	120 GB SSD
2. Laptop	Win 7	Core i5-430UM	4 GB	60 GB SSD
3. Desktop	Win 7	Core i5 2500k	4 GB	1 TB HDD
4. Laptop	Win 7	Core i5-430UM	4 GB	500 GB HDD
5. Desktop	Win 7	Core i5 2500k	4 GB	1 TB HDD
6. Desktop	Win 7	Core i5 2500k	4 GB	1 TB HDD
7. Laptop	Win 7	Core i7-3470QM	16 GB	2 TB HDD
8. Desktop	Win 7/Win 8	Core i5 2500k	8 GB	2 TB HDD
9. Desktop	Win 7	Core i5 2500k	4 GB	500 GB HDD
10. VM	Server 2008 R2	Core 2 Quad Q9400	4 GB	40 GB HDD
11. VM	Win 7	Core 2 Quad Q9400	1.5 GB	60 GB HDD

Murphey [10] conducted technical research into the format of NT5 Windows event logs (used in Windows XP and Windows Server 2003 systems) and devised an automated method for forensic extraction (including recovery and repair) of the event logs. Schuster [12] provides technical insights into the newer Windows XML event log format introduced with Windows Vista. Unfortunately, aside from this work, there have been relatively few papers published that discuss specific aspects of Windows event logs for the purpose of forensic analysis.

The research efforts mentioned above provide invaluable knowledge and guidance on the use of event logs and log data in forensic investigations. However, because of the large quantities of data contained in the logs, it can be challenging and time consuming for a forensic practitioner to discover exactly where the evidence resides. To ensure the most effective use of event logs in forensic investigations, practitioners need a well-defined process to follow, more so when they have limited technical expertise.

3.   Experimental Setup

Our experiments sampled event logs from several source computers; the specifications of the computers are listed in Table 1. The computers ranged from systems with low processing power used for recreation and simple office work (e.g., Internet browsing, social media browsing and low-intensity document and spreadsheet editing) to systems used for video gaming and other resource-intensive tasks (e.g., hobbyist programming).

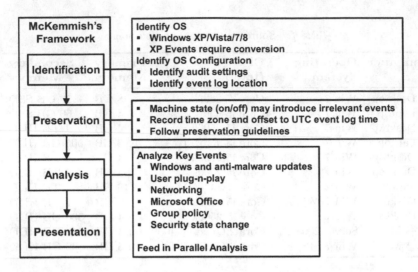

Figure 1.   Proposed Windows event forensic process.

The laptops used in our experiments had wired and wireless network connections. The desktop computers only had wired connections. Virtual machines (VMs) were also provisioned to investigate auditing and group policies. Event log files collected over a two-month period – from November 1, 2012 to December 31, 2012 – were analyzed. This enabled commonly-occurring events to be discovered without having to sort through massive amounts of log data.

4.   Proposed Windows Event Forensic Process

Current digital forensic frameworks do not discuss the analysis of event logs in detail. For example, the McKemmish framework [7] focuses on physical media such as hard drives and DVDs; there is little emphasis on operating system and configuration specifications, which are crucial to a Windows event log forensic process. Kent, *et al.* [5] have provided guidelines related to operating system event logs, but they do not discuss specific operating systems (which have different events and, depending on the configuration of an operating system, different information would be present in the logs). Thus, we present the Windows event log forensic process (WinEFP) to specifically support forensic examinations of event logs and log data stored in Windows systems.

The proposed WinEFP (Figure 1) fits within the McKemmish framework [7]. The four key elements of the framework are: (i) identification; (ii) preservation; (iii) analysis; and (iv) presentation of digital evidence.

Using the McKemmish framework renders the event log forensic process straightforward for even an inexperienced practitioner to follow.

4.1 Identification

The goal of the identification step in the McKemmish framework is to determine the digital evidence that is present along with its type and format. The location and format of the evidence are crucial because they determine the recovery methods. The WinEFP identification step focuses on identifying and understanding relevant event data from Windows machines.

Depending on the version of Windows installed on the system under investigation, the number and types of events will differ. In fact, the events logged by a Windows XP machine may be incompatible with an event log analysis tool designed for Windows 8. For example, Event ID 551 on a Windows XP machine refers to a logoff event; the Windows Vista/7/8 equivalent is Event ID 4647. Windows XP events can be converted to Vista events by adding 4096 to the Event ID [1]. Windows versions since Vista include a number of new events that are not logged by Windows XP systems. Windows Server editions have larger numbers and types of events. Thus, the exact version of the Windows system must be considered very carefully when developing a digital forensic process centered on event logs.

By default, a Windows system is set to log a limited number of events, but it can be modified to include actions such as file deletions and changes. Windows event logs are stored in a binary XML format that is unreadable by a text editor. However, the included Windows Event Viewer is able to read the logs and convert them to plaintext XML. The default location of Windows event logs is typically `C:\Windows\System32\winevt\Logs`. This can be changed by a user by modifying the File value of the following registry keys in `HKEY_LOCAL_MACHINE` (`HKLM`) on the local machine:

- **Application Events:** `SYSTEM\CurrentControlSet\services\eventlog\Application`

- **Hardware Events:** `SYSTEM\CurrentControlSet\services\eventlog\HardwareEvents`

- **Security Events:** `SYSTEM\CurrentControlSet\services\eventlog\Security`

- **System Events:** `SYSTEM\CurrentControlSet\services\eventlog\System`

We found that other event "channels" only generate File keys when their paths are changed from the default. When a custom path is used, a key is generated at the registry location: `HKLN\Microsoft\Windows\CurrentVersion\WINEVT\Channels\[logname]` (e.g., `Microsoft-Windows-Audio\CaptureMonitor`).

4.2　Preservation

The preservation step seeks to keep alterations to the digital evidence to a minimum. The event logs on a standard Windows machine are generally contained in just a few files, so it is generally not necessary to alter any data. However, because the event logging tools that come with Windows systems can remove and even completely clear data, care must be taken when retrieving event logs.

A running Windows machine logs events almost continuously. Therefore, if a forensic practitioner were to use the machine, new events would be added to the event log that could contaminate the digital evidence. Because the event log files are non-volatile [5], the computer should be powered down as soon as possible (after obtaining all the volatile data) to reduce evidence contamination. All the actions taken by the practitioner upon accessing the machine should be recorded thoroughly.

Digital forensic practitioners often make use of timestamps in investigations. Our research shows that timestamps in event logs are recorded in Coordinated Universal Time or UTC. This means that the current time zone of the machine must be used to compute the local time on the computer when the event occurred.

If a Windows machine is in a powered down state, it is possible to retrieve the Windows event log files without adding additional events by collecting the log files from the hard drive using an external machine. The log files typically reside in the `C:\Windows\System32\winevt\Logs` directory. However, as mentioned above, the Windows registry can be modified to change the event log locations.

4.3　Analysis

The analysis step in the McKemmish framework contributes specific knowledge about Windows system events that are of interest to a digital forensic practitioner.

Key Events. Locating digital evidence in a Windows event log file requires an understanding of Windows events and knowing what to look for. Our WinEFP attempts to describe key Windows event logs (`.evtx` in Windows Vista onwards) and their associated Event IDs.

Windows and Anti-Malware Update Events. When enabled, a Windows 7 system records details of updates applied by the Windows update service and every update to the Microsoft Security Essentials anti-malware software. Each event in this log provides details of the contents of an update and the time when the event was generated. This information and the conclusions derived from it are potentially interesting from a forensic standpoint. For example, the event timestamp and the details of the installed update can help a forensic practitioner determine if the system in question was secure or vulnerable to specific security threats during a particular period of time.

The events covered in this section were sourced from the System Event Log. Events that provide information regarding Windows updates have the "Windows Update Client" as their source and the events that indicate Microsoft Security Essentials updates have "Microsoft Anti-Malware" as their source.

Event 19 is the most common event that is used to ascertain installed updates on Windows 7 machines. This event is generated when an update is applied to the system; the event description provides details about the update file that generated the event. Often, Windows will download multiple update files in a batch; this generates an instance of Event 18. The event provides a description that lists all the update files that have been downloaded and are ready for installation. Therefore, the relationship between Event 18 and Event 19 is one to many: each update file mentioned in the Event 18 description generates an instance of Event 19 when it is installed. Event 22 is generated when the installation of a Windows update requires the system to be restarted.

Two events are of interest when determining the update status of Microsoft Security Essentials, namely Event 2000 and Event 2002. Event 2000 is logged when the Microsoft anti-malware signature database has been updated; the event provides the version numbers of the new and previous signatures. When coupled with the event timestamp, it is possible to determine periods of vulnerability where the installed anti-malware was not updated to a particular signature version. Event 2000 also provides the version number of the anti-malware engine in operation at the time of the signature update.

Event 2002 is generated when the Microsoft anti-malware engine is updated. We discovered that this occurs less frequently than signature updates – when reviewing logs collected over a two-month period, there were 42 times more Event 2000 instances on the average compared with Event 2002 instances. Much like Event 2000, the description of Event 2002 provides the version numbers of the previous security engine and the updated engine.

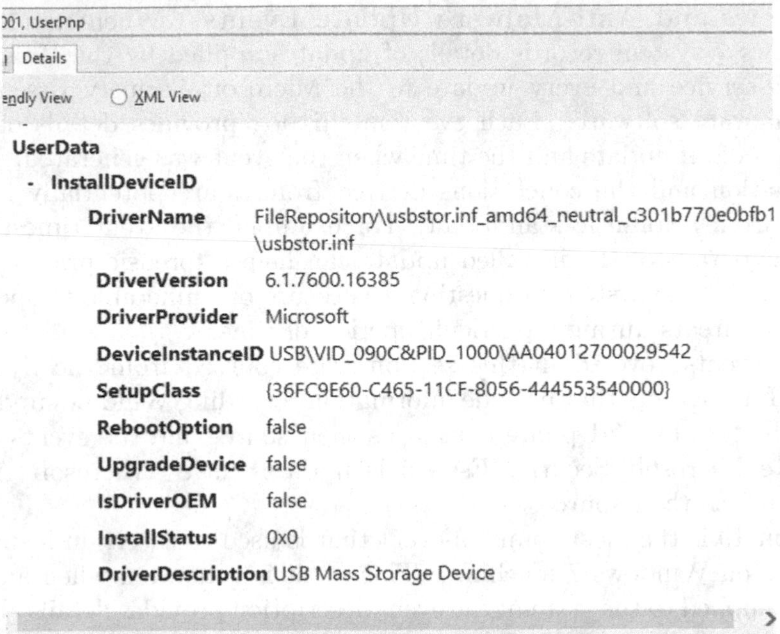

Figure 2.   Example of Event 20001 (involving a USB device).

User Plug-n-Play Events.   The User Plug-n-Play Device Events located in the System Event Log show USB/PCI connections to the computer. An event is triggered when a driver is installed or updated. Events that provide information about a hardware installation and driver have UserPnp as their source. The device installation and update event is 20001 and the service installation and update event is 20003.

Data provided by Event 20001 includes the DeviceInstanceID, driver information and setup class. The DeviceInstanceID is a unique identifier for each device; it is a slash-delimited string. Figure 2 shows an event recorded after the insertion of a USB storage device. A unique identifier is recorded in the DeviceInstanceID. The first field (USB in this example) represents the type of connection. VID represents the vendor ID (USB vendor IDs are recorded at www.usb.org) and PID represents the physical interface device class number (see www.usb.org/developers/devclass_docs/pid1_01.pdf). This is followed by the device identifier (AA04012700029542 in the example).

Networking Events.   An attempt to connect to a wireless network results in Event 8000 being logged in WLAN-AutoConfig, which also stores the SSID of the wireless connection. Event 8001 is logged on a

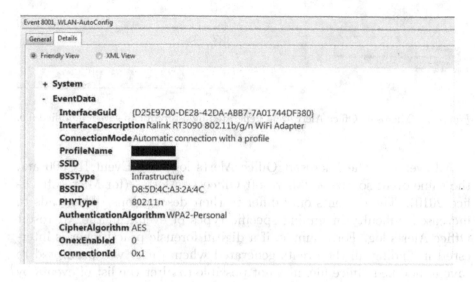

Figure 3. Example of Event 8001.

connection to the wireless network (Figure 3). Event 8001 contains information about the network interface, connection SSID, connection BSSID (which uniquely identifies the access point), wireless connection type (802.11a/b/g/n/ac) as well as the authentication type (WEP, WPA, WPA2, etc.) and cipher type (AES, TKIP, etc.). Event 8003 is logged on a disconnection from a wireless connection. In the case of laptops and mobile devices, interactions with wireless access points could be used by a practitioner to estimate the locations of the devices [2].

Because all events are timestamped, both the location and time are known. Event 11001 is logged when a wired connection succeeds; it provides the unique MAC address of the network interface and the MAC address of the peer. When a wired connection requires user authentication, Event 12012 is also logged. This event saves user login information, including the domain, username and computer name.

Microsoft Office Events. When a Microsoft Office application is installed, the Windows event log files contain a separate entry for Microsoft Office Alerts. The entry contains the events that are generated when an Office program displays a dialog box informing the user of an alert.

From a digital forensic standpoint, the events in the Microsoft Office Alerts log are useful for determining when documents were created, modified and opened, and their file names and types. For example, an event is logged when an Office application displays a dialog box that prompts the user to save a Microsoft Office file. This event records the details of the save prompt, including the file name.

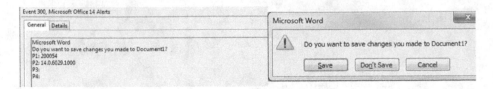

Figure 4.   Microsoft Office Alert event generated by a prompt to save a modified file.

All events in the Microsoft Office Alerts log have Event ID 300 and the same event source of "Microsoft Office 14 Alerts" (for Microsoft Office 2010). These events only differ in their descriptions. This leads to increased difficulty in finding specific types of events in the Microsoft Office Alerts log. For example, if a digital forensic practitioner is interested in finding all the events generated when a user was prompted to save a modified Office file, it is not possible to filter the list of events by searching for a unique combination of event ID and source.

All event descriptions in the Microsoft Office Alert log have the same general structure. The first line of the event description is the name of the Office application that generated the event. The second line is the literal of the dialog box that generated the event. The final four lines contain four parameters.

The most common event in the Microsoft Office Alerts log is typically the modification of an Office file. This event provides information about the name of the Office application file that a user opened and modified, along with the event timestamp. From among the event logs sampled in this research, it is the only event whose description provides the name of the file that the user was editing.

Every Office application generates its own version of this event. The descriptions differ in the first line (i.e., application name) and in the first parameter (i.e., unique numerical value based on the event description and application). In the case of Microsoft Word 2010, the unique first parameter value is 200054 (see Figure 4), for Microsoft Excel 2010 it is 100216 and for Microsoft PowerPoint 2010 it is 400072.

Group Policy and Auditing Events.   Windows 7 Professional edition and higher and Windows Server editions allow the use of a group policy to control and administer user accounts in corporate environments [9]. Depending on the network group policy, it may be important in a digital forensic investigation to check the configuration, e.g., when the group policy is configured so that certain events are forwarded to another Windows device. Thus, if the event logs on a given machine are wiped, the logs may be obtained from the other Windows device.

Table 2. Windows Client editions vs. Windows Server editions.

Configuration(s)	Client Windows	Server Windows
Audit Account Login Events		
Credential Validation; Kerberos Authentication Service; Other Account Login Events	No Auditing	Success
Kerberos Service Ticket Operations	No Auditing	No Auditing
Audit Account Management		
Application Group Management; Distribution Group Management	No Auditing	No Auditing
Computer Account Management	No Auditing	Success
Security Group Management; User Account Management	Success	Success
Audit Directory Service Access		
Detailed Directory Service Replication; Directory Service Change; Directory Service Replication	No Auditing	No Auditing
Directory Service Access	No Auditing	Success
Audit Login Events		
Account Lockout; Logoff; Special Login	Success	Success
IPSec Extended/Main/Quick Mode; Other Login/Logoff Events	No Auditing	No Auditing
Login	Success	Success, Failure
Network Policy Server	Success, Failure	Success, Failure
Audit Object Access		
Application Generation; Certification Services; Detailed File Share; File Share; File System; Filtering Platform Connection/Packet Drop; Handle Manipulation; Kernel Object; Registry; SAM; Other Object Access Events	No Auditing	No Auditing
Audit Policy Change		
Audit/Authentication Policy Change	Success	Success
Authorization Policy Change; Filtering Platform Policy Change; MPSSVC Rule-Level Policy Change; Other Policy Change Events	No Auditing	No Auditing
Audit Privilege Use		
Non-Sensitive Privilege Use; Other Privilege Use Events; Sensitive Privilege Use	No Auditing	No Auditing
Audit Process Tracking		
DPAPI Activity; Process Creation; Process Termination; RPC Events	No Auditing	No Auditing
Audit System Events		
IPSec Driver; Security System Extension	No Auditing	No Auditing
Other System Events; System Integrity	Success, Failure	Success, Failure
Security State Change	Success	Success

Another example is the audit policy setting in a group policy object, which specifies if certain types of events should be logged as success or failure, or both. In most cases, the default setting for audit policies is "No Auditing." Table 2 lists each audit policy category and the events audited in each category for Windows Client editions and Windows Server editions (default configurations).

Security State Change Events. Windows Vista and newer editions have an event category known as Security State Change events. Event 4608 occurs when a system starts up and Event 4616 occurs when the system time is changed, either by the user or when Windows communicates with a time synchronization server.

Event 4609, the final event in this category, occurs when the system is shut down [8]. This event category is listed under "Audit System Events" in the group policy settings.

Event Summary. The following is a summary of the key events discussed above:

- **Windows and Anti-Malware Events:**

    - Event ID 19 is logged when an update is applied to the system.

    - Event ID 18 is logged when a batch Windows update is downloaded.

    - Event ID 22 is logged when a restart is required for an update installation.

    - Event ID 2000 is logged when Microsoft anti-malware signatures are updated.

    - Event ID 2002 is logged when the Microsoft anti-malware engine is updated.

- **User Plug-n-Play Events:**

    - Event ID 20001 is logged when a driver is installed/updated.

    - Event ID 20003 is logged when a service is installed/updated.

- **Networking Events:**

    - Event ID 8000 is logged when a wireless network connection is attempted.

    - Event ID 8001 is logged on a successful wireless network connection.

    - Event ID 8003 is logged on a disconnection from a wireless network.

    - Event ID 11001 is logged on a successful wired network connection.

    - Event ID 12012 is logged when a wired connection requires user authentication.

- **Microsoft Office Events:**

    - Event ID 300 is logged when an Office application generates a dialog box; the contents of this event differ based on the Office application that generates it.

- **Auditing Events:**

    - Refer to Table 2.

- **Security State Change Events:**

  – Event ID 4608 is logged when Windows starts up.

  – Event ID 4609 is logged when Windows shuts down.

  – Event ID 4616 is logged when the system time is modified.

4.4 Presentation

The final presentation step in the McKemmish framework involves presenting the evidence in a court of law [7]. In the case of Windows event logs, presenting textual information may not be ideal because demonstrating computer usage over time may involve many pages of text. It is advisable to present the information in the form of graphs, tables and other graphical visualization schemes.

5. Conclusions

Windows is the dominant operating system in consumer and corporate computing environments. Unless a Windows user has manually disabled the event logging service, the proposed Windows event forensic process (WinEFP) can be applied to practically every forensic investigation involving a Windows personal computer. In developing WinEFP, a number of forensically-relevant Windows event log entries were identified and cataloged. Our future research will extend the process to address other Windows versions as well as other operating systems.

References

[1] Dorian Software Blog, 4094 Security Events Lane (`eventlogs.blogspot.com.au/2007/04/4096-security-events-lane.html`), April 13, 2007.

[2] X. Fu, N. Zhang, A. Pingley, W. Yu, J. Wang and W. Zhao, The digital marauder's map: A WiFi forensic positioning tool, *IEEE Transactions on Mobile Computing*, vol. 11(3), pp. 377–389, 2012.

[3] N. Hashim and I. Sutherland, An architecture for the forensic analysis of Windows system artifacts, *Proceedings of the Second International ICST Conference on Digital Forensics and Cyber Crime*, pp. 120–128, 2011.

[4] N. Ibrahim, A. Al-Nemrat, H. Jahankhani and R. Bashroush, Sufficiency of Windows event log as evidence in digital forensics, *Proceedings of the Seventh International Conference on Global Security, Safety and Sustainability and the Fourth Conference on e-Democracy*, pp. 253–262, 2011.

[5] K. Kent, S. Chevalier, T. Grance and H. Dang, Guide to Integrating Forensic Techniques into Incident Response, NIST Special Publication 800-86, National Institute of Standards and Technology, Gaithersburg, Maryland, 2006.

[6] A. Marrington, G. Mohay, A. Clark and H. Morarji, Event-based computer profiling for the forensic reconstruction of computer activity, *Proceedings of the AusCERT Asia Pacific Information Technology Security Conference*, pp. 71–87, 2007.

[7] R. McKemmish, What is forensic computing? *Trends and Issues in Crime and Criminal Justice*, vol. 118, pp. 1–6, 1999.

[8] Microsoft, Audit Security State Change, Microsoft, Redmond, Washington (`technet.microsoft.com/en-us/library/dn311493.aspx`), 2013.

[9] Microsoft, Windows 7 Product Guide, Microsoft, Redmond, Washington (`www.microsoft.com/en-us/download/details.aspx?id=4984`), 2014.

[10] R. Murphey, Automated Windows event log forensics, *Digital Investigation*, vol. 4(S), pp. S92–S100, 2007.

[11] J. Newman, Windows 8 grabs more market share, but so do older versions, *PC World*, August 1, 2013.

[12] A. Schuster, Introducing the Microsoft Vista event log file format, *Digital Investigation*, vol. 4(S), pp. S65–S72, 2007.

Chapter 8

SCHEMA RECONSTRUCTION IN DATABASE FORENSICS

Oluwasola Mary Adedayo and Martin Olivier

Abstract   Although considerable research has been conducted in the area of database forensics over the past few years, several aspects of database forensics remain to be considered. One of the challenges facing database forensics is that the results of forensic analysis may be inconsistent with the raw data contained in a database because of changes made to the metadata. This paper describes the various types of changes that can be made to a database schema by an attacker and shows how metadata changes can affect query results. Techniques for reconstructing the original database schema are also described.

Keywords: Database forensics, database reconstruction, inverse relational algebra

1.   Introduction

Databases are a core component of many computing systems and play an important role in many organizations. However, the use of databases to store critical and sensitive information has led to an increase in the rate at which they are exploited to facilitate computer crimes [5]. Database forensics is the branch of digital forensics [11, 15] that deals with the identification, preservation, analysis and presentation of evidence from databases [8]. Over the past few years, researchers [2, 14] have emphasized the need to incorporate database forensic analysis as part of traditional digital forensics due to the amount of information that is often retrieved from a database during an investigation. Although considerable research has been conducted in the area of database forensics, much work remains to be done with regard to formalizing the database forensic process.

The use of database logs as a source of information for forensic analysis has been the subject of many research efforts (see, e.g., [5, 7, 9,

G. Peterson and S. Shenoi (Eds.): Advances in Digital Forensics X, IFIP AICT 433, pp. 101–116, 2014.

10, 12]). Database logs can be explored in a variety of ways in order
to reconstruct the queries executed on a database and the values in the
database at an earlier time. In addition, a database can serve as a tool
to support the forensic analysis of the database itself because it permits the execution of complex queries for information retrieval [14]. An
important aspect of database forensics deals with the ability to revert
the operations performed on a database so that the information that
existed in the database at an earlier time can be reconstructed [1, 5,
7]. One aspect of database forensics that has not yet been considered
deals with the reconstruction of the database schema or metadata. Although the importance of the database schema has been discussed in the
database forensic literature [2, 5, 7, 12], no method currently exists for
reconstructing a database schema.

In earlier work [5, 7], we presented an algorithm for reconstructing
the data that was present in a database at an earlier time. Several
techniques to ensure the completeness of the reconstructed information
have also been considered [1]. This paper builds on the previous work
by describing techniques for reconstructing the database schema. It
shows how the schema of a relation that has been deleted or lost can
be reconstructed based on the information in the log file. Examples are
provided to illustrate the reconstruction techniques.

2.   Database Management Systems

One of the fundamental characteristics of a database system is that it
contains the stored data as well as a complete definition and description
of the database and the stored data. This description, which is referred
to as "metadata" or the "database schema," is stored in the system
catalog. The metadata contains details about the structure, type and
format of each file and data item, along with the relationships between
the data and other constraints [4, 13]. The metadata is used by the
database management system (DBMS) to provide information about the
database structure to database users and application programs. Because
the DBMS software is not written for one specific database application,
the metadata provides the information needed by the DBMS to understand the structure, type and format of files and data that it will access.

It well known that the result of a database query is a function of the
metadata and the data stored in the database. This characteristic can
be exploited to facilitate criminal activities. One example is when a
criminal creates a view (stored as metadata) that provides easy access
to data of interest. Although the raw data may still exist, it may not be
retrievable after the metadata is deleted [14].

3.   Dimensions of Database Forensics

In a recent work [6], we discussed three dimensions of database forensics: the investigation of modified databases, damaged databases and compromised databases. A modified database is a database that has undergone changes due to normal business processes after an event of interest occurred. This type of database is often of interest when a database is not directly involved in the crime being investigated, but is used to store information that may assist in solving the crime [5–7].

In contrast, a damaged database is a database whose data or files may have been modified, deleted or copied from their original locations to other places. Such a database may or may not be operational depending on the extent of the damage.

A compromised database is a database in which some metadata or DBMS software have been modified by an attacker although the database may still be operational. Olivier [14] and Beyers, *et al.* [2] have pointed out that, although a database itself may be the best tool for collecting data for forensic analysis of the database, the integrity of the results obtained cannot be guaranteed because the database could have been modified into giving false information. Litchfield [12] also identified this problem when discussing the steps for performing a live response to an attack on an Oracle database. The major portion of the investigation of a compromised database focuses on obtaining the correct version of the metadata.

This paper provides insight into this problem by describing the various ways in which a database can be compromised by changing the metadata. Also, it shows how the problem can be addressed by reconstructing the database schema. The schema reveals the design decisions regarding the tables and their structures and, as such, can be used to obtain a better understanding of the results obtained from database queries. The paper describes typical examples of database compromise and shows how the schema can be reconstructed by considering operations that were previously performed on the database. In earlier work [7], we presented an algorithm for reconstructing database data. This paper considers the application of some of the previously-described data reconstruction techniques to the problem of reconstructing the database schema.

4.   Database Reconstruction

This section provides a brief overview of the main concepts underlying the paper. In particular, it describes the relational model, the relational algebra, the relational algebra log and the inverse operators of the relational algebra.

Table 1.   Relational algebra operators and their inverses.

Operators	Notation	Inverse Operator
Cartesian Product ($\times$)	$T \leftarrow R(A) \times S(B)$	$\times^{-1}(T) = (R, S)$ where $R = \pi_A(T)$ and $S = \pi_B(T)$
Union ($\cup$)	$T \leftarrow R \cup S$	$\cup^{-1}(T) = (R^*, S)$ where $R^* = T - S$ provided that S is known and vice versa
Intersection ($\cap$)	$T \leftarrow R \cap S$	$\cap^{-1}(T) = (R^*, S^*)$ where $R^* = S^* = T$
Difference ($-$)	$T \leftarrow R - S$	$-^{-1}(T) = R^* = T$. If R is known, then $S^* = R - T$
Join ($\bowtie$)	$T \leftarrow R(A) \bowtie_{p(A,B)} S(B)$	$\bowtie^{-1}(T) = (R^*, S^*)$ where $R^* = \bowtie_A(T)$ and $S^* = \pi_B(T)$
Projection (π)	$T \leftarrow \pi_{A_1, A_2, A_3}(R)$	$\pi^{-1}(T) = S^* = T$
Selection (σ)	$T \leftarrow \sigma_{p(A)}(R)$	$\sigma_{p(A)}^{-1}(T) = S^* = T$
Division ($/$)	$T \leftarrow R[A, B/C]S$	$/^{-1}(T) = (R^*, S^*)$ where $R^* = RM$ and RM is the remainder of the division

Relational Algebra and Relational Algebra Log.   The relational model developed by Codd [3] is based on the relational theory of mathematics. The model is composed of only one type of compound data known as a relation. Given a set of domains $\{D_1, D_2 \ldots, D_n\}$ over which the attributes $A = \{A_1, A_2, \ldots A_n\}$ are defined, a relation R (or $R(A)$) is a subset of the Cartesian product of the domains [3].

The relational algebra consists of basic operators for manipulating relations and a relational assignment operator ($\leftarrow$). The basic operators transform one or two relations into a new relation. The basic relational operators as defined by Codd [3] are listed in Table 1 along with the inverse operators (explained below). In the table, R, S and T denote relations, while A, B and C denote attributes of relations. Note that $p(attributes)$ is a logical predicate on one or more attributes representing a condition that must be satisfied by a row before the specified operation can be performed on it.

As introduced in our earlier work [5, 7], a relational algebra log (RA log) is a log of queries expressed as operations involving relational algebra operators instead of the traditional SQL notation. It presents several advantages over the traditional SQL notation [7].

Inverse Relational Algebra. The inverse operators of the relational algebra defined in our earlier work [5, 7] are used to obtain the value of an attribute A (corresponding to a tuple in relation R) at a specific time by computing the inverse of the most recent query performed on the current relation and sequentially retracing the queries backward until the desired time is reached. Depending on whether or not the result generated by an inverse operator is complete (i.e., without any missing information), the inverse operators of the relational algebra are categorized as a "complete inverse" or a "partial inverse." Note that, regardless of this classification, there are often instances where a complete inverse can be found for an operator that is categorized as a partial inverse operator. Given a relation R generated by a inverse operation, the notation R^* is used to denote that the inverse generated is incomplete. Table 1 lists the inverse operators of the relational algebra. Interested readers are referred to [5, 7] for a detailed description of the inverses and the conditions under which complete inverses exist.

5. Compromising a Database Schema

This section describes several ways in which a database schema may be compromised. Also, it demonstrates how a compromise can cause a database to give incorrect answers to queries. The study was performed using Postgres 9.2 running on a Windows 8 operating system.

Several actions can be performed on a database schema to compromise the database. Usually, an attacker may simply damage a database to prevent it from being used for its intended purpose. An attacker may also compromise a database in an attempt to hide some data stored by a user or by the attacker. In general, an attacker could make three types of changes:

- Localized changes to data

- Changes to blocks of data

- Changes to links between blocks of data

Localized Changes to Data. An attacker can make changes to specific columns of a relation within a database schema. The changes may be made to hide the information contained in the columns or to make the data unavailable to database users. This can be accomplished in several ways. A compromise involving the swapping of two columns can have serious effects on database operations [14]. An example is swapping the "Purchase Price" and "Selling Price" columns in a store database, which would cause the store to sell its goods at a lower price. Figure 1

```
update pg_attribute set attnum = '5' where attrelid = '16432'
    and attname = 'purchasePrice';
update pg_attribute set attnum = '2' where attrelid = '16432'
    and attname = 'sellingPrice';
update pg_attribute set attnum = '3' where attrelid = '16432'
    and attname = 'purchasePrice';
```

Figure 1.   Modifying a schema to swap two column names.

shows a code segment that can be used to compromise a database by swapping the column names in the database schema. The swap causes a **select** statement on one of the columns to return values from the second column.

```
update pg_attribute set attnum = '5' where attrelid = '24587'
    and attname = 'purchasePrice';
```

Figure 2.   Modifying a schema to hide a column.

A database schema could also be manipulated by changing the identification of an attribute (within the schema) to something unknown to the schema. Although the raw data may still be present in the database, it becomes impossible to query the database. Information initially thought to have been deleted or non-existent could, in fact, turn out to be non-retrievable because it is hidden from the DBMS by schema modification. Figure 2 shows a command that can be used to hide the attribute **purchasePrice** from authorized users by changing the identification used by the DBMS to access the column.

```
update pg_attribute set atttypid = '18' where attrelid = '16432' and
    attname = 'firstName'
```

Figure 3.   Modifying a schema to change the datatype of an attribute.

Details such as the datatypes of the attributes of a relation can be modified by changing specific values in the schema (Figure 3). Such a change affects the type of information that can be inserted into a column as well as the information that is retrieved when the column is queried. Modifying the datatype of an attribute in the schema causes data (whether it is being inserted or retrieved) to be formatted according to the new datatype; this makes it impossible to comprehend previously-stored information.

Depending on the DBMS, several parts of a database schema, including the column names, datatypes and constraints can be compromised by changing specific values in the schema. An attacker with an under-

```
update pg_class set relname = 's-unknown'||nextval('serial')
where relname in
select relname from pg_class where relnamespace=2200 and
  reltype!=0 and relkind ='r' and relname like 's%'
```

Figure 4. Changes to blocks of data in a schema.

standing of the DBMS structure can execute an SQL query that affects the schema and the results obtained from subsequent database queries.

Changes to Blocks of Data. Blocks of data such as complete tables and sets of columns can be modified via the database schema. Two simple examples are an attack that changes identically-named columns in multiple tables to a different name and an attack that changes the names of several tables to a different name that is not understandable to users. The code in Figure 4 changes the names of all tables with names starting with the letter s to a different name. This makes it impossible to retrieve the tables using the original name. In a similar manner to changing the names of blocks of data, blocks of data could be removed or even combined to compromise the database.

Changes to Links Between Blocks of Data. Another method of compromising a database involves changes that affect the links between data. This is accomplished by modifying the foreign keys and/or primary keys of database relations. It can involve localized changes to information in the database schema or changes to groups of data in the schema or a combination of both. An example attack is the modification of a table constraint (within the schema) by removing the foreign key, making it impossible to link information in another table. It is also possible to modify the links such that the table is linked to a wrong table.

Regardless of the types of changes made by an attacker, an important aspect of database forensics is the ability to reconstruct the data in a table and its schema. The next section describes techniques that can be used to reconstruct the schema by considering the operations that were previously performed on the database.

6. Schema Reconstruction

According to Elmasri and Navathe [4], the widespread use of relational DBMSs is due to their simplicity and the mathematical foundation of the relational algebra. This section leverages these characteristics to reconstruct the database schema. Section 6.1 describes how the schema of a relation can be reconstructed by examining the conditions associated with each relational algebra operator. Section 6.2 investigates the application of inverse relational algebra operators used for reconstructing database data [5, 7] to reconstruct a database schema. Finally, Section 6.3 describes how a schema can be reconstructed by checking the consistency of database information.

6.1   Reconstruction from Manipulations

Given an RA log, the attributes of the operations performed on a relation can be used to determine the schema. Many of the relational algebra operators with two operands require the structures of the operands to be the same. The Union, Intersection and Difference operators fall in this category. Given a relational algebra query, $C \leftarrow A$ op B, where A, B and C are relations and op is a Union ($\cup$), Intersection ($\cap$) or Difference operation ($-$), then the three relations A, B and C have the same structure. Thus, if the structure of one of the relations is known, the same structure can be used for the other two relations and the data in the relations can be reconstructed [5, 7] based on this structure.

This is also true with the Selection operator. Given a Select query, $B \leftarrow \sigma_{p(attr)}(A)$, where some tuples in A are selected as B based on the condition $p(attr)$, then the relations A and B have exactly the same structure and the known structure of one relation can be used as the structure of the other relation in order to reconstruct data or to infer the structure of other relations.

An interesting aspect of this approach is that it is possible to combine different operations and analyze the likely schema for the resulting relations.

6.2   Reconstruction Using Inverse RA

A formal approach for reconstructing the schema of a relation is to apply the reconstruction algorithm for database forensics described in previous work [5, 7]. Since the algorithm uses inverse relational algebra operators, we proceed to describe how the inverses can be used for schema reconstruction.

Transposing Schemas into Relations.   Since the inverse operators of the relational algebra require a relation as an operand, the schema of a relation must be expressed as a relation in order to use the inverse operators in schema reconstruction. Many DBMSs provide the ability to retrieve the structure of a relation in the database as a table. In Postgres, for example, the command shown in Figure 5 can be used to

```
select ordinal_position, column_name, data_type, is_nullable,
    descrip.description AS comment
from information_schema.columns columns
left join pg_class class on (columns.table_name = class.relname)
left join pg_description descrip on (class.oid = descrip.objoid)
left join pg_attribute attrib on  (class.oid = attrib.attrelid
    and columns.column_name = attrib.attname
    and attrib.attnum = descrip.objsubid)
where table_name= 'actor'  /* The table name*/
group by ordinal_position, column_name, data_type,
    is_nullable, table_schema, descrip.description;
```

Figure 5. Retrieving a schema as a table.

retrieve the structure of a relation into a table where each attribute of the relation is a tuple in the retrieved table.

As a consequence of retrieving the schema of a relation as another relation, it is also necessary to find the "transpose" of the operations performed on the original relations so that the transposed operations can be applied to the retrieved schemas and used for schema reconstruction. We now consider each relational algebra operator and identify the operation that can be considered to be its transposition:

- **Cartesian Product** ($\times$): Given a query $T \leftarrow R \times S$, the resulting relation T has all the attributes of both R and S. Thus, if the schemas of relations R and S are retrieved, then the schema of T would be the union of the two schemas. Consequently, the transpose of a Cartesian Product operation is a Union operation.

- **Union** ($\cup$): Given a query $T \leftarrow R \cup S$, the schema of T is the same as those of R and S. If the schemas of the two operands could be retrieved, then the schema of T would be the intersection of the two schemas. Thus, the transpose of a Union operation is an Intersection operation.

- **Intersection** ($\cap$): Using the same reasoning as for the Union operation, the transpose of an Intersection operation, $T \leftarrow R \cap S$, is also an Intersection operation.

- **Difference** ($-$): Given a Difference operation expressed as the query, $T \leftarrow R - S$, the schema of T is the same as those of R and S. As in the case of the Union and Intersection operations, the transpose of the Difference operation is an Intersection operation.

- **Join** ($\bowtie$): A Join operation is similar to a Cartesian Product, except that the Cartesian Product is performed under a specified

Table 2.   Transpose of the relational algebra operators.

Operators	Transposed Operators
Cartesian Product ($\times$)	Union ($\cup$)
Union ($\cup$)	Intersection ($\cap$)
Intersection ($\cap$)	Intersection ($\cap$)
Difference ($-$)	Intersection ($\cap$)
Join ($\bowtie$)	Union ($\cup$)
Projection (π)	Selection (σ)
Selection (σ)	Selection (σ)
Division ($/$)	Difference ($-$)

condition and, as such, the result of the Join may not include all the tuples that might be in a Cartesian Product. However, this has no effect on the attributes of the operands or on the resulting relation. Given a Join query, $T \leftarrow R \bowtie_{p(A,B)} S$, it is clear that T has all the attributes of both R and S. Thus, if the schema of both R and S can be retrieved, then the schema of T would be the union of the two schemas. This implies that the transpose of a Join operation is a Union operation.

- **Projection (π):** A Projection operation selects some of the attributes of a relation to produce another relation. Given a query, $T \leftarrow \pi_{A_1, A_2, A_3}(R)$, it is clear that the attributes of T correspond to a subset of the attributes of R. Thus, the transpose of a Projection operation is a Selection operation.

- **Selection (σ):** The output of a Selection operation, $T \leftarrow \sigma_{p(A)}(R)$, has exactly the same set of attributes as that of the operand; this is because a Selection only affects the tuples of a relation. Thus, the transpose of a Selection operation is a Selection (without any conditions) of all the tuples in the schema of the operand.

- **Division ($/$):** Given a query, $T \leftarrow R[A, B/C]S$, where a relation R is divided by an attribute C of relation S, it is clear that the attribute of T will include all the attributes of A except the attribute (also in S) that was used in the Division operation. If the schema of the two relations R and S are known, then the schema of T would be the schema of R minus the schema of S. Thus, the transpose of a Division operation is a Difference operation.

Table 2 summarizes the transposed operations that can be applied to reconstruct the schema of a relation. The value of a particular attribute of a relation at time t is obtained by computing the inverse of the most recent query performed on the current relation and going backward in sequence until the desired time t is reached. The same technique can be applied to schema reconstruction, except that the transposed operations are used to handle the schemas involved in the relational algebra operations.

Applying the Inverse RA and Transpose Operators. This section describes how the transposed operators described above can be used together with the inverse operators to reconstruct table schemas. According to Table 2, there are four relational algebra operators that must be considered: (i) Union ($\cup$); (ii) Intersection ($\cap$); (iii) Selection (σ); and (iv) Difference ($-$). This is because the relational algebra operators can be transposed using these four operators.

The inverse of a Union operation $T \leftarrow R \cup S$ can only be determined if one of the expected outputs (i.e., R or S) is known. If relation S is known, then $\cup^{-1}(T) = (R^*, S)$ where $R^* = T - S$. On the other hand, if R is known, then $\cup^{-1}(T) = (R, S^*)$. A complete Inverse Union exists only when R and S have no tuples in common [5, 7]. Since the transpose of the Cartesian Product and Join operators is a Union operation, this definition can be applied to reconstruct the schemas of relations involved in either operation. Given an operation $C \leftarrow A$ op B, where op is the Cartesian Product or Join operator, if the schema of C can be retrieved as relation T, then the schema of A can be reconstructed using the Inverse Union operator provided that the schema of B is known, or vice versa. As an example, if the schemas of relations C (S_C) and B (S_B) are retrieved using the code in Figure 5 and stored as the tables in Figure 6, then the schema of relation A can be reconstructed as ($S_C - S_B$), which yields the result in Figure 7.

The inverse of an Intersection operation $T \leftarrow R \cap S$, generates partial tuple inverses containing all the tuples in T, i.e., $\cap^{-1}(T) = (R^*, S^*)$ where $R^* = S^* = T$. Complete inverses exist when R and S are known to be the same [5, 7]. The Inverse Intersection operator can be applied to reconstruct the schemas of relations involved in a Union, Intersection or Difference operation because their transpose is an Intersection operation. That is, given an operation $C \leftarrow A$ op B, where op is the Union, Intersection or Difference operator, if the schema of C can be retrieved as a relation T, then the schemas of A and B can be reconstructed using the definition of the Inverse Intersection operator. A unifying characteristic of the Union, Intersection and Difference operators is that their operands must have the same schema. Thus, if the schema of relation C (or that of A or B) is retrieved as a table, then the schemas of the

ordinal_position integer	column_name character varying	data_type character varying
1	id	integer
2	lastname	character varying
3	firstname	character varying
4	lastupdate	timestamp
5	emp_id	integer
6	dept	character varying
7	address	character varying

(a) Schema of Relation C (S_C).

ordinal_position integer	column_name character varying	data_type character varying
1	id	integer
2	lastname	character varying
3	firstname	character varying
4	lastupdate	timestamp

(b) Schema of Relation B (S_B).

Figure 6.   Retrieved schemas of Relations C and B.

ordinal_position integer	column_name character varying	data_type character varying
5	emp_id	integer
6	dept	character varying
7	address	character varying

(a) Reconstructed schema of Relation A (S_A).

emp_id	dept	address
⋮	⋮	⋮
⋮	⋮	⋮

(b) Structure of Relation A.

Figure 7.   Reconstructed schema of Relation A using Inverse Union.

other relations can be reconstructed completely by applying the Inverse Intersection operator.

Given a Selection operation $R \leftarrow \sigma_{p(A)}(S)$, the Inverse Selection is given by $\sigma_{p(A)}^{-1}(R) = S^*$ where $S^* = R$. That is, all the tuples in R are also in S. The Inverse Selection yields a complete inverse if all the tuples in the operand of the Selection operator (i.e., S) satisfy the predicate $p(A)$ [5, 7]. The Inverse Selection operator can be applied to reconstruct the schemas of relations involved in a Projection or Selection operation because the transpose of both operations is a Selection operation. That is, given a Projection operation $C \leftarrow \pi_{A_1, A_2}(B)$ or a Selection operation $C \leftarrow \sigma_{p(A)}(B)$, if the schema of relation C is known (say S_C), then the schema of B contains all the tuples in S_C. In the case of a Projection operation, the reconstructed schema may be incomplete because a Projection is usually a Selection of some of the columns of the operand. In the case of a Selection operation, the reconstructed schema is complete because the Selection operator picks some of the tuples of its operand with all their attributes.

The Inverse Difference operation can be applied to reconstruct the schema of the operands of a Division operation because its transpose is a Difference operation. Given a Difference operation $T \leftarrow R - S$, the left operand is easily determined by the Inverse Difference operator as $R^* = T$ because $T \subseteq R$. A complete R can be determined only if the relation S is known and all the tuples in S are also known to be in R (i.e., $S \subseteq R$) so that $R = T \cup S$. The relation S^* with partial tuples can also be determined if R is known, in which case $S^* = R - T$. If $S \subseteq R$ in known, then a complete relation S is found from the inverse as $S = R - T$ [5, 7]. This implies that, if the schema of C (S_C) in the Division operation $C = A/B$ is known, then the schema of A contains all the tuples in S_C. The schema may be incomplete because relation A may contain other attributes that were not included in the Division operation. The reconstructed schema for A is given by $S_C \cup S_B$ and is complete if the schema of B (S_B) is known and it is also known that all the columns in B are also in A. On the other hand, the schema of relation B can be reconstructed as $S_A - S_C$ if the schema of A (S_A) is known. Also, if all the columns in B are also in A, then the reconstructed schema for relation B is complete.

Although a reconstructed schema is generated in the form of a table, the structure of the corresponding table is simply a matter of transposing the reconstructed schema so that tuples in the reconstructed table become the columns of the required relation. The technique described above can be applied to a sequence of operations in order to arrive at the particular relation whose schema is required. This is equivalent to working with the database reconstruction algorithm described by Fasan and Olivier [5, 7], and using the transposed operations and the schemas expressed as tables instead of the actual operators and operands involved in relational algebra operations.

6.3   Reconstruction Through Consistencies

Another approach that can be used to reconstruct a database schema is to check the consistency of the information contained in the database. Typically, a DBMS provides the ability to represent complex relationships between data. The descriptions of these relationships are stored in the schema and imply that certain conditions hold between related data. Identifying instances that do not satisfy these conditions could point to actions performed by an attacker.

This approach is particularly useful for reconstructing the constraints associated with a relation. For example, if a referential integrity constraint [4] exists from a relation R to a relation S, then the relevant attributes in the two relations would be expected to have the same datatypes. This information can be used to determine the datatypes of the attributes if the schemas of R and/or S need to be reconstructed. The referential integrity constraint also implies that the referenced column is the primary key of one of the two relations.

Another example is the application of the entity integrity constraint [4], which specifies that a primary key value cannot be a null value. Thus, an attribute that can take a null value is not the primary key of the relation whose schema is to be reconstructed, and vice versa.

Database constraints and attribute characteristics can also help identify characteristics relating to the schema of a relation. While it may be possible to retrieve some of the constraints in a schema using the two techniques described above, it may be necessary to use additional techniques such as checking for data consistencies when reconstructing the constraints relating to a relation.

7.   Conclusions

A database schema can be compromised by attackers in several ways, causing queries to yield results that may be different from the actual data stored in the database. The techniques described for reconstructing relation schemas are useful in forensic investigations of compromised databases. These techniques leverage the inverses of relational algebra operators that were originally defined to reconstruct data that may have existed in a database at an earlier point in time.

Future research will focus on measuring the effectiveness of the schema reconstruction approaches in various error scenarios. In addition, it will investigate the problem of schema reconstruction from the big data and NoSQL perspectives.

Acknowledgement

This research was supported by the Organization for Women in Science for the Developing World (OWSD).

References

[1] O. Adedayo and M. Olivier, On the completeness of reconstructed data for database forensics, *Proceedings of the Fourth International Conference on Digital Forensics and Cyber Crime*, pp. 220–238, 2013.

[2] H. Beyers, M. Olivier and G. Hancke, Assembling metadata for database forensics, in *Advances in Digital Forensics VII*, G. Peterson and S. Shenoi (Eds.), Springer, Heidelberg, Germany, pp. 89–99, 2011.

[3] E. Codd, *The Relational Model for Database Management, Version 2*, Addison-Wesley, Reading, Massachusetts, 1990.

[4] R. Elmasri and S. Navathe, *Fundamentals of Database Systems*, Addison-Wesley, Boston, Massachusetts, 2011.

[5] O. Fasan and M. Olivier, Correctness proof for database reconstruction algorithm, *Digital Investigation*, vol. 9(2), pp. 138–150, 2012.

[6] O. Fasan and M. Olivier, On dimensions of reconstruction in database forensics, *Proceedings of the Seventh International Workshop on Digital Forensics and Incident Analysis*, pp. 97–106, 2012.

[7] O. Fasan and M. Olivier, Reconstruction in database forensics, in *Advances in Digital Forensics VIII*, G. Peterson and S. Shenoi (Eds.), Springer, Heidelberg, Germany, pp. 273–287, 2012.

[8] K. Fowler, *SQL Server Forensic Analysis*, Addison-Wesley, Boston, Massachusetts, 2009.

[9] P. Fruhwirt, M. Huber, M. Mulazzani and E. Weippl, InnoDB database forensics, *Proceedings of the Twenty-Fourth IEEE International Conference on Advanced Information Networking and Applications*, pp. 1028–1036, 2010.

[10] P. Fruhwirt, P. Kieseberg, S. Schrittwieser, M. Huber and E. Weippl, InnoDB database forensics: Reconstructing data manipulation queries from redo logs, *Proceedings of the Seventh International Conference on Availability, Reliability and Security*, pp. 625–633, 2012.

[11] S. Garfinkel, Digital forensics research: The next 10 years, *Digital Investigation*, vol. 7(S), pp. S64–S73, 2010.

[12] D. Litchfield, Oracle Forensics, Parts 1–6, NGSSoftware Insight Security Research Publication, Next Generation Security Software, Manchester, United Kingdom, 2007–2008.

[13] S. Nebiker and S. Bleisch, *Introduction to Database Systems*, Geographic Information Technology Training Alliance, Zurich, Switzerland, 2010.

[14] M. Olivier, On metadata context in database forensics, *Digital Investigation*, vol. 5(3-4), pp. 115–123, 2009.

[15] G. Palmer, A Road Map for Digital Forensic Research, Report from the First Digital Forensic Research Workshop, DFRWS Technical Report, DTR-T001-01 Final, Utica, New York, 2001.

Chapter 9

ANALYSIS OF THE USE OF XOR AS AN OBFUSCATION TECHNIQUE IN A REAL DATA CORPUS

Carolina Zarate, Simson Garfinkel, Aubin Heffernan, Scott Horras, and Kyle Gorak

Abstract   The only digital forensic tools known to provide an automated approach for evaluating XOR obfuscated data are DCCI_Carver and DC3_Carver, two general-purpose carving tools developed by the Defense Cyber Crime Center (DC3). In order to determine the use of XOR as an obfuscation technique and the need to adapt additional tools, we analyzed 2,411 drive images from devices acquired from countries around the world. Using a modified version of the open source tool bulk_extractor, evidence of XOR obfuscation was found on 698 drive images, with a maximum of 21,031 XOR-obfuscated features on a single drive. XOR usage in the corpus was observed in files with timestamps between the years 1995 and 2009, with the majority of the usage found in unallocated space. XOR obfuscation was used in the corpus to circumvent malware detection and reverse engineering, to hide information that was apparently being exfiltrated, and by malware detection tools for their quarantine directories and to distribute malware signatures. The results indicate that XOR obfuscation is important to consider when performing malware investigations. However, since the corpus does not contain data sets that are known to have been used by malicious entities, it is difficult to draw conclusions regarding the importance of extracting and examining XOR obfuscated files in criminal, counterintelligence and counterterrorism cases without further research.

Keywords: XOR, obfuscation, steganography, bulk_extractor

1. Introduction

A variety of single-byte operators have been used for simple data hiding or obfuscation. A classic technique involved the use of the ROT13

G. Peterson and S. Shenoi (Eds.): Advances in Digital Forensics X, IFIP AICT 433, pp. 117–132, 2014.

operator [34] to hide off-color jokes disseminated on the early Internet. Common techniques used today include single-byte XOR and single-byte rotate operators. These operators are essentially poor encryption algorithms with 8-bit keys: they are trivial to decode, but to do so the analyst or tool must specifically probe for evidence of their use. If no detection algorithm is employed, even 8-bit encryption is sufficient to hide data.

The only digital forensic tools known to the authors that provide forensic investigators with an automated approach for finding XOR-obfuscated data are DCCI_Carver and DC3_Carver, two general-purpose forensic carving tools developed by the Defense Cyber Crime Center (DC3). Existing commercial and open source digital forensic tools largely ignore single-byte obfuscation techniques. Although it is relatively easy to modify forensic and anti-malware tools to scan for data that have been obfuscated, most digital forensic tools and malware scanners eschew steganography detection because it is computationally expensive and the use of steganography is thought to be low. However, simple obfuscation techniques are sufficient to bypass most commercial and open source malware detection techniques, rendering the lack of de-obfuscation features in tools a vulnerability.

This paper focuses on a specific obfuscation technique, which we call XOR(255). XOR is the exclusive-or binary operation. XOR binary operations are performed with "keys." A key is a series of bytes with which a source file is XORed. XOR(255) is a special case of a single-byte key with the value 0xFF. Bytewise XOR(255) has the effect of inverting every bit in a source file. XOR(255) has the advantages of being fast (it typically executes in less than one clock cycle on modern architectures), reversible and performed in-place. XOR(255) has the additional property of leaving the file entropy unchanged, allowing processed data to remain invisible to tools that search for encrypted data using entropy techniques. We focused on XOR(255) because of its ease of use and effectiveness at obscuring data.

We created a plug-in for the open source tool bulk_extractor [18] that processes data with XOR(255). The structure of bulk_extractor is such that each scanner is applied independently to each block of data during processing. The modified tool was employed to scan a corpus of several thousand drive images extracted from used storage devices that had been purchased on the secondary market. The analysis was limited to email addresses, URLs, JPEG photographs, Windows executables, ZIP files and other kinds of easily recognizable data that had been obfuscated by XOR(255). The tool optimistically applied XOR(255) before and after every decompression or decoding step in its search for recognizable structured data.

The analysis revealed that simple obfuscation techniques were present on the drives purchased on three continents over a ten-year period, with some examples of obfuscation as recent as 2009. The use of XOR(255) was limited to a small fraction of the corpus, but the applications of obfuscation are very relevant to forensic investigations. In particular, obfuscation was used to hide signatures in malware and user-generated content that appeared to be targeted for exfiltration. Also, obfuscation was used by legitimate programs to prevent reverse engineering.

2.   Prior Work

Simple data obfuscation techniques predate the modern Internet. The ROT13 operator was used in the 1980s to distribute off-color jokes and the answers to riddles on Usenet.

2.1   Use of XOR

The academic literature on XOR obfuscation is relatively sparse. Indeed, documented examples of XOR use are largely confined to online blogs of malware investigators. Mueller [29] notes that Norton Antivirus uses XOR to obfuscate its log files and *Quarantine* folder; we verify this observation in this paper. Hussey [22] suggests that XOR is sometimes used as an obfuscation technique to hide data as it is being exfiltrated; we discovered evidence of XOR used for this purpose.

Several types of malware have been reported as using simple obfuscation techniques to hide data being exfiltrated from a victim machine. Trojan.NTESSESS XORs the results of its commands, including uploaded files, with a changing nine-byte key [12]. Even advanced malware such as Stuxnet, Duqu, Flame and Red October use XOR as the basis of obfuscation algorithms to hide data [35]. Stuxnet uses a 31-byte key with XOR [16]. Duqu XORs data from its keylogger, which it sends to its server [35]. Like Duqu, Flame employs XOR obfuscation techniques on captured keystrokes, screenshots, email messages and conversations recorded via the computer microphone [35]. Red October also uses XOR obfuscation techniques when exfiltrating information from Nokia phones, iPhones and networks [35].

Simple obfuscation techniques have proven to be popular for protecting malicious code and exfiltrated data from anti-virus software and forensic investigators. The SymbOS/OpFake.A!tr.dial malware from Opera Updater is one such example. Apvrille [2] found the Opera Updater malware to contain a 91-byte XOR key as a more complicated algorithm for hiding itself. Similarly, variations of Trojan.PingBed and Trojan.NTESSESS employ XOR obfuscation and embedding techniques in PNG files to evade anti-virus scanners [11, 12]. Cannell [6] suggests that malware may contain XORed URLs as references to malicious files and executables online, creating the appearance of benign files. An example is Trojan.Win32.Patched.mc, which disguises itself as a harmless Flash file. The Trojan file `main.swf` analyzed by StopMalvertising [25] contains an XORed hexadecimal string, which allows an XORed malicious executable to be downloaded. This poses a problem for anti-virus scanners because the files appear harmless, but proceed to download files from URLs that are known to be malicious. XOR has also been used by advanced malware as a method for hiding their main code from anti-virus software – Stuxnet, Duqu, Flame and Red October all obfuscate their payloads and main executables with XOR [35]. In addition, the Storm botnet and other advanced botnets have begun to take advantage of the technique, obfuscating their traffic with XOR in order to avoid identification [24].

Previous research has examined how well anti-virus systems deal with simple obfuscation in malware. Common commercial anti-virus systems tested by Christodorescu and Jha [8] frequently did not identify obfuscated malware, demonstrating that simple obfuscation is an effective technique to defeat anti-virus scanners. The Internot Security Team [23] examined a similar case and found that simple obfuscation allowed malware to easily bypass many anti-virus scanners.

Other researchers have provided insight into techniques that could help undermine XOR obfuscation. Cannell [5] suggests that patterns inside XORed material can be used to find the XOR key. Malware normalization has also been proposed by Christodorescu, *et al.* [9] as a method for undermining obfuscation techniques by normalizing a file, enabling anti-virus scanners to detect malicious content.

2.2   Manual Analysis Tools

Although numerous digital forensic tools can de-obfuscate a region of bytes with an XOR mask or use XOR pre-processing in malware analysis, only one tool applies XOR as part of automated processing. The other tools that de-obfuscate data require the techniques to be manually invoked by the operator.

Some tools offer methods for de-obfuscating data, but leave the interpretation up to the operator. Hex editors often implement such a feature, enabling the user to view data in hex and offering de-obfuscation functions. The open source Hexplorer [13] has the ability to XOR regions before they are displayed. The `translate.py` script [31] also allows an investigator to XOR a file with a single-byte key. Other tools are specifically tailored to de-obfuscating certain components of a forensic investigation. The MemoryDump plugin [1], for instance, has an option for XORing a memory dump before outputting the data to the user.

Other tools examine data to look for XOR keys, leaving it up to the user to de-obfuscate and analyze the information. XORBruteForcer [15] uses a brute-force algorithm to determine the keys that were most likely to have been used in XORing the data. In contrast, NoMoreXOR [14] attempts to guess an XOR key using frequency analysis.

String searching is also a frequently-used feature in obfuscation analysis tools. XORSearch [30] uses a brute-force approach to search for specific strings that have been obfuscated using XOR, ROL and ROR. Similarly, XORStrings [32], an extension of the XORSearch tool, scans a given file for strings that have been XORed with a specific sequence. The `iheartxor` tool [20] offers a similar function, using brute-force to search for certain obfuscated regular expressions and plain strings.

2.3 Automated Analysis Tools

As mentioned above, DCCI_Carver and DC3_Carver are the only digital forensic tools that provide investigators with an automated approach for uncovering a wide variety of XOR obfuscated files in storage media. In addition to these tools, a literature search turned up tools that provide automated assistance in identifying obfuscated malicious files. Several programs can search for XORed executables embedded in files. Hexacorn's DeXRAY tool [21] acts as a file carver and can identify obfuscated malicious files under a single XOR layer. OfficeMalScanner [3] has a feature to scan for traces of XORed malicious data in Office documents using a brute-force method. Another document scanner tool, Cryptam [26], uses cryptanalysis to identify obfuscated embedded executable files and is effective at detecting XOR obfuscation [27].

3. Materials and Methods

We modified an open source tool to preprocess all the examined data with XOR(255). We then processed data from 2,411 forensic images and found 324,144 XOR artifacts on 698 of the images, with a maximum of 21,031 validated artifacts on a single forensic image.

The goal of the research was to identify the different ways that XOR obfuscation is used in real data in order to determine if the quantity and quality of obfuscation cases are sufficient to suggest implementing XOR de-obfuscation functions as a standard step in automated forensic processing. In particular, we analyzed a corpus of data seeking to determine the extent to which XOR(255) is implemented as an obfuscation technique.

3.1   Real Data Corpus

The Real Data Corpus [17] is a collection of several thousand digitized digital storage devices collected from countries around the world between 1998 and 2013. The corpus contains data from computer hard drives, cell phones, CD-ROMs, DVDs and thumb drives purchased from secondhand computer stores and markets. The corpus thus permits the sampling of XOR usage over a 15-year period in countries around the world, essentially representing a real-world data set.

A limitation of the Real Data Corpus is that it does not include data sets that are known to have been used by malicious entities. Thus, it would be difficult to draw conclusions regarding the importance of extracting and examining XOR obfuscated files in criminal, counterintelligence and counterterrorism investigations without further research. In addition, since the analysis was limited to email addresses, URLs, JPEG photographs, Windows executables, ZIP files and other kinds of easily recognizable data, we did not search for all the types of files that would be considered relevant to these types of investigations.

3.2   bulk_extractor

The bulk_extractor forensic tool can scan digital media for email addresses, phone numbers, Internet domain names and other data of interest to investigators. The tool is employed by triage and malware investigators [18]. The tool employs compiled regular expressions and hard-coded finite state machines to extract features from digital media. Features are pieces of key information such as credit cards, emails and URLs that are encountered in forensic investigations. For each feature, bulk_extractor determines the feature encoding and records the information in its output. The program labels features found using XOR(255) de-obfuscation with the string "XOR(255)."

The bulk_extractor tool tracks the features that result from the application of each scanner; this information is recorded in the program output. By using the tool in this manner, it was possible to search the entire corpus systematically for different uses of XOR obfuscation. For example, we were able to detect and distinguish the case of a JPEG photograph being XORed and then archived in a ZIP file from a series of JPEGs that were archived in a ZIP file and then XORed.

Table 1.   *bulk_extractor* features used in the study.

Feature
URLs
WINPE headers
Local file headers of ZIP archives
Exif headers (from JPEGs)

The identify_filenames.py tool included in the bulk_extractor package was used to associate identified features with the files in which they were located. For each feature, the tool indicated if the feature occurred in an allocated file, a deleted file or disk sectors that could not be associated with any file. This allowed the identification of the files containing XORed information and also helped understand the purpose and extent of the obfuscation.

3.3   Feature Selection

We examined the encodings of domains, URLs, email addresses, ZIP file data structures and Windows Portable Executable (WINPE) headers in order to find examples of XOR(255) usage. The problem with looking for XORed features is to distinguish actual XORed features from "false positives" or matching data that appear by chance, but that are not actual features.

We observed a much greater percentage of false positives (i.e., significantly lower precision) for the features that were found with XOR encodings than is typical for bulk_extractor output (which normally has high precision). We assume that the error rate or the number of false positives detected by bulk_extractor is constant for random input and a large set of data. When the input contains a substantial signal, such as when running bulk_extractor to find plaintext features, the precision is high. However, with an XOR filter, the signal is low because the majority of the features in the data are not XORed. Since the signal is lower, but the error rate remains constant, the precision is lower.

The higher incidence of false positives complicated the analysis. We addressed the error incidence by restricting the analysis to features with significant internal structure that are automatically checked for internal consistency (Table 1). The features are, thus, self-validating; as a result, they are extracted with an extremely low false positive error rate. Self-validating features can also be easily confirmed to be legitimate at a glance, such as opening a JPEG file or clicking a URL to visit a site.

Thus, we could safely assume that most of the identified features were true positives.

Because our goal was to evaluate files containing certain XOR(255)-encoded features, we ignored features that were not being evaluated in order to restrict the data set. In particular, we removed features that were not XORed, features that were not being considered and "false positive" features that we did not recognize as legitimate features.

3.4   Analysis of Identified Files

After identifying the features that had been XOR-encoded, we proceeded to identify the files that contained them. The Sleuth Kit [7] was used to extract the files that identify_filenames.py associated with intriguing XORed features. We analyzed the original files and the files after decoding with XOR(255) to determine the purpose for which the XOR obfuscation was used.

3.5   Evaluation of URLs

The vast majority of the XOR-encoded features discovered were URLs. Malware files may contain some mechanisms to further infiltrate a victim, while appearing benign at the same time. For example, malware often contained URLs of malicious sites for downloading additional malicious executables and other files. We examined the XORed URL features outputted by bulk_extractor because it has been reported that some malware samples use XOR to obscure embedded URLs. We evaluated the XORed URLs using the Google Safe Browsing API [19] and the McAfee TrustedSource Real-Time Threat Service [28].

4.   Results and Discussion

This section presents the results and discusses their implications.

4.1   XOR Obfuscation as a Watermark

We found several cases in which an innocuous URL was XOR(255)-encoded and embedded in a legitimate program. For example, drive image AE10-1023 contained a copy of Nero 7 with the byte sequence 97 8b 8b 8f c5 d0 d0 88 88 88 d1 91 9a 8b 90 d1 9c 90 92 0a at decimal offset 15,416,790,675. This maps to byte offset 112 of the file Program Files/Nero/Nero 7/Nero CoverDesigner/def.dat, a 13,630-byte file with an MD5 value of 8f4b534ed6a82e1885e155541aab0940 that is reported to be part of the Nero Premium distribution [33]. The

Table 2. Cross-tabulation of the classification of the 30,684 URLs.

McAfee Risk	Google OK	Google Malware	Total
High Risk	1,938	143	2,081
Medium Risk	1,301	9	1,310
Minimal Risk	24,090	6	24,096
Unverified	2,216	5	2,221
Total	29,545	163	29,708

string was transformed to http://www.nero.com after being processed by XOR(255).

4.2 XORed URL Analysis

A total of 281,712 XORed URLs were found in the drive images, 30,684 of them were distinct. Google's Safe Browsing (GSB) database only checks the domains of sites and is quite conservative. For each XORed URL, GSB reports if the URL's domain is "OK" or "Malware." McAfee's Real-Time Threat Service considers the entire URL and provides better discrimination. For each URL, we recorded if McAfee considered it to be "High Risk," "Medium Risk," "Minimal Risk" or "Unverified."

Table 2 shows how the URLs were evaluated by Google's Safe Browsing API and McAfee's Real-Time Threat Service. Overall, roughly 10% of the distinct URLs found in the XORed data were tied to malware.

4.3 XOR Obfuscation in Anti-Virus Software

Confirming Mueller's observatin [29], we found many XOR-obfuscated URLs in Norton Anti-Virus log files and virus definitions. We also discovered some files in the *Quarantine* directory that had been obfuscated with XOR(255). The drive image il3-0161 contained one such collection of XORed quarantined malware. bulk_extractor determined that the file 05FB1F54.exe contained an XORed WINPE header. The file was also indicated to be located under *Program Files/Norton Antivirus/Quarantine/* with an MD5 value of a96ae9519ea968ac0089-d6b53cef9b2b. Examination of the hex dump of the original file revealed that it had no executable code or strings. However, after the file was XORed, the entire file appeared to be malware, containing strings such as "RegDeleteKeyA," "DownloadFile" and "Download.Trojan."

Malware is often distributed via "drive-by downloads" from compromised web servers and, thus, the presence of a malicious URL is a key indicator of malware. Norton and other anti-virus scanners use this approach to identify malware. By obfuscating malware signatures and log files, anti-virus scanners avoid accidentally identifying themselves as malware.

4.4   Obfuscated URLs in Malware

We found a significant number of XORed domains and URLs in programs that were clearly associated with malware. In many cases, the URLs were verified as malicious by Google's Safe Browing API or had names that were clearly malicious. One example is the file SENDFILE.EXE in the drive image IN10-0145, which has an MD5 value of 3d419f96-355b93e641ba097c08121937. The unobfuscated version of the file contained several malicious strings, including URLs linked to malware and instances that modify the registry and processes. For example, the 47-byte sequence b7 ab ab af c5 d0 d0 ac bc be b1 b1 ba ad d1 a9 d2 a7 d2 ac bc be b1 b1 ba ad d1 bc b0 b2 d0 ac ba ab aa af d0 b9 b6 b3 ba d1 af b7 af appears at the decimal offset 4426 in SENDFILE.EXE. After it was processed by XOR(255), the string became HTTP://SCANNER.VAV-X-SCANNER.COM/SETUP/FILE.PHP. Based on this analysis, it is clear that some examples of malware use XOR(255) obfuscation in their normal operations.

The use of XOR(255) by anti-virus scanners and malware is problematic. In our testing, many program samples containing malicious XORed URLs were not identified as malicious by any of the 46 anti-virus engines at VirusTotal.com. However, after the files were de-obfuscated, many of the engines were able to identify the malware. Clearly, the engines simply look for the malicious URLs (because applying XOR(255) to the entire executable would also corrupt the Windows PE header and damage the executable code). It is troubling that common anti-virus engines and professional forensic tools do not even offer this simple technique for finding obfuscated malicious data, especially given the widespread use of XOR(255) in malware that we encountered in the Real Data Corpus and in our literature search.

4.5   Anti-Reverse Engineering

In many of the drive images, we observed XOR-obfuscated variations of an email address belonging to Reznik (co-developer of the RealAudio and RealVideo algorithms [10]) in DLLs associated with software from his company. The email address and its variations appeared to have been repeated several times in blocks throughout the Real codecs. One example was found in the drive image AE10-1029 in the file `Program Files/Real/RealPlayer/converter/Codecs/erv4.dll`. The `erv4.dll` file is 483,328 bytes in size and has an MD5 value of `e8b759859b53e19c261162 783dae9869`. The byte sequence `a6 8a 8d 96 86 df ad 9a 85 91 96 94 df c3 86 8d 9a 85 91 96 94 bf 8d 9a 9e 93 d1 9c 90 92 c1 ff`, which appeared at offset 61,120, was de-obfuscated to `Yuriy Reznik <yreznik@real.com>`. We contacted Dr. Reznik and learned that his obfuscated email address was embedded in the binary as a key for decrypting code tables used by the RealVideo 8 codec.

We also found several instances of XOR(255)-encoded JPEG digital photographs that appeared to be from Adobe Flash video games. Drive image IN10-0060 contained the Battle Rush Adobe Flash game menu screen background, drive image SG1-1062 had an XORed menu screen of Gutterball 2 and drive image TH0001-0010 had many Beach Party Craze backgrounds. We believe that the JPEG pictures were encoded as an anti-reverse engineering measure.

4.6 XOR(255)-Encoded ZIP File

On one drive image, we observed remnants of multiple ZIP files in unallocated space that contained confidential information that had been archived and XOR-encoded. The disk was from a computer running Windows 95 that had been purchased on the secondary market and imaged in 2007. The most recent use of the drive was in 2006.

On the drive image, we found a total of 802 documents with time-stamps in the ZIP archive ranging from 1991 through 1999, with the majority of the files from 1998 (112 files) and 1999 (623 files). No archived files were found with timestamps after 1999.

After finding these files, we proceeded to modify the ZIP scanner of `bulk_extractor` to carve the remnants into files that could be transferred to another system and analyzed. Upon reviewing the extracted files, we found spreadsheets, personal emails and other sensitive documents containing employee names, home addresses and government identification numbers. We located a batch file, `EMPACA2.BAT`, that zipped the documents to create the archive on the drive image. We were unable to find evidence of the tools that had been used to obfuscated the archive and, thus, could not prove that the obfuscation was the result of an exfiltration attempt.

There are several possible explanations for the obfuscation. The data could have belonged to the individual who was obfuscating the data; this individual could have been developing an application to protect a set of

Table 3. Processing times for `bulk_extractor` with and without the XOR scanner.

Test Image	Size	Without XOR	With XOR	Δ
nps-2009-domexusers	40 GB	522 sec	799 sec	+53%
nps-2011-2tb	2 TB	34,140 sec	58,147 sec	+70%

data or to protect his/her own data. Alternatively, the obfuscated ZIP file could be the result of software processing the data. On the other hand, the data could have been obfuscated by a rogue employee to hide the data or in an attempt to exfiltrate the data.

4.7   Performance Impact

We saw a significant increase in the processing time after adding the XOR scanner. One standard test drive image required 53% additional processing time, while another required 70% additional time (Table 3). Timing was performed on a 12-core HP Z800 with dual Intel Xenon E5645 CPUs running at 2.4 GHz with 24 GiB of RAM. The operation system was Fedora 19 Linux.

Because `bulk_extractor` recursively processes decompressed data and the XOR scanner attempts to de-obfuscate the data at each step of the pipeline, the actual increase in time is dependent on the data in a disk image. The increase in time is also proportional to the amount of data that is compressed and have to be re-processed, but it is not proportional to the amount of XOR-obfuscated data. For example, the NPS Realistic drive image nps-2011-2tb contains a large number of Adobe PDF files, each of which has multiple `zlib`-compressed regions. Applying XOR deobfuscation to these bytes quadruples the processing time required by other `bulk_extractor` scanners: the bytes were processed with the scanners as they sat in the disk image, after XOR de-obfuscation, after decompression, and after decompression and XOR de-obfuscation.

4.8   Accuracy of `bulk_extractor`

We were interested in substantiating the accuracy of `bulk_extractor` in detecting features obfuscated with XOR(255). Two standard forensic drive images, nps-2009-domexusers (40 GB) and nps-2011-2tb (2 TB), were used to study the accuracy of `bulk_extractor`'s XOR scanner. We took a random sample of 500 features from each type of feature from each drive image. Each feature was determined to be a true positive or false positive by hand. We found that, for each type of feature, bulk_extractor had almost all the features as true positives or all the features as false positives. There was a higher incidence of features on the 2 TB drive image that were almost completely false positives than on the 40 GB drive image.

4.9 XOR(255)-UNZIP-XOR(255) Property

We were surprised to discover several instances in which the sequence XOR(255)-UNZIP-XOR(255) applied to a fragment of a ZIP-encoded file yielded the same result that would be produced by the straightforward application of UNZIP. We hypothesize that is the result of zlib's use of an adaptive decompression algorithm. We subsequently suppressed XOR(255)-UNZIP-XOR(255) processing with a modification to the bulk_extractor XOR scanner.

5. Conclusions

The analysis of the Real Data Corpus revealed multiple cases of XOR(255) obfuscation. XOR(255) was used to encode URLs in antivirus scanner files and malware in order to avoid detection. XOR(255) obfuscation was also used to hinder the reverse engineering of RealVideo 8 codecs and several Adobe Flash video games. In one case, XOR(255) was likely used in a successful attempt to exfiltrate sensitive data.

The study of XOR obfuscation in the Real Data Corpus revealed several instances where XOR obfuscation is relevant to digital forensic investigations. However, the increase in processing time by bulk_extractor and other forensic tools may be problematic when large data sets have to be examined in a limited amount of time. Therefore, while forensic tools should implement features that would allow investigators to perform simple de-obfuscation, the de-obfuscation should be adjustable by the investigator to run in a manual or automatic mode (similar to the XOR feature in DCCI_Carver and DC3_Carver). Additionally, because the analysis has demonstrated a need for de-obfuscating malware and exfiltrated data, a forensic tool should be operated with the de-obfuscation function enabled in order to capture all the information. Likewise, XOR de-obfuscation should be enabled in child exploitation and objectionable content cases to address the so-called "botnet" or "SODDI" defense [4]. Our XOR scanner is included in the bulk_extractor 1.4 release and is enabled using the flag -e xor.

Our future research will focus on enhancing bulk_extractor's XOR scanner to run with little noticeable performance impact. Another line of research is to conduct a thorough survey of the prevalence and purpose of other simple obfuscation and steganography techniques such as rotate and the ROT13 algorithm, as well as, XORing with different keys. Finally, efforts should focus on enhancing anti-virus systems to detect malware that has been obfuscated; the fact that simple XOR obfuscation can successfully evade today's anti-virus systems is troubling indeed.

The opinions and views expressed in this paper are those of the authors and do not reflect the views of the Naval Postgraduate School, the U.S. Military Academy, the Department of the Navy, the Department of the Army or the U.S. Department of Defense.

Acknowledgements

We wish to thank Robert Beverly, Michael Shick and Yuriy Reznik for their help with this research. We also wish to thank Dave Ferguson from DC3, and Colonel Greg Conti, Lieutenant Colonel Matt Burrow and Lieutenant Michael Nowatkowski from the U.S. Military Academy.

References

[1] aeon, MemoryDump (`www.woodmann.com/collaborative/tools/index.php/MemoryDump`), 2009.

[2] A. Apvrille, Symbian malware uses a 91-byte XOR key, Fortinet, Sunnyvale, California (`blog.fortinet.com/symbian-malware-uses-a-91-byte-xor-key`), 2012.

[3] F. Boldewin, Frank Boldewin's `www.reconstructer.org` (`www.reconstructer.org/code.html`), 2009.

[4] S. Brenner, B. Carrier and J. Henninger, The Trojan horse defense in cybercrime cases, *Santa Clara High Technology Law Journal*, vol. 21(1), pp. 1–53, 2004.

[5] J. Cannell, Nowhere to hide: Three methods of XOR obfuscation, Malwarebytes, San Jose, California (`blog.malwarebytes.org/intelligence/2013/05/nowhere-to-hide-three-methods-of-xor-obfuscation`), 2013.

[6] J. Cannell, Obfuscation: Malware's best friend, Malwarebytes, San Jose, California (`blog.malwarebytes.org/intelligence/2013/03/obfuscation-malwares-best-friend`), 2013.

[7] B. Carrier, The Sleuth Kit (`www.sleuthkit.org/sleuthkit`), 2013.

[8] M. Christodorescu and S. Jha, Testing malware detectors, *ACM SIGSOFT Software Engineering Notes*, vol. 29(4), pp. 34–44, 2004.

[9] M. Christodorescu, J. Kinder, S. Jha, S. Katzenbeisser and H. Veith, Malware Normalization, Technical Report #1539, Deparment of Computer Sciences, University of Wisconsin, Madison, Wisconsin (`ftp.cs.wisc.edu/pub/techreports/2005/TR1539.pdf`), 2005.

[10] G. Conklin, G. Greenbaum, K. Lillevold, A. Lippman and Y. Reznik, Video coding for streaming media delivery on the Internet, *IEEE Transactions on Circuits and Systems for Video Technology*, vol. 11(3), pp. 269–281, 2001.

[11] Cyber Engineering Services, Malware obfuscated within PNG files, Columbia, Maryland (`www.cyberengineeringservices.com/mal ware-obfuscated-within-png-files`), 2011.

[12] Cyber Engineering Services, Malware obfuscated within PNG files > Sample 2, Columbia, Maryland (`www.cyberengineeringserv ices.com/malware-obfuscated-within-png-files-sample-2-2`), 2011.

[13] M. Dudek, Hexplorer (`sourceforge.net/projects/hexplorer`), 2013.

[14] G. Edwards, NoMoreXOR (`github.com/hiddenillusion/NoMore XOR`), 2013.

[15] J. Esparza, XORBruteForcer (`eternal-todo.com/var/scripts/ xorbruteforcer`), 2008.

[16] N. Falliere, L. O'Murchu and E. Chien, W32.Stuxnet Dossier, Symantec, Mountain View, California, 2011.

[17] S. Garfinkel, P. Farrell, V. Roussev and G. Dinolt, Bringing science to digital forensics with standardized forensic corpora, *Digital Investigation*, vol. 6(S), pp. S2–S11, 2009.

[18] S. Garfinkel, Digital media triage with bulk data analysis and `bulk_extractor`, *Computers and Security*, vol. 32, pp. 56–72, 2013.

[19] Google, Safe Browsing API, Mountain View, California (`develop ers.google.com/safe-browsing`), 2013.

[20] A. Hanel, iheartxor (`hooked-on-mnemonics.blogspot.com/p/ iheartxor.html`), 2012.

[21] Hexacorn, DeXRAY, Hong Kong, China (`www.hexacorn.com/bl og/category/software-releases/dexray`), 2012.

[22] B. Hussey, Decoding data exfiltration – Reversing XOR encryption, Crucial Security Forensics Blog (`crucialsecurityblog. harris.com/2011/07/06/decoding-data-exfiltration-%E2%80 %93-reversing-xor-encryption`), 2011.

[23] Internot Security Team, Bypassing anti-virus scanners (`dl. packetstormsecurity.net/papers/bypass/bypassing-av.pdf`), 2011.

[24] B. Kang, E. Chan-Tin, C. Lee, J. Tyra, H. Kang, C. Nunnery, Z. Wadler, G. Sinclair, N. Hopper, D. Dagon and Y. Kim, Towards complete node enumeration in a peer-to-peer botnet, *Proceedings of the Fourth International Symposium on Information, Computer and Communications Security*, pp. 23–34, 2009.

[25] Kimberly, Analysis of `imm32.dll` – `Trojan.Win32.Patched.mc`, StopMalvertising (`stopmalvertising.com/malware-reports/ana lysis-of-imm32.dll-trojan.win32.patched.mc.html`), 2011.

[26] Malware Tracker, Cryptam document scanner, North Grenville, Canada (`malwaretracker.com/doc.php`), 2012.

[27] Malware Tracker, New malware document scanner tool released, North Grenville, Canada (`blog.malwaretracker.com/2012/02/ new-malware-document-scanner-tool.html`), 2012.

[28] McAfee, TrustedSource – Check Single URL, Santa Clara, California (`www.trustedsource.org/en/feedback/url?action= checksingle`), 2011.

[29] L. Mueller, XOR entire file or selected text, ForensicKB (`www.for ensickb.com/2008/03/xor-entire-file-or-selected-text.ht ml`), 2008.

[30] D. Stevens, XORSearch and XORStrings (`blog.didierstevens. com/programs/xorsearch`), 2007.

[31] D. Stevens, Translate (`blog.didierstevens.com/programs/trans late`), 2008.

[32] D. Stevens, New tool: XORStrings (`blog.didierstevens.com/?s= xorstrings`), 2013.

[33] Systweak CheckFileName, View Nero Premium Details (`www.check filename.com/view-details/Nero-Premium`), 2013.

[34] I. Venkata Sai Manoj, Cryptography and steganography, *Internal Journal of Computer Applications*, vol. 1(12), pp. 61–65, 2010.

[35] N. Virvilis and D. Gritzalis, The big four – What we did wrong in advanced persistent threat detection? *Proceedings of the Eighth International Conference on Availability, Reliability and Security*, pp. 248–254, 2013.

Chapter 10

SIMILARITY HASHING BASED ON LEVENSHTEIN DISTANCES

Frank Breitinger, Georg Ziroff, Steffen Lange, and Harald Baier

Abstract   It is increasingly common in forensic investigations to use automated pre-processing techniques to reduce the massive volumes of data that are encountered. This is typically accomplished by comparing fingerprints (typically cryptographic hashes) of files against existing databases. In addition to finding exact matches of cryptographic hashes, it is necessary to find approximate matches corresponding to similar files, such as different versions of a given file.

   This paper presents a new stand-alone similarity hashing approach called saHash, which has a modular design and operates in linear time. saHash is almost as fast as SHA-1 and more efficient than other approaches for approximate matching. The similarity hashing algorithm uses four sub-hash functions, each producing its own hash value. The four sub-hashes are concatenated to produce the final hash value. This modularity enables sub-hash functions to be added or removed, e.g., if an exploit for a sub-hash function is discovered. Given the hash values of two byte sequences, saHash returns a lower bound on the number of Levenshtein operations between the two byte sequences as their similarity score. The robustness of saHash is verified by comparing it with other approximate matching approaches such as sdhash.

Keywords: Fuzzy hashing, similarity digest, Levenshtein distance

1.   Introduction

A crucial task during the forensic evidence acquisition process is to distinguish relevant information from non-relevant information – this is often equivalent to searching for a needle in a haystack. In order to identify known files, a forensic examiner typically hashes all the files using cryptographic hash functions such as MD5 [16] and SHA-1 [14] and compares the hash values (fingerprints) against hash databases such

G. Peterson and S. Shenoi (Eds.): Advances in Digital Forensics X, IFIP AICT 433, pp. 133–147, 2014.
© IFIP International Federation for Information Processing 2014

as the National Software Reference Library (NSRL) [13]. This enables the examiner to automatically filter out irrelevant files (e.g., operating system files) and focus on files of interest (e.g., illegal images or company secrets).

While this procedure is well-established and straightforward, it has one main drawback. Regardless of the number of bits that are different between two files, the hash outputs behave in a pseudorandom manner. An active adversary can leverage this property of cryptographic hash functions to change one bit within each file to circumvent the automated filtering process. Consequently, it is necessary to perform approximate matching to identify files that are slightly manipulated or files that are similar (e.g., different versions of a given file).

In general, there are two levels of file similarity: (i) byte-level similarity that focuses on structure; and (ii) semantic-level similarity that focuses on meaning. Working at the byte-level is faster and is independent of the file type. However, it is easy to hide similarity, e.g., by changing the file type from JPG to PNG or the file encoding from ASCII to Base64.

Several approaches have been proposed to measure byte-level similarity: `ssdeep` [11], `sdhash` [18], `bbhash` [5], `mrsh-v2` [6] and `mvhash-B` [2]. These approaches typically pre-process an input file by dividing it into pieces, take unique features and then employ cryptographic hash functions to create the file fingerprint. However, it is possible to change just one bit within each piece or feature and corrupt the fingerprint.

This paper presents a stand-alone similarity hashing approach called `saHash` (statistical analysis hashing), which is not based on cryptographic hash functions. It employs four sub-hash functions, each of which creates its own sub-hash value. The four sub-hash values are concatenated to create the final hash value. `saHash` enables the detection of "small" changes between files – up to several hundred Levenshtein operations.

The `saHash` approach offers three advantages. First, it is almost as fast as SHA-1 and is faster than existing byte-level similarity approaches. Second, it creates nearly fixed-size hash values with a length of 769 bytes (1,216 bytes for 1 GiB files). Although using a fixed hash length has some disadvantages, the approach allows for faster comparisons and better ordering in a database. Third, similarity is defined in terms of the well-known Levenshtein distance. In contrast, all the approaches listed above yield similarity values between 0 and 100; these values express levels of confidence about similarity instead of true levels of similarity.

2.   Background

This paper uses the term "approximate matching" as a synonym for similarity hashing and fuzzy hashing. Such an approach uses an "approximate matching function" to create hash values or fingerprints of files and a "comparison function" to output a similarity score for two file fingerprints.

In general, file similarity can be expressed in terms of byte-level similarity (structure) or semantic similarity (meaning). In what follows, we treat each input as a byte sequence and, therefore, only consider the byte-level similarity of files.

Several approaches are used to measure the similarity or dissimilarity of strings. We employ an approximate matching function based on the Levenshtein distance, one of the most popular string metrics. Given two byte sequences x and y, the Levenshtein distance is the smallest number of deletions, insertions and reversals (also called substitutions) that transform x into y [12].

The measurement of similarity has a long history. One of the early metrics is the Jaccard index [10], which was published in 1901. However, since the approach is very time consuming, Rabin [15] suggested the use of random polynomials to create flexible and robust fingerprints for binary data.

Over the years, several approaches have been proposed for approximate matching at the byte level. In 2002, Harbour [9] developed `dcfldd` that extended the well-known disk dump tool `dd` with the goal of ensuring integrity at the block level during forensic imaging. Instead of creating a single hash value over the entire file, the file is divided into fixed-size blocks and a hash value is generated for each block. Thus, this approach is also called "block-based hashing." Fixed-size blocks are well suited to flipping bits because only the hash value of the corresponding block changes. However, any insertion or deletion of a byte at the beginning causes all the block hashes to be different. Therefore, this approach has low alignment robustness [22], i.e., resistance to the addition or deletion of bytes.

Kornblum [11] introduced the notion of context-triggered piecewise hashing, which is based on a spam detection algorithm proposed by Tridgell [22]. The approach is similar to block-based hashing, except that instead of dividing an input into fixed-size blocks, a pseudorandom function based on a current context of seven bytes is used to split the input. Several enhancements have been proposed to Kornblum's approach, including modifications of the `ssdeep` implementation to enhance efficiency [8, 21], and security and efficiency [3]. Baier and Breitinger [4] and Breitinger [1] have demonstrated attacks against context-triggered piecewise hashing with respect to blacklisting and whitelisting, along with some improvements to the pseudorandom function.

Roussev [17, 18] has proposed a novel **sdhash** method for approximate matching. Instead of dividing an input, the method selects multiple characteristic (invariant) features from the data object and compares them with features selected from other objects (the unique 64-byte features are selected based on their entropy). Two files are deemed to be similar if they have the same features (byte sequences). Experiments demonstrate that **sdhash** performs significantly better than **ssdeep** in terms of recall, precision, robustness and scalability [19]. Roussev [20] has also developed **sdhash** 2.0, a parallelized version of **sdhash**.

3.   Approximate Matching Algorithm

This section presents the **saHash** algorithm for approximate matching. The algorithm estimates byte-level similarity based on the Levenshtein distance.

The **saHash** algorithm uses k independent sub-hash functions, also called "statistical approaches." Each sub-hash function produces its own hash value; the final fingerprint is created by concatenating the k sub-hash values. A fingerprint is compared by splitting it into its k component sub-hash values and k comparison functions are used to estimate the Levenshtein distance and produce the similarity score.

saHash is designed to detect near duplicates; the term "near" means that the two byte sequences being compared are essentially the same, but vary by a few hundred Levenshtein operations. In this case, **saHash** provides a lower bound for the Levenshtein distance between the two byte sequences as their similarity score.

The selection of the k sub-hash functions was a relatively simple procedure. We started by using trivial sub-hash functions such as the byte sequence length and byte frequency. We stopped adding new sub-hash functions when we could not find an attack that would defeat the combination of sub-hash functions. The term "attack" is expressed as follows. Let bs and bs' be two byte sequences. Furthermore, let $LD(bs, bs')$ be the Levenshtein distance of bs and bs' and $saH(bs, bs')$ be the Levenshtein assumption of **saHash**. An attack is valid if it is possible to find bs and bs' such that $LD(bs, bs') \leq saH(bs, bs')$.

We also checked if all the sub-hash functions were necessary because one sub-hash function could subsume another sub-hash function. Note that the modular design of **saHash** allows a new sub-hash function and comparison function to be incorporated if an attack is discovered on an existing sub-hash function. Interested readers are referred to [23] for additional details.

saHash currently employs $k = 4$ sub-hash functions. The implementation (available at www.dasec.h-da.de/staff/breitinger-frank) was tested using Microsoft Visual Studio C++ and GCC on 32-bit systems. Thus, there might be problems running it in the 64-bit mode.

3.1 Sub-Hash Functions

This section describes the four sub-hash functions (i.e., statistical approaches) used by saHash.

Let bs denote a byte sequence (i.e., file) of length l comprising the bytes $b_0, b_1, \ldots b_{l-1}$. A modulus m defined by:

$$m = 2^{\max\left(8, \left\lceil \frac{\log_2 l}{2} \right\rceil\right)} \tag{1}$$

may be used to reduce sub-hash values. The value of m depends on the exponent $\max\left(8, \left\lceil \frac{\log_2 l}{2} \right\rceil\right)$, which results in a minimum modulus of $m = 256$. The modulus ensures uniformity in the use of the range of values. For instance, Breitinger and Baier [3] have observed that the average file size in a Windows XP installation is 250 KB $\approx 250 \cdot 10^3$ bytes. Assuming a uniform distribution of bytes, every byte will appear approximately 10^3 times. The modulo computation counters overflow and the probability distribution for all the modulo counters approach a uniform distribution. As a consequence, the lower bound ensures an adequate magnitude of m. Large files, which require more information to be stored due to more Levenshtein operations, have higher values of m.

The following sub-hash functions h_k $(0 \leq k \leq 3)$ are used:

- **Sub-Hash Function (h_0):** This function returns the byte sequence length equal to l as an unsigned integer. The bit size of the integer depends on the compilation mode and is either 32 bits or 64 bits. h_0 is an order criteria and is used to drop unnecessary comparisons: if the lengths of two byte sequences deviate widely (based on a threshold), the comparison is canceled.

  Trivial Attack: A byte sequence bs' with the same length l has the same hash value $h_0(bs')$.

- **Sub-Hash Function (h_1):** This function returns the byte frequency $freq$, a histogram showing the bytes 0x00 to 0xff (i.e., 0 to 255). For example, to obtain the byte frequency of 0xaa, the occurrences of 0xaa in bs are counted. The result of $h_1(bs)$ is an array containing the frequencies of all 256 bytes ($freq_0$ to $freq_{255}$) modulo m. In order to reduce the fingerprint size, only the values from $freq_0$ to $freq_{254}$ are stored. This is because $freq_{255}$ can be predicted using the equation:

$$freq_{255}(bs) = (h_0(bs) - \sum_{i=0}^{254} freq_i(bs)) \mod m.$$

Note that the byte length $|h_1(bs)|$ is equal to $\frac{255 \cdot \log_2 m}{8}$.

Trivial Attack: A byte sequence bs' of length l containing the same bytes in any order defeats the combination of h_0 and h_1.

- **Sub-Hash Function (h_2):** This function returns the transition frequency $tfreq$. First, a left circular bit shift by four is performed; following this, the computations proceed as for h_1. In other words, the shift corresponds to one specific transition within bs where the transition is the four lowest bits of b_x and the four highest bits of b_{x+1}.

As in the case of sub-hash function h_1, only $tfreq_0$ to $tfreq_{254}$ modulo m are stored and, therefore, $|h_1(bs)| = |h_2(bs)|$.

Trivial Attack: A bs' of length l containing the same bytes in any order where blocks with the same transition are switched defeats the combination of h_0, h_1 and h_2.

- **Sub-Hash Function (h_3):** This function returns the unevenness array $uneva$ that captures relevant statistical features. In addition to the frequency of occurrence, the frequency of repeated occurrences is considered. Also, the unevenness of a byte b within bs is used as a measure of how evenly the occurrences of b in bs are spread.

The result is an ordered array of 256 bytes starting with the less "uneven" bytes. Because the last uneven byte is predictable (the byte is not found in $uneva$), the byte length $|h_3(bs)| = 255$.

Figure 1 shows the algorithm for computing the unevenness of all 256 bytes in a byte sequence bs. Three **for** loops are involved in the algorithm. The first loop calculates the average distance between the same b. The second loop computes the deviations for each b, which is equal to the square of deviations between each

```
01:array uneva[256] = means[256] = {0, 0, ...}

02: for i = 0 to 255  {Create mean values}
03:    means[i] = [length(bs) + 1]/[freq(bs, i) + 1]
04: end for

05: array lastOcc[256]={-1,-1,...}
06: for i = 0 to length(bs) - 1   {Create deviations for each byte}
07:    bytes= bs[i]
08:    dev=means[byte] - (i-lastOcc[byte])
09:    uneva[byte] += dev*dev
10:    lastOcc[byte] = i
11: end for

12: for i = 0 to 255   {Deviation from last occurrence until end}
13:    dev = means[i] - (length(bs) - lastOcc[i])
14:    uneva[i] += dev*dev
15:    uneva[i] *= (freq(bs,i) + 1)
16: end for
```

Figure 1. Computation of the *uneva* array.

occurrence of a b. The third loop computes the deviation from the last occurrence until end of a b.

The final saHash value $H(bs)$ is the concatenation of the four sub-hashes:

$$H(bs) = h_1(bs) \parallel h_2(bs) \parallel h_3(bs) \parallel h_4(bs).$$

3.2   Distances between Sub-Hashes

Let bs_1 and bs_2 be two byte sequences and let d_k be a distance function that returns a measure of the distance between the sub-hash values $h_k(bs_1)$ and $h_k(bs_2)$. Note that $d_k(h_k(bs_1), h_k(bs_2))$ measures the "inverse similarity" of two sub-hash values, i.e., the more distant the sub-hash values the less similar they are.

- **Sub-Hash Function (h_0):** An obvious distance function for d_0, which represents the byte sequence length is given by:

$$d_0 = |h_0(bs_1) - h_0(bs_2)|.$$

- **Sub-Hash Function (h_1):** In order to define the measure for h_1 (an array containing the frequencies of all the bytes), the auxiliary function $sub_i(h_1(bs_1), h_1(bs_2))$ is used to subtract the ith element in $h_1(bs_1)$ from the ith element in $h_1(bs_2)$. The distance function

d_1 is given by:

$$tmp = \sum_{i=0}^{255} |sub_i(h_1(bs_1), h_1(bs_2))|$$

$$d_1 = \left\lceil \frac{tmp - d_0}{2} \right\rceil + d_0.$$

First, the absolute values for all position-differences for all the frequencies are added. This yields the number of byte frequencies that are different. In general, there are two possibilities. If $|bs_1| = |bs_2|$, then $\left\lceil \frac{tmp-d_0}{2} \right\rceil$ substitutions are needed. If $|bs_1| \neq |bs_2|$, then d_0 must be added.

For example, AAAAA and AABA yield $d_0 = 1$ and $tmp = 2$. Thus, $d_1 = \lceil (2 - 1)/2 \rceil + 1 = 2$. The difference in length is considered by $d_0 = 1$ while all other differences can be corrected due to a substitution (B into A).

- **Sub-Hash Function (h_2):** Sub-hash function h_2 is similar to h_1, which is why the same auxiliary function sub is used. One difference is the division by four instead of two, which is due to the initial left circular bit shifting operation: one deletion or insertion can influence up to four positions in the $tfreq$ array. The distance function d_2 is given by:

$$tmp = \sum_{i=0}^{255} |sub_i(h_2(bs_1), h_2(bs_2))|$$

$$d_2 = \left\lceil \frac{tmp - d_0}{4} \right\rceil + d_0.$$

- **Sub-Hash Function (h_3):** To compute the similarity of two uneva arrays, an auxiliary function $pos_b(h_3(bs))$ is used to return the position of byte b in an array. The maximum distance is $256 \cdot 128$, which occurs if the array is shifted by 128. The distance function d_3 is given by:

$$tmp = \sum_{b=0}^{255} |pos_b(h_3(bs_1)) - pos_b(h_3(bs_2))|$$

$$d_3 = \left(1 - \frac{tmp}{256 \cdot 128}\right) \cdot 100$$

3.3 Final Similarity Decision

We decided to have a binary decision and, therefore, saHash outputs whether or not the two input two byte sequences are similar. To produce a result, saHash requires two thresholds, t_{LB} and t_{CS}. The first threshold is for the lower bound on the number of Levenshtein operations LB while the second is for a certainty score C that expresses the quality. The lower bound on the number of Levenshtein operations LB is assumed to be $\max(d_0, d_1, d_2)$ and CS is simply set to d_3. If $LB \leq t_{LB}$ and $CS \geq t_{CS}$, then the two byte sequences are considered to be similar.

Default threshold settings of $t_{LB} = 282$ and $t_{CS} = 97$ are recommended. These default values can be adjusted by users, but this may increase the probability of obtaining false positives.

A set of 12,935 files was used to obtain the default thresholds t_{LB} and t_{CS}. First, an all-versus-all-others comparison was performed and the corresponding LB values were entered into a matrix. Next, all file pairs were compared by hand starting at the lowest LB in the matrix and terminating at the first false positive, which had an LB value of 283. Thus, the threshold t_{LB} was set to 282. The threshold t_{CS} was set to 97 because the CS values for all the true positives exceeded 97.

The use of a large test corpus provides confidence that $t_{LB} = 282$ is a realistic threshold to avoid false positives. Note, however, that this represents a lower bound, so the actual number of Levenshtein operations would be higher; this is discussed later in the section on correctness.

3.4 Adjusting Sub-Hashes to the Modulus

This section discusses the special case when different moduli exist. Let bs_1 and bs_2 be two inputs that yield the moduli m and m' where $m < m'$ according to Equation (1). Because saHash is designed to identify small changes between two inputs, the moduli will at most differ by a factor of 2 and, therefore, $m' = 2m$.

In order to compute the distances d_1 and d_2, it is necessary to adjust $h_1(bs_2)$ and $h_2(bs_2)$. Because $(x \bmod 2m) \bmod m = x \bmod m$, the array is searched for $h_1(bs_2)$ and $h_2(bs_2)$, and m is used to recompute the frequency values; the sub-hash values can then be compared.

4. Evaluation

This section evaluates the correctness and performance of saHash with respect to efficiency (ease of computation and compression). Furthermore, saHash is compared with the ssdeep and sdhash approaches to assess its benefits and drawbacks.

The experimental environment comprised a Dell laptop running Windows 7 (64 bit) with 4 GB RAM and Intel Core 2 Duo 2×2 GHz. All the tests used a file corpus containing 12,935 files (2,631 DOC, 67 GIF, 362 JPG, 1,729 PDF and 8,146 TXT files) that were collected using a Python script via Google. The random byte sequences discussed in the evaluation were generated using the function `int rand()` with seed `srand(time(NULL))`.

4.1   Impact of a Changing Modulus

According to Equation (1), the modulus is fixed for all byte sequences with less than 2^{16} bytes. For larger byte sequences, the factor increases by two as the input size increases by a factor of four. We assume that a larger modulus is able to determine more modifications and, thus, has a better detection rate.

Because small files do not provide enough information and do not exhaust the counters, the test only used files from the corpus that were larger than 1 MB, a total of 749 files. To analyze the consequences of increasing the modulus, we manually changed the modulus to 7, 8, 9 and 10 bits. Based on the discussion above regarding the final similarity decision, we searched for the smallest LB that yielded a false positive and obtained the values $2,527$, $4,304$, $7,207$ and $13,503$, respectively. Hence, the higher the modulus, the more robust is `saHash`.

During the transition from 9 to 10 bits, it was possible to identify more true positives, but this was negatively impacted when a smaller modulus was used. Thus, it makes sense to use a larger modulus.

4.2   Correctness

This section discusses a randomly-driven test case where the evaluation mainly focused on false positives. The term "randomly" in this instance means that random changes were made all over the file.

First, we analyzed the impact of random changes to a byte sequence bs of length 250 KB, the average file size for the Windows XP operating system [3]. A random change involved a typical deletion, insertion or substitution operation, each with a probability of $\frac{1}{3}$ and all bytes in bs having the same probability to be changed.

We generated a test corpus T_{700} of 700 files using the `rand()` function; each file was 250 KB in size. For each n in the range $1 \leq n \leq 700$ and $bs \in T_{700}$, n random changes were applied to produce the file bs'. Next, all pairs (bs, bs') were used as inputs to `saHash` to obtain similarity decisions. As n increases, the dissimilarity of the files is expected to increase.

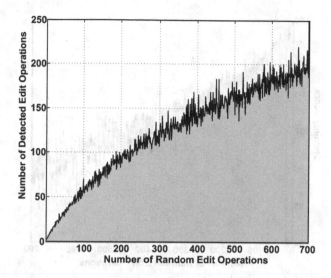

Figure 2. Edit operations vs. detected edit operations.

The saHash algorithm outputs two values, LB and CS. Figure 2 shows the results for up to $n = 700$ edit operations (x-axis) and the number of edit operations detected by saHash (y-axis). Even $n = 700$ yields a number of operations lower than 282 whereas only true positives were obtained previously. Thus, although the default value for LB is 282, saHash can detect many more modifications without any false positives. Note that the output is the lower bound on the number of Levenshtein operations.

As described above, the default threshold for CS was set to 97. Figure 3 shows the certainty score in relation to the number of random edit operations. Using the threshold of 97, saHash was able to reliably detect similarity for $n < 600$.

4.3 Cross Comparison

This section discusses the performance and correctness of saHash.

Compression. The overall hash value length $|H(bs)|$ for a byte sequence bs of length l is the sum of the lengths of the k sub-hashes. Thus, the length (in bits) is given by:

$$
\left.
\begin{aligned}
|h_0(bs)| &= 4 \text{ bytes (32 bits)} \\
|h_1(bs)| &= \frac{255 \cdot \max\left(8, \left\lceil \frac{\log_2 l}{2} \right\rceil\right)}{8} \text{ bytes} \\
|h_2(bs)| &= \frac{255 \cdot \max\left(8, \left\lceil \frac{\log_2 l}{2} \right\rceil\right)}{8} \text{ bytes} \\
|h_3(bs)| &= 255 \text{ bytes}
\end{aligned}
\right\}
\left\lceil 4 + \frac{2 \cdot 255 \cdot \max\left(8, \left\lceil \frac{\log_2 l}{2} \right\rceil\right)}{8} + 255 \right\rceil
$$

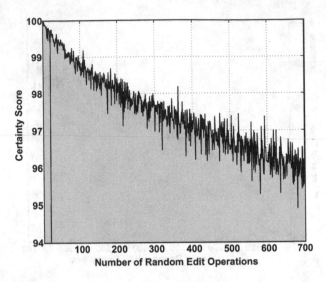

Figure 3.   Ratio of the certainty score to the number of edit operations.

For instance, the fingerprint of a 1 MiB file $(=2^{20})$ is 897 bytes and, thus, has a compression ratio of 0.08554%.

The compression property is best satisfied by `ssdeep`, which generates hash values up to a maximum of 104 Base64 characters regardless of the input length.

Roussev [18] states that `sdhash` creates hash values whose length corresponds to about 2.6% of the input. Our experiments with several thousand files reveal that `sdhash 2.3` creates fingerprints of length approximately 2.5%. Therefore, `saHash` has better compression for all files larger than approximately $\frac{769 \cdot 100}{3.3} \approx 23{,}303$ bytes. Recall that the average file size of a Windows XP installation is 250 KB [3].

Ease of Computation.   A highly desirable property of an approximate matching algorithm is ease of computation, which is why we gave a high priority to runtime efficiency during the design of `saHash`. In fact, the time complexity to compute $H(bs)$ for a byte sequence bs is $O(|bs|)$.

We generated a 100 MiB file from `/dev/urandom/` to compare the runtime performance of `saHash` with that of other algorithms. The C++ `clock()` function was used in the experiments; this function has the benefit that the times of parallel processes do not influence the timing. The results in Table 1 show that `saHash` is almost as fast as SHA-1 and faster than `ssdeep 2.9` and `sdhash 3.2`.

Table 1. Ease of computation of SHA-1 and approximate matching schemes.

	SHA-1	saHash	ssdeep 2.9	sdhash 3.2
Runtime	1.23 s	1.76 s	2.28 s	4.48 s

Correctness. It is well known that `ssdeep` is vulnerable to random changes made all over a file. For instance, if $n > 70$, the match score is always zero. In addition, Breitinger and Baier [4] have shown that it is possible to obtain an absolute non-match by editing ten bytes and to obtain a false positive with a similarity score of 100. Additionally, Roussev [19] notes that `ssdeep` yields no false positives for a similarity score greater than 90%. However, our random test demonstrates that, for $n = 5$, the similarity score could be reduced to less than 90%.

Two groups of researchers [7, 19] have shown that `sdhash` is robust. In fact, `sdhash` allows up to 1.1% random changes while still detecting similarity. However, because the score is not a percentage value, it is difficult to assess the actual similarity between two inputs.

In summary, `saHash` is very robust when small changes have been made all over a file. However, it has one main drawback – it only can compute the similarity of inputs that have similar sizes. Therefore, we recommend that `sdhash` be used to detect embedded objects and fragments.

5.   Conclusions

The `saHash` algorithm is a new stand-alone approach for approximate matching that is based on the Levenshtein metric. The principal advantages of `saHash` are its modular design that enables it to be enhanced to cope with new attacks and its robustness to changes made all over a file. The final hash value of `saHash` does not exceed 1,216 bytes for files smaller than 1 GiB and, therefore, has a nearly fixed size. Also, `saHash` has good runtime efficiency and is nearly as fast as SHA-1 and is significantly faster than other approximate matching approaches.

Topics for future research include designing an approach that outputs the upper limit of Levenshtein operations and conducting a detailed security analysis of `saHash`. Additionally, because `saHash` can improve existing algorithms by replacing their underlying cryptographic hash functions, it would be interesting to attempt to combine `saHash` and `sdhash`, and to analyze the performance of the new version of `sdhash`.

Acknowledgement

This research was partially supported by the European Union under the Integrated Project FIDELITY (Grant No. 284862) and by the Center for Advanced Security Research Darmstadt (CASED).

References

[1] F. Breitinger, Security Aspects of Fuzzy Hashing, M.Sc. Thesis, Department of Computer Science, Darmstadt University of Applied Sciences, Darmstadt, Germany, 2011.

[2] F. Breitinger, K. Astebol, H. Baier and C. Busch, mvhash-b – A new approach for similarity preserving hashing, *Proceedings of the Seventh International Conference on IT Security Incident Management and IT Forensics*, pp. 33–44, 2013.

[3] F. Breitinger and H. Baier, Performance issues about context-triggered piecewise hashing, *Proceedings of the Third International ICST Conference on Digital Forensics and Cyber Crime*, pp. 141–155, 2011.

[4] F. Breitinger and H. Baier, Security aspects of piecewise hashing in computer forensics, *Proceedings of the Sixth International Conference on IT Security Incident Management and IT Forensics*, pp. 21–36, 2011.

[5] F. Breitinger and H. Baier, A fuzzy hashing approach based on random sequences and Hamming distance, *Proceedings of the Conference on Digital Forensics, Security and Law*, 2012.

[6] F. Breitinger and H. Baier, Similarity preserving hashing: Eligible properties and a new algorithm mrsh-v2, *Proceedings of the Fourth International ICST Conference on Digital Forensics and Cyber Crime*, 2012.

[7] F. Breitinger, G. Stivaktakis and H. Baier, FRASH: A framework to test algorithms for similarity hashing, *Digital Investigation*, vol. 10(S), pp. S50–S58, 2013.

[8] L. Chen and G. Wang, An efficient piecewise hashing method for computer forensics, *Proceedings of the First International Workshop on Knowledge Discovery and Data Mining*, pp. 635–638, 2008.

[9] N. Harbour, dcfldd (dcfldd.sourceforge.net), 2006.

[10] P. Jaccard, Distribution de la flore alpine dans le bassin des drouces et dans quelques regions voisines, *Bulletin de la Société Vaudoise des Sciences Naturelles*, vol. 37(140), pp. 241–272, 1901.

[11] J. Kornblum, Identifying almost identical files using context triggered piecewise hashing, *Digital Investigation*, vol. 3(S), pp. S91–S97, 2006.

[12] V. Levenshtein, Binary codes capable of correcting deletions, insertions and reversals, *Soviet Physics Doklady*, vol. 10(8), pp. 707–710, 1966.

[13] National Institute of Standards and Technology, National Software Reference Library, Gaithersburg, Maryland (`www.nsrl.nist.gov`).

[14] National Institute of Standards and Technology, Secure Hash Standard (SHS), FIPS Publication 180-4, Gaithersburg, Maryland, 2012.

[15] M. Rabin, Fingerprinting by Random Polynomials, Technical Report TR-15-81, Center for Research in Computing Technology, Harvard University, Cambridge, Massachusetts, 1981.

[16] R. Rivest, The MD5 Message-Digest Algorithm, RFC 1321, 1992.

[17] V. Roussev, Building a better similarity trap with statistically improbable features, *Proceedings of the Forty-Second Hawaii International Conference on System Sciences*, 2009.

[18] V. Roussev, Data fingerprinting with similarity digests, in *Advances in Digital Forensics VI*, K. Chow and S. Shenoi (Eds.), Springer, Heidelberg, Germany, pp. 207–226, 2010.

[19] V. Roussev, An evaluation of forensic similarity hashes, *Digital Investigation*, vol. 8(S), pp. S34–S41, 2011.

[20] V. Roussev, Managing terabyte-scale investigations with similarity digests, in *Advances in Digital Forensics VIII*, G. Peterson and S. Shenoi (Eds.), Springer, Heidelberg, Germany, pp. 19–34, 2012.

[21] K. Seo, K. Lim, J. Choi, K. Chang and S. Lee, Detecting similar files based on hash and statistical analysis for digital forensic investigations, *Proceedings of the Second International Conference on Computer Science and its Applications*, 2009.

[22] A. Tridgell, spamsum (`mirror.linux.org.au/linux.conf.au/2004/papers/junkcode/spamsum/README`), 2002.

[23] G. Ziroff, Approaches to Similarity-Preserving Hashing, B.Sc. Thesis, Department of Computer Science, Darmstadt University of Applied Sciences, Darmstadt, Germany, 2012.

Chapter 11

USING APPROXIMATE MATCHING
TO REDUCE THE VOLUME
OF DIGITAL DATA

Frank Breitinger, Christian Winter, York Yannikos, Tobias Fink,
and Michael Seefried

Abstract   Digital forensic investigators frequently have to search for relevant files
in massive digital corpora – a task often compared to finding a needle
in a haystack. To address this challenge, investigators typically apply
cryptographic hash functions to identify known files. However, cryptographic hashing only allows the detection of files that exactly match
the known file hash values or fingerprints. This paper demonstrates the
benefits of using approximate matching to locate relevant files. The
experiments described in this paper used three test images of Windows
XP, Windows 7 and Ubuntu 12.04 systems to evaluate fingerprint-based
comparisons. The results reveal that approximate matching can improve
file identification – in one case, increasing the identification rate from
1.82% to 23.76%.

Keywords: File identification, approximate matching, ssdeep

1.   Introduction

Traditional physical media such as books, photos, letters and long-
playing records (LPs) have been replaced by digital media in the form of
e-books, digital photos, email and MP3 files. The result is that forensic
investigators are faced with overwhelming amounts of digital data even in
routine cases. Investigators need automated processes that can quickly
classify and filter terabytes of data, yielding only the relevant files that
can then be inspected manually.

A common approach is to employ cryptographic hash functions to
automatically classify files: an investigator computes the hash values of
all the files residing on digital media and compares these fingerprints

G. Peterson and S. Shenoi (Eds.): Advances in Digital Forensics X, IFIP AICT 433, pp. 149–163, 2014.
© IFIP International Federation for Information Processing 2014

against file hash values stored in a reference database. A matching hash confirms that the referenced file is present in the storage media. Depending on the hash values stored in the reference database, the files can be classified as relevant (blacklisting) and non-relevant (whitelisting). Files not found in the database are not classified.

White [18] and Baier and Dichtelmuller [1] have analyzed the impact of using cryptographic hash functions for file classification in digital forensic investigations. White obtained identification rates as high as 70%. However, Baier and Dichtelmuller measured identification rates between 15% and 52%; these lower identification rates were due to small changes in files that typically occur during computer use.

As a consequence, the digital forensic research community has proposed the use of approximate matching that maps similar files to similar hash values. This paper shows that approximate matching can increase the file identification rate. In one case, the identification rate increased from 1.82% with traditional cryptographic hash value comparisons to 23.76% with approximate matching.

The principal contribution of this paper is the quantitative evaluation of identification rates for approximate matching on complete disk images. While reference results are available for cryptographic hashing [1, 18], approximate matching has not been evaluated on such a large scale. Also, the paper analyzes the error rates for approximate matching and establishes similarity score thresholds for use in real-world digital forensic investigations.

2.   Background

Two strategies exist for filtering known content: (i) blacklisting, which compares a file to a reference database containing the fingerprints of illegal and suspicious files (e.g., child pornography) that should be retained for further analysis; and (ii) whitelisting, which compares a file to a reference database containing fingerprints of innocuous files (e.g., operating system files) that should be eliminated from consideration.

The most prominent reference database is the National Software Reference Library (NSRL) [11] maintained by the U.S. National Institute of Standards and Technology (NIST). NIST regularly publishes reference data sets containing the cryptographic hashes of software products. The current reference data set, RDS 2.42 of September 2013, covers approximately 115 million files.

Known file filtering predominantly utilizes cryptographic hash functions. However, the security properties of cryptographic hash functions imply that only identical files can be matched using these hash functions – a difference in just one bit produces a completely different hash value. Although this property is desired for cryptographic purposes, it complicates forensic investigations. For example, an investigator is often interested in locating similar files, file fragments and embedded objects. Therefore, it is helpful to have algorithms that provide approximate matches to correlate related versions of data objects.

Approximate matching techniques find matches based on bytewise similarity or semantic similarity. Bytewise matching operates at the byte level: two inputs are similar if they have similar byte structures. Semantic matching, also called perceptual hashing or robust hashing, attempts to understand the input format and is, therefore, bound to specific media types, images or movies. While a semantic hashing solution is highly domain specific, bytewise approximate matching has the advantage of generality.

This paper investigates bytewise approximate matching, in particular, using the ssdeep tool [9, 10]. This was motivated by the prominence of ssdeep, the fact that NIST has published a reference set of ssdeep hashes, and the ability to process large file volumes in reasonable time using the F2S2 tool [19].

It is important to note that the concept of approximate matching should not be confused with locality sensitive hashing. Approximate matching reduces large files to small digests such that similar files are mapped to similar digests. On the other hand, locality sensitive hashing is an indexing strategy, which places items into hash buckets such that similar items have a high probability of being in the same bucket. Hence, locality sensitive hashing could speed up approximate matching depending on the matching approach and the locality sensitive hashing method that are employed.

2.1   ssdeep

Context triggered piecewise hashing was proposed by Kornblum [9, 10] and implemented in the ssdeep tool. It originates from the spam detection algorithm of Tridgell [17] implemented in spamsum.

The ssdeep tool divides a byte sequence (file) into chunks and hashes each chunk separately using the Fowler-Noll-Vo (FNV) algorithm [12]. Context triggered piecewise hashing then encodes the six least significant bits of each FNV hash as a Base64 character. All the characters are concatenated to create the file fingerprint.

The trigger points for splitting a file into chunks are determined by a rolling hash function. This function, which is a variation of the Adler-32 algorithm [8], is computed over a seven-byte sliding window to generate a sequence of pseudorandom numbers. A number r in the sequence triggers a chunk boundary if $r \equiv -1 \pmod{b}$. The modulus b, called the block size, correlates with the file size.

Kornblum suggests dividing a file into approximately $S = 64$ chunks and using the same modulus b for similar-sized files. The modulus b is a saltus function:

$$b = b_{\min} \cdot 2^{\lfloor \log_2(N/S/b_{\min}) \rfloor} \tag{1}$$

where $b_{min} = 3$ and N is the input length in bytes. Since two fingerprints can only be compared if they were generated using blocks of the same size, ssdeep calculates two fingerprints for each file using the block sizes b and $2b$ and stores both fingerprints in one ssdeep hash.

The similarity of two fingerprints is calculated in two steps. First, the fingerprints are treated as text strings and compared with each other using an edit distance function. An edit distance of zero indicates matching strings and the distance increases with the dissimilarity of strings. In the second step, the computed distance of the two fingerprints is converted into a similarity score in the range 0 to 100, where a higher score indicates greater similarity.

The ssdeep similarity measure defines a score boundary for small fingerprints. Hence, small files that are identical often do not receive a score of 100, although this is expected. The score boundary is enforced in lines 600 through 604 of fuzzy.c (ssdeep version 2.10). Tridgell's comment in the source code says that this is done so as not to "exaggerate the match size" for a small block size. However, we eliminated this constraint in our research because the score boundary introduces uncertainty when interpreting the match results.

While ssdeep is a pioneer in the domain of approximate matching, several improvements to ssdeep hashing have been proposed in the literature [7, 16].

2.2   F2S2

The task of comparing files to a reference list can be very time consuming. In particular, the comparison of similarity digests cannot be performed as efficiently as the exact matching of cryptographic hashes. Approximate matching tools – including ssdeep – typically compare every hash computed for the investigation target to every hash in the reference list.

Unlike exact matching, approximate matching cannot be accelerated using classical indexing strategies developed for relational databases. However, it is possible to find suitable indexing strategies. The F2S2 tool [19] implements one such solution that involves n-gram indexing.

F2S2 has been applied to `ssdeep` hashes and has achieved a speedup of 2,000 times in realistic test cases.

3. Experimental Methodology

The experiments were performed on an Ubuntu 12.04 host using `ssdeep` 2.7-1. The drive images came from computers running the Windows and Linux operating systems. Since Windows is the most commonly used operating system, the experiments analyzed two Windows versions: Windows XP (Professional, 32 bit) and Windows 7 (Professional, 32 bit). The experiments also analyzed the Linux Ubuntu operating system (version 12.4, 32 bit).

3.1 Overview

The experiments focused on determining the appropriateness of SHA-1 and `ssdeep` for known file identification with approximate matching. The detection rates with respect to true positives and false positives for cryptographic hashing (SHA-1) and approximate matching (`ssdeep`) were examined. Note that the assessment only considered positive errors.

Some large files, such as `hyberfil.sys` (Windows XP), device files and named pipes (Ubuntu), did not generate `ssdeep` hashes. Since the algorithm was considered to be a blackbox, these problems were treated as bugs and were not investigated further.

Hash values could not be generated for a very small number of files. When a file hash value could not be generated, the file was treated as if it did not exist. In the worst case (Ubuntu$_U$), only 0.12% of the files had to be dropped.

3.2 System Description and Snapshots

The Windows XP samples came from two snapshots of an extensively-used system, which were 14 and 27 months old, respectively, when the snapshots were taken (the age of a system is defined as the time elapsed between system installation and snapshot generation). The Windows XP system was used on a daily basis for office work; it contained software installations, system and software update artifacts, user created files and other software usage traces. The Ubuntu system was about six months old when the snapshot was taken. This snapshot included system updates, and system development and web browsing artifacts. The Windows 7 system was used for half a day; during that time, the latest updates were applied, some files were created and some web pages were visited. The trusted reference snapshots were created from default

Table 1.   Operating system snapshots.

Operating System	File Count	Disk Usage
WinXP$_D$ (Windows XP, Default installation)	8,946	1.9 GB
WinXP$_{U1}$ (Windows XP SP3, 14 months old)	195,186	128.4 GB
WinXP$_{U2}$ (Windows XP SP3, 27 months old)	466,266	109.5 GB
Win7$_D$ (Windows 7, Default installation)	45,470	8.1 GB
Win7$_U$ (Windows 7 SP1, Used installation)	66,312	9.4 GB
Ubuntu$_D$ (v12.04, Default installation)	185,468	3.3 GB
Ubuntu$_U$ (v12.04, Used installation)	411,209	25.2 GB

installations of the operating systems (i.e., without any updates, service packs or additional programs).

Table 1 provides information about the operating system snapshots. Note that WinXP$_{U1}$ used more disk space than WinXP$_{U2}$ because an 82 GB image file was deleted between the times that the two snapshots were taken.

3.3   Reference Databases

The following reference databases were used to determine the identification rates for each operating system image:

- **NIST Database:** This NIST-published database (RDS 2.27 of December 2009) contains more than eight million entries. The hashes are provided in the form of a text file with one SHA-1 hash and one ssdeep hash per line. The SHA-1 hash is used to link each entry to the regular NIST RDS. The experiments used the SHA-1 and ssdeep hashes from the NIST database.

- **Custom Reference Databases:** Because the NIST database above is an outdated subset of the current RDS 2.42 (September 2013) and no newer ssdeep dataset was available, we created our own reference sets based on the default installations of the operating systems. The procedure used to create the reference sets was essentially the same as that used to create the NIST database.

3.4   Quality of Matches

The matches reported by ssdeep correspond to the number of positive collisions. The collisions require truth data in order to be classified as true positives and false positives. Because there were too many files to perform a manual inspection, the true positives were considered to be the files that matched the SHA-1 hashes.

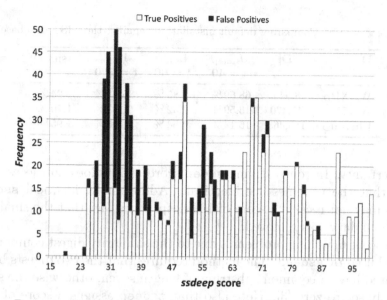

Figure 1. Distribution of `ssdeep` scores according to Roussev [14].

To perform approximate matching, a threshold t was set to yield a match score M such that $M \geq t$ indicates a positive match (i.e., similar files). However, identifying an appropriate threshold t was challenging because a low t value increases the false positive rate while a high t value decreases the true positive rate.

Roussev [14] has studied the ratio between true and false positives based on the comparison of 4,457 files (= 9,930,196 pairs). His results are presented in Figure 1. Accordingly, we set the thresholds to $t = 60$ and $t = 40$. Although the $t = 60$ threshold yielded a few false positives, we rated the false positive rate of the $t = 40$ threshold as acceptable.

4. Experimental Results

This section presents the experimental results. First, the difference between SHA-1 matches and `ssdeep` matches is examined. Next, identification rates are compared for the various images and databases. Following this, the identification rates are presented in correlation with file names and paths. Finally, the relationship between identification rate and file type is clarified.

4.1 Seemingly Identical Files

Minor differences exist between a SHA-1 match and an `ssdeep` score of 100. A SHA-1 match implies that two files are identical with extremely

Table 2.   TC1: Comparing default installations against the NIST database.

D	|D|	I_{ssdeep} $t = 40$	I_{ssdeep} $t = 60$	I_{ssdeep} $t = 100$	$I_{\text{SHA-1}}$
WinXP$_D$	8,946	68.69 %	63.85 %	35.84 %	35.24 %
Win7$_D$	45,470	16.59 %	9.32 %	1.73 %	1.70 %
Ubuntu$_D$	185,468	16.14 %	9.54 %	1.90 %	1.95 %

high certainty. In contrast, an **ssdeep** score of 100 does not necessarily mean that the two files are identical. Additionally, identical **ssdeep** hashes may not receive a score of 100 despite the fact that the small file score boundary was removed.

The score matching problem is due to the similarity digest comparison method used by **ssdeep**. The method requires that the two digests being compared have a common substring of length seven, otherwise the score is simply set to zero [3]. Note also that **ssdeep** assigns a score of zero to two empty files whereas SHA-1 matches the two files.

An **ssdeep** score of 100 can be obtained even when the SHA-1 hashes are different; this is due to fingerprint collisions and the comparison method. Note that each **ssdeep** digest consists of two fingerprints and it is sufficient to have one matching pair to obtain a score of 100. Thus, there are two types of collisions for **ssdeep**. In some cases, the **ssdeep** hashes match completely; in other cases, only one pair of **ssdeep** fingerprints matches. We consider a similarity score 100 for two non-identical files to be a false positive.

4.2   Detection Thresholds

We also analyzed the detection rates based on the thresholds $t = 40$ and $t = 60$. When presenting the results, note that D denotes the analyzed system and $|D|$ denotes the number of files in the system. Also, I_A is the identification rate using algorithm $A \in \{\text{ssdeep}, \text{SHA-1}\}$. For example, $I_{\text{ssdeep}} = 10\%$ means that 10% of the files in system D were found in the database using **ssdeep**. Thus, the higher the value of I, the greater the number of files that are identified automatically.

- **Test Case 1 (TC1):** This test case compared the files in the default operating system installations with the files represented in the NIST database. The results are shown in Table 2. The identification rates for the Windows XP system are significantly higher compared with those for the other operating systems; this because the underlying database was created in December 2009

Table 3. TC2: Comparing used installations against the NIST database.

D	|D|	$\mathbf{I}_{\text{ssdeep}}$ $t = 40$	$\mathbf{I}_{\text{ssdeep}}$ $t = 60$	$\mathbf{I}_{\text{ssdeep}}$ $t = 100$	$\mathbf{I}_{\text{SHA-1}}$
WinXP$_{U1}$	195,186	17.79 %	14.70 %	7.69 %	8.03 %
WinXP$_{U2}$	466,266	23.02 %	17.39 %	7.05 %	7.30 %
Win7$_U$	66,312	17.88 %	10.21 %	1.45 %	1.44 %
Ubuntu$_U$	411,209	23.76 %	17.11 %	1.79 %	1.82 %

when Windows XP was very popular. Still, the trend is obvious, regardless of the operating system, the identification rate is much higher for ssdeep (e.g., nearly ten times better for Win7 with the threshold $t = 40$).

- **Test Case 2 (TC2):** This test case compared the files in the used operating system installations with the files represented in the NIST database. The results in Table 3 are comparable with those obtained in Test Case 1 (Figure 2). Once again, the Windows XP systems have the best identification rates due to the underlying database. However, the identification rates are smaller than in the previous test case because the systems contained large numbers of files. For example, WinXP$_{U2}$ had in excess of 50 times more files than WinXP$_D$. Still, the identification rates are approximately two to ten times higher for ssdeep with threshold $t = 60$ compared with SHA-1.

Table 4. TC3: Comparing used installations against default installations.

D	|D|	$\mathbf{I}_{\text{ssdeep}}$ $t = 40$	$\mathbf{I}_{\text{ssdeep}}$ $t = 60$	$\mathbf{I}_{\text{ssdeep}}$ $t = 100$	$\mathbf{I}_{\text{SHA-1}}$
WinXP$_{U1}$	195,186	5.12 %	4.71 %	4.13 %	4.14 %
WinXP$_{U2}$	466,266	2.27 %	2.01 %	1.72 %	1.74 %
Win7$_U$	66,312	93.85 %	90.19 %	67.41 %	67.72 %
Ubuntu$_U$	411,209	55.67 %	53.38 %	47.74 %	47.83 %

- **Test Case 3 (TC3):** This test case compared the files in the used installations against those in the default installations. The main results are shown in Table 4. The low rates for the Windows XP systems are a consequence of the "small" default installation. Recall that the default installation had only about 9,000 files. How-

Table 5. TC4: Comparing WinXP$_{U2}$ against WinXP$_{U1}$ as the reference database.

D	$|$D$|$	I$_{ssdeep}$ $t = 40$	I$_{ssdeep}$ $t = 60$	I$_{ssdeep}$ $t = 100$	I$_{SHA-1}$
WinXP$_{U2}$	466,266	31.98 %	28.87 %	24.04 %	24.37 %

ever, some files in the default installation are similar or identical to files in the used installation. Examples are the `desktop.ini` files, DLLs and file shortcuts (`.lnk`). Typical locations for such files in the default installation are `WINDOWS/system32/config/systemprofile`, `WINDOWS/pchealth/helpctr/System` and `WINDOWS/system32/dllcache`. Hence, it was possible to identify more files in the used system than were present in the default system.

The high identification rates for the Windows 7 system reflect the fact that the system was not used very much. Also, the updates introduced many files that are similar to the files found in the default system.

- **Test Case 4 (TC4):** This test case compared the files in the two Windows XP snapshots where WinXP$_{U1}$ emulates the database. The main results are shown in Table 5. Despite the difference of 13 months between the two snapshots, identification rates are 24% for SHA-1 and 32% for `ssdeep`, a difference of 8%. The percentage may seem small, but 8% of the 466,266 files in the system corresponds to approximately 37,000 files.

The experiments confirmed that the detection rates for `ssdeep` are higher than for SHA-1 in all four test cases. This is especially relevant for blacklisting (files that are similar to suspicious files could constitute evidence). Also, as shown in the comprehensive study by Roussev [14], the thresholds used in the experiments are reasonable and have acceptable false positive rates.

4.3   File Names and Paths

This section analyzes the reliability of positive matches obtained using the two thresholds. Recall that the number of approximate matches is the total number of `ssdeep` matches minus the number of exact SHA-1 matches. Table 6 shows the results. The first column specifies the comparisons, e.g., WinXP U1 versus WinXP U2. The second and third columns list the numbers of files in the systems ($|D|$) and the numbers of matches with scores greater than or equal to t (`ssdeep` Hits), respec-

Table 6. Identification rates for file paths and names in different images.

D	|D|	ssdeep Hits	Without SHA-1	Path Matches	Name Matches
WinXP($U1$ v. $U2$); t=40	466,266	31.98 %	7.97 %	10.57 %	37.09 %
WinXP($U1$ v. $U2$); t=60	466,266	28.87 %	4.86 %	15.58 %	50.68 %
Win7(B v.U); t=40	66,312	93.85 %	26.44 %	1.51 %	5.79 %
Win7(B v. U); t=60	66,312	90.19 %	22.78 %	1.51 %	5.91 %
Ubuntu(B v. U); t=40	411,209	55.67 %	7.99 %	16.99 %	71.37 %
Ubuntu(B v. U); t=60	411,209	53.38 %	5.71 %	22.91 %	85.89 %

tively. The fourth column shows the benefit of **ssdeep**, i.e., matches that are not identified by SHA-1 (relative to $|D|$) – this is the "critical amount" of files. The last two columns list the file path and name matches relative to the numbers of files excluding the SHA-1 matches.

Consider, for example, the last row of Figure 6, which examines the default Ubuntu installation against the used Ubuntu installation that contains 411,209 files. When $t = 60$, **ssdeep** detects 53.38% as similar files. Reducing this figure by the number of SHA-1 matches yields 5.71% (i.e., 23,480 files). 22.91% of these files have the same path and 85.89% have the same file name. Hence, these files are considered to be true positives. The remaining $100\% - 85.89\% = 14.11\%$ files are either false positives or files that have been moved or renamed. A total of 3,313 files remain and these files need to be analyzed manually.

4.4 File Types

While approximate matching at the syntactic level can be applied to any file, it is not useful for all file types. This depends on the file type and the type of modification – whether small modifications preserve most of the binary content of a file or lead to a completely different binary pattern. For example, text is favorable while compressed data causes problems. The reason is that small text modifications result in small changes to the binary data of a text file, but compression algorithms create very different byte sequences given similar inputs. Thus, approximate matching at the raw byte level cannot discern the real similarity when compression algorithms have been used.

The final experiment sought to identify the file types for which **ssdeep** is better than cryptographic hashing. The test considered only **ssdeep** scores between 60 and 99. Table 7 shows the ten most frequent file types with scores between 60 and 99 for each operating system based on Test Case 2. The numbers correspond to the file percentages compared with

Table 7. File types with high identification rates for non-identical files.

WinXP$_{U2}$		Win7$_U$		Ubuntu$_U$	
Type	Amount	Type	Amount	Type	Amount
	11.60 %	.mum*	40.05 %	.html*	60.62 %
.html*	10.44 %	.inf*	10.09 %	.h*	19.40 %
.h*	6.40 %	.dll	8.18 %		10.63 %
.yaml*	6.09 %	.png	6.06 %	.pm*	1.42 %
.svn-base*	4.52 %	.mui	4.77 %	.gz	0.73 %
.dll	4.15 %	.gpd*	4.42 %	.png	0.63 %
.png	3.82 %	.fon	3.37 %	.py*	0.63 %
.py*	2.53 %	.nls	3.30 %	.al	0.55 %
.mf*	1.86 %	.ttf	2.48 %	.ent	0.44 %
.htm*	1.69 %	.ini*	1.32 %	.ps	0.36 %

all the files identified within the score range. The file types that include text are marked with an asterisk; they constitute the majority of the listed files. However, binary file types (e.g., .dll in Table 7) also have high identification rates. Other results (not shown in this paper) reveal that .exe, .pyc and .so are also among the top ten file types. Note that files without suffixes are typically text files or binary executables.

5.　　Related Work

Approximate matching has been shown to be useful for detecting similar inputs (e.g., different versions of a file), detecting embedded objects (e.g., a .jpg file in a Word document) and detecting fragments (e.g., network packets) [14]. Apart from ssdeep, we are aware of six other approximate matching algorithms. Two of them have similar qualities as ssdeep. The first is sdhash [13], which identifies statistically improbable features (e.g., a byte sequence of 64 characters), hashes them using SHA-1 and sets five bits in a Bloom filter. The second, mrsh-v2 [5], is a combination of ssdeep and sdhash. This algorithm uses a rolling hash to divide the input into chunks and each chunk is hashed using the FNV algorithm and inserted in a Bloom filter.

The remaining algorithms are less practical. For example, bbHash [4] is very slow – it requires about two minutes to process a 10 MiB file. mvHash-B [2] needs a specific configuration for each file type, while SimHash [15] and MinHash [6] can only handle near duplicates.

White [18] has analyzed the benefits of using hash functions in digital forensics. Instead of hashing complete files, block hashing applies cryptographic algorithms to smaller-than-filesize portions of data, where a portion is a 4,096-byte block. According to White, file-based data reduction leaves an average of 30% of disk space for human investigation and incorporating block hashes reduces the amount of data for human review to 15% of disk space. However, White focused on basic installations, which is not a realistic scenario. Baier and Dichtelmuller [1] showed that the reduction rates for used workstations were much worse than those obtained by White. In particular, Baier and Dichtelmuller obtained rates of approximately 50% for a basic Windows XP installation and rates as low as 15% for used Windows 7 and Ubuntu systems. In both cases, Baier and Dichtelmuller used the latest reference data set that contained many more entries than the reduced NIST database employed in this research.

6.   Conclusions

This paper describes the first experimental evaluation of approximate matching with large test cases. The results show that approximate matching provides substantial benefits compared with cryptographic hashing. Approximate matching significantly increases the number of files identified as known files. Also, it reduces the number of files that have·to be inspected manually by digital forensic investigators. Text files and binary files can be filtered effectively using approximate matching at the syntactic level. However, it is important that an up-to-date reference database is used to obtain the best identification rates.

Better results than ssdeep can be obtained using a more accurate approximate matching algorithm such as sdhash. However, an efficient similarity comparison method must be devised before sdhash can be evaluated using large test cases.

Acknowledgement

This research was partially supported by the European Union under the Integrated Project FIDELITY (Grant No. 284862) and by the Center for Advanced Security Research Darmstadt (CASED).

References

[1] H. Baier and C. Dichtelmuller, Datenreduktion mittels kryptographischer Hashfunktionen in der IT-Forensik: Nur ein Mythos? *DACH Security*, pp. 278–287, September 2012.

[2] F. Breitinger, K. Astebol, H. Baier and C. Busch, mvhash-b – A new approach for similarity preserving hashing, *Proceedings of the Seventh International Conference on IT Security Incident Management and IT Forensics*, pp. 33–44, 2013.

[3] F. Breitinger and H. Baier, Security aspects of piecewise hashing in computer forensics, *Proceedings of the Sixth International Conference on IT Security Incident Management and IT Forensics*, pp. 21–36, 2011.

[4] F. Breitinger and H. Baier, A fuzzy hashing approach based on random sequences and Hamming distance, *Proceedings of the Conference on Digital Forensics, Security and Law*, 2012.

[5] F. Breitinger and H. Baier, Similarity preserving hashing: Eligible properties and a new algorithm `mrsh-v2`, *Proceedings of the Fourth International ICST Conference on Digital Forensics and Cyber Crime*, 2012.

[6] A. Broder, On the resemblance and containment of documents, *Proceedings of the International Conference on the Compression and Complexity of Sequences*, pp. 21–29, 1997.

[7] L. Chen and G. Wang, An efficient piecewise hashing method for computer forensics, *Proceedings of the First International Workshop on Knowledge Discovery and Data Mining*, pp. 635–638, 2008.

[8] P. Deutsch and J. Gailly, ZLIB Compressed Data Format Specification Version 3.3, RFC 1950, 1996.

[9] J. Kornblum, Identifying almost identical files using context triggered piecewise hashing, *Digital Investigation*, vol. 3(S), pp. S91–S97, 2006.

[10] J. Kornblum, `ssdeep` (`ssdeep.sourceforge.net`), 2013.

[11] National Institute of Standards and Technology, National Software Reference Library, Gaithersburg, Maryland (`www.nsrl.nist.gov`).

[12] L. Noll, FNV hash (`www.isthe.com/chongo/tech/comp/fnv/index.html`), 2013.

[13] V. Roussev, Data fingerprinting with similarity digests, in *Advances in Digital Forensics VI*, K. Chow and S. Shenoi (Eds.), Springer, Heidelberg, Germany, pp. 207–226, 2010.

[14] V. Roussev, An evaluation of forensic similarity hashes, *Digital Investigation*, vol. 8(S), pp. S34–S41, 2011.

[15] C. Sadowski and G. Levin, SimHash: Hash-Based Similarity Detection, Technical Report UCSC-SOE-11-07, Department of Computer Science, University of California Santa Cruz, Santa Cruz, California (`simhash.googlecode.com/svn/trunk/paper/SimHashWithBib.pdf`), 2007.

[16] K. Seo, K. Lim, J. Choi, K. Chang and S. Lee, Detecting similar files based on hash and statistical analysis for digital forensic investigations, *Proceedings of the Second International Conference on Computer Science and its Applications*, 2009.

[17] A. Tridgell, `spamsum` (`mirror.linux.org.au/linux.conf.au/20 04/papers/junkcode/spamsum/README`), 2002.

[18] D. White, Hashing of file blocks: When exact matches are not useful, presented at the *Annual Meeting of the American Academy of Forensic Sciences*, 2008.

[19] C. Winter, M. Schneider and Y. Yannikos, F2S2: Fast forensic similarity search through indexing piecewise hash signatures, *Digital Investigation*, vol. 10(4), pp. 361–371, 2013.

Chapter 12

ACTIVE LINGUISTIC AUTHENTICATION USING REAL-TIME STYLOMETRIC EVALUATION FOR MULTI-MODAL DECISION FUSION

Ariel Stolerman, Alex Fridman, Rachel Greenstadt, Patrick Brennan, and Patrick Juola

Abstract   Active authentication is the process of continuously verifying a user based on his/her ongoing interactions with a computer. Forensic stylometry is the study of linguistic style applied to author (user) identification. This paper evaluates the Active Linguistic Authentication Dataset, collected from users working individually in an office environment over a period of one week. It considers a battery of stylometric modalities as a representative collection of high-level behavioral biometrics. While a previous study conducted a partial evaluation of the dataset with data from fourteen users, this paper considers the complete dataset comprising data from 67 users. Another significant difference is in the type of evaluation: instead of using day-based or data-based (number-of-characters) windows for classification, the evaluation employs time-based, overlapping sliding windows. This tests the ability to produce authentication decisions every 10 to 60 seconds, which is highly applicable to real-world active security systems. Sensor evaluation is conducted via cross-validation, measuring the false acceptance and false rejection rates (FAR/FRR). The results demonstrate that, under realistic settings, stylometric sensors perform with considerable effectiveness down to 0/0.5 FAR/FRR for decisions produced every 60 seconds and available 95% of the time.

Keywords: Active authentication, stylometry, authorship verification

1.   Introduction

The challenge of identity verification for the purpose of access control is the trade-off between maximizing the probability of intruder detec-

G. Peterson and S. Shenoi (Eds.): Advances in Digital Forensics X, IFIP AICT 433, pp. 165–183, 2014.
© IFIP International Federation for Information Processing 2014

tion and minimizing the cost to the legitimate user in terms of time and distraction due to false alerts, along with the extra hardware requirements for physical biometric authentication. In recent years, behavioral biometric systems have been explored to address this challenge [3]. These systems rely on inexpensive input devices such as a keyboard and mouse. However, their performance in terms of detecting intruders and maintaining a low-distraction human-computer interaction experience has been mixed [8]. In particular, they have error rates ranging from 0% [29] to 30% [30], depending on the context, variability in task selection and other dataset characteristics.

The bulk of biometric-based authentication research has focused on verifying a user based on a static set of data. This type of one-time authentication is not well suited to a live multi-user environment, where a person may leave the computer for an arbitrary period of time without logging off. Such an environment requires continuous authentication when the computer is in a non-idle state. The Active Linguistic Authentication Dataset [18] used in this work was created to represent this general real-world scenario. The dataset, which was generated in a simulated office environment, contains behavioral biometrics associated with typical human-computer interactions by office workers.

Stylometry is a form of authorship recognition that relies on the linguistic information found in a document. While stylometry existed before computers and artificial intelligence (AI), the field is currently dominated by techniques such as neural networks and statistical pattern recognition. State-of-the-art stylometry approaches can identify individuals in sets of 50 authors with more than 90% accuracy [2] and even scaled to more than 100,000 authors [28]. Stylometry is currently used in intelligence analysis and forensics, with increasing applications in digital communication analysis [40]; the results are accurate and reliable enough to be admissible as legal evidence [11, 12]. The application of stylometry as a high-level modality for authenticating users in a continuous user verification system is novel. Initial evaluations of authorship attribution technologies are promising, realizing in excess of 90% identification accuracy over fourteen users [18].

This paper considers a set of stylometric classifiers, also referred to as sensors, as a representative selection of high-level behavioral biometrics. The primary goal is to evaluate authorship attribution approaches in realistic settings for active authentication, which require constant monitoring and frequent decision making about the legitimacy of a user at a computer in a dynamic, time-constrained environment. This work is designed as a preliminary evaluation of one modality among many to consider for an active authentication system. In the future, the stylometric modalities discussed in this paper would be interleaved with other low- and high-level modalities, such as keyboard dynamics [33], mouse movements [3] and web browsing behavior [41], in a centralized decision fusion system. The use of such modalities, including stylometry, may provide a cost-effective alternative to sensors based on physiological biometrics [39].

Although this research focuses on active authentication, a live security application of stylometric analysis and its implications for the usability and configuration of stylometric sensors are relevant to forensic contexts. Consider, for example, a standard post-mortem forensic analysis of user input data aggregated over an entire day. This research seeks to identify the features to consider in such "noisy" settings, which include window sizes, effects of overlapping windows and how idle periods in data input should be considered.

2.   Related Work

A defining problem of active authentication is that the verification of an identity must be carried out continuously on a sample of sensor data that varies drastically with time. Therefore, the classification has to be made using a "window" of recent data, dismissing or discounting the value of older data outside the window. Depending on the user task being performed, some biometric sensors may provide more data than others. For example, when a user browses the web, mouse and web activity sensors are flooded with data, while keystroke and stylometric sensors may only receive a few infrequent key presses.

This motivates recent work on multimodal authentication systems where the decisions of multiple classifiers are fused together [34]; the resulting verification process is more robust to the dynamic nature of real-time human-computer interactions. This paper examines only the effectiveness of stylometric sensors under active authentication settings, the goal being to eventually construct a multi-modal biometric system. The notion of decision fusion is motivated by the research of Ali and Pazzani [4], which achieved reduced error rates using distinctly different classifiers (i.e., using different behavioral biometrics) with several fusion options [10, 15, 20].

Authorship attribution based on linguistic style, or stylometry, is a well-researched field [6, 16, 17, 23, 32, 35]. Its principal application domain is written language – identifying an anonymous author of a text by mining it for linguistic features. The theory behind stylometry is that every person has a unique linguistic style or "stylome" [38] that can be quantified and measured in order to distinguish between different authors. The feature space is potentially endless, with frequency measurements and numeric evaluations based on features across different levels of the text, including function words [9, 27], grammar [25], character n-grams [36] and more. Although stylometry has not been used for active user authentication, its application to this task brings higher-level inspection into the process compared with lower-level biometrics such as mouse movements and keyboard dynamics [7, 42].

The most common practice of stylometry is in supervised learning, where a classifier is trained on texts of candidate authors and used to attribute the stylistically closest candidate author to unknown writings. In an unsupervised setting, a set of writings whose authorship is unknown are classified into style-based clusters, each representing texts of a unique author.

In an active authentication setting, authorship verification is applied where unknown text is to be classified by a unary author-specific classifier. The text is attributed to an author only if it is stylistically close enough to the author. Although pure verification is the ultimate goal, standard authorship attribution as a closed-world problem is an easier (and sometimes sufficient) goal. In either case, classifiers are trained in advance and used for real-time classification of processed sliding windows of input keystrokes. If enough windows are recognized as an author other than the real user, the presence of an intruder is indicated.

Another use of stylometry is in author profiling [6, 19, 37]. This application is quite different from author recognition because writings are mined for linguistic features to identify characteristics of their authors such as age and gender [5], native language [24] and personality characteristics [13].

In a pure authorship attribution setting, where classification is done off-line on complete texts (rather than sequences of input keystrokes) and in a supervised setting where all candidate authors are known, state-of-the-art stylometry techniques perform very well. For instance, at PAN-2012 (`pan.webis.de`), some methods achieved more than 80% accuracy on a set of 241 documents, sometimes with added distractor authors.

Two key challenges arise in an active authentication setting. First, open-world stylometry is a much harder problem, with a tendency to yield high false negative (false reject) rates. The unmasking technique [22] has been shown to be effective – 95.7% accuracy – on a dataset of 21 books by ten nineteenth-century authors. However, the amount of data collected by sliding windows of sufficiently small durations requires efficient authentication and the lack of quality coherent literary writings render this approach infeasible for active linguistic authentication. Second, the inconsistent frequency nature of keyboard input along with the relatively large amount of data required for good performance of stylometric techniques render a large portion of the input windows unusable for learning writing style.

On the other hand, an active authentication setting offers some advantages with regard to potential features and analysis method. Since the raw data consists of keystrokes, some linguistic and technical idiosyncratic features can be extracted; these include misspellings caught before they are auto-corrected and vanish from the dataset and patterns of deletions such as selecting a sentence and hitting delete as opposed to repeatedly hitting backspace to delete individual characters. Additionally, in an active authentication setting, it is intuitive to consider overlaps between consecutive windows, resulting in a large dataset and providing grounds for local voting based on a set of windows and controlling the frequency at which decisions are made.

3.   Evaluation Dataset

The complete Active Linguistic Authentication Dataset [18] is used in the evaluation. The dataset, which contains data collected in a simulated work environment, is designed specifically for behavioral biometric evaluation. The data collection utilized an office space, which was allocated, organized and supervised by some of the authors of this paper. The office space contained five desks, each with a laptop, mouse and headphones. The equipment and supplies were chosen to be representative of a standard office environment. However, one of the important properties of the dataset is uniformity. Because the computers and input devices in the simulated office environment were identical, the variations in behavioral biometrics data can be attributed to variations in the characteristics of the users instead of the effects of variations in the physical environment.

The dataset contains data collected from 80 users. Due to equipment and software crashes and sick days taken by the subjects, a little more than 80 subjects were used for data collection to reach the 80 user goal. However, when examining the data obtained from the 80 users, it was observed that some users had produced significantly less data than the others. In order to eliminate user activity variance effects, a threshold of 60,000 seconds (16.67 hours) of minimum activity was set. This threshold left 67 qualifying users for the evaluation presented in this paper.

Five temporary employees (subjects) were hired during each week of the data collection. The subjects had to work for a total of 40 hours. Each subject was assigned two tasks each day. The first, for six hours of the eight-hour workday, was an open-ended task to write blog-style

Table 1. Character count statistics over five workdays.

Minimum per user	17,027
Maximum per user	263,165
Average	84,206
Total	5,641,788

articles related to the city in which the testing was carried out. The second task, involving two hours of the workday, was less open-ended. Each subject was asked to write summaries from a list of topics or web articles. The articles were from various reputable news sources and were kept consistent between users.

Both tasks encouraged the subjects to conduct extensive online research using web browsers. They were allowed to copy and paste content, but they were told that the final work product had to be their own authorship. As expected, the subjects almost exclusively used two applications: Microsoft Word 2010 for word processing and Internet Explorer for browsing the web. Although the user-generated documents are available in the dataset, the evaluation in this paper is based on the stream of keystrokes recorded during the workday, with the purpose of simulating the settings with which a real-time authentication system would have to operate.

The 67-user dataset was further parsed in order to produce one large stream of mouse/keyboard events. For every user, the entire five days of data was concatenated into one stream (in JSON format), and marked to be divided into five equally-sized folds for later cross-validation evaluation. In addition, periods of inactivity lasting more than two minutes were marked as idle. For the purposes of this research, a subset of events that only included keyboard strokes was maintained (the mouse events will be used by other sensors in future work). The format of one continuous stream permitted the complete utilization of the data in a real-time, continuous active authentication system. Table 1 summarizes the keystroke event statistics for the parsed 67-user dataset. The keystroke events include the alphanumeric keys as well as special keys such as shift, backspace, ctrl and alt. The keystroke counts only include the down presses, the key releases were ignored.

4.　　Methodology

This section describes the methodology in detail, including the challenges and limitations.

4.1 Challenges and Limitations

An active authentication system presents a few concerns. First, a potential performance overhead is expected to accompany the deployment of such a system because it requires constant monitoring and logging of user input, and on-the-fly processing of all its sensor components. With stylometric sensors, large amounts of memory and computation power are often consumed by language processing tools (e.g., dictionary-based features and part-of-speech taggers). Therefore, the system should be carefully configured to balance accuracy and resource consumption. This issue becomes more acute in a multi-modal system that uses multiple sensors.

A second concern with an active authentication system is the user input requirements. In a non-active authentication scheme, a user is required to provide credentials only when logging in and perhaps when certain operations are to be executed. The credentials include some sort of personal key (e.g., password or private key) that identifies the user. However, in the case of an active authentication system based on stylometric modalities, the user keyboard input is required. In a multi-modal system, all user interactions may be required, including mouse events and web browsing behavior. The precise sequence and timing of keyboard events are essential to enhance system performance. However, such input is not designed for stylometric analysis and authentication. Additionally, it often contains sensitive and private information, which is collected when the user types in passphrases to log into accounts, writes something personal or simply browses the web. Some actions may be taken during system design to address security and privacy concerns. For example, the collected data could be managed carefully, storage of raw collected data could be avoided (except for parsed feature vectors extracted from the data) and all stored data could be encrypted. The privacy issue specifically applies to stylometric modalities, where the content of user input is of importance. Other modalities may void these issues by not targeting content, such as mouse movement biometrics that focus on physical characteristics of the user instead of the possibly sensitive semantics of the generated input.

4.2 Previous Evaluation

In earlier work [18], we presented an initial evaluation of a portion of the Active Linguistic Authentication Dataset (i.e., data for fourteen users). Two methods of evaluation were applied.

First, each day's worth of work was analyzed as one unit or document, for a total of 69 documents (five days for fourteen users, minus a missing day by one user). One-vs.-all analysis was applied using a simple nearest-neighbor classifier with the Manhattan or intersection distance metric and character n-grams as features ($1 \leq n \leq 5$). The best result achieved was 88.4% accuracy.

In the second analysis, a number-of-characters-based sliding window technique was applied to generate the input segments to be classified; this provides a better simulation of the performance of a realistic active stylometric authentication system. The generated windows were non-overlapping, with the window sizes set to 100, 500 and 1,000 words (tokens separated by whitespaces). The minimum window size was used to allow sufficient data for the stylistic profiling of the window. An extensive linguistic feature set, inspired by the one used in the Writeprints [2] stylometry method, was employed along with a linear SVM and a nearest-neighbor classifier. The best result achieved was 93.33% accuracy with 0.009 FAR and 0.067 FRR.

The results demonstrate that it is beneficial to use stylometric biometrics for active authentication. However, the analysis approach, although satisfactory as a preliminary study, omitted some key requirements for an active authentication system. First, only fourteen subjects were used; thus, the system performance for a large set of users remains unknown. Stylometry research has thus far provided solutions for large author sets, but no research to date has focused on a dataset with incoherent and noisy qualities. Indeed, the approaches discussed above may prove to be inefficient for larger author sets.

Perhaps the main issue with the method of analysis is the units determined for learning/classification. Day-based windows are certainly not useful for active authentication, which aims to provide intruder alerts as quickly as possible (in minutes, if not seconds). Even the second data-based-windows analysis is insufficient: each window may have an arbitrary length in terms of its time span and collecting the minimum amount of words may allow an intruder enough time to apply an attack. Moreover, due to the possibility of large windows that may cross idle periods, data associated with different users could be mixed. For example, the first half of a window could contain legitimate user input while the second half, an idle-period later, could be supplied by an intruder. This causes the contamination of "bad" windows with "good" data that could throw off the classifier and cause it to miss an alert.

This paper provides an analysis of the authentication system in a more realistic setting. The focus is on a time-wise (instead of a data-wise) sliding window, and overlapping windows are allowed so that the system can output decisions with increased frequency. With this approach, the system is compelled to decide whether to accept or reject the latest window in a timely manner based on the data it has acquired thus far, or to determine that it cannot make a decision. The issue of balancing the amount of collected data, the required time-wise size of windows and the desired decision frequency is examined in the following section.

4.3 Real-Time Approach

The stylometric classifiers, or sensors, presented in this section are based on the simplest settings of closed-world stylometry: the classifiers are trained on the closed set of 67 users, where each classification results with one of the users being identified as the author. A more sophisticated approach would use open-world verifiers, where each legitimate user is paired to its own classifier in a one-class/one-vs.-all formulation. Such a verification approach is naturally suited to the open-world scenario, where possible imposters can originate outside the set of legitimate users (e.g., an intruder from outside an office who takes over an unlocked computer, instead of a malicious colleague). However, this paper considers the case of a closed set of possible users as a baseline for future verification-based classifiers.

In the preprocessing phase, the keystroke data files were parsed to produce a list of documents (text windows) consisting of overlapping windows for each user with time-based sizes of 10, 30, 60, 300, 600 and 1,200 seconds. For the first three settings, a sliding window was advanced with steps of 10 seconds of the stream of keystrokes; the last three settings used steps of 60 seconds. The step size determines how often a decision can be made by the sensor. In addition, although the window generation was configured with fixed parameters (e.g., a time-wise size of 300 and step of 60), in practice, the timestamps of the generated windows correlated with the keystroke events by relaxing the generation to no greater than 300 and no less than 60 with empty windows being discarded. In a live system, a similar approach is expected to be used: a window is "closed" and a decision is made when the size limitation time is up; hence, it is no greater than 300. In addition, when determining the beginning of a window followed by another window, a difference of at least one character is expected (otherwise the second window is a subset of the first). Therefore, if the time span between the first character in a window and the one that follows is greater than the determined step size, effectively a greater step size is applied; hence, it is no less than 60.

In this research, the generated windows were set to ignore idle periods, as if the data stream was continuous with no more than two minutes of delay between one input character and the next. This was applied in the dataset by preprocessing the keystroke timestamps such that an idle period longer than two minutes was artificially narrowed down to precisely two minutes. Furthermore, the data was aggregated and divided into five equally-sized folds for analysis purposes, thus potentially containing windows with an idle period between days. Although this preprocessing suffers from the problems associated with mixed legitimate/non-legitimate user-input windows or mixed time-of-day windows (e.g., end of one day and beginning of the next day) if applied in a real system, in our analysis, the processing was applied to allow the generation of as many windows as possible. Since the analysis presented does not involve legitimate/non-legitimate mixed windows, idle-crossing windows are reasonable for the purpose of this work.

In the case of stylometry-based biometrics, selecting a window size involves a delicate trade-off between the amount of captured text (and the probability of correct stylistic profiling for the window) and the system response time. In contrast, other biometrics can perform satisfactorily with small windows (with sizes in the order of seconds). The problem is somewhat overcome using small steps (and overlapping windows), leaving the problem only at the beginning of a day (until the first window is generated). Similar to the analysis in [18], only keystrokes were considered during preprocessing (key releases were filtered) and all special keys were converted to unique single-character placeholders. For example, **BACKSPACE** was converted to β and **PRINTSCREEN** was converted to π. Representable special keys such as \t and \n were taken as is (i.e., tab and newline, respectively).

The chosen feature set is probably the most crucial part of the configuration. The constructed feature set, which we refer to as the AA feature set, is a variation of the Writeprints [2] feature set that includes a vast range of linguistic features across different levels of text. Table 2 summarizes the features of the AA feature set. This rich linguistic feature set can better capture a user's writing style. With the special-character placeholders, some features capture aspects of a user's style that are not found in standard authorship problem settings. For example, frequencies of backspaces and deletes provide an evaluation of a user's typo-rate (or lack of decisiveness).

The features were extracted using the JStylo framework [26]. JStylo was chosen for analysis because it is equipped with fine-grained feature definition capabilities. Each feature is uniquely defined by a set of its own document preprocessing tools, one unique feature extractor (core of the feature), feature post-processing tools and normalization/factoring options. The features available in JStylo are frequencies of a class of related features (e.g., frequencies of "a," "b," ..., "z" for the "letters" feature class) or some numeric evaluation of an input document (e.g., av-

Table 2. AA feature set.

Group	Features
Lexical	Average word length
	Characters
	Most common character bigrams
	Most common character trigrams
	Percentage of letters
	Percentage of uppercase letters
	Percentage of digits
	Digits
	Two-digit numbers
	Three-digit numbers
	Word length distribution
Syntactic	Function words
	Part-of-speech (POS) tags
	Most common POS bigrams
	Most common POS trigrams
Content	Words
	Word bigrams
	Word trigrams

erage word length or Yule's Characteristic K). Its output is compatible with the Weka platform [14], which was employed during the classification process. The definition and implementation of all the features in the AA feature set are available in JStylo, making it easily reproducible.

Two important procedures were applied in the feature extraction phase. First, every word-based feature (e.g., function words class or different word-grams) was assigned a tailor-made preprocessing tool developed for the dataset; each tool applied the relevant special characters on the text. For example, the character sequence ch$\beta\beta$Cch$\beta\beta$hicago becomes Chicago, where β represents backspace. Second, since the windows are determined by time and not by the amount of collected data as in [18], normalization is crucial for all frequency-based features (which constitute the majority of the feature set). Each of these features was simply divided by the most relevant measurement related to the feature. For example, character bigrams were divided by the total character count of the window.

The classification used sequential minimal optimization support vector machines [31] with a linear kernel and complexity parameter $C = 1$ available in Weka. Support vector machines are commonly used for authorship attribution [1, 21, 43] and are known to provide high performance and accuracy. As mentioned earlier, they are closed-world classifiers, i.e., they classify each window to one of the known candidate users (with the legitimate user as the true class). No acceptance thresholds were integrated in the classification process.

Finally, the data was analyzed with the stylometric sensors using a varying threshold for minimum characters-per-window spanning from 100 to 1,000 with steps of 100. For every threshold set, all the windows with less than the threshold amount of characters were discarded and the sensors outputted no decisions for these windows. The different thresholds help assess the trade-off in sensor performance in terms of accuracy and availability: as the threshold increases, the window has richer data and is potentially classified with higher accuracy, but the portion of total windows that pass the threshold decreases, making the sensor less available. Note that even the largest threshold (1,000 characters) is considerably smaller than that used in most previous stylometry analyses (minimum of 500 words). After filtering, only configurations with training data available for all users were retained; as expected, this resulted in the removal of sensors configured to small windows with high minimum number of character thresholds.

After eliminating sensors according to the rule mentioned above, 37 stylometric sensors were retained. These sensors spanned a variety of time-wise window sizes and minimum character-wise window sizes. In the remainder of this paper, the stylometric sensors are denoted as $S_{n,m}$, where n denotes the time-wise window size in seconds and m denotes the minimum characters-per-window configuration.

5.   Evaluation

The generated user data streams, divided into five equally-sized folds, are intended to be evaluated in a multi-modal decision fusion active authentication system. Such a system requires knowledge of the expected FAR and FRR rates of its sensors in order to make a cumulative weighted decision. Therefore, the intended evaluation is based on five-fold cross-validation where, in each of the five validations, three folds were used for training, one fold for characterization of the FAR and FRR of the sensor, and the last fold for testing. Thus, each of the five validations outputted a decision for each test instance (from the last fold) and a global FAR and FRR characterization of the sensor. Eventually, the results of all five validations were averaged to determine the performance of the system. The configuration of the validations was cyclic, such that, in the first validation, folds 1, 2 and 3 were used for training, fold 4 for characterization and fold 5 for testing; in the second, folds 2, 3 and 4

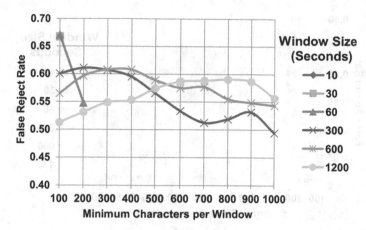

Figure 1. Averaged FRR for all characterization phases.

were used for training, fold 5 for characterization and fold 1 for testing, and so on.

To evaluate the performance of the stylometric sensors, we use the results averaged over all train-characterize-test configurations described above to provide performance evaluations of the sensors when combined in a centralized decision fusion algorithm. Since the FRR and FAR produced in the characterization phase of the main experiments provide an evaluation of the reliability of the decisions made during the test phase, it is reasonable to use them to evaluate the standalone performance of the stylometric sensors.

Figures 1 and 2 show the averaged FRR and FAR results. In particular, Figure 1 shows the averaged FRR for all characterization phases using the stylometric sensors with varying time-wise window sizes and varying thresholds for the minimum number of characters per window. Only windows passing the threshold (i.e., with at least that many characters) participated in the analysis. This measurement accounts for the portion of legitimate user windows that were not detected as belonging to the user (i.e., false alarms).

Figure 2 shows the averaged FAR for all characterization phases using the stylometric sensors with the same configurations. Note that the FAR accounts for the portion of intruder windows that were classified as belonging to a legitimate user (i.e., security breaches).

Figure 3 shows the averaged percentage of the remaining windows after all the windows that did not pass the minimum characters-per-window threshold were removed.

The high FRR and low FAR suggest that the majority of the sensors are rather strict: they almost never falsely identify an intruder as le-

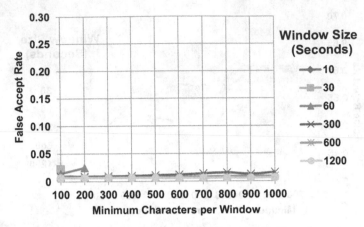

Figure 2.   Averaged FAR for all characterization phases.

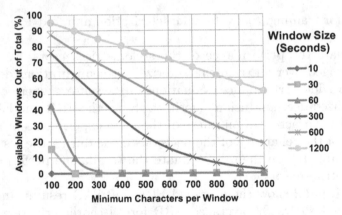

Figure 3.   Percentage of remaining windows.

gitimate, but a cost is paid in terms of a high FAR. The FRR results indicate that as the window size (in seconds) increases, the less the minimum characters-per-window threshold affects performance. The same trend is seen with the FAR results: the large windows (300, 600 and 1,200) show insignificant differences for different minimum characters-per-window thresholds.

The availability of decisions as a function of the minimum characters-per-window thresholds (shown in Figure 3) completes the evaluation of the performance of the stylometric sensors. For example, $S_{1200,100}$ triggered every 60 seconds (the step configuration of the 1,200-second-windows sensors) produces a decision 95% of the time with an accuracy of approximately 0.5/0 FRR/FAR.

6. Conclusions

A preliminary study by Juola, *et al.* [18] indicates the effectiveness of stylometric biometrics for active authentication. This paper puts the shortcomings of the preliminary study to the test by using settings that simulate a more realistic active authentication environment, with many users and high frequency decision making constraints. The results obtained under these settings demonstrate that the effectiveness of stylometric sensors deteriorates drastically, down to 0.5 FRR and 0 FAR. Nevertheless, the results are promising because the sensors may be used in a mixture-of-experts approach that fuses multi-modal sensors.

Although the configuration of data with overlapping sliding windows is realistic, the classification methodology is still limited and focused on closed-world SVM classifiers with an extensive linguistic feature set. Future analysis must include other classifiers, especially open-world verifiers that can be applied in scenarios where the set of suspects is not closed. In addition, because of the noisiness of the data, other feature sets should be considered, including sets that focus less on high linguistic characteristics of the text (like POS-taggers) and more on typing patterns. A mixture of writing style and typing style quantification could, perhaps, achieve better profiling with this type of data.

The immediate next step in evaluation is to use a multi-modal fusion system employing multiple sensors. Sensors to be considered include mouse movements, keyboard dynamics (i.e., low-level key patterns) and web-browsing behavior. The configuration of such a system based on closed-world sensors and data-based windows evaluated on a subset of nineteen users achieves approximately 1% FAR/FRR, but its performance in open-world settings with the complete dataset is as yet unknown and is currently the subject of investigation.

References

[1] A. Abbasi and H. Chen, Identification and comparison of extremist-group web forum messages using authorship analysis, *IEEE Intelligent Systems*, vol. 20(5), pp. 67–75, 2005.

[2] A. Abbasi and H. Chen, Writeprints: A stylometric approach to identity-level identification and similarity detection in cyberspace, *ACM Transactions on Information Systems*, vol. 26(2), pp. 7:1–7:29, 2008.

[3] A. Ahmed and I. Traore, A new biometric technology based on mouse dynamics, *IEEE Transactions on Dependable and Secure Computing*, vol. 4(3), pp. 165–179, 2007.

[4] K. Ali and M. Pazzani, On the Link Between Error Correlation and Error Reduction in Decision Tree Ensembles, Department of Information and Computer Science, University of California at Irvine, Irvine, California, 1995.

[5] S. Argamon, M. Koppel, J. Pennebaker and J. Schler, Mining the blogosphere: Age, gender and the varieties of self-expression, *First Monday*, vol. 12(9), 2007.

[6] S. Argamon, M. Koppel, J. Pennebaker and J. Schler, Automatically profiling the author of an anonymous text, *Communications of the ACM*, vol. 52(2), pp. 119–123, 2009.

[7] N. Bakelman, J. Monaco, S. Cha and C. Tappert, Continual keystroke biometric authentication on short bursts of keyboard input, *Proceedings of the Student-Faculty Research Day*, Seidenberg School of Computer Science and Information Systems, Pace University, New York, 2012.

[8] F. Bergadano, D. Gunetti and C. Picardi, User authentication through keystroke dynamics, *ACM Transactions on Information Systems Security*, vol. 5(4), pp. 367–397, 2002.

[9] J. Binongo, Who wrote the 15th Book of Oz? An application of multivariate analysis of authorship attribution, *Chance*, vol. 16(2), pp. 9–17, 2003.

[10] Z. Chair and P. Varshney, Optimal data fusion in multiple sensor detection systems, *IEEE Transactions on Aerospace and Electronic Systems*, vol. AES-22(1), pp. 98–101, 1986.

[11] C. Chaski, Who's at the keyboard: Authorship attribution in digital evidence investigations, *International Journal of Digital Evidence*, vol. 4(1), 2005.

[12] C. Chaski, The keyboard dilemma and forensic authorship attribution, in *Advances in Digital Forensics III*, P. Craiger and S. Shenoi (Eds.), Springer, Boston, Massachusetts, pp. 133–146, 2007.

[13] C. Gray and P. Juola, Personality identification through on-line text analysis, presented at the *Chicago Colloquium on Digital Humanities and Computer Science*, 2012.

[14] M. Hall, E. Frank, G. Holmes, B. Pfahringer, P. Reutemann and I. Witten, The Weka Data Mining Software: An update, *SIGKDD Explorations Newsletter*, vol. 11(1), pp. 10–18, 2009.

[15] S. Hashem and B. Schmeiser, Improving model accuracy using optimal linear combinations of trained neural networks, *IEEE Transactions on Neural Networks*, vol. 6(3), pp. 792–794, 1995.

[16] M. Jockers and D. Witten, A comparative study of machine learning methods for authorship attribution, *Literary and Linguistic Computing*, vol. 25(2), pp. 215–223, 2010.

[17] P. Juola, Authorship attribution, *Foundations and Trends in Information Retrieval*, vol. 1(3), pp. 233–334, 2008.

[18] P. Juola, J. Noecker, A. Stolerman, M. Ryan, P. Brennan and R. Greenstadt, Towards active linguistic authentication, in *Advances in Digital Forensics IX*, G. Peterson and S. Shenoi (Eds.), Springer, Heidelberg, Germany, pp. 385–398, 2013.

[19] P. Juola, M. Ryan and M. Mehok, Geographically localizing tweets using stylometric analysis, presented at the *American Association for Corpus Linguistics Conference*, 2011.

[20] J. Kittler, M. Hatef, R. Duin and J. Matas, On combining classifiers, *IEEE Transactions on Pattern Analysis and Machine Intelligence*, vol. 20(3), pp. 226–239, 1998.

[21] M. Koppel and J. Schler, Ad-hoc authorship attribution competition – Approach outline, presented at the *Joint International Conference of the Association for Literary and Linguistic Computing and the Association for Computers and the Humanities*, 2004.

[22] M. Koppel and J. Schler, Authorship verification as a one-class classification problem, *Proceedings of the Twenty-First International Conference on Machine Learning*, 2004.

[23] M. Koppel, J. Schler and S. Argamon, Computational methods in authorship attribution, *Journal of the American Society for Information Science and Technology*, vol. 60(1), pp. 9–26, 2009.

[24] M. Koppel, J. Schler and K. Zigdon, Determining an author's native language by mining a text for errors, *Proceedings of the Eleventh ACM SIGKDD International Conference on Knowledge Discovery and Data Mining*, pp. 624–628, 2005.

[25] O. Kukushkina, A. Polikarpov and D. Khmelev, Using literal and grammatical statistics for authorship attribution, *Problemy Peredachi Informatii*, vol. 37(2), pp. 96–198, 2001; Translated in *Problems of Information Transmission*, vol. 37(2), pp. 172–184, 2001.

[26] A. McDonald, S. Afroz, A. Caliskan, A. Stolerman and R. Greenstadt, Use fewer instances of the letter "i:" Toward writing style anonymization, in *Privacy Enhancing Technologies*, S. Fischer-Hubner and M. Wright (Eds.), Springer-Verlag, Berlin, Germany, pp. 299–318, 2012.

[27] F. Mosteller and D. Wallace, *Inference and Disputed Authorship: The Federalist*, Addison-Wesley, Reading, Massachusetts, 1964.

[28] A. Narayanan, H. Paskov, N. Gong, J. Bethencourt, E. Stefanov, R. Shin and D. Song, On the feasibility of Internet-scale author identification, *Proceedings of the IEEE Symposium on Security and Privacy*, pp. 300–314, 2012.

[29] M. Obaidat and B. Sadoun, Verification of computer users using keystroke dynamics, *IEEE Transactions on Systems, Man and Cybernetics, Part B: Cybernetics*, vol. 27(2), pp. 261–269, 1997.

[30] T. Ord and S. Furnell, User authentication for keypad-based devices using keystroke analysis, *Proceedings of the Second International Network Conference*, pp. 263–272, 2000.

[31] J. Platt, Fast training of support vector machines using sequential minimal optimization, in *Advances in Kernel Methods: Support Vector Learning*, B. Scholkopf, C. Burges and A. Smola (Eds.), MIT Press, Cambridge, Massachusetts, pp. 185–208, 1999.

[32] J. Rudman, The state of authorship attribution studies: Some problems and solutions, *Computers and the Humanities*, vol. 31, pp. 351–365, 1998.

[33] D. Shanmugapriya and G. Padmavathi, A survey of biometric keystroke dynamics: Approaches, security and challenges, *International Journal of Computer Science and Information Security*, vol. 5(1), pp. 115–119, 2009.

[34] T. Sim, S. Zhang, R. Janakiraman and S. Kumar, Continuous verification using multimodal biometrics, *IEEE Transactions on Pattern Analysis and Machine Intelligence*, vol. 29(4), pp. 687–700, 2007.

[35] E. Stamatatos, A survey of modern authorship attribution methods, *Journal of the American Society for Information Science and Technology*, vol. 60(3), pp. 538–556, 2009.

[36] E. Stamatatos, On the robustness of authorship attribution based on character n-gram features, *Brooklyn Law School Journal of Law and Policy*, vol. 21(2), pp. 421–439, 2013.

[37] H. van Halteren, Author verification by linguistic profiling: An exploration of the parameter space, *ACM Transactions on Speech and Language Processing*, vol. 4(1), pp. 1:1–1:17, 2007.

[38] H. van Halteren, R. Baayen, F. Tweedie, M. Haverkort and A. Neijt, New machine learning methods demonstrate the existence of a human stylome, *Journal of Quantitative Linguistics*, vol. 12(1), pp. 65–77, 2005.

[39] J. Wayman, Fundamentals of biometric authentication technologies, *International Journal of Image and Graphics*, vol. 1(1), pp. 93–113, 2001.

[40] J. Wayman, N. Orlans, Q. Hu, F. Goodman, A. Ulrich and V. Valencia, Technology Assessment for the State of the Art Biometrics Excellence Roadmap, Volume 2, MITRE Technical Report v1.3, The MITRE Corporation, Bedford, Massachusetts, 2009.

[41] R. Yampolskiy, Behavioral modeling: An overview, *American Journal of Applied Sciences*, vol. 5(5), pp. 496–503, 2008.

[42] N. Zheng, A. Paloski and H. Wang, An efficient user verification system via mouse movements, *Proceedings of the Eighteenth ACM Conference on Computer and Communications Security*, pp. 139–150, 2011.

[43] R. Zheng, J. Li, H. Chen and Z. Huang, A framework for authorship identification of online messages: Writing-style features and classification techniques, *Journal of the American Society for Information Science and Technology*, vol. 57(3), pp. 378–393, 2006.

Chapter 13

BREAKING THE CLOSED-WORLD ASSUMPTION IN STYLOMETRIC AUTHORSHIP ATTRIBUTION

Ariel Stolerman, Rebekah Overdorf, Sadia Afroz, and Rachel Greenstadt

Abstract   Stylometry is a form of authorship attribution that relies on the linguistic information found in a document. While there has been significant work in stylometry, most research focuses on the closed-world problem where the author of the document is in a known suspect set. For open-world problems where the author may not be in the suspect set, traditional classification methods are ineffective. This paper proposes the "classify-verify" method that augments classification with a binary verification step evaluated on stylometric datasets. This method, which can be generalized to any domain, significantly outperforms traditional classifiers in open-world settings and yields an F1-score of 0.87, comparable to traditional classifiers in closed-world settings. Moreover, the method successfully detects adversarial documents where authors deliberately change their styles, a problem for which closed-world classifiers fail.

Keywords: Forensic stylometry, authorship attribution, authorship verification

1.   Introduction

The web is full of anonymous communications that are often the focus of digital forensic investigations. Forensic stylometry is used to analyze anonymous communications in order to "de-anonymize" them. Classic stylometric analysis requires an exact set of suspects in order to perform reliable authorship attribution, settings that are often not met in real-world problems. This paper breaks the closed-world assumption and explores a novel method for forensic stylometry that addresses the possibility that the true author is not in the set of suspects.

G. Peterson and S. Shenoi (Eds.): Advances in Digital Forensics X, IFIP AICT 433, pp. 185–205, 2014.

Stylometry is a form of authorship recognition that relies on the linguistic information found in a document. While stylometry existed before computers and artificial intelligence, the field is currently dominated by artificial intelligence techniques such as neural networks and statistical pattern recognition. State-of-the-art stylometric approaches can identify individuals in sets of 50 authors with better than 90% accuracy [1], and even scaled to more than 100,000 authors [22]. Stylometry is currently used in intelligence analysis and forensics, with increasing applications in digital communications analysis. The increase in rigor, accuracy and scale of stylometric techniques has led legal practitioners to turn to stylometry for forensic evidence [15], albeit stylometry is considered to be controversial at times and may not be admitted in court [9].

The effectiveness of stylometry has key implications with regard to anonymous and pseudonymous speech. Recent work has exposed limits on stylometry through active circumvention [4, 21]. Stylometry has thus far focused on limited, closed-world models. In the classic stylometry problem, there are relatively few authors (usually fewer than 20 and nearly always fewer than 100), the set of possible authors is known, every author has a large training set and all the text is from the same genre. However, real-world problems often do not conform to these restrictions.

Controversial pseudonymous documents that are published on the Internet often have an unbounded suspect list. Even if the list is known with certainty, training data may not exist for all suspects. Nonetheless, classical stylometry requires a fixed list and training data for each suspect, and an author is always selected from this list. This is problematic for forensic analysts who have no way of knowing when widening their suspect pool is required, as well as for Internet activists who may appear in the suspect lists and be falsely accused of authorship.

This paper explores a mixed closed-world and open-world authorship attribution problem with a known set of suspect authors, but with some probability (known or unknown) that the author is not in the set.

The primary contribution of this paper is the novel classify-verify (CV) method, which augments authorship classification with a verification step and obtains similar accuracy on open-world problems as traditional classifiers in closed-world problems. Even in the closed-world case, CV can improve results by replacing wrongly identified authors with "unknown." The method can be tuned to different levels of rigidity to achieve the desired false positive and false negative error rates. However, it can also be automatically tuned, whether or not the expected proportion of documents by authors in the suspect list versus those who are absent is known.

CV performs better in adversarial settings than traditional classification. Previous work has shown that traditional classification performs near random chance when faced with writers who change their styles. CV filters most of the attacks in the Extended-Brennan-Greenstadt Adversarial Corpus [4], an improvement over previous work that requires training on adversarial data [2].

This paper also presents the sigma verification method, which is based on Noecker and Ryan's [24] distractorless verification method that measures the distance between an author and a document. Sigma verification incorporates pairwise distances within an author's documents and the standard deviations of the author's features. Although it is not proven to statistically outperform the distractorless method in all scenarios, it has been shown to be a better alternative for datasets with certain characteristics.

2. Problem Statement

The closed-world stylometry or authorship attribution problem is: given a document D of unknown authorship and documents by a set of known authors $\mathcal{A} = \{A_1, ..., A_n\}$, determine the author $A_i \in \mathcal{A}$ of D. This problem assumes that the author of D is in $\mathcal{A}$.

The open-world stylometry problem is: given a document D, identify the author of D.

Authorship verification is a slightly relaxed version: given a document D and an author A, determine whether or not D is written by A.

The problem explored in this paper is a mixture of the two problems above: given a document D of unknown authorship and documents by a set of known authors $\mathcal{A}$, determine the author $A_i \in \mathcal{A}$ of D or that the author of D is not in $\mathcal{A}$. This problem is similar to the attribution problem but with the addition of the class "unknown." An extended definition includes $p = Pr[A_D \in \mathcal{A}]$, the probability that the author of D is in the set of candidates.

In the remainder of this paper, test documents are examined in two settings: when the authors of the documents are in the set of suspects, denoted by "in-set," and when the documents are by an author outside the suspect set, denoted by "not-in-set."

Applying closed-world stylometry in open-world settings suffers from a fundamental flaw: a closed-world classifier always outputs some author in the suspect set. If it outputs an author, it merely means that the document in question is written in a style that is more similar to that author's style than the other suspects, and the probability estimates of the classifier reflect only the suspect who is the "least-worst" choice.

Meanwhile, the absence of the document author from the set of suspects remains unknown. This problem is significant in online domains where the number of potential suspects can be virtually unbounded. Failing to address the limitations of closed-world models can result in falsely-attributed authors with consequences for both forensic analysts and innocent Internet users.

3.   Related Work

Open-world classification deals with scenarios in which the set of classes is not known in advance. Approaches include unsupervised, semi-supervised and abstaining classification. Unsupervised stylometry clusters instances based on their feature vector distances [1]. Semi-supervised methods are used to identify clusters [26] that are later used in supervised classification. Abstaining classifiers refrain from classification to improve classifier reliability in certain situations, for example, to minimize the misclassification rate by rejecting the results when the confidence of the classifier is low [8, 12]. The CV method is an abstaining classifier that rejects/accepts an underlying classifier output using a verification step based on the distance between the test author and the predicted author. The novelty of this approach is that, unlike other techniques, CV considers the open-world situation where the author may not be in the suspect set.

Another method is to create a model of the closed-world and reject everything that does not fit the model. In biometric authentication systems, such distance-based anomaly detection methods perform well [3].

In authorship classification, one of the authors in a fixed suspect set is attributed to the test document. Current stylometry methods achieve in excess of 80% accuracy with 100 authors [1], more than 30% accuracy with 10,000 authors [18] and greater than 20% precision with 100,000 authors [22]. None of the methods consider the case where the true author is missing. Although stylometric techniques work well, they are easily circumvented by imitating another person or by deliberate obfuscation [5].

The goal of authorship verification is to determine whether or not a document D is written by an author A. This problem is harder than the closed-world stylometry discussed above. Authorship verification is essentially a one-class classification problem. Research in this area primarily employs support vector machines [20, 28], but little work has focused on stylometry.

Most previous work addresses verification for plagiarism detection [10, 29]. The unmasking algorithm [19] is an example of a general approach to verification, which relies on the "depth-of-difference" between document and author models. The algorithm yields 99% accuracy with similar false positive and false negative rates, but it is limited to problems with large training datasets.

Noecker and Ryan [24] propose the distractorless verification method, which avoids using negative samples to model the "not the author" class. They use simplified feature sets constructed only of character or word n-grams, normalized dot-product (cosine distance) and an acceptance threshold. The approach has been evaluated on two corpora [13, 27] with accuracy results up to 88% and 92%, respectively. Noecker and Ryan provide a robust verification framework across different types of writings (language, genre and length independent). However, their results also suffer from low F-scores (up to 47% and 51%), which suggest a skew in the test data (testing more non-matching document-author pairs than matching ones). Section 6.2 takes a closer look at this method along with the error rates.

4. Corpora

The experiments described in this paper focused on two corpora, the Extended-Brennan-Greenstadt (EBG) Adversarial Corpus [4] and the ICWSM 2009 Spinn3r Blog Dataset (Blog Corpus) [6].

The EBG Corpus contains writings of 45 different authors, with at least 6,500 words per author. It also contains adversarial documents, where the authors change their writing styles either by imitating another author (imitation attack) or hiding their styles (obfuscation attack). Most of the evaluations in this paper are performed using the EBG Corpus.

The Spinn3r Blog Corpus from `Spinn3r.com` is a set of 44 million blog posts made between August 1, 2008 and October 1, 2008. The posts include the text as syndicated, as well as metadata such as the blog homepage, timestamps, etc. This dataset was previously used in Internet-scale authorship attribution [22]. Our experiments used a subcorpus of 50 blogs with at least 7,500 words as the Blog Corpus. This Blog Corpus was used as control and evaluated under the same settings as the EBG Corpus in order to avoid overfitting configurations on the latter and generalizing the conclusions.

5. Closed-World Setup

A closed-world classifier was used throughout the research – for the baseline results used to evaluate different methods and as the underlying classifier for the CV method. The linear kernel sequential minimal optimization (SMO) support vector machine from Weka [11] was used with complexity parameter $C = 1$. Support vector machines were selected due to their proven effectiveness for stylometry [14].

In addition to classifier selection, another important part of a stylometric algorithm is the feature set used to quantify the documents prior to learning and classification. The EBG Corpus was originally quantified using the Writeprints feature set [4] based on the Writeprints algorithm [1], which has been shown to be accurate for a large number of authors (more than 90% accuracy for 50 authors). Writeprints uses a complex feature set that quantifies the different linguistic levels of text, including lexical, syntactic and content related features; however, for simplicity, a feature set consisting of one type of feature was chosen. The EBG Corpus was evaluated using ten-fold cross validation with the k most common word n-grams or character n-grams, with k between 50 and 1,000 and n between 1 and 5. The most-common feature selection heuristic is commonly used in stylometry to improve performance and avoid over-fitting [1, 17, 24], as are the chosen ranges of k and n.

Character n-grams performed best, yielding the highest F1-score at approximately 0.93 (for $k = 400$ and higher). The word and character feature sets both outperformed the original EBG evaluation with Writeprints (F1-score of 0.832 [4]). We chose the 500 most common character bigrams as the feature set (F1-score of 0.928) for all the experiments; this is denoted by $\langle 500, 2 \rangle$-Chars. The choice was made due to its simplicity, performance and effectiveness. Note that $\langle 500, 2 \rangle$-Chars also outperformed Writeprints on the control corpus with an F1-score of 0.64 compared with 0.509. All the feature extractions were performed using the JStylo [21] and JGAAP authorship attribution framework APIs.

6.   Verification

Authorship verification seeks to determine if a document D is written by an author A. Two naïve approaches suggest themselves. The first and most intuitive is to reduce the problem to closed-world settings by creating a model for not-A (simply from documents not written by A) and to train a binary classifier. This method suffers from a fundamental flaw: if D is attributed to A, it merely means that D's style is less distant from A than it is from not-A. The second approach is to train a binary model of D versus A, and test the model on itself using cross-validation. If D is written by A, the accuracy should be close to random due to the indistinguishability of the models. However, this method does not work well and requires D to contain a substantial amount of text for cross-validation, an uncommon privilege in real-world scenarios.

The following sections discuss and evaluate several verification methods. The first family of methods comprises classifier-induced verifiers, which require an underlying (closed-world) classifier and utilize its class probabilities output for verification. The second family of methods comprises standalone verifiers, which rely on a model built using author training data, independent of other authors and classifiers. Two verification methods are evaluated. The first is the distractorless verification method [24] denoted by V. It is presented as a baseline because it is a straightforward verification method that has been shown to be robust across different domains and does not use a distractor set (model of not-A). The second is the novel sigma verification method, which applies adjustments to V for increased accuracy: adding per-feature standard deviation normalization (denoted by V_σ) and adding per-author threshold normalization (denoted by V^a). Finally, V is evaluated and compared with its new variants.

6.1 Classifier-Induced Verification

A promising aspect of the closed-world model that can be used in open-world scenarios is the confidence in solutions provided by distance-based classifiers. A higher confidence in an author may, naturally, indicate that the author is a suspect while a lower confidence may indicate that he is not and this problem is, in fact, an open-world one.

Following classification, verification can be formulated simply by setting an acceptance threshold t, measuring the confidence of the classifier in its result, and accepting the classification if it is above t.

Next, we discuss several verification schemes based on the classification probabilities output by a closed-world classifier. For each test document D with suspect authors $\mathcal{A} = \{A_1, ..., A_n\}$, a classifier produces a list of probabilities P_{A_i} which is, according to the classifier, the probability D is written by A_i ($\sum_{i=1}^{n} P_{A_i} = 1$). We denote the probabilities $P_1, ..., P_n$ as the reverse order statistic of P_{A_i}, i.e., P_1 is the highest probability given to some author (chosen author), P_2 the second highest, and so on.

These methods are obviously limited to classify-verify scenarios because verification is dependent on classification results (thus, they are not evaluated in this section, but in Section 8 as part of the CV evaluation). For this purpose and in order to extract the probability measurements required by the following methods, SMO support vector machine classifiers were used with the $\langle 500, 2\rangle$-Chars feature set for all the experiments described in Section 8. Logistic regression models were fitted to the support vector machine outputs to obtain proper probability estimates.

The following classifier-induced verification methods are evaluated:

- **P_1:** This measurement is simply the classifier probability output for the chosen author, namely P_1. The hypothesis behind this measurement is that as the likelihood that the top author is the true author increases, relative to all others, so does its corresponding probability.

- **P_1-P_2-Diff:** This measurement captures the difference between the classifier probability outputs of the chosen and second-choice authors, i.e., $P_1 - P_2$; it is referred to as the P_1-P_2-*Diff* method.

- **Gap-Conf:** In the case of the gap confidence method [25], one support vector machine classifier is not trained; instead, for all n authors, the corresponding n one-versus-all support vector machines are trained. For a given document D, each classifier i produces two probabilities: the probability that D is written by A_i and the probability that it is written by an author other than A_i. For each i, if $p^i(\text{Yes}|D)$ denotes the probability that D is written by A_i, then the gap confidence is the difference between the highest and second-highest $p^i(\text{Yes}|D)$, which we denote briefly as *Gap-Conf*. The hypothesis is similar to P_1-P_2-*Diff*: the probability of the true author should be much higher than that of the second-best choice.

6.2   Standalone Verification

The following methods are evaluated:

- **Distractorless Verification (V):** As discussed above, V uses the straightforward distance combined with a threshold: set an acceptance threshold t, model document D and author A as feature vectors, measure their distance and determine that D is written by A if it is below t.

  For n denoting the size of the chosen feature set, a model $M = \langle m_1, m_2, ..., m_n \rangle$ is built from the centroid of the character or word n-gram feature vectors of A's documents. For each i, m_i is the average relative frequency of feature i across A's documents, where the relative frequency is used to eliminate document length variation effects. In addition, a feature vector $F = \langle f_1, f_2, ..., f_n \rangle$ is extracted from D, where f_i corresponds to the relative frequency of feature i in D.

Finally, a distance function δ and a threshold t are set, such that if $\delta(x, y) < \delta(x, z)$, x is considered to be closer to y than to z. A normalized dot-product (cosine distance) is used:

$$\delta(M, F) = \frac{M \cdot F}{\|M\|\|F\|} = \frac{\sum_{i=1}^n m_i f_i}{\sqrt{\sum_{i=1}^n m_i^2}\sqrt{\sum_{i=1}^n f_i^2}}.$$

This measure has been shown to be effective for stylometry [23] and efficient for large datasets. Note that "closer to" is defined using $>$ instead of $<$, which is consistent with the cosine distance (where a value of one is a perfect match). However, we use $<$ as the more intuitive direction (according to which a smaller distance means a better match), and adjust the cosine distance δ in the equation above to $1 - \delta$.

The threshold t is set such that D is written by A is determined when $\delta(M, F) < t$. Ideally, it is empirically determined by analysis of the average δ between the author's training documents; however, the evaluation in [24] uses a hardcoded threshold that does not take the author-wise δ values into account (which V^a does, as shown below).

- **Per-Feature SD Normalization (V_σ):** The first suggested improvement to V is based on the variance of the author's writing style. If an author has a style that does not vary much, a tighter bound for verification is required, whereas for a more varied style, the model can be loosened to be more accepting. To do so, the standard deviation (SD) of an author on a per-feature basis is used. For each author, the SD of all of the author's features is determined. When computing the distance between an author and a document, each feature-distance is divided by its SD, so if the SD is smaller, then A and D move closer together, otherwise they move farther apart. This idea is applied in [3] for authentication using typing biometrics; however, its application to stylometric verification is novel.

- **Per-Author Threshold Normalization (V^a):** The second proposed improvement is to adjust the verification threshold t on a per-author basis based on the average pairwise distance between all the author's documents; this is denoted by δ_A. V does not take this into account and instead uses a hard threshold. Using δ_A to determine the threshold is, intuitively, an improvement because it accounts for the spread of the documents written by an author. This allows the model to relax if the author has a more varied style. As in the case of V, this "varying" threshold is still applied by setting a fixed threshold t across all authors, determined empirically over the training set. However, for V^a, every author-document distance measurement δ is adjusted by subtracting δ_A before being compared with t, thus allowing per-author thresholds but still requiring the user to set only one fixed threshold value.

The three methods described above were evaluated based on their false positive (FP) and false negative (FN) rates measured on the EBG Corpus and the Blog Corpus as control. The EBG Corpus was evaluated only on the non-adversarial documents, and the Blog Corpus was evaluated in its entirety. Ten-fold cross-validation with the $\langle 500, 2 \rangle$-Chars feature set was used; the author models were built using the training documents. In each fold, every test document was tested against every one of the author models, including its own (trained on other documents by the author).

When applied to the EBG Corpus, V_σ significantly outperformed V for $FP \geq 0.05$ with a confidence level of $p\text{-}val < 0.01$. Similarly, V_σ^a outperformed V for $FP \geq 0.114$. However, different results were obtained for the Blog Corpus, where V significantly outperformed both V_σ and V_σ^a. The differences could be explained by the corpora characteristics: the EBG Corpus is a cleaner and more stylistically consistent corpus consisting of all English formal writing samples (essays originally written for business or academic purposes), whereas the Blog Corpus contains less structured and formal language, which reduces the distinguishable effects of style variance normalization. This notion is supported by the better performance for the EBG Corpus compared with the Blog Corpus (larger area under the receiver operator curve). Clearly, the results suggest that one method is not preferred over the other, and selecting a verifier for a problem should rely on empirical testing over stylistically similar training data.

For both corpora, V_σ^a outperformed V_σ starting at $FP = 0.27$ and $FP = 0.22$ for the EBG and Blog Corpora, respectively. These properties allow verification approaches to be used according to need, dependent on the FP and FN error rate constraints that a specific problem may impose.

7.   Classify-Verify

The CV method employs an abstaining classifier [8], i.e., a classifier that refrains from classification in certain cases to reduce misclassifications. CV combines classification with verification to expand closed-world authorship problems to the open-world essentially by adding the "unknown" class. Another aspect of the novelty of the CV method is the utilization of abstaining classification methods to upgrade from closed-world to open-world, where the methods for thwarting misclassifications are evaluated based on how they apply to those that originate outside the assumed suspect set, instead of simply missing the true suspect.

First, closed-world classification is applied to the document D in question and the author suspect set $\mathcal{A} = \{A_1, ..., A_n\}$ (i.e., sample documents). Then, the output of the classifier $A_i \in \mathcal{A}$ is given to the verifier to determine the final output. Feeding only the classifier result to the verifier leverages the high accuracy of classifiers, which outperform verifiers in closed-world settings, thus focusing the verifier only on the top choice author in $\mathcal{A}$. The verifier determines whether to accept A_i or reject by returning $\perp$ based on a verification threshold t. CV is essentially a classifier over the suspect set $\mathcal{A} \cup \{\perp\}$.

The threshold t selection process can be automated with respect to varying expected portions of in-set and not-in-set documents. The likelihood of D's author being in $\mathcal{A}$, the expected in-set documents fraction, is denoted by $p = Pr[A_D \in \mathcal{A}]$ (making the likelihood of the expected not-in-set documents $1 - p$). In addition, $p\langle measure \rangle$ refers to the weighted average of the measure with respect to p. For instance, p-$F1$ is the weighted F1-score, weighted over F1-scores of p expected in-set documents and $1 - p$ expected not-in-set documents. Thus, the threshold t can be determined in several ways:

- **Manual:** The threshold t can be manually set by the user. The threshold determines the sensitivity of the verifier, so setting t manually adjusts it from strict to relaxed, where the stricter it is, the less likely it is to accept the classifier output. This enables the algorithm to be tuned to different settings, imposing the desired rigidity.

- **p-Induced Threshold:** The threshold can be set empirically over the training set to maximize the target measurement, e.g., F1-score, in an automated process. If p is given, then the algorithm applies cross-validation on the training data alone using the range of all relevant manually-set thresholds and chooses the threshold that yields the best target measurement. This essentially applies CV recursively on the training data one level deeper with a range of manual thresholds. The relevant threshold search range is determined automatically by the minimum and maximum distances observed in the verify phase of CV.

- **In-Set/Not-In-Set-Robust:** If the expected in-set and not-in-set documents proportion is unknown, the same idea as in the

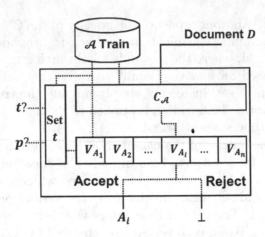

Figure 1. CV method flow.

previously described threshold can be applied. Upon examining the CV F1-score curve for some p along a range of thresholds, if p increases, then it favors smaller (more accepting) thresholds, therefore the curve behaves differently for different values of p. However, all the curves intersect at one t – at which the in-set and not-in-set curves intersect. This can be utilized to automatically obtain a robust threshold for any value of p by taking the thresholds that minimize the difference between the p-$F1$ and q-$F1$ curves for arbitrary $p, q \in [0, 1]$ (for simplicity, values of 0.3 and 0.7 are used). The robust threshold does not guarantee the highest measurement; it does, however, guarantee a relatively high expected value of the measure independent of p, and is, thus, robust for any open-world settings. This measurement is denoted by p-$\langle measure \rangle_R$ (for robust), e.g., p-$F1_R$.

Figure 1 shows the flow of the CV algorithm on a test document D and a suspect set $\mathcal{A}$ with optional threshold t and in-set portion p.

8.   Evaluation and Results

This section describes the evaluation methodology and the experimental results.

8.1   Evaluation Methodology

Main Experiment. The main experiment evaluated the CV method on the EBG Corpus (excluding the adversarial documents) and the Blog Corpus as control. The corpora were evaluated in two settings: when the authors of the documents under test were in the set of suspects (in-set) and when they were not (not-in-set).

Each classification over n authors $\mathcal{A} = \{A_1, ..., A_n\}$ produces one of $n+1$ outputs: an author $A_i \in \mathcal{A}$ or $\perp$ ("unknown"). Therefore, when the verifier accepts, the final result is the author A_i chosen by the classifier, and when it rejects, the final result is $\perp$.

In the evaluation process, the CV algorithm was credited when the verification step thwarted misclassifications in in-set settings. For instance, if D was written by A, classified as B, but the verifier replaced B with $\perp$, the result was considered to be true. This approach for abstaining classifiers [12] relies on the fact that a result of "unknown" is better than an incorrect author.

The overall performance was evaluated using ten-fold cross-validation. For each fold experiment, with nine of the folds as the training set and one fold as the test set, every test document was evaluated twice: once as in-set and once as not-in-set.

For the classification phase of CV over n authors, n $(n-1)$-class classifiers were trained, where each classifier C_i was trained on all the authors except for A_i. A test document by some author A_i was then classified as in-set using one of the $n-1$ classifiers that were trained on A_i training data; for simplicity, we chose C_{i+1} (and C_1 for A_n). For the not-in-set classification, the classifier that was not trained on A_i, i.e., C_i, was employed.

For the verification phase of CV, several methods were evaluated: one standalone method (V_σ for the EBG Corpus and V for the Blog Corpus), *Gap-Conf*, P_1 and P_1-P_2-*Diff*. V_σ was used for the EBG Corpus and V for the Blog Corpus because these methods outperformed the other standalone methods evaluated per corpus as discussed in Section 6.

The more the verifiers reject, the higher the precision (because bad classifications are thrown away), but the recall decreases (as good classifications are thrown away as well), and vice-versa – higher acceptance increases recall but decreases precision. Therefore, the overall performance is measured using the F1-score, since it provides a balanced measurement of precision and recall:

$$F1\text{-}score = 2 \times \frac{precision \times recall}{precision + recall}$$

where

$$precision = \frac{tp}{tp + fp}; \qquad recall = \frac{tp}{tp + fn}.$$

The two automatic verification threshold selection methods discussed in Section 7 were used. For the scenario in which the proportion of in-set and not-in-set is known with the in-set proportion $p = 0.5$ (the not-in-set proportion is $1 - p$), we used the p-induced threshold that maximizes the F1-score on the training set. For the scenario in which p is unknown, we used the robust threshold configured as described in Section 7. In order to calculate the F1-score of evaluating the test set, the confusion matrices produced by the in-set and not-in-set evaluations were combined to form a p-weighted average matrix, from which the weighted F1-score was calculated. The p-induced F1-scores is denoted by p-$F1$ and robust threshold induced F1-scores evaluated at some p is denoted by p-$F1_R$.

The threshold optimization phase of the CV method discussed in Section 7 was performed using nine-fold cross-validation with the same experimental settings as in the main experiment. Since the F1-score was used to evaluate the overall performance, it was also used as the target measurement to maximize in the automatic threshold optimization phase. When p was known, the threshold that maximizes p-$F1$ was selected, and when it was unknown, the robust threshold was selected as the one for which the F1-scores of different p values intersect (arbitrarily set to 0.3-$F1$ and 0.7-$F1$).

As a baseline, the F1-scores were compared with ten-fold cross-validation results of closed-world classification using the underlying classifier, SMO support vector machine with the $\langle 500, 2 \rangle$-Chars feature set. Let p-$Base$ be the baseline F1-score of the closed-world classifier where the in-set proportion is p. It follows that 1-$Base$ is the performance in pure closed-world settings (i.e., only in-set documents) and for any $p \in [0, 1]$, p-$Base = p \cdot 1$-$Base$ (since the classifier is always wrong for not-in-set documents).

Adversarial Settings.   To evaluate the CV method in adversarial settings, the models were trained on the non-adversarial documents in the EBG Corpus, and tested on the imitation and obfuscation attack documents to measure how well CV thwarted attacks (by returning $\perp$ instead of a wrong author). In this context, $\perp$ can be considered as either "unknown" or "possible-attack." The term 0.5-$F1$ was measured, i.e., how well CV performed on attack documents in an open-world scenario where the verification threshold was set independent of a possible attack, tuned only to maximize performance on expected in-set and not-in-set document portions of 50% each. As a baseline, the results with standard classification using SMO support vector machine were compared with the $\langle 500, 2 \rangle$-Chars feature set.

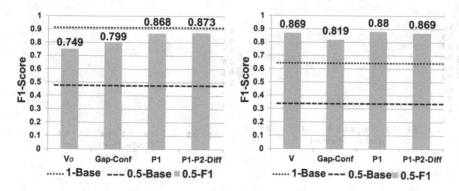

Figure 2. 0.5-F1 results for the EBG Corpus (left) and Blog Corpus (right).

8.2 Results

Main Experiment. For the EBG Corpus, the baseline closed-world classifier attained 1-$Base$ = 0.928 in perfect in-set settings, which implies that 0.5-$Base$ = 0.464. For the Blog Corpus, 1-$Base$ = 0.64, which implies that 0.5-$Base$ = 0.32. Figure 2 shows the 0.5-F1 results for the CV method on the EBG and Blog Corpora, where the authors are equally likely to be in-set or not-in-set ($p = 0.5$) and the verification thresholds were automatically selected to maximize 0.5-F1. For the EBG and Blog Corpora, the CV 0.5-F1 results significantly outperform 0.5-$Base$ (dashed lines) for all the underlying verification methods at a confidence level of p-val < 0.01.

Furthermore, the results are not only better than the obviously bad 0.5-$Base$, but produce similar results to 1-$Base$, giving an overall 0.5-F1 for open-world settings up to approximately 0.87. For the EBG Corpus, moving to open-world settings only slightly decreases the F1-score compared with the closed-world classifier performance in closed-world settings (dotted line in Figure 2), which is a reasonable penalty for upgrading to open-world settings. However, for the Blog Corpus, where the initial 1-$Base$ is low (0.64), CV manages to upgrade to open-world settings and outperform 1-$Base$. These results suggest that out of the in-set documents, many misclassifications were thwarted by the underlying verifiers, leading to an overall increase in the F1-score.

Next, the robust threshold selection scheme was evaluated. In this scenario, the portion of in-set documents p was not known in advance. Figure 3 shows the p-$F1_R$ results for the EBG and Blog Corpora, where different p scenarios were "thrown" at the CV classifier with robust verification thresholds. The expected portion of in-set documents p var-

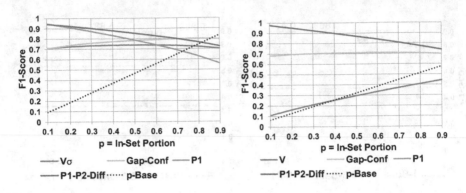

Figure 3. p-$F1_R$ results for the EBG Corpus (left) and Blog Corpus (right).

ied from 10% to 90% and was assumed to be unknown, and robust p-independent thresholds were used for the underlying verifiers.

In the robust thresholds scenario with the EBG Corpus, CV still significantly outperforms the respective closed-world classifier (p-$Base$ results) for $p < 0.7$ with any of the underlying verifiers at a confidence level of p-$val < 0.01$. For the Blog Corpus, CV significantly outperforms p-$Base$ using any of the classifier-induced verifiers for all p at a confidence level of p-$val < 0.01$.

Moreover, the robust threshold selection hypothesis holds true, and for both corpora all the methods (with the exception of V on the Blog Corpus) manage to guarantee a high F1-score at approximately 0.7 and above for almost all values of p. For the EBG Corpus, at $p \geq 0.7$ the in-set portion is large enough that the overall p-$Base$ becomes similar to p-$F1_R$. For the Blog Corpus, using V fails and has a similar performance as 0.5-$Base$.

P_1-P_2-$Diff$ is the preferred verification method. It consistently outperforms the other methods across almost all values of p for both corpora, which implies that it is robust to domain variation.

Adversarial Settings. Evaluated on the EBG Corpus under imitation and obfuscation attacks, the baseline closed-world classifier yields F1-scores of 0 and 0.044 for the imitation and obfuscation attack documents, respectively. The results imply that the closed-world classifier is highly vulnerable to these types of attacks. Figure 4 shows the F1-scores for CV on the attack documents. Note that all attack documents were written by in-set authors and were, thus, handled as in-set documents.

The results suggest that CV successfully manages to thwart the majority of the attacks, with F1-scores up to 0.826 and 0.874 for the imitation and obfuscation attacks, respectively. These results are very close to the

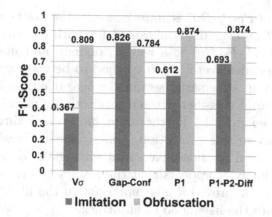

Figure 4. F1-scores for the EBG Corpus under imitation and obfuscation attacks.

deception detection results reported in [2] with F1-scores of 0.895 for imitation and 0.85 for obfuscation attacks. A major difference is that the results in this paper were obtained in open-world settings with a threshold configuration that does not consider inside-attacks. Moreover, unlike the methods applied in [2], no attack documents were used as training data.

Interestingly, the results presented above were obtained for a standard $p = 0.5$ open-world scenario, without possible attacks in mind. Still, the overall results were affected very little, if at all, depending on the underlying verifier. For example, when using *Gap-Conf*, 0.5-*F1* is at 0.799 in non-attack scenarios and the F1-scores range from 0.784 to 0.826 under attack.

9.   Discussion

The evaluation results suggest that classifier-induced verifiers consistently outperform standalone verifiers. However, this trend may be limited to large datasets with many suspect authors in the underlying classifier, like those evaluated in this paper, on which classifier-induced verifications rely. It may be the case that standalone verifiers perform better for small author sets; this direction should be explored in future research. Moreover, standalone verifiers provide reasonable accuracy that enables them to be used in pure one-class settings, where only true author data exists (a scenario in which classifier-induced methods are useless).

The CV 0.5-*F1* results for the EBG and Blog Corpora (Figure 2) suggest that using P_1 or P_1-P_2-*Diff* as the underlying verification method yield domain-independent results for which 0.5-*F1* is approximately 0.87.

The superiority of P_1-P_2-*Diff* is emphasized by the p-$F1_R$ results in Figure 3, where p-$F1_R$ over 0.7 is obtained for both corpora independent of p. Therefore, P_1-P_2-*Diff* is a robust, domain and in-set/not-in-set proportion independent verification method to be used with CV.

CV is effective in adversarial settings, where it outperforms the traditional closed-world classifier without any training on adversarial data (which is required in [2]). Furthermore, no special threshold tuning is needed to achieve this protection, i.e., standard threshold selection schemes can be used for non-adversarial settings while still thwarting most attacks. Finally, it appears that the results in adversarial settings can potentially be improved if p is tuned not to the likelihood of in-set documents, but to the likelihood of an attack.

10.   Conclusions

From a forensic perspective, the possibility of authors outside the suspect set renders closed-world classifiers unreliable. In addition, whether linguistic authorship attribution can handle open-world scenarios has important privacy ramifications for authors of anonymous texts and individuals who are falsely implicated by erroneous results. Indeed, when the closed-world assumption is violated, traditional stylometric approaches do not fail in a graceful manner.

The CV method proposed in this paper can handle open-world settings where the author of a document may not be in the training set, and can also improve the results in closed-world settings by abstaining from low-confidence classification decisions. Furthermore, the method can filter attacks as demonstrated on the adversarial samples in the EBG Corpus. In all these settings, the CV method replaces wrong assertions with the more honest and useful result of "unknown."

The CV method is clearly preferable to the standard closed-world classifier. This is true regardless of the expected in-set/not-in-set ratio, and in adversarial settings as well. Moreover, the general nature of the CV algorithm enables it to be applied with any stylometric classifiers and verifiers.

Our future research will pursue three avenues. The first is to apply the CV method to other problems such as behavioral biometrics using, for example, the Active Linguistic Authentication dataset [16]. The second is to attempt to fuse verification methods using the Chair-Varshney optimal fusion rule [7] to reduce error rates. The third avenue is to investigate the scalability of the CV method to large problems while maintaining its accuracy.

References

[1] A. Abbasi and H. Chen, Writeprints: A stylometric approach to identity-level identification and similarity detection in cyberspace, *ACM Transactions on Information Systems*, vol. 26(2), pp. 7:1–7:29, 2008.

[2] S. Afroz, M. Brennan and R. Greenstadt, Detecting hoaxes, frauds and deception in writing style online, *Proceedings of the IEEE Symposium on Security and Privacy*, pp. 461–475, 2012.

[3] L. Araujo, L. Sucupira, M. Lizarraga, L. Ling and J. Yabu-Uti, User authentication through typing biometrics features, *IEEE Transactions on Signal Processing*, vol. 53(2), pp. 851–855, 2005.

[4] M. Brennan, S. Afroz and R. Greenstadt, Adversarial stylometry: Circumventing authorship recognition to preserve privacy and anonymity, *ACM Transactions on Information and System Security*, vol. 15(3), pp. 12:1–12:22, 2012.

[5] M. Brennan and R. Greenstadt, Practical attacks against authorship recognition techniques, *Proceedings of the Twenty-First Conference on Innovative Applications of Artificial Intelligence*, pp. 60–65, 2009.

[6] K. Burton, A. Java and I. Soboroff, The ICWSM 2009 Spinn3r Dataset, *Proceedings of the Third Annual Conference on Weblogs and Social Media*, 2009.

[7] Z. Chair and P. Varshney, Optimal data fusion in multiple sensor detection systems, *IEEE Transactions on Aerospace and Electronic Systems*, vol. AES-22(1), pp. 98–101, 1986.

[8] C. Chow, On optimum recognition error and reject tradeoff, *IEEE Transactions on Information Theory*, vol. 16(1), pp. 41–46, 1970.

[9] A. Clark, Forensic Stylometric Authorship Analysis Under the Daubert Standard, University of the District of Comumbia, Washington, DC (`papers.ssrn.com/sol3/papers.cfm?abstract_id=2039824`), 2011.

[10] P. Clough, Plagiarism in Natural and Programming Languages: An Overview of Current tools and Technologies, Technical Report, Department of Computer Science, University of Sheffield, Sheffield, United Kingdom, 2000.

[11] M. Hall, E. Frank, G. Holmes, B. Pfahringer, P. Reutemann and I. Witten, The Weka Data Mining Software: An update, *SIGKDD Explorations Newsletter*, vol. 11(1), pp. 10–18, 2009.

[12] R. Herbei and M. Wegkamp, Classification with reject option, *Canadian Journal of Statistics*, vol. 34(4), pp. 709–721, 2006.

[13] P. Juola, Ad hoc Authorship Attribution Competition, *Proceedings of the Joint International Conference of the Association for Literary and Linguistic Computing and the Association for Computers and the Humanities*, 2004.

[14] P. Juola, Authorship attribution, *Foundations and Trends in Information Retrieval*, vol. 1(3), pp. 233–334, 2008.

[15] P. Juola, Stylometry and immigration: A case study, *Journal of Law and Policy*, vol. 21(2), pp. 287–298, 2013.

[16] P. Juola, J. Noecker, A. Stolerman, M. Ryan, P. Brennan and R. Greenstadt, A dataset for active linguistic authentication, in *Advances in Digital Forensics IX*, G. Peterson and S. Shenoi (Eds.), Springer, Heidelberg, Germany, pp. 385–398, 2013.

[17] M. Koppel and J. Schler, Authorship verification as a one-class classification problem, *Proceedings of the Twenty-First International Conference on Machine Learning*, 2004.

[18] M. Koppel, J. Schler and S. Argamon, Authorship attribution in the wild, *Language Resources and Evaluation*, vol. 45(1), pp. 83–94, 2011.

[19] M. Koppel, J. Schler and E. Bonchek-Dokow, Measuring differentiability: Unmasking pseudonymous authors, *Journal of Machine Learning Research*, vol. 8(2), pp. 1261–1276, 2007.

[20] L. Manevitz and M. Yousef, One-class document classification via neural networks, *Neurocomputing*, vol. 70(7-9), pp. 1466–1481, 2007.

[21] A. McDonald, S. Afroz, A. Caliskan, A. Stolerman and R. Greenstadt, Use fewer instances of the letter "i:" Toward writing style anonymization, in *Privacy Enhancing Technologies*, S. Fischer-Hubner and M. Wright (Eds.), Springer-Verlag, Berlin, Germany, pp. 299–318, 2012.

[22] A. Narayanan, H. Paskov, N. Gong, J. Bethencourt, E. Stefanov, R. Shin and D. Song, On the feasibility of Internet-scale author identification, *Proceedings of the IEEE Symposium on Security and Privacy*, pp. 300–314, 2012.

[23] J. Noecker and P. Juola, Cosine distance nearest-neighbor classification for authorship attribution, presented at the *Digital Humanities Conference*, 2009.

[24] J. Noecker and M. Ryan, Distractorless authorship verification, *Proceedings of the Eight International Conference on Language Resources and Evaluation*, pp. 785–789, 2012.

[25] H. Paskov, A Regularization Framework for Active Learning from Imbalanced Data, M. Engg. Thesis, Department of Electrical Engineering and Computer Science, Massachusetts Institute of Technology, Cambridge, Massachusetts, 2010.

[26] E. Sorio, A. Bartoli, G. Davanzo and E. Medvet, Open world classification of printed invoices, *Proceedings of the Tenth ACM Symposium on Document Engineering*, pp. 187–190, 2010.

[27] B. Stein, M. Potthast, P. Rosso, A. Barron-Cedeno, E. Stamatatos and M. Koppel, Workshop report: Fourth International Workshop on Uncovering Plagiarism, Authorship and Social Software Misuse, *ACM SIGIR Forum*, vol. 45(1), pp. 45-48, 2011.

[28] D. Tax, One-Class Classification, Ph.D. Dissertation, Faculty of Applied Physics, Delft University of Technology, Delft, The Natherlands, 2001.

[29] H. van Halteren, Linguistic profiling for authorship recognition and verification, *Proceedings of the Forty-Second Annual Meeting of the Association for Computational Linguistics*, art. 199, 2004.

III

MOBILE DEVICE FORENSICS

Chapter 14

PRESERVING DATES AND TIMESTAMPS FOR INCIDENT HANDLING IN ANDROID SMARTPHONES

Robin Verma, Jayaprakash Govindaraj, and Gaurav Gupta

Abstract The "bring your own device" (BYOD) policy is rapidly being adopted by enterprises around the world. Enterprises save time and money when they allow employees to bring their own electronic devices to the workplace; employees find it convenient and efficient to use a single device for professional and personal use. However, securing the personal and professional data in the devices is a huge challenge for employers and employees. Dates and timestamps constitute important evidence when devices have been compromised or used for illegal activities. This paper focuses on the malicious tampering of dates and timestamps in Android smartphones. The proposed reactive approach gathers kernel-generated timestamps of events and stores them in a secure location outside an Android smartphone. In the case of a security incident, the stored timestamps can assist in an offline digital forensic investigation. To our knowledge, this is the first attempt to preserve authentic Android event timestamps in order to detect potential malicious actions, including anti-forensic measures.

Keywords: Android smartphones, dates and timestamps, preservation

1. Introduction

The growth and adoption of smartphones have gathered pace during the past five years. According to a Gartner report [12], during the second quarter of 2013, the sales of smartphones surpassed the sales of feature phones and accounts, corresponding to 51.8% of market share, which amounted to approximately 225 million units. In the same report, Gartner notes that Android, an open source mobile operating system, leads the smartphone operating system market with a 79.0% share. According to the International Data Corporation [16], Android dominated the

G. Peterson and S. Shenoi (Eds.): Advances in Digital Forensics X, IFIP AICT 433, pp. 209–225, 2014.
© IFIP International Federation for Information Processing 2014

smartphone operating system market during 2013, with around 75.3%
of the share, and will continue to dominate until 2017.

In a May 2013 survey, the Pew Research Center [27] noted that 61%
of American cell phone owners have smartphones, out of which 28% own
Android devices. Most people prefer to have one device for both personal
and professional needs, so instead of taking a new device from their
employers, they bring their personal devices to the workplace. This has
given rise to the "bring your own device" (BYOD) trend that is catching
on around the world [19]. According to another Gartner report [29], 50%
of the companies are expected to allow their employees to carry their own
devices by 2017, and the majority of these devices will be smartphones
and tablets.

In an enterprise environment, the BYOD policy helps employers save
on the cost of devices and services, and enables employees to conveniently
manage their personal and professional data on a single device. However,
BYOD also has opened up new windows of opportunities for fraudsters
to access, modify, edit and steal information, and then cover their tracks
by tampering with data on the devices. Indeed, personal mobile devices
are one of the weakest links for gaining unauthorized access to enterprise
networks and carrying out malicious actions.

In a BYOD environment, the incentive for stealing information from
a phone is high because both personal and corporate data are stored on
the same device [19]. Access control restrictions imposed on files can
protect against unauthorized access by someone other than the owner
of the device; however, access control fails if the device owner decides
to compromise security or adopts a cavalier attitude regarding device
security. To hide their tracks, malicious individuals could attempt to
tamper with metadata, including modification, access, change and/or
creation dates and timestamps (MAC DTSs) to match the MAC DTSs
that existed before the malicious access.

MAC DTSs of digital data on a smartphone constitute fundamental
evidence in digital forensic investigations. Thus, establishing the authenticity of the recovered MAC DTSs is of prime importance. Malicious
tampering of MAC DTSs mainly involves modifying dates and timestamps and/or file contents. Commercial tools, including the Cellebrite
Universal Forensic Extraction Device (UFED) system and FTK Mobile
Phone Examiner, can recover mobile device data; however, most of them
prove to be inadequate when attempting to establish the authenticity of
MAC DTSs.

This paper demonstrates that tampering with MAC DTSs on Android
smartphones is possible using anti-forensic techniques. A mechanism
is described for preserving dates and timestamps for incident handling

involving Android smartphones. System-generated MAC DTSs are collected with the aid of a loadable kernel module (LKM) [14], which hooks system calls to capture the values. The dates and timestamps, along with location details, are stored as event logs in a secure location outside the smartphone (e.g., a local enterprise server or the cloud). In the event of a security incident, the stored data and timestamps can assist in an offline digital forensic investigation.

2. Related Work

Weil [28] has shown that dynamic date and timestamp analysis can determine the actual times of events on a personal computer (especially when they are not available or tampered with) by utilizing an external source of data-time data. Carrier and Spafford [7] have suggested that dynamic timeline analysis is essential to reconstructing digital events after a security incident and identifying the suspects. To implement these ideas, a customized forensic tool named Zeitline was developed by Buchholz and Falk [6] that creates timelines from various sources and presents the details via a graphical interface; however, the tool has certain limitations in handling clock differences and clock drifts. An improved tool, Cyber-Forensic Time Lab (CFTL), was created by Olsson and Boldt [20]. A different approach to address the same problem is described by Marrington, *et al.* [18], who trace computer activity timelines by utilizing the "causality" of events in computer systems. Their tool extracts the MAC timestamps from a hard drive and correlates events according to their causality. However, the problem of MAC timestamp tampering was not been addressed in their implementation, which leads to certain irregularities in the results.

Barik, *et al.* [4] were the first to propose the logging of MAC DTSs for filesystems. Das, *et al.* [8] and Ansari, *et al.* [2] have enhanced this approach for use in filesystem intrusion detection. All three works focus on Linux systems with conventional hard disk drives as storage media. In contrast, this paper describes an Android solution that has considerable differences in terms of functionality and implementation.

Grover [11] has proposed an enterprise monitoring application, "Droid-Watch," that continuously collects data from Android phones. The collected data sets are uploaded to an enterprise server for assisting security personnel in monitoring, auditing and responding to incidents and conducting forensic investigations. However, the approach is not secure against root attacks and application uninstallation attacks.

Android phone anti-forensics is also an important related area of research. Distefano, *et al.* [9] have devised an anti-forensic technique that uses the private folder of an installed Android application to hide counterfeit evidence; they propose a safe uninstallation process to hide evidence of tampering. Albano, *et al.* [1] have demonstrated that the timestamps of tampered files can be restored without raising suspicion and without leaving any traces in the filesystem. However, their method is only able to change the contents of the storage media; data that has been uploaded to a location external to device is untouched.

Linux security modules (LSMs) were created as a framework to support security functionality [26]. Security modules that have been implemented include Security Enhanced Linux (SELinux), AppArmor, Smack and TOMOYO Linux. Shabtai, *et al.* [24] have implemented SELinux on an Android platform to perform strict access control. The steps involved compiling the kernel with SELinux support, followed by designing an Android-specific security policy. The standard startup processes and supporting scripts were modified to load the new policy at startup. In the final step, the Android disk image (popularly called ROM) was created to be flushed on the phone.

In 2012, the National Security Agency specified the SEAndroid standard [25] for implementing SELinux on Android devices; the SELinux-enabled Android has been successfully tested against most contemporary exploits that seek to gain root access. Shabtai, *et al.* [24] and Smalley [25] require that the disk image of an Android phone or tablet be flushed with their own customized ROM, which is impractical in a BYOD environment. Our solution, on the other hand, focuses on preserving the MAC DTSs without reflushing, which keeps the phone data intact and is more suited to a BYOD environment. Additionally, the user's personal data residing on the device is preserved, enabling regular phone use to continue without any impact after the LKM installation.

3.   MAC DTS Tampering

Our research initially focused on developing and testing an attack tool that could tamper with files and their timestamps without leaving forensic evidence. Following this, a tool was developed that could detect such tampering. We selected the HTC Wildfire and Samsung Galaxy S2 GT-I9100 Android phones as prototypes for the research. The two phones were chosen because they represent two ends of the smartphone segment in terms of processing power, storage capacity, battery power and cost. HTC Wildfire is a low-end smartphone with a 0.60 GHz CPU, single core processor, 512 MB RAM and 1230 mAh battery capacity. The Samsung Galaxy S2 is a high-end smartphone with a 1.20 GHz CPU, dual core processor, 1 GB RAM and 1,650 mAh battery capacity.

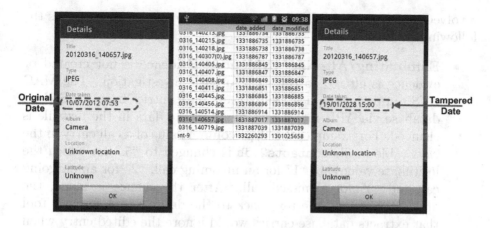

Figure 1. Tampering with the date of a camera image file.

The Android filesystem stores data and the corresponding metadata (including MAC DTS values) in SQLite databases. The data includes phone calls, short message service (SMS) messages, multimedia messaging service (MMS) messages, photographs/video captured by the camera, audio recorded by the microphone and other types of files (e.g., Word, Excel, PDF and text). User applications access the data through various APIs and interfaces controlled by the operating system. Applications need explicit permissions to use the APIs and interfaces; the permissions are generally granted to them at the time of their installation. The Android filesystem ensures that users have no direct access to the SQLite databases by storing them in the restricted internal memory of the phone.

Although Android is claimed to be secure by design, it is possible to bypass the Android security mechanisms (see, e.g., [5, 17]). In fact, several timestamp tampering applications are available. For example, one application named SQLite Editor (available at goo.gl/ppxAXo) can be used to overwrite the timestamps of received SMS messages. We also built a custom application that can tamper with the timestamps of calls, SMS messages, camera images and video files on Android phones. Figure 1 shows screenshots of a camera image file before and after tampering with the date.

3.1 Attack Methodology and Anti-Forensics

Anti-forensic actions seek to destroy or tamper with digital evidence [9, 13]. Specific actions include destroying evidence, hiding evidence, altering evidence and counterfeiting evidence. Our attack methodology involved creating a MAC DTS tampering application that performs the following actions:

- **Eliminating/Altering Evidence:** Evidence is not created or evidence is altered to thwart a forensic investigation. The MAC DTS tampering application extracts data entries from the SQLite database via APIs into a text file, and the data in the text file is changed. For example, the Type column value of a call entry in the *calls* table in file `contacts2.db` is changed to "5," for which the legitimate values are "1" for an incoming call, "2" for an outgoing call and "3" for a missed call. After the change is made, the application writes the text back to the database. A forensic tool that extracts database entries would ignore the edited entry when extracting call records. Several other similar operations can be performed on other potential evidence in a SQLite database.

- **Counterfeiting Evidence:** Fake evidence is implanted to thwart a forensic investigation. For example, the tampering application can overwrite entries in a SQLite database. Also, it can overwrite the logcat buffer that stores the debugging logs.

- **Destroying Evidence:** Evidence is deleted to thwart a forensic investigation. For example, the tampering application can delete the contents of a SQLite database and the logcat buffer.

Note that data retrieval is possible after these anti-forensic actions are performed. However, the retrieval is both costly and time-consuming [10, 22].

Attack Scenario 1. The first scenario assumes that an individual left his Android phone unattended for five to ten minutes, during which time an attacker gained physical access to the phone. The following steps are involved in the attack scenario:

- The phone is connected to a laptop that has Android SDK (open source software development kit) installed.

- The MAC DTS tampering application is installed on the phone via the laptop. The application can be installed even if the phone is locked. However, like all contemporary mobile forensic tools, the USB debugging mode must be enabled.

- The contents of camera image database are extracted to the internal memory folder of the application, following which the file is pulled to the laptop.

- The file metadata and MAC DTSs are modified.

- The updated file is pushed back to the phone and the phone database is updated.

- The logcat entries in the phone are cleared.

The process requires the execution of a small set of simple commands (that could easily be combined into a script). The entire process takes about three minutes (five iterations), ample time to carry out the attack in the real world. Note that physical acquisition from the phone could reveal the deleted data, but this would be expensive and time consuming [22].

Attack Scenario 2. The second scenario assumes that a company employee intends to steal a confidential document. Since the time at which he accessed the document would be suspicious, he accesses the file via his Android phone and modifies the MAC DTS values to hide his tracks. The following steps are involved in the attack scenario:

- The MAC DTS tampering application is installed on the phone.

- The confidential file is accessed and stolen.

- The MAC DTS values are changed to their values before the access.

- The tampering application is uninstalled and the logcat entries are cleared.

4.   Implementation

Our solution for preserving dates and timestamps engages a custom LKM that hooks the sys_open() system call and captures the kernel-level timestamp values of selected files. The timestamps are then uploaded to a secure local server.

Figure 2 shows a schematic diagram of the implementation architecture. Details about the LKM algorithm and the procedures for compiling the LKM and loading the LKM on a phone are provided below. After the LKM is loaded, it reads the MAC DTS values from the phone. The captured values are written to a temporary log file that is stored in the internal memory of the phone. The log file is uploaded to a local server when network connectivity is available.

4.1   LKM Algorithm

The LKM algorithm shown in Figure 3 incorporates four functions: root_start, hacked_open, hacked_unlink and root_stop. Function

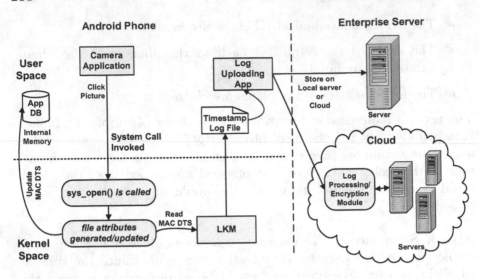

Figure 2.   Preserving dates and timestamps.

`root_start` initializes the log file pointer, sets the `sys_open()` call address to point to the `hacked_open()` call and sets the `sys_unlink()` call address to point to the `hacked_unlink()` call. Function `hacked_open` takes the file path and file attributes as input parameters. If the file path name matches the selected file or folder in the filter array, then the date and timestamp details are written to a log file; following this, control is passed back to the original `sys_open()` call. Function `hacked_unlink` takes the file path name as an input parameter. If the file path matches the log file path, then the delete operation is denied; otherwise, control is passed back to the original `sys_unlink()` call. Function `root_stop` function closes the log file pointer, restores the address back to the original `sys_unlink()` call routine and restores the address back to the original `sys_open()` call routine.

4.2   LKM Compilation

The LKM must be compiled against the kernel source code on which it has to be loaded. The compilation instructions are posted on the Android Open Source Project website (`goo.gl/TQVVV`). The first step is to set up the kernel environment on a computer. Following this, it is necessary to acquire the original kernel source code of the Android version installed on the device. For the two scenarios described above, we downloaded the Android 2.1 Eclair kernel source from HTC [15] and the Android 2.3 Gingerbread kernel source from Samsung [23].

```
Function root_start
  Output: File Pointer to the record.log file
    {Log File Pointer = File Open ("/data/data/record.log")
     Original Sys Open Pointer = sys_call_table[__NR_open]
     Original Sys Unlink Pointer = sys_call_table[__NR_unlink]
     sys_call_table[__NR_open] = Our Sys Open call hacked_open
     sys_call_table[__NR_unlink] = Our Sys Open call hacked_unlink
    }

Function hacked_open
  Input: File Path Name, Flags
  Output: File Pointer to the record.log file
    {Filter = File/Folder path for enabling timestamp logging
     Path Name = Current working directory
     If (Filter = Path Name)
         Log Path Name, Date and Time and File Operation Type ID
     Else
         Return to Original Sys Open Operation
     EndIf
    }

Function hacked_unlink
  Input: File Path Name
    {If (Path Name = Log File Path)
         Return -1    /* Deny log file deletion. */
     Else
         Return to Original Sys Unlink Operation
     EndIf
    }

Function root_stop
  Original Sys Open Pointer, Log File Pointer
    {Restore to Original System Call
     sys_call_table[__NR_open] = Original Sys Open Pointer
     sys_call_table[__NR_unlink] = Original Sys Unlink Pointer
     Close Log File Pointer
    }
```

Figure 3. Algorithm for logging MAC DTS values using the LKM.

The next step is to locate the physical address of the system call table on each phone in order to hook system calls. A mandatory condition for loading the LKM successfully on the phones is that the "vermagic string" (see Table 1 for details) of the kernels and LKMs should match [21].

Table 1.   Smartphones used in the experiment.

Phone	Android Version	Vermagic String	sys_call_table Address
HTC Wildfire	2.1 Eclair	2.6.29-4266b2e1	0xc002bfa4
Samsung Galaxy S2 GT-I9100	2.3 Gingerbread (XWKL1)	2.6.35.7-I9100XWKL1-CL809037	0xc0028fe4

4.3   Loading the LKM

Root permissions (administrative privileges) are required to load the LKM on an Android phone. Generally, temporary rooting is a good option because it involves the least number of changes to the filesystem, which is preferred in digital forensics. We decided to apply temporary rooting on the Samsung Galaxy S2; however, we permanently rooted the HTC wildfire to explore how our solution performs on permanently rooted devices. (As a matter of fact, our solution works seamlessly on temporary and permanently rooted devices.) We followed the rooting instructions listed on the XDA Developers mobile software development community portal (www.xda-developers.com).

Figure 4.   Storing the record.log file in internal memory.

After the phone was rooted, the LKM was loaded. The LKM monitors the events occurring on a selected set of files and directories. It reads the MAC DTS values for these files and writes them to a log file (recordfile.log) on the phone (Figure 4).

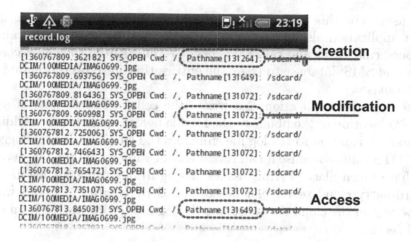

Figure 5. Snapshot of the `record.log` file for camera image `IMAG0699.jpg`.

4.4 Hiding Log File Deletions

The log file is stored in the internal memory of the Android smartphone, which is not accessible directly by applications; thus, the file is secure from deletion attempts. In the event that an attacker manually locates the log file, an attempt to delete it is denied by the LKM module, which bypasses the call to `sys_unlink` (`hacked_unlink()` call); this ensures the security of the log file. The overall approach can be categorized as "anti-anti-forensics," in that, by not allowing deletions, a possibly destructive anti-forensic attempt is foiled.

4.5 Uploading the Log File

The log file generated by the LKM is subsequently uploaded at regular intervals, depending on the availability of network connectivity, to a local server with the help of our uploader application. We used the WAMP software stack on our local server, which runs Apache, PHP and MySQL. The system can easily be extended to use the cloud as external storage for the uploaded logs. The MAC DTS entries for the files (Figure 5) can be identified on the basis of unique flag values associated with operations such as file creation, modification and deletion.

The LKM can read MAC DTS values for individual files such as image files, audio files, text files and SQLite databases. However, it cannot capture timestamps for individual database transactions. In the case of SMS messages and calls, records are added to their respective databases. All images, audio, video and other common files are updated directly on the storage device and the entries are added to the corresponding databases. For this reason, along with uploading the log file, the up-loader application also extracts and uploads specific details (e.g., called numbers, call status and call/SMS message times) from the call-records folder and SMS database to track the entries that have been updated in the databases.

The uploader application also writes the cell tower information and the GPS location of the phone to the log file before uploading it. Adding location information to the log file enhances the credibility of the logged MAC DTS values because it can reveal the location where the tampering may have taken place. Privacy issues arising from storing the log file on a third-party cloud server can be addressed by creating a middleware component in the cloud that encrypts the log file before storing it on the cloud server.

4.6   Incident Handling

When tampering is suspected, the MAC DTS values of suspected files on the phone must be cross-checked with the corresponding MAC DTS log file values stored on the local server or cloud. If the values match, no tampering is indicated; otherwise, the discrepancy should be investigated.

In some cases, tampering can be detected even when the solution is not deployed on a phone, or if there is some discrepancy that was present on the phone before the solution was operational. For example, every SQLite database on a device has a primary key (named _id), which increases in sequential order whenever a new record is inserted into the database. If a call is made or an SMS message is sent to an existing number, then a new record is written to the database. Camera image, video and audio files also have distinct records in their respective databases and, when they are edited, new entries with new _id values are written to the databases. If the timestamp values of one record with a lower _id value are after those of another record with a higher _id value (i.e., it was inserted later), then it is certain that timestamp values were tampered with. These results can then be forwarded to a digital forensic professional for further investigation.

4.7   Anti-Forensics

In addition to the anti-forensic techniques discussed above, we are considering an additional category, namely, forensic tools that are op-erating on a device [3]. When attempting to destroy evidence, the first thing that an attacker might do is to delete the evidence file itself. Our implementation cannot recover deleted data, but it can tell the time

Table 2.   Performance benchmark parameters.

Test Parameter	Operations
RAM R/W Operations	MB per 10 seconds for integer array copying and adding in RAM
CPU Integer	Million operations per 10 seconds
CPU Float	Million operations per 10 seconds
2D Graphics	Performance evaluation for 2D animation
3D Graphics	Performance evaluation for 3D animation
Database I/O	Performance of SQLite queries such as INSERT, SELECT and UPDATE
SD Card W Operations	MB of data written to SD card per 10 seconds
SD Card R Operations	MB of data read from SD card per 10 seconds

when a file was deleted. If the attacker tries to tamper with the metadata of an evidentiary file, the implementation can detect the attempt and provide the original values from the stored log. If the attacker somehow identifies the location of the log file and attempts to delete it, the deletion would not be supported by the operating system.

Our solution is resistant to anti-forensic techniques that seek to hide evidence. This is because log redirection is not possible when the LKM is running. In the event that an attacker attempts to alter or counterfeit the evidence (e.g., using the technique described in [1]), the LKM would be unloaded and the logging would stop. This would result in log files not being uploaded to the local server or cloud. To address this, a provision could be made at the local server or in the cloud that, if no update is received over a certain period of time, an alarm is raised that could be used to isolate the device until further examination. The detection of running forensic tools is not directly applicable to our solution because only activities that occur after its installation can be captured. If an enterprise deploys our solution on an Android device before the device enters its ecosystem, then the activities that occurred earlier are assumed to be of no concern to the enterprise.

5.   Impact on Performance

To examine the impact of installing the LKM on a phone, we ran 30 iterations of the System Test benchmarking tool (see goo.gl/0f67R) on the HTC Wildfire smartphone with and without the LKM. We selected this tool specifically because it provides results for various system peripherals at the same time. The system components considered in the benchmarking are listed in Table 2. The graph in Figure 6 summarizes the results.

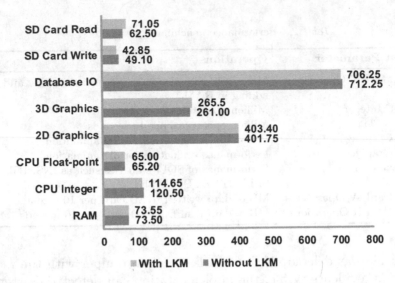

Figure 6.   Performance benchmarking results for the HTC Wildfire smartphone.

Our experiments demonstrated that the solution does not impact the performance of the HTC Wildfire smartphone to a significant degree. Similar results were observed for the Samsung Galaxy S2 smartphone.

6.   Conclusions

Android smartphones used in a BYOD environment are vulnerable to confidentiality and integrity attacks, especially those involving tampering with potential evidentiary data stored on the phones. The solution described in this paper helps detect malicious data tampering by storing authentic copies of the MAC DTS values of selected files and directories on a local server or in the cloud for later verification and validation. The solution is also applicable to Android tablets. Indeed, the concept of storing kernel-generated authentic timestamps at secure external locations for the purpose of identifying malicious activities can be implemented for a variety of mobile device operating systems.

Our future research will focus on developing an anomaly-based intrusion detection system for Android devices. MAC DTS logs can be used to construct models of expected behavior, enabling malicious activities to be detected and blocked in real time. Another topic of future research is to create a customized kernel using SE Linux as part of an integrated solution.

References

[1] P. Albano, A. Castiglione, G. Cattaneo and A. De Santis, A novel anti-forensics technique for the Android OS, *Proceedings of the International Conference on Broadband and Wireless Computing, Communications and Applications*, pp. 380–385, 2011.

[2] M. Ansari, A. Chattopadhayay and S. Das, A kernel level VFS logger for building efficient filesystem intrusion detection systems, *Proceedings of the Second International Conference on Computer and Network Technology*, pp. 273–279, 2010.

[3] S. Azadegan, W. Yu, H. Liu, M. Sistani and S. Acharya, Novel anti-forensics approaches for smartphones, *Proceedings of the Forty-Fifth Hawaii International Conference on System Science*, pp. 5424–5431, 2012.

[4] M. Barik, G. Gupta, S. Sinha, A. Mishra and C. Mazumdar, An efficient technique for enhancing the forensic capabilities of the Ext2 filesystem, *Digital Investigation*, vol. 4(S), pp. S55–S61, 2007.

[5] M. Becher, F. Freiling, J. Hoffmann, T. Holz, S. Uellenbeck and C. Wolf, Mobile security catching up? Revealing the nuts and bolts of the security of mobile devices, *Proceedings of the IEEE Symposium on Security and Privacy*, pp. 96–111, 2011.

[6] F. Buchholz and C. Falk, Design and implementation of Zeitline: A forensic timeline editor, *Proceedings of the Fifth Digital Forensic Research Workshop*, 2005.

[7] B. Carrier and E. Spafford, An event-based digital forensic investigation framework, *Proceedings of the Fourth Digital Forensic Research Workshop*, 2004.

[8] S. Das, A. Chattopadhayay, D. Kalyani and M. Saha, Filesystem intrusion detection by preserving MAC DTS: A loadable kernel module based approach for Linux kernel 2.6.x, *Proceedings of the Fifth Annual Workshop on Cyber Security and Information Intelligence Research*, art. 57, 2009.

[9] A. Distefano, G. Me and F. Pace, Android anti-forensics through a local paradigm, *Digital Investigation*, vol. 7(S), pp. S83–S94, 2010.

[10] E. Gal and S. Toledo, Algorithms and data structures for flash memories, *ACM Computing Surveys*, vol. 37(2), pp. 138–163, 2005.

[11] J. Grover, Android forensics: Automated data collection and reporting from a mobile device, *Digital Investigation*, vol. 10(S), pp. S12–S20, 2013.

[12] A. Gupta, C. Milanesi, R. Cozza and C. Lu, Market Share Analysis: Mobile Phones, Worldwide, 2Q13, Gartner, Stamford, Connecticut, August 13, 2013.

[13] R. Harris, Arriving at an anti-forensics consensus: Examining how to define and control the anti-forensics problem, *Digital Investigation*, vol. 3(S), pp. S44–S49, 2006.

[14] B. Henderson, Linux Loadable Kernel Module HOWTO (`tldp.org/HOWTO/Module-HOWTO`), September 24, 1006.

[15] HTC Corporation, The HTC Developer Center, Taoyuan, Taiwan (`www.htcdev.com/devcenter`), 2013.

[16] International Data Corporation, Worldwide mobile phone market forecast to grow 7.3% in 2013 driven by 1 billion smartphone shipments, according to IDC, Press Release, Framingham, Massachusetts, September 4, 2013.

[17] M. La Polla, F. Martinelli and D. Sgandurra, A survey on security for mobile devices, *IEEE Communications Surveys and Tutorials*, vol. 15(1), pp. 446–471, 2013.

[18] A. Marrington, I. Baggili, G. Mohay and A. Clark, CAT Detect (Computer Activity Timeline Detection): A tool for detecting inconsistency in computer activity timelines, *Digital Investigation*, vol. 8(S), pp. S52–S61, 2011.

[19] K. Miller, J. Voas and G. Hurlburt, BYOD: Security and privacy considerations, *IT Professional*, vol. 14(5), pp. 53–55, 2012.

[20] J. Olsson and M. Boldt, Computer forensic timeline visualization tool, *Digital Investigation*, vol. 6(S), pp. S78–S87, 2009.

[21] C. Papathanasiou and N. Percoco, This is not the droid you're looking for..., presented at *DEF CON 18*, 2010.

[22] J. Reardon, S. Capkun and D. Basin, Data node encrypted filesystem: Efficient secure deletion for flash memory, *Proceedings of the Twenty-First USENIX Security Symposium*, 2012.

[23] Samsung, Samsung Open Source Release Center, Suwon, South Korea (`opensource.samsung.com`), 2013.

[24] A. Shabtai, Y. Fledel and Y. Elovici, Securing Android-powered mobile devices using SELinux, *IEEE Security and Privacy*, vol. 8(3), pp. 36–44, 2010.

[25] S. Smalley, The case for SE Android, presented at the *Linux Security Summit*, 2011.

[26] S. Smalley, T. Fraser and C. Vance, *Linux Security Modules: General Security Hooks for Linux*, NAI Labs, Santa Clara, California (`tali.admingilde.org/linux-docbook/lsm.pdf`), 2001.

[27] A. Smith, Smartphone Ownership 2013, Pew Research Center, Washington, DC, June 5, 2013.

[28] M. Weil, Dynamic time and date stamp analysis, *International Journal of Digital Evidence*, vol. 1(2), 2002.

[29] D. Willis, Bring Your Own Device: The Facts and the Future, Gartner, Stamford, Connecticut, April 11, 2013.

Chapter 15

AN OPEN SOURCE TOOLKIT FOR iOS FILESYSTEM FORENSICS

Ahmad Raza Cheema, Mian Muhammad Waseem Iqbal,
and Waqas Ali

Abstract   Despite the fact that every iOS release introduces new security restrictions that must be overcome in order to recover data from iPhones, the locations where the data of interest resides are generally consistent. This paper analyzes the iOS filesystem and identifies files and directories that contain data that can aid investigations of traditional crimes involving iPhones as well as hacking and cracking attacks launched from iPhones. Additionally, best practices for minimizing the false positive rate during data carving are identified. These findings are implemented in an open source forensic investigation toolkit that operates in a forensically-sound manner.

Keywords: Mobile phone forensics, iOS, iPhone

1.   Introduction

The Apple iOS operating system is a Unix-like operating system based on FreeBSD. Despite the open source roots of iOS, the operating system is locked down and accessing the core Unix functions requires an iOS device such as an iPhone to be jailbroken. An iPhone has two filesystem partitions: one partition stores iOS-specific files such as kernel images and configuration files, and the other stores user-specific settings and applications [6]. From a forensic perspective, the second partition is more important because it contains user applications and data. The call history, short messaging service (SMS) messages, contact list, emails, audio and video, and pictures taken with the built-in camera are all located in the second partition.

Since iOS is closed source and proprietary, general purpose forensic techniques and tools do not work on iOS devices. This paper analyzes the iOS filesystem and identifies files and directories that contain data

G. Peterson and S. Shenoi (Eds.): Advances in Digital Forensics X, IFIP AICT 433, pp. 227–236, 2014.

that can aid investigations of hacking and cracking attacks launched from iPhones. The paper also describes an open source forensic toolkit and forensic procedures that can extract and analyze data stored on iPhones running iOS versions 3.1.3 through 4.3. The toolkit has been tested on an iPhone 3G running iOS version 3.1.3.

2.   Related Work

The iOS filesystem stores a large number of relevant files in multiple locations. The files are stored in a variety of formats (both open and proprietary); therefore, without knowledge of the location and purpose of each file, a forensic investigation is bound to fail.

Companies that market forensic software for iPhones and Android devices claim that the software can securely recover data from these devices [3]. However, because of the lack of independent verification and the closed source nature of the forensic investigation tools, the procedures used by the tools are questionable.

Schmidt [9] discusses the bruteforcing of iPhone passcodes in a safe manner without any loss of data; it is not possible to guess the passcode through the graphical interface because the data is automatically erased after ten unsuccessful attempts. Zdziarski [11] has developed a custom firmware loading and acquisition method that is forensically secure. However, the tools and techniques developed by Zdziarski are only available to the law enforcement community and are applicable to the older iOS 2.x firmware versions. Hay, *et al.* [4] have updated Zdziarski's process to work on firmware versions through 4.x; they also provide details about the locations where valuable data resides. Mallepally [7] discusses a number of challenges involved in extracting evidence from iOS devices, including novel anti-forensic techniques.

3.   Implementation

Designing a forensic investigation toolkit requires care in order to ensure data integrity and that evidence is not lost. The NIST Computer Forensics Tool Testing Program for Mobile Devices [8] requires that a forensic toolkit must perform a complete data extraction and must maintain the forensic integrity of the data. The open source toolkit [5] described in this paper meets both requirements. The data integrity requirement is achieved by unmounting the iOS filesystem and then copying the two partitions using the dd utility via a secure shell (SSH) connection between the phone and investigator machine over Wi-Fi. Unmounting the filesystem prevents the accidental writing of data to the filesystem and, thus, maintains forensic integrity during data extraction.

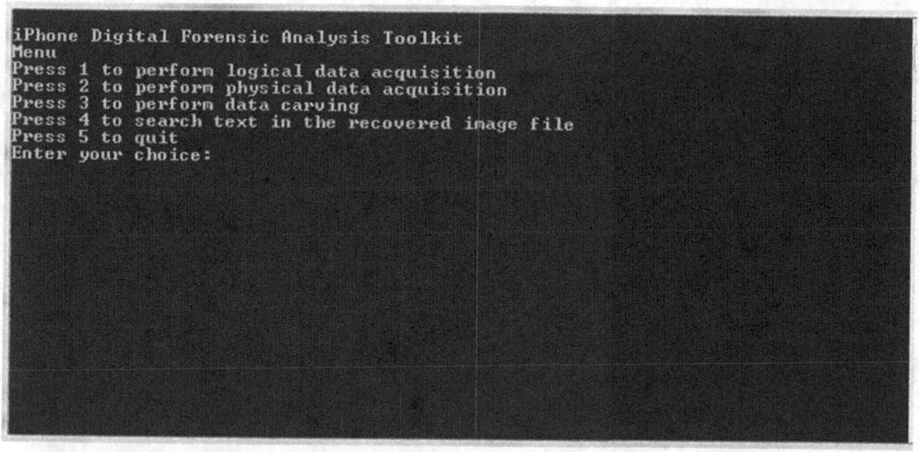

```
iPhone Digital Forensic Analysis Toolkit
Menu
Press 1 to perform logical data acquisition
Press 2 to perform physical data acquisition
Press 3 to perform data carving
Press 4 to search text in the recovered image file
Press 5 to quit
Enter your choice:
```

Figure 1. Screenshot of the forensic investigation toolkit.

The forensic toolkit is written in C#. Because iOS requires executables to be digitally signed, an iPhone must be jailbroken to circumvent this restriction and obtain root privileges. Root privileges can be gained using manual or automated jailbreaking methods. A manual method provides more control over the jailbreaking process. However, an automated method [1, 10] can be used because jailbreaking only changes files in the first partition. User data and other information in the second partition remain intact no matter which method is used.

After obtaining root access to the iPhone, an OpenSSH server is installed on the device. A secure shell client implemented in the forensic investigation toolkit is then used to connect to the OpenSSH server and extract data from the device to the forensic investigation machine. This process is secure because all the data is transferred through an encrypted SSH tunnel, which ensures data confidentiality and integrity

Figure 1 shows a screenshot of the forensic investigation toolkit. The toolkit menu is organized as follows:

- **Logical Acquisition:** Important files stored in the iOS filesystem are transferred from the iPhone to the forensic investigation machine. No deleted data is recovered and only the files stored in the filesystem are recovered. This type of acquisition is useful for quickly searching and retrieving evidence.

- **Physical Acquisition:** A bit-for-bit copy of the data is obtained. This type of acquisition provides the forensic investigator with a complete copy of all the data stored on the device.

Table 1.   iOS filesystem evidence files.

File Name	File Location	Description
General.log	/Library/logs/ AppleSupport/	iPhone firmware information
localtime@	/private/var/db/timezone/	Local time zone configuration details
*.deb	/private/var/mobile/ Library/Backup	Downloaded application install packages
Status	/private/var/lib/dpkg/	Application installation status
Each directory	/private/var/stash/ Applications/	Install location of each application
AddressBook .sqlitedb	/private/var/mobile/ Library/AddressBook/	User contact list
Calendar.sqlite	/private/var/mobile /Library/Calendar/	User calendar data
Call_history.db	/private/var/mobile /Library/CallHistory/	Details of the last 100 calls placed, received and missed
Voicemail.db	/private/var/mobile /Library/voicemail/	Information about voicemail senders
sms.db	/private/var/mobile /Library/SMS/	Default SMS database file containing SMS messages sent and received
DraftMessage. plist	/private/var/mobile /Library/Draft/PENDING /.draft/	SMS messages written in the Messages application but not yet sent
Email	/private/var/mobile /Library/Mail/	"Protected Index" file with email information
SafariHistory .plist	/private/var/mobile /Library/Safari/	Safari browser website history information
SafeBrowsing.db	/private/var/mobile /Library/SafeBrowsing/	Websites visited using the Safari Safe Browsing feature
Cookies.plist	/private/var/mobile /Library/Cookies	Website cookies saved for the Safari browser

- **Data Carving:** After the bit-for-bit copy is obtained, the Scalpel open source forensic data carving tool is used to recover deleted data.

4.   Analysis

After manually analyzing the iOS file contents, the files listed in Table 1 were identified as being relevant to iPhone investigations. The file content of interest includes address book data, SMS messages, email, images and audio/video. iPhones have been used to attack networks

Table 2.   Recommended file sizes for data recovery.

File Name	Type	Size
sms.db	Default SMS file	1.2 MB to 2 MB
AddressBook.sqlitedb	Default address book	220 KB
Notes.db	Notes file	50 KB
Calendar.sqlitedb	Calendar entries	204 KB
Call_history.db	User call history	28 KB
History.plist	Safari browser history	1 MB
Voicemail.db	Voice mail information	100 KB

and the digital infrastructure [2]; the installed application files listed in Table 1 are also useful for investigating these crimes.

Most of the files are in the open source SQLite database format. SQLite is an efficient and lightweight database engine. However, SQLite database files lack a trailing signature and can only be identified by their file header (53 51 4C 69 74 65 20 66 6F 72 6D 61 74 20 33 00). This makes it difficult to recover deleted files; searching for files using only the header signature yields a large number of false positives. However, our research indicates that the false positive rate is greatly reduced if the maximum file sizes listed in Table 2 are chosen.

4.1   System Information

The General.log file is the first file that should be analyzed. It contains information about the iOS version installed on the device, which is important because it provides insights into the protection measures that are in place and the vulnerabilities that can be exploited in a forensic investigation. The iOS version information can also help the forensic practitioner select the appropriate tools for data recovery and analysis. The General.log file also stores the date when the firmware was installed; this gives an estimate of how long the device has been in use.

Another important file is localtime, which contains local time settings data that is useful for developing an accurate timeline of user activity involving an iPhone.

4.2   Installed Applications

The /private/var/mobile/Library/Backup directory contains multiple .deb files. These files correspond to Debian package management system install packages; their presence indicates that they were downloaded by the user in preparation for installation on the iPhone. Even if an application is subsequently removed from the device, its downloaded package persists until the maximum archive size specified in the `apt.conf` file is reached. Of particular interest in investigations are `.deb` files corresponding to hacking and cracking applications.

Together with the `.deb` archive files, the status file can be used to establish that a user not only downloaded applications but also installed them. The status file contains the status of every package ever installed on the iPhone, including applications downloaded and installed from Cydia repositories

Each installed application has a sub-directory in the `/private/var /stash/Applications` directory. This is useful when a user has deliberately hidden applications from the normal display. For example, applications are available for hiding applications from the SpringBoard GUI until a particular key combination or password is entered. This protection can be circumvented by examining the contents of the `/private/ var/stash/Applications` directory.

4.3   User Data

The most important files for investigating traditional crimes are located in the `/private/var/mobile/Library/` directory. This directory and its sub-directories contain the address book, calendar, call history, SMS messages, email and web browser history.

The `AddressBook.sqlitedb` file contains contact information and numbers stored in the iPhone. Two tables, ABPerson and ABMulti-Value, are especially important. ABPerson contains contact names while the ABMultiValue table has the corresponding contact numbers.

The `Calendar.sqlitedb` file stores user calendar entries. Another important file is `Call_history.db`, which contains the last 100 calls dialed, received and missed. The `Voicemail.db` file stores the sent and received voicemail messages.

The message table in the `sms.db` file contains the sent and received SMS messages. Data extracted from this table must be correlated with the data stored in the ABPerson and ABMultiValue tables to determine the contact information of the person who sent an SMS message. Relating the data with `AddressBook.sqlitedb` requires the execution of the following command line query:

```
ATTACH DATABASE "AddressBook.sqlitedb" AS AB;
ATTACH DATABASE "sms.db" AS sms;
SELECT First,Last FROM AB.ABPerson WHERE rowid=(SELECT
record_id FROM AB.ABMultiValue WHERE value=(SELECT
address FROM sms.message WHERE text LIKE \%\%));
```

The `DraftMessage.draft` file contains SMS messages that have not yet been sent. By default, iOS does not have a draft saving feature. However, messages written using the Messages application, but that have not yet been sent are saved in this file.

Email messages are stored in the "Protected Index" file. This file has no file extension, but opening it in a hex editor and examining the header reveals that it is a SQLite database file. Two tables, messages and messages_data, contain important forensic artifacts. User browsing history artifacts are found in the `History.plist`, `SafeBrowsing.db` and `Cookies.plist` files.

5.   Evaluation

This section presents two use cases: one involving an iPhone seized in a traditional criminal investigation and the other involving an iPhone used in a hacking incident. The two cases highlight how the results of this research can support digital forensic investigations.

- **Traditional Crime Use Case:** A phone is often one of the most important evidence containers in traditional crimes such as theft and murder. Traditional criminal cases typically focus on the contact list, SMS messages, email, images, audio/video and call history. Recovering data from an iPhone can be difficult if proper tools and techniques are not employed. The open source tool described in this paper was tested on an iPhone 3G with 8 GB internal storage running firmware version 3.1.3.

  The first task in a forensic investigation is to jailbreak the iPhone to obtain root access and bypass the security restrictions. This should be done using offline jailbreak tools such as JailbreakMe [1], which can jailbreak iPhones up to firmware version 4.3. Jailbreaking only alters the data in the first partition; no data (including user data) residing in the second partition is modified or lost.

  After the phone is jailbroken, the next step is to use the Cydia repository to install OpenSSH on the device. Then, the open source toolkit [5] described in this paper is used to download the files in the **/private/var/mobile/Library** directory in order to perform offline analysis. The most important data is the call history, contact list, SMS messages and email, all of which are stored in SQLite files that can be analyzed with a SQLite browser (e.g., the open source SQLite Browser) or hex dump software. Audio and video files are also recovered from their sub-directories and analyzed.

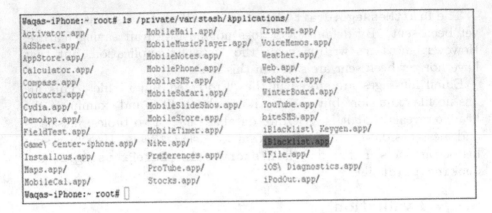

Figure 2. Applications installed on an iPhone.

- **Hacking Incident Use Case:** In the case of an iPhone involved in a hacking or cracking case, it is necessary to the analyze specific application files used in the illegal activities as well as the configuration and log parameters. Commonly-used hacking tools such as Nmap, Metasploit and Aircrack-ng can only be installed if the device has already been jailbroken. The problem is that when an iPhone is jailbroken to conduct an investigation, important log files and application files related to the incident are modified because they are also stored in the first logical partition that is affected by a jailbreaking process. Since an iPhone involved in a hacking or cracking case has already been broken to load the attack tools, there is no need to jailbreak the device and the forensic integrity of the device is not impacted.

The most important files in hacking and cracking investigations are files located in the installed application directory `/private/var/stash/Applications` and the `.bash_history` file located in the `root` directory. The installed application directory lists the applications installed on an iPhone (Figure 2) while the `.bash_history` file lists all the commands executed via the terminal.

6.   Conclusions

The Apple iPhone is a modern smartphone that provides sophisticated computing, communications and user functionality. The proprietary and closed nature of the iPhone hardware and software greatly complicates forensic recovery and analysis. The analysis of the iOS filesystem has identified files and directories that contain evidentiary data of interest to traditional criminal investigations as well as investigations of hacking and cracking attacks launched from an iPhone. The open source forensic toolkit described in this paper is specifically designed to extract and analyze evidentiary data stored on iPhones running iOS versions 3.1.3 through 4.3.

References

[1] comex, JailbreakMe (`www.jailbreakme.com`), 2011.

[2] D. Compton, Own with an iPhone (`www.youtube.com/watch?v=zB m1UXmgz1k`), 2010.

[3] ElcomSoft, ElcomSoft Phone Password Breaker, Moscow, Russia (`www.elcomsoft.com/eppb.html`), 2014.

[4] A. Hay, D. Krill, B. Kuhar and G. Peterson, Evaluating digital forensic options for the Apple iPad, in *Advances in Digital Forensics VII*, G. Peterson and S. Shenoi (Eds.), Springer, Heidelberg, Germany, pp. 257–274, 2011.

[5] W. Iqbal, Open source toolkit for iPhone filesystems file analysis (`sites.google.com/a/mcs.edu.pk/open-source-toolkit-for-iphone-file-system-files-analysis/open-source-toolkit-for-iphone-file-systems-file-analysis`), 2013.

[6] R. Kubasiak, S. Morrissey, W. Barr, J. Brown, M. Caceres, M. Chasman and J. Cornell, *Mac OS X, iPod and iPhone Forensic Analysis*, Syngress Publishing, Burlington, Massachusetts, 2009.

[7] R. Mallepally, Implementation of Applications to Improve iPhone Forensic Analysis and Integrity of Evidence, M.S. Thesis, Department of Computing Sciences, Texas A&M University – Corpus Christi, Corpus Christi, Texas, 2011.

[8] National Institute of Standards and Technology, Mobile Devices, Computer Forensics Tool Testing Program, Gaithersburg, Maryland (`www.cftt.nist.gov/mobile_devices.htm`).

[9] J. Schmidt, iOpener: How safe is your iPhone data? *The H Security*, Heise Media UK, London, United Kingdom (`www.h-online.com/security/features/iOpener-How-safe-is-your-iPhone-data-1266713.html`), July 4, 2011.

[10] J. Sigwald, Analysis of the jailbreakme v3 font exploit, Sogeti ESEC Lab (`esec-lab.sogeti.com/post/Analysis-of-the-jailbreakme-v3-font-exploit`), 2011.

[11] J. Zdziarski, *iPhone Forensics*, O'Reilly Media, Sebastopol, California, 2008.

Chapter 16

SMARTPHONES AS DISTRIBUTED WITNESSES FOR DIGITAL FORENSICS

Heloise Pieterse and Martin Olivier

Abstract   Smartphones have become an integral part of people's lives. Their wide range of capabilities and support of diverse applications result in a wealth of data being stored in smartphone memory. Although tools are available to extract and view the data stored in smartphones, no comprehensive process exists for event reconstruction using the extracted data. Data in smartphones is typically stored in SQLite databases and can, therefore, be easily transformed. To perform event reconstruction, multiple SQLite databases have to be integrated. This paper proposes a novel mobile event reconstruction process that allows for event reconstruction by querying the integrated SQLite databases collected from multiple smartphones. The process can create detailed accounts of the events that took place before, during and after an incident.

Keywords: Smartphones, event reconstruction, distributed databases

1.   Introduction

Smartphones have become constant companions for people around the world. Their popularity can be attributed to multiple factors, but the most important is their continuous enhancement in functionality. In addition to telephony, smartphones offer functionality similar to a small computer. They support complete operating systems, allow for the installation of third-party applications and have ubiquitous connectivity and communications capabilities.

The extensive and diverse use of smartphones make them a rich source of evidence. Smartphones inherently sense the environment in which they operate and store trace elements (or more) of what they have sensed. The "environment" may include the digital realm (such as social network ecosystems and location-based messages received via Bluetooth

G. Peterson and S. Shenoi (Eds.): Advances in Digital Forensics X, IFIP AICT 433, pp. 237–251, 2014.

or NFC), the physical realm (such as photographs taken, and videos and sound clips recorded) and events that straddle the digital and physical realms (such as wireless access points and cellular towers seen or accessed). The exact events recorded by a smartphone depend on many factors, including the smartphone settings, sensors and applications.

Since smartphones are ubiquitous, there is a high probability that: (i) one or more smartphones would almost certainly have "witnessed" an event that otherwise may not have left any traces; and (ii) multiple smartphones would have "witnessed" the event, which can increase the reliability of the evidence pertaining to the event. To illustrate the latter point, if hundreds of smartphones have recorded an event, it may be possible to determine the time that the event occurred with much greater precision than if information was available from just one or a few smartphone logs.

A set of smartphones essentially forms a distributed database of independent nodes that contain potential evidence about events sensed by the devices. One option is to amalgamate all this information and "mine" it for evidence. However, a more controlled examination of the smartphone data would provide: (i) a structured approach to test hypotheses; and (ii) greater clarity about the reliability of evidence obtained from the distributed database. The autonomy of each smartphone suggests that the set of smartphones should be treated as a federated database. However, practical considerations (such as the time available to obtain evidence from the smartphones) may require that the distributed information be amalgamated into a single database.

Database integration is a well-known problem with significant subproblems. However, a fortunate circumstance reduces the complexity of this process in the current context: smartphones (almost) exclusively use SQLite databases to store information. In addition, the integration does not entail amalgamating information in the usual sense of the word – the different data sets are to be retained as different data sets so that information seen in a data set may be correlated with information seen (or not seen) in other data sets. While these observations do not render database integration a trivial problem, they do suggest that integration in the forensic sense is feasible within the constraints of a forensic examination; they do not equate to the massive projects typically associated with integration efforts.

The immediate challenges are to show that: (i) the remarks about database integration in a forensic context made above are indeed correct; and (ii) useful queries may be answered by an integrated database. This paper provides preliminary evidence that the suggested approach can help address these challenges. The first challenge is addressed by providing a simple process model based on database integration theory that shows how integration may be achieved. The second challenge is addressed by providing examples of potential queries that demonstrate the utility of the approach.

The outcome of the process is the reconstruction of events surrounding a particular incident by querying the integrated SQLite databases. Event reconstruction supports investigations by allowing multiple events to be tied together and crucial relationships to be identified based on multiple smartphones serving as distributed witnesses.

2. Reconstruction Techniques

Reconstruction is an important component of the digital forensic examination process, allowing for the establishment of the most probable sequence of events that occurred during a specific time period. Forensic Science Central [9] defines reconstruction as the "process of establishing a sequence of events about the occurrences" during and after an incident. Gladyshev [11] describes reconstruction as the process of "determining the events that happened during an incident." Prasad and Satish [21] view event reconstruction as the examination of evidence to determine why it has certain characteristics; this is achieved by using the collected evidence to reconstruct what has happened in a particular system. Finally, Cohen [5] defines reconstruction as an experimental component that is used to test hypotheses.

There have been several attempts to formalize event reconstruction. Formal frameworks are discussed by Stephenson [26], Gladyshev and Patel [12] and Arnes, *et al.* [2]. Stephenson uses a Petri net approach to reconstruct attacks and identify the root cause of attacks. Gladyshev and Patel use state machines and mathematical modeling to reconstruct events. Arnes, *et al.* model a virtual digital crime scene in order to reconstruct events in a realistic fashion.

Techniques such as attack trees and visual investigative analysis also support event reconstruction. Attack trees [22] provide a mechanism for thinking, building, capturing and making decisions about the security of a system. With the help of possible incident scenarios and hypotheses integral to event reconstruction, attack trees can aid the discovery, documentation and analysis of the incident scenarios. Visual investigative analysis is a charting technique that graphically displays sequences of events and relationships using a network approach [16]. This technique was developed to improve the ability to visualize complex crimes [11].

The works described above consider event reconstruction to be a process that is followed to rebuild the possible sequence of events surrounding a particular incident. In the remainder of this paper, event reconstruction will, therefore, refer to the rebuilding of events surrounding a specific incident.

Little attention has been directed at the reconstruction of events using smartphones. The techniques discussed above primarily focus on reconstructing events surrounding computer incidents and, although applicable, do not consider the differences associated with using smartphones for event reconstruction. To accommodate the differences, a new process is proposed that allows for the reconstruction of events using data collected from smartphones.

3.   Mobile Event Reconstruction Process

Mobile phone forensics is a constantly evolving area of digital forensics [6]. The new millennium introduced a new generation of mobile phones known as smartphones. These devices, with their ability to execute third-party applications, store large amounts and diverse types of data. Evidence commonly found on smartphones includes, but is not limited to, contacts, call history, calendar entries and messages [6]. Several forensic tools are available for retrieving smartphone data (e.g., Oxygen Forensic Suite [17], AccessData Mobile Phone Examiner Plus (MPE+) [1] and viaExtract from viaForensics [28]).

Most of the data extracted from smartphones using forensic tools is in the structured format of SQLite databases, which forms a distributed database of independent nodes containing potential evidence that was acquired and stored by the smartphones. The mobile event reconstruction process described in this paper draws on database integration theory to combine the multiple SQLite databases into a single, integrated multidatabase. The process, which is summarized in Figure 1, involves four distinct phases: (i) extraction; (ii) homogenization; (iii) schema integration; and (iv) exploration. The first three phases perform the database integration while the last phase, exploration, allows for the examination of the data by executing custom queries against the integrated database. The outcome of the process is the reconstruction of events surrounding a particular incident by visualizing the queried data.

3.1   Phase 1: Extraction

The first phase of the mobile event reconstruction process is the extraction of data from smartphones. In addition to SQLite databases, valuable data resides in backup database files in the form of rollback journals and write-ahead log files. These files store the changes made to a SQLite database to enable the database to be returned to a pre-

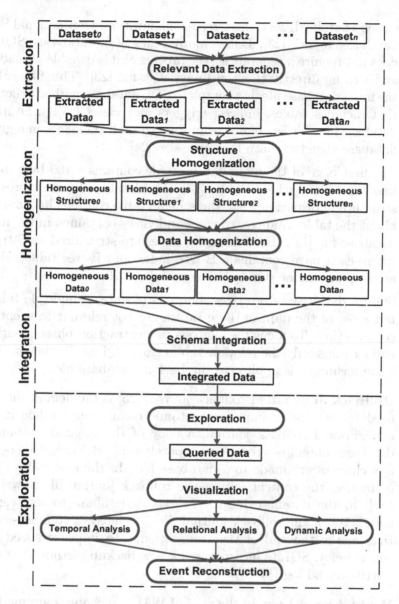

Figure 1. Mobile event reconstruction process.

vious stable state after a crash or failure. Indeed, the files provide an opportunity to extract previously altered or deleted data that can aid in reconstructing events.

- **SQLite Databases:** SQLite is an open source, lightweight database that allows for the quick processing of stored data [14]. Data processing is facilitated by an in-process library that implements a "self-contained, serverless, zero-configuration, transactional SQL database engine" [23]. Unlike many other SQL databases, SQLite does not require a separate server process and is capable of reading and writing directly to an ordinary disk file [23]. This file, called the main database file, is a complete SQL database with a structure that includes tables, indices, triggers and views [23]. The main database file consists of one or more pages; all the pages in a given database structure have the same size [24].

The first page of the main database file contains a 100-byte database header and schema tables [14]. The database header stores file structure information while the schema table contains information about the tables, indices, triggers and views contained in the main database file [14]. The remaining pages are structured as B-trees, where each page contains a B-tree index and B-tree table, which are responsible for storing the actual data [20].

SQLite databases store large amounts of data in multiple tables, but most of the data in these tables are not relevant to event reconstruction. To focus the analysis, the extraction phase identifies and extracts only the relevant tables from SQLite databases. This same technique is applied to the backup database files.

- **Rollback Journal:** A rollback journal [25] is the default method used by SQLite to implement atomic commit and rollback. In a traditional rollback journal, a copy of the original unchanged database content is written to a separate rollback journal file before any changes are made to a database file. In the event of a crash or failure, the content within the rollback journal file is written back to the database file to revert the database to its original state. When the rollback journal file is deleted, a commit occurs that marks the end of the transaction. To improve speed and concurrency, SQLite incorporates a new backup method that uses a write-ahead log (WAL).

- **Write-Ahead Log:** In the case of WAL, no changes are made to a database file; instead, the changes are appended to a separate WAL file. A special record indicating a commit marks the end of the transaction when the record is appended to the WAL file. Moving the pages from the WAL file back to the database is called a "checkpoint." A checkpoint occurs automatically when the WAL file reaches a size of 1,000 pages [25].

  Two files, <databasefilename> -wal and <databasefilename> -shm, are found in the same directory as the main database file [3].

The WAL file contains the new and updated database pages [3] while the SHM file is the shared memory file associated with the main database [25]. The WAL file contains a 32-byte file header followed by zero or more WAL frames. Since a checkpoint only occurs after 1,000 entries, the WAL file maintains a long record of previously altered and deleted data that can be very valuable in event reconstruction.

3.2   Phase 2: Homogenization

After the SQLite databases have been extracted, differences between the structures and data formats must be reconciled. The second phase, homogenization, reconciles the heterogeneous structures and data formats into a canonical form to allow for efficient analysis [18]. Homogenization involves two steps: structure homogenization and data homogenization. The first step resolves the heterogeneities in the structures of the SQLite databases. The second step transforms the data collected from the databases into a general format.

- **Step 1 (Structure Homogenization):** Structure homogenization facilitates the integration of data from the various SQLite databases. Similar databases from different devices do not always use the same structure. The table structure used by Android devices to store text and multimedia messages differs from the structure used by iPhones. For example, an Android device stores message content in a column named "body" [15] while an iPhone stores the same content in a column named "text" [27]. To support query processing and visualization, which are required during the last two phases, the extracted databases must be transformed to a general structure.

  To achieve structure homogenization, both schema and data type heterogeneity need to be addressed [8]. Schema heterogeneity refers to the structure of the tables that can be different, even if the same type of data is stored. For example, one database may store the first and last names of contacts in separate columns while another database stores the first and last names as a full name in a single column. Although the same type of data is stored, the differences in the schema structure can lead to misinterpretations. To overcome this problem, a single canonical schema must be identified and the data pulled into the canonical schema.

  In addition to the differences found in schemas, different data types are often used to store similar data. For example, a cellphone number can be stored as a string in one database but as a number in another. To simplify query processing, a single data type must be identified and used to store similar data.

Having achieved structure homogenization, the next step is to reconcile data heterogeneity.

- **Step 2 (Data Homogenization):** As in the case of file structures, differences exist with regard to data formats. For example, timestamps may have different formats, which increases the difficulty of performing analysis and event reconstruction. Thus, timestamps must be converted into a standard format. A standard format such as `YYYY-MM-DD-HH:mm:ss:pppp...` facilitates analysis because it allows the timestamps to be sorted alphabetically and numerically [5].

Timestamps are also complicated to analyze due to the presence of different time zones and varying clock skews [5]. Thus, the relevant time mechanisms should be examined closely and an appropriate Δ must be determined to limit false positives [5]. Timestamps can be evaluated and ordered using the equation [5]:

$$\forall t_1, t_2, |t_1 - t_2| < \Delta \Rightarrow t_1 \approx t_2. \tag{1}$$

In addition to differences in timestamps and time offsets, similar logical values are often stored in different formats. This is referred to as value heterogeneity [8]; an example is the representation of true and false as 1 and 0, respectively. To overcome possible confusion and misinterpretation, heterogeneous values must be transformed to canonical forms.

3.3   Phase 3: Schema Integration

After successful data extraction and homogenization, the next step is to integrate the SQLite databases and backup files. Integration, or schema integration, takes multiple schemas as input and produces an integrated schema as output [7].

Schema integration involves four phases [7]: (i) schema translation; (ii) schematic interschema relationship generation; (iii) interschema relationship generation; and (iv) integrated schema generation. Schema translation converts the database schemas into an intermediate canonical representation [18]. Schematic interschema relationship generation identifies objects in the schemas that may be related and categorizes their relationships [7]. Interschema relationship generation describes the interschema relationships [19]. The final phase produces the integrated schema along with mapping information to support data access via the integrated schema [7, 19].

The output of schema integration is a single, cohesive schema [10], which is also referred to as a "multidatabase" [18]. Schema integration brings together large collections of data, enhancing query processing and simplifying data exploration.

3.4 Phase 4: Exploration

In many cases, potentially useful information may be obtained from an integrated database using simple custom-crafted queries. In a physical environment, location information about an incident such as a gunshot can be acquired from GPS locations recorded on smartphones, cellular tower associations and hotspot connections. Audio and video records could be obtained from smartphones in the proximity of the incident that were in the recording mode. The exact formulation of the query may depend on the density of smartphones in a given location as well as the expected range of the sound. In a tourist hotspot, it is likely that many videos would be recorded.

Clearly, all sources of evidence are not equally precise: a recording may enable an investigator to pinpoint the time very accurately. However, if an individual who was engaged in a telephone conversation heard the sound, the positioning of the gunshot event in time could only be tied to the period of the phone call. Of course, if multiple individuals engaged in phone calls were to hear the gunshot, the intersection of the phone call periods would provide a more accurate estimate of the time. Therefore, an investigator should prioritize queries to initially find recordings that provide the required information, and then proceed to find activities that may yield less precise results.

Queries about average message propagation delays (in mobile networks, Internet and social networks) could be used to infer location information. Querying communications data, such as call logs and messages, can identify mutual relationships between individuals that were previously unknown. Such queries can also determine the propagation of a specific piece of information and identify not only the individuals involved in propagating the information, but also the order in which the propagation took place. Indeed, data exploration using queries can be very useful in myriad scenarios.

Multiple smartphones can help determine the exact times of events more accurately; also they can confirm the correctness of evidence obtained from one (or a few) smartphones if the database entries of all the smartphones are consistent. Conversely, the absence of consistent entries for a large enough set of independent smartphones where some entries are expected or the presence of inconsistent entries on other smartphones may cast doubt on the evidence.

Despite the utility of simple queries, the real forensic power of a distributed database created from smartphones lies in the complex questions that can be answered. SQL querying and visualization are two important mechanisms that assist in phrasing complex queries and understanding the results.

SQL Querying. SQL can be used to create complex queries that are of forensic use. Considerable flexibility is provided by the WHERE clause of the SQL SELECT statement; indeed, this clause imposes hardly any limits on what may be compared in a distributed database. However, this paper focuses on the powerful abilities of the SELECT statement to summarize results. SELECT can, of course, be used with aggregation functions such as count, sum, average, maximum and minimum. We explore the forensic uses of the GROUP BY, HAVING and ORDER BY clauses.

The GROUP BY clause is often used in conjunction with aggregation functions to group the result set according to one or more columns [13]. From a forensic perspective, the GROUP BY clause provides assistance in categorizing a large collection of data according to specified groups. For example, a table storing text messages from a particular smartphone can quickly grow to a significant size, making it difficult for an investigator to identify the communications that occurred between individuals of interest. The GROUP BY clause can be used to group text messages by individual, reducing the data volume and simplifying the analysis.

The HAVING clause was added to SQL because the WHERE clause could not be used with aggregation functions [13]. Building on the example above, the HAVING clause can be used to select the individuals whose communication rates (average numbers of text messages sent during specific time periods) were particular high. If the period in time correlates with an event being investigated, the individuals with high communication rates could be involved in the event in some manner.

The ORDER BY clause is used to structure data to appear in a specific order [13]. The order in which data is presented can speed analysis. Continuing with the example, the data may be ordered to show the text messages that were sent by individuals near the time when the event of interest was known to have taken place. Identifying these individuals can lead to the discovery of data with forensic value.

Visualization. Visualization techniques can enable an investigator to quickly explore and analyze specific characteristics of the query results [5]; they can also be used to prove or disprove hypotheses. Useful visualization techniques include temporal, relational and dynamic analysis. Part of the power of visualization stems from the fact that a visual representation often reveals patterns, exceptions to patterns and inconsistencies that are not obvious from the raw data. We recommend a two-pronged approach. First, queries may be structured to find artifacts without using visualization. Visualization can then be used to confirm any patterns. Visualization is also used to present complex evidence in court proceedings. In this case, a query could be formulated to test some hypothesis and the result (possibly with visualization) could be used to confirm or reject the hypothesis. The alternative is to "read" the visualizations, i.e., use visualization to formulate hypotheses that are tested in some other manner.

The first visualization technique, temporal analysis, helps reconstruct events using a timeline. In some cases, a partial ordering (or better) suffices; as Cohen [5] points out, it is inconsistent to claim that A caused B if B precedes A. In other cases, exact times may be required.

A query-based strategy to determine a timeline in the given context would proceed as follows. First, a set of smartphones that automatically set their times from external sources (e.g., telecommunications networks or GPS). The consistency of the times on the devices can be confirmed by finding common events in their databases and comparing the recorded times. Care should be taken to ensure that the common events are actually shared events; in many cases, common events may be communicated sequentially to smartphones with expected differences in recorded times. Note also that smartphones that use different shared time servers may have times that are consistent with those that use the same server, but not necessarily with smartphones that use other servers. However, if the time servers are to be trusted, the differences between them should remain constant (i.e., no drift). If this is the case, it is easy to harmonize time.

The next query may then be formulated to determine if the times on the devices containing the evidence can be harmonized with the times on other devices, which is also done by finding common events on the smartphones and the independent events. If this is done successfully, the timeline can be reconstructed using the harmonized time on the devices containing the evidence. Note that the times on different independent smartphones cannot be expected to match perfectly, slight variance is almost always present. This variance can be carried forward during the various queries that set the time of an event on an evidentiary device not as a specific instant, but as a time range with some probability. In most cases, the ranges would be small enough to identify specific times for evidentiary use; but, of course, these would have to be verified empirically.

Note that the strategy described in the previous paragraph assumes that all the checks will pass. However, this may not be the case in the real world. Hence, the process may be followed by an investigator, with alternatives needing to be explored when the "normal" process fails. More specifically, the investigator may use the process under the supervision of a forensic scientist. When it works (and all standards have been adhered to) the scientist can sign off on the results. This is similar to what happens at a DNA laboratory, where the majority of tests are handled by technicians under the supervision of a forensic pathologist. The forensic pathologist gets involved in the process when the standard protocol does not yield good results.

The second visualization technique, relational analysis, is the identification of meaningful relationships existing between various entities. A query-based strategy to identify the relationships would use custom queries to first select all communications data between a set of smartphones that have evidence pertaining to an event. This data would include text messages, instant messages, email and call logs, all of which could be used to determine relationships between individuals. Next, GPS data or a timeline generated by temporal analysis would be used to identify the relationships between individuals described using times and locations.

Visualizations provided by temporal and relational analyses offer static pictures of events that occurred at a specific times and locations. The third technique, dynamic analysis, can replay a sequence of events by changing one or more properties related to the events. The properties include time and location, which may be changed to visualize the effects on the events. Dynamic analysis provides an interactive view of the reconstruction of the events surrounding an incident. The richer the interactive features, the more thoroughly the events can be explored and analyzed.

It is important to note that the computation of a timeline and the elucidation of relationships, although inspired by visualization, are quite distinct from the visualization process itself. Visualization helps the uninitiated to comprehend the results, but they may read more (or less) in the results than what the results actually convey. Visualization is useful for conveying results that have already been determined to be probative. Visualization is also useful for finding investigative leads. Problems arise when these two applications of visualization are confused.

4. Discussion

The mobile event reconstruction process provides several advantages in support of digital forensic investigations. The process can handle a diverse collection of smartphones, increasing the quality and quantity of evidence. Furthermore, the process allows for the proper integration of datasets extracted from multiple smartphones by leveraging database integration theory. The process also enhances data analysis by using a set of custom queries to analyze the data and reveal latent information. Finally, the process can assist digital forensic investigations by helping visualize the queried data. The output of the process is the reconstruction of events surrounding a particular incident, including the events that occurred before, during and after the incident.

5. Conclusions

Smartphones store vast amounts of valuable data in SQLite databases, making them important assets in digital forensic investigations. A collection of smartphones corresponds to a distributed database of nodes containing potential evidence about events of interest. The mobile event reconstruction process described in this paper allows for event reconstruction by querying an integrated database created from the individual SQLite smartphone databases. The process, which incorporates tried and tested visualization techniques, creates detailed accounts of the events that took place before, during and after an incident.

Future work will focus on refining the mobile event reconstruction process and exploring the addition of evidence from devices other than smartphones. Also, the performance and functionality of the process will be evaluated using real-world scenarios.

References

[1] AccessData, Mobile Phone Examiner Plus (MPE+), Lindon, Utah (www.accessdata.com/products/digital-forensics/mobile-phone-examiner).

[2] A. Arnes, P. Haas, G. Vigna and R. Kemmerer, Digital forensic reconstruction and the virtual security testbed ViSe, *Proceedings of the Third International Conference on Detection of Intrusions and Malware and Vulnerability Assessment*, pp. 144–163, 2006.

[3] A. Caithness, The Forensic Implications of SQLite's Write Ahead Log, CCL Group, Stratford-upon-Avon, United Kingdom (www.cclgroupltd.com/the-forensic-implications-of-sqlites-write-ahead-log), 2012.

[4] E. Casey, *Digital Evidence and Computer Crime*, Elsevier, Waltham, Massachusetts, 2011.

[5] F. Cohen, *Digital Forensic Evidence Examination*, Fred Cohen & Associates, Livermore, California, 2009.

[6] K. Curran, A. Robinson, S. Peacocke and S. Cassidy, Mobile phone forensic analysis, *International Journal of Digital Crime and Forensics*, vol. 2(3), pp. 15–27, 2010.

[7] A. Elmagarmid, M. Rusinkiewicz and A. Sheth (Eds.), *Management of Heterogeneous and Autonomous Database Systems*, Morgan Kaufmann Publishers, San Francisco, California, 1999.

[8] M. Eltabakh, Data Integration, CS561-Spring 2012, Department of Computer Science, Worcester Polytechnic Institute, Worcester, Massachusetts (web.cs.wpi.edu/~cs561/s12/Lectures/Integra tionOLAP/DataIntegration.pdf), 2012.

[9] Forensic Science Central, Crime Scene and Accident Scene Reconstruction (www.forensicsciencecentral.co.uk/reconstruct ion.shtml), 2005.

[10] A. Gal, A. Trombetta, A. Anaby-Tavor and D. Montesi, A model for schema integration in heterogeneous databases, *Proceedings of the Seventh International Database Engineering and Applications Symposium*, pp. 2-11, 2003.

[11] P. Gladyshev, Formalizing Event Reconstruction in Digital Investigations, Ph.D. Dissertation, Department of Computer Science, University College Dublin, Dublin, Ireland, 2004.

[12] P. Gladyshev and A. Patel, Finite state machine approach to digital event reconstruction, *Digital Investigation*, vol. 1(2), pp. 130–149, 2004.

[13] H. Halvorsen, Structured Query Language, Department of Electrical Engineering, Information Technology and Cybernetics, Telemark University College, Porsgrunn, Norway (home. hit.no/~hansha/documents/database/documents/Structured% 20Query%20Language.pdf), 2012.

[14] S. Jeon, J. Bang, K. Byun and S. Lee, A recovery method of deleted record for SQLite database, *Personal and Ubiquitous Computing*, vol. 16(6), pp. 707–715, 2012.

[15] MD's Technical Sharing, Raw access to SMS/MMS database on Android phones (minhdanh2002.blogspot.com/2012/02/raw-access-to-sms-database-on-android.html), February 14, 2012.

[16] J. Morris, *Crime Analysis Charting: An Introduction to Visual Investigative Analysis*, Palmer Enterprises, Loomis, California, 1982.

[17] Oxygen Forensics, Oxygen Forensic Suite, Alexandria, Virginia (`www.oxygen-forensic.com/en`).

[18] M. Ozsu and P. Valduriez, *Principles of Distributed Database Systems*, Springer, New York, 2011.

[19] C. Parent and S. Spaccapietra, Issues and approaches of database integration, *Communications of the ACM*, vol. 41(5), pp. 166–178, 1998.

[20] P. Patodi, Database Recovery Mechanism for Android Devices, Ph.D. Dissertation, Department of Computer Science and Engineering, Indian Institute of Technology Bombay, Bombay, India, 2012.

[21] M. Prasad and Y. Satish, Reconstruction of events in digital forensics, *International Journal of Engineering Trends and Technology*, vol. 4(8), pp. 3460–3467, 2013.

[22] B. Schneier, Attack trees, *Dr. Dobb's Journal of Software Tools*, vol. 24(12), pp. 21–29, 1999.

[23] SQLite, About SQLite, Charlotte, North Carolina (`www.sqlite.org/about.html`).

[24] SQLite, The SQLite Database File Format, Charlotte, North Carolina (`www.sqlite.org/fileformat.html`).

[25] SQLite, Write-Ahead Logging, Charlotte, North Carolina (`www.sqlite.org/wal.html`), 2013.

[26] P. Stephenson, Modeling of post-incident root cause analysis, *International Journal of Digital Evidence*, vol. 2(2), 2003.

[27] The iPhone Wiki, Messages (`theiphonewiki.com/wiki/Messages`), August 16, 2013.

[28] viaForensics, viaExtract, Oak Park, Illinois (`viaforensics.com`).

Chapter 17

SMARTPHONE MESSAGE SENTIMENT ANALYSIS

Panagiotis Andriotis, Atsuhiro Takasu, and Theo Tryfonas

Abstract   Humans tend to use specific words to express their emotional states in written and oral communications. Scientists in the area of text mining and natural language processing have studied sentiment fingerprints residing in text to extract the emotional polarity of customers for a product or to evaluate the popularity of politicians. Recent research focused on micro-blogging has found notable similarities between Twitter feeds and SMS (short message service) text messages. This paper investigates the common characteristics of both formats for sentiment analysis purposes and verifies the correctness of the similarity assumption. A lexicon-based approach is used to extract and compute the sentiment scores of SMS messages found on smartphones. The data is presented along a timeline that depicts a sender's emotional fingerprint. This form of analysis and visualization can enrich a forensic investigation by conveying potential psychological patterns from text messages.

Keywords: SMS messages, Twitter feeds, emotion, timeline

1.   Introduction

The evolution of mobile phones from simple telephone devices to sophisticated handheld computers has transformed how users communicate. Modern smartphones are widely used to send email and chat with friends via instant messages. However, the older SMS (short message service) is still one of the most popular mobile phone services because of its simplicity. The textual information in SMS messages convey the thoughts and emotions of the sender.

A forensic investigation typically involves the examination of electronic devices such as computers, hard drives, tablets and smartphones. The goal is to retrieve relevant information, recover deleted files and

G. Peterson and S. Shenoi (Eds.): Advances in Digital Forensics X, IFIP AICT 433, pp. 253–265, 2014.
© IFIP International Federation for Information Processing 2014

present the extracted data in an efficient and intuitive manner. Text messages are an integral part of mobile communications and potentially constitute valuable evidence.

Research efforts in the areas of natural language processing and information retrieval have studied micro-blogging services such as Twitter because of their openness, ubiquity and information content [11, 14]. The extraction of the emotional polarity of text messages is an active research topic. Other researchers (e.g., [19]) note the marked similarity between a tweet (Twitter post) and an SMS message, claiming that Twitter feed analysis techniques can be used to analyze SMS messages. The two formats do indeed have common characteristics. Both involve a limited number of characters (140 for tweets and 160 for SMS messages). In addition, the "@" feature in Twitter can be viewed as a direct message to a specific person, just like an SMS message sent to a contact. Moreover, special symbols such as emoticons and other abbreviations are widely used in Twitter and SMS communications.

This paper extends the textual sentiment analysis work to the domain of digital forensics. It has four main contributions. First, the efficiency of a lexicon-based sentiment analysis algorithm on various datasets (Twitter feeds and SMS messages) is investigated, and the claim that mood analysis methods used on Twitter feeds can also be used on SMS messages is evaluated. Second, the importance of word pre-processing methods is examined along with their contribution to sentiment scoring. Third, the significance of a lexicon is studied and the optimization of a lexicon-based method to improve SMS mood scores is discussed. Finally, a forensic tool that performs sentiment analysis is described; the tool can be used by investigators to search for keywords, compute the sentiment scores of messages and present the sentiment scores in a timeline view.

2.   Background

Sentiment analysis is the process of identifying positive and negative opinions about a subject or topic from a piece of text. Prior work in this field used lexical knowledge and the emotional valence of the words included in vocabularies [12].

Knowledge-based methods use linguistic models to categorize the sentiment of passages of text. These methods construct and use dictionaries in order to capture the sentiments of words. The models can be crafted in a manual [4] or semi-automated manner [20]. Pang, *et al.* [16] implemented three classifiers (naive Bayes, maximum entropy and support vector machines) to evaluate their efficiency in categorizing movie reviews as negative or positive; they conclude that support vector machines work better in most cases. They emphasize that using a more complicated linguistic model such as n-grams does not dramatically improve the results, suggesting that a unigram approach may be sufficient.

Sentiment analysis has been applied to diverse problems ranging from online forum hotspot detection [11] to sentiment classification in microblogs [2, 5]. Melville, *et al.* [12] have developed a framework for sentiment analysis of blogs that combines lexical knowledge with supervised learning for text categorization; they report that it is preferable to incorporate both methods to obtain good results for blog analysis. Taboada, *et al.* [19] have used dictionaries of words with predefined characteristics (polarity and strength) and show that lexicon-based methods for sentiment analysis are robust and can be used in a variety of domains without any training with domain-specific data. Their lexicon-based implementation performs well on diverse tasks ranging from video game reviews to blog post classification.

Twitter is an open micro-blogging service that makes all posts available to the public. The public nature of the data provides researchers with the opportunity to use Twitter as a corpus [14]. Bermingham and Smeaton [2] suggest that it is easier to infer the sentiment polarity of micro-blogging posts compared with blogs, which have richer textual content (they also note the similarity between micro-blogging posts and SMS messages). However, the automatic processing of micro-blogging posts can be problematic because of the use of non-standard words and unusual punctuation [9]. Leong, *et al.* [10] use sentiment mining to analyze SMS messages in teaching evaluations.

In the area of digital forensics, text analysis has been used to extract patterns from email and to construct user-profiles from text [6]. Several researchers (see, e.g., [3]) have focused on investigations and the modeling of texting languages. Despite an extensive search of the literature on mood analysis, we were unable to find any research that engaged principles from opinion and text mining to conduct mobile device forensics.

3. Experimental Setup and Datasets

This section describes the datasets used in the research, the algorithm and the experimental setup.

The Twitter dataset (TWT) used in the research contained 6,566 tweets collected from 33 popular Twitter accounts on August 5, 2013. The accounts belonged to musicians, actors, athletes and managers. A dataset (SENT140) of tweets classified as positive (PoSENT140) and negative (NegSENT140) was also used [7].

The SMS dataset contained 5,574 messages with duplicates [1]. Removing the duplicates yielded 4,827 unique messages that were manually classified as conveying positive or negative sentiments. Negative messages were assumed to express anger, fear, sadness, disgust and boredom (919 messages). Positive messages were assumed to express joy and happiness (1,867 messages). Numerous messages that were not classified as positive or negative were marked as neutral.

The algorithm uses a bag-of-words approach and employed three lexicons containing words linked to positive or negative emotions. The AFINN lexicon [8] contains words with valences ranging from –5 to 5. The Wordnet-Affect lexicon [18] consists of synsets linked to affective labels and words. The NRC lexicon [13] was originally used in a competition on sentiment analysis on Twitter feeds. The lexicons were sanitized by eliminating hashtag symbols (#) and words that appeared to be irrelevant to sentiment analysis (e.g., "5yo" and plain letters like "t"). The sanitized vocabularies consisted of 25,675 words and abbreviations corresponding to positive emotions, and 20,636 corresponding to negative emotions.

The methodology for calculating sentiment scores used the three lexicons to score each tweet and SMS. Let L_p be the set of positive textual markers (positive lexicon) with $l_{pi} \in L_p$ for $i = 1, 2, \ldots, m$ and let L_n be the set of negative textual markers (negative lexicon) with $l_{nj} \in L_n$ for $j = 1, 2, \ldots, n$. The corpus C consists of tweets and SMS messages and $t_k \in C$ denotes an individual message for $k = 1, 2, \ldots, q$. If a positive marker l_{pi} appears in a tweet or SMS (t_k) in the corpus:

$$l_{pi}(t_k) = 1. \tag{1}$$

Otherwise, $l_{pi}(t_k)$ is set to zero. The same calculations were performed for negative markers l_{nj}. The Boolean assignment is based on the fact that the documents are of limited size; thus, there is a limited range of markers in each tweet that contribute to the tweet sentiment score. The tweet sentiment score $s(t_k)$ is equal to the number of positive markers found in a tweet minus the number of negative markers found in the tweet:

$$s(t_k) = \sum_i l_{pi}(t_k) - \sum_j l_{nj}(t_k). \tag{2}$$

4.   Experimental Results

This section describes the experimental results related to determining the impact of stemming on the dataset, identifying the lexicon that results in the best classification accuracy, and analyzing the impact of emoticons.

Table 1. Effect of stemming on Twitter sentiment scores.

	Dataset	None	Total	Neutral
No Stem	TWT	39.1%	60.9%	48.0%
	PoSENT140	28.4%	71.6%	41.5%
	NegSent140	25.3%	74.7%	39.3%
Stem	TWT	31.8%	68.2%	42.3%
	PoSENT140	23.3%	76.7%	36.6%
	NegSent140	18.7%	81.3%	34.7%

4.1 Stemming Results

Stemming is a popular text pre-processing method to obtain the root of a word. For example, the words "connect," "connected" and "connection" have the same root that can be represented by the lemma "connect" [17]. The stemming test discussed in this section evaluates if stemming combined with Equation (2) increases classification accuracy. The experiments used the AFINN lexicon on the Twitter dataset and subsequently on the SMS dataset.

Table 2. Distribution of textual markers in the Twitter datasets.

	Dataset	1	2	3	4	5	6	7+
No Stem	TWT	47.7%	28.7%	14.3%	5.9%	2.1%	0.8%	0.5%
	PoSENT140	40.8%	29.0%	16.1%	8.0%	3.6%	1.5%	1.0%
	NegSent140	43.4%	28.3%	15.4%	7.4%	3.4%	1.3%	0.8%
Stem	TWT	41.6%	28.6%	16.6%	7.8%	3.3%	1.3%	0.8%
	PoSENT140	36.6%	28.0%	17.7%	9.5%	4.7%	2.1%	1.4%
	NegSent140	36.9%	28.1%	17.4%	9.4%	4.7%	2.1%	1.4%

Each tweet from the TWT and SENT140 datasets was stemmed using Porter's stemming algorithm from the Apache Lucene Library prior to calculating the sentiment score. Table 1 compares the sentiment scores obtained with and without stemming. The column "None" lists the percentages of tweets that did not contain matching words from the lexicon. "Total" lists the percentages of tweets that contained at least one matching word (positive or negative). "Neutral" lists the percentages of tweets that had a sentiment score of zero. Table 2 shows the number of textual markers found in a single tweet.

Table 1 shows that stemming improves the identification of tweets. Another observation is that the Boolean sentiment scores have high "Neutral" classifications. The algorithm sorted 48% of the tweets as

Table 3. Effect of stemming on SMS sentiment scores.

	None	Total	Neutral $s(t_k)$
No Stem	40.6%	59.4%	50.2%
Stem	31.9%	68.1%	42.8%

Table 4. Distribution of textual markers in the SMS dataset.

	1	2	3	4	5	6	7	8/9	10+
No Stem	45.1%	25.2%	14.5%	6.8%	3.7%	2.5%	0.8%	1.0%	0.4%
Stem	42.2%	25.0%	14.6%	7.5%	4.4%	2.6%	1.7%	1.6%	0.4%

neutral, but the percentage of the messages that did not contain any matching words was 39.1%. This difference is because several tweets have zero sentiment scores (i.e., equal numbers of positive and negative markers). In fact, Table 2 shows that the positive and negative datasets have almost the same numbers of matching words. This finding is an indication that a balanced lexicon (i.e., AFINN) is used in the bag-of-words approach.

Tables 3 and 4 present the results of the same experiment conducted on the SMS dataset. The lexicon used the AFINN vocabulary and the SMS dataset was first analyzed without stemming and then with stemming after applying Porter's algorithm. Table 3 shows that stemming enhances the efficiency of SMS sentiment analysis because the number of classified messages is increased from 59.4% to 68.1%. Table 4 supports the assessment that AFINN is a balanced lexicon with similar numbers of positive and negative scores. The results also confirm that the methods used for Twitter sentiment analysis help discern the emotional trends of users during forensic examinations of smartphones.

4.2   Lexicon Results

Three vocabularies were compared to test the generalizability of the sentiment score: (i) the AFINN lexicon (Tables 1 through 4); (ii) the WordNet-Affect lexicon, which contains formal words that are not widely used in the micro-blogging world; and (iii) the NRC lexicon, which contains many words and hashtags (#) associated with positive or negative emotions. The NRC lexicon was sanitized to fit the bag-of-words approach, but many lemmas such as "okayyy" were present in both categories (positive and negative), making us skeptical about its use. The NRC lexicon also included symbols and Internet slang.

In the case of the WordNet-Affect lexicon, roughly one to three matching words were found in each tweet and 68.5% of the tweets had neutral sentiment scores. For the NRC lexicon, 20.6% of the tweets had neutral emotional scores while 96.9% of the tweets contained at least one word from the lexicon. However, the distributions of matching words were very different compared with the previous results. For example, there were as many as 20 "matching" words in a single tweet. This occurred because many textual markers were present in the positive and negative lexicons. The fact that such an extensive and diverse lexicon could not decrease the percentage of tweets rated with $s(t_k) = 0$ motivated us to use the AFINN lexicon in the remainder of the study.

4.3   Emoticon Results

Many people, particularly young smartphone users, include symbols and special words to abbreviate their messages and produce more concise text. The most popular symbols are called "emoticons." An emoticon is a symbol that expresses an emotion; for example, happiness is represented using a smiling face ":)" emoticon. Based on the characteristics of the SMS dataset, the AFINN lexicon was extended to include emoticons.

Due to the number of neutral sentiment scores, the computation of sentiment scores was modified to include valence. In lexicons such as NRC and AFINN, words are presented with their emotional valence. In AFINN, for example, the textual marker "amazing" has a valence of 4 and the word "approval" has a valence of 2. The maximum valence is 5 and the minimum valence is –5, denoting the most powerful negative emotion. We rated the emoticons as having higher valences on the assumption that users add these symbols to their text messages to express strong feelings. Hence, emoticons should have the highest weight when incorporated in the sentiment scores. In this case, Equation (2) does not change, and the difference arises in the manner in which the contribution of each marker to the final score is computed. Instead, $l_{pi}(t_k) = 1$ in Equation (1) is changed to $l_{pi}(t_k) = v$ where $v \in \{-5, -4, \ldots, 4, 5\}$ is the valence of each textual marker.

Table 5 shows the results obtained after repeating the tests on the SMS dataset with the emoticon-enhanced AFINN lexicon and the revised sentiment score computation that includes valence. Note that the addition of emoticons and valence both have a positive effect on the success rates and reduce the numbers of false positives and false negatives.

Table 5.   Success and failure rates of lexicon-based sentiment analysis.

	Datasets	Total	FPR	FNR	Hit Rate
AFINN	Positive	1,867	12.1%	32.6%	55.3%
	Negative	919	22.7%	32.4%	44.8%
Emoticons	Positive	1,867	11.5%	31.1%	57.4%
	Negative	919	22.0%	31.7%	46.3%
Emoticons	Positive	1,867	7.3%	23.9%	68.8%
and Valence	Negative	919	29.2%	25.0%	45.8%

5.   Combining Sentiment Analysis with Forensics

A common practice during forensic analysis is to use Linux commands such as `strings` and `grep` to view and elaborate text. Additionally, an analyst may use open source tools such as the SQLite Database Browser and SQLiteman to view the contents of databases. Our forensic tool extends the database view and incorporates the sentiment analysis approach presented in this paper. This enables the tool to be used to search for keywords in a database, compute the sentiment scores of messages, and present the sentiment scores in a timeline view.

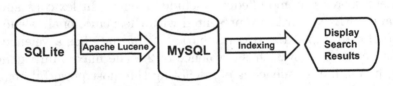

Figure 1.   Schematic diagram of the forensic tool.

Figure 1 shows a schematic diagram of the forensic tool. First, all the requested content from an SMS SQLite database (`/data/com.android.providers.telephony/databases/mmssms.db`) is stored in a MySQL database. Next, Apache Lucene is used to produce unstemmed SMS message keywords for searching, and stemmed words for SMS mood analysis. After all the data is processed, search indexes are constructed to answer text queries posed by forensic examiners.

The forensic tool was tested on an image extracted from a Samsung Galaxy Y S5360 smartphone running the Android 2.3.5 operating system. Unfortunately, the database contained non-English messages; since these messages had no lexical matches, no sentiment scores were generated. We substituted SMS messages in `mmssms.db` with random tweets from the TWT database. After running the tool, we had a MySQL

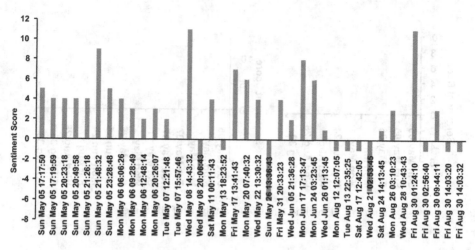

Figure 2. Timeline emotional analysis of SMS messages.

database containing the data from `mmssms.db` and the keywords extracted from each "message" along with the computed sentiment scores.

The forensic tool is designed to provide forensic examiners with a timeline analysis interface that conveys the emotion of each SMS message found on a smartphone. This could provide a quick indication of the emotional states of a user over time. For example, if the person being investigated was generally in a good mood, except for a certain period of time when negative emotions were observed, it might be worthwhile for a forensic examiner to focus on that specific time period.

Figure 2 shows the mood timeline of SMS messages extracted from the SQLite database, including the messages sent to and received from all contacts. Note that the smartphone user mostly exchanged messages that have positive emotional fingerprints. However, there are some periods (e.g., from 12th August until 17th August) when the sentiment scores are negative. The timeline view provides the forensic examiner with a general perspective of user behavior as well as the opportunity to focus on periods that may be of special interest.

The forensic tool enables an examiner to focus on the communications between two parties, or to view the sentiment scores of only the received or sent messages. For example, Figure 3(a) shows the sentiment scores of all the messages exchanged with a specific device. Figure 3(b) shows the scores of all the messages sent by the user.

Finally, the MySQL database may be searched using the index. Figure 4 shows the results obtained for the search term "happy." The tool returned four hits, each with details such as the message ID in the origi-

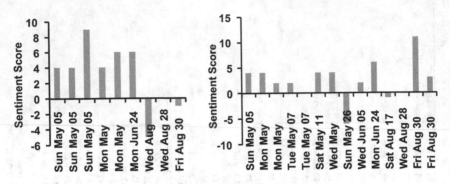

Figure 3. Timeline emotional analysis of SMS messages.

```
Found 4 hits.
1. It is a boy! So happy for my cousin Kate and the future King of England!
---- Database id: 11 on Mon May 06 20:26:07 JST 2013 received from: +3        48
2. Happy Halloween from me &amp; the dummy http://t.co/jQxPvHqi
---- Database id: 32 on Mon Aug 26 03:10:23 JST 2013 received from: +44        94
3. Happy 4th of July! In 1776, Betsy Ross signed the Gettysburg Address and celebrated at the Boston Tea Party. It was a magical day.
---- Database id: 19 on Mon May 20 07:40:32 JST 2013 received from: +3        8
4. Congratulations to my dear friend @JimmyKimmel and his beautiful new wife! I am so happy for him. I had no idea he was straight.
---- Database id: 14 on Wed May 08 14:43:32 JST 2013 received from: +3        40
```

Figure 4. Searching the MySQL database.

nal SQLite database, the date the message was sent or received, and the contact involved in the communication.

6. Conclusions

Current methods used for Twitter sentiment analysis are very useful for depicting the emotional polarity of SMS messages. The results obtained using emoticons and the sentiment valence of words demonstrate the value of a bag-of-words approach. Furthermore, the results can be enhanced by employing a dynamic lexicon.

The digital forensic tool described in this paper merges traditional string searches with text mining to expedite the retrieval of sentiment indications from SMS messages. In particular, the tool can be used by investigators to search for keywords, compute the sentiment scores of messages and present the sentiment scores in a timeline view. This functionality can enrich a forensic investigation by revealing the psychological patterns of users from their text messages.

Our future research will employ the mood analysis approach to produce a timeline view of all smartphone content, including email, instant messages, notes and social network activities. Also, we plan to investigate the application of support vector machine classifiers to enhance the efficiency of the digital forensic tool.

Acknowledgement

This research was supported by the European Union's Prevention of and Fight against Crime Programme "Illegal Use of Internet" – ISEC 2010 Action Grants (HOME/2010/ISEC/AG/INT-002), the National Institute of Informatics, the Systems Centre of the University of Bristol and Project NIFTy (HOME/2012/ISEC/AG/INT/4000003892).

References

[1] T. Almeida, J. Hidalgo and A. Yamakami, Contributions to the study of SMS spam filtering: New collection and results, *Proceedings of the Eleventh ACM Symposium on Document Engineering*, pp. 259–262, 2011.

[2] A. Bermingham and A. Smeaton, Classifying sentiment in microblogs: Is brevity an advantage? *Proceedings of the Nineteenth ACM International Conference on Information and Knowledge Management*, pp. 1833–1836, 2010.

[3] M. Choudhury, R. Saraf, V. Jain, A. Mukherjee, S. Sarkar and A. Basu, Investigation and modeling of the structure of texting language, *International Journal of Document Analysis and Recognition*, vol. 10(3-4), pp. 157–174, 2007.

[4] S. Das and M. Chen, Yahoo! for Amazon: Sentiment extraction from small talk on the web, *Management Science*, vol. 53(9), pp. 1375–1388, 2007.

[5] X. Ding, B. Liu and P. Yu, A holistic lexicon-based approach to opinion mining, *Proceedings of the International Conference on Web Search and Web Data Mining*, pp. 231–240, 2008.

[6] D. Estival, T. Gaustad, S. Pham, W. Radford and B. Hutchinson, Author profiling for English emails, *Proceedings of the Tenth Conference of the Pacific Association for Computational Linguistics*, pp. 263–272, 2007.

[7] A. Go, R. Bhayani and L. Huang, Twitter Sentiment Classification using Distant Supervision, CS224N Final Project Report, Department of Computer Science, Stanford University, Stanford, California, 2009.

[8] L. Hansen, A. Arvidsson, F. Nielsen, E. Colleoni and M. Etter, Good friends, bad news-affect and virality in Twitter, in *Future Information Technology*, J. Park, L. Yang and C. Lee (Eds), Springer, Berlin-Heidelberg, Germany, pp. 34–43, 2011.

[9] G. Laboreiro, L. Sarmento, J. Teixeira and E. Oliveira, Tokenizing micro-blogging messages using a text classification approach, *Proceedings of the Fourth Workshop on Analytics for Noisy Unstructured Text Data*, pp. 81–88, 2010.

[10] C. Leong, Y. Lee and W. Mak, Mining sentiments in SMS texts for teaching evaluation, *Expert Systems with Applications*, vol. 39(3), pp. 2584–2589, 2012.

[11] N. Li and D. Wu, Using text mining and sentiment analysis for online forums hotspot detection and forecast, *Decision Support Systems*, vol. 48(2), pp. 354–368, 2010.

[12] P. Melville, W. Gryc and R. Lawrence, Sentiment analysis of blogs by combining lexical knowledge with text classification, *Proceedings of the Fifteenth ACM SIGKDD International Conference on Knowledge Discovery and Data Mining*, pp. 1275–1284, 2009.

[13] S. Mohammad, S. Kiritchenko and X. Zhu, NRC-Canada: Building the state-of-the-art in sentiment analysis of tweets, *Proceedings of the Seventh International Workshop on Semantic Evaluation Exercises*, 2013.

[14] A. Pak and P. Paroubek, Twitter as a corpus for sentiment analysis and opinion mining, *Proceedings of the Seventh International Conference on Language Resources and Evaluation*, pp. 1320–1326, 2010.

[15] B. Pang and L. Lee, Opinion mining and sentiment analysis, *Foundations and Trends in Information Retrieval*, vol. 2(1-2), pp. 1–135, 2008.

[16] B. Pang, L. Lee and S. Vaithyanathan, Thumbs up? Sentiment classification using machine learning techniques, *Proceedings of the Association for Computational Linguistics Conference on Empirical Methods in Natural Language Processing*, vol. 10, pp. 79–86, 2002.

[17] M. Porter, An algorithm for suffix stripping, *Program: Electronic Library and Information Systems*, vol. 14(3), pp. 130–137, 1980.

[18] C. Strapparava and R. Mihalcea, Semeval-2007 Task 14: Affective text, *Proceedings of the Fourth International Workshop on Semantic Evaluations*, pp. 70–74, 2007.

[19] M. Taboada, J. Brooke, M. Tofiloski, K. Voll and M. Stede, Lexicon-based methods for sentiment analysis, *Computational Linguistics*, vol. 37(2), pp. 267–307, 2011.

[20] H. Yu and V. Hatzivassiloglou, Towards answering opinion questions: Separating facts from opinions and identifying the polarity of opinion sentences, *Proceedings of the Conference on Empirical Methods in Natural Language Processing*, pp. 129–136, 2013.

Chapter 18

FORENSIC ANALYSIS OF THE TOMTOM NAVIGATION APPLICATION

Nhien-An Le-Khac, Mark Roeloffs, and Tahar Kechadi

Abstract   Exactly where an individual has been is important when attempting to forensically reconstruct an incident. With the advent of portable navigation systems and mobile phones, information about where a person has been is recorded more comprehensively than ever before. This paper focuses on the data recorded by the Android TomTom Navigation Application. It also describes how mobile device usage data can assist a digital forensic practitioner in determining where the device has been.

Keywords: Forensic acquisition, TomTom, GPS devices, smartphones

1.   Introduction

Devices equipped with Global Positioning System (GPS) navigation capabilities assist motorists, pilots and sailors in determining their geographical locations and provide information such as maps, directions, alternative routes and their status, and the locations of amenities (e.g., food and fuel). Because these devices store historic navigation data, the acquisition and analysis of forensic evidence from the devices is of great interest. One of the market leaders in the domain of personal GPS navigation systems is the TomTom Portable Navigation Device (TomTom PND).

Smartphones are used for all kinds of activities, from placing calls to browsing on the Internet and playing games. But more important is the fact that users carry their smartphones wherever they go [2]. Smartphones often incorporate an embedded GPS chip. From a forensic perspective, this feature is very important because it is possible to know the geographical location of the device at any given time. However, a large number of diverse mobile device applications are available, each of which stores relevant data in proprietary formats. The primary chal-

G. Peterson and S. Shenoi (Eds.): Advances in Digital Forensics X, IFIP AICT 433, pp. 267–276, 2014.

lenge in mobile device forensics is to extract and analyze data from these applications.

Android is currently the most widely used smartphone platform in the United States [4]. One of the most popular navigation applications on Android devices is the TomTom Navigation Application (TomTom NA). It was launched in October 2012 and has been downloaded thousands of times. The application stores multiple geographical points and time-stamps during navigation, making any device that uses the application very valuable in an investigation.

This paper focuses on the forensic acquisition and analysis of navigation data from the TomTom NA. A step-by-step procedure for retrieving forensic data from TomTom NA is described. Multiple driving tests with a Samsung Galaxy S3 (GT-i9300) mobile phone were conducted to locate and decode the significant files. These files contain information about favorite locations, addresses and routes. The paper also compares the data that is available in a TomTom PND and a TomTom NA.

2.   Related Work

The vast majority of TomTom device research has focused on the TomTom PND. Analysis of a TomTom PND requires the device to be rooted in order to copy the data [6]. The process described by Nutter [8] extracts a physical image to retrieve the most important files, which are subsequently decoded. The retrieved files include a settings file and data residing in unallocated clusters [8]. The commercial tool TomTology [5] can decode images extracted from the first generation of TomTom PNDs, but not later generations of the device.

Research related to Android mobile phone forensics (see, e.g., [1, 7]) has not considered the TomTom NA. To our knowledge, this is the first effort to focus on the TomTom NA used in Android smartphones.

3.   Methodology

Documenting the navigation data available from the TomTom NA involves three steps: (i) physical image extraction; (ii) file identification; and (iii) file decoding and analysis.

Most of the data collection was performed by planning routes, entering favorites, changing the home location, etc. in the town of Gouda, The Netherlands. Two routes in the vicinity of Gouda, approximately 3 km each, were driven while using the TomTom NA.

Physical image extraction used the UFED Physical Analyzer [3]. This tool was chosen over manual bootloader methods because of their complexity and the fact that different devices require different methods.

3.1   Identifying Important Files

The files found in a mobile device are not all forensically useful, so the crucial task is to identify the files of interest. The favorite location data, address and location files were identified by comparing the images before and after entering the test data for altered files; the important files identified by the comparison procedure were designated for extraction using a forensic tool. Because many changes occur throughout the system, it was easiest to perform the comparison of mobile phone filesystems. The process of searching for important files involved three steps: (i) loading the physical image into software (e.g., UFED Physical Analyzer) that decodes the filesystem; (ii) searching for the TomTom folder using the string "tomtom;" and (iii) examining the files in the TomTom folder to identify the altered files.

3.2   File Decoding

The identified files were decoded and analyzed to determine how the data is stored within the files. Because the information is stored in the XML format, useful metadata is also present [10]. Scripts were written to decode the files and extract the relevant information. The outputs of the scripts were presented in the form of tables to help interpret the recovered data.

4.   Results

The TomTom NA stores most of the relevant data in base64 strings in XML files. Because of the base64 encoding, each of the strings must be decoded to become readable.

The TomTom NA also uses a consistent location data structure to identify the places of interest to a user. The location data structure includes the following components:

- **Location_UserName:** The name given (by a user) to a location (not applicable if it is an address).

- **Location_UserPos:** The position of the location in a specified coordinate system (usually decimal degrees). This is the point that the user enters into the device.

- **Location_LocName:** In the case of a street address, the street name is saved in this field. If the location is a city, the city name is stored in this field.

- **Location_LocType:** The type of the location. The following types have been identified:

- LOCTYP_MAPTICK: Navigated to a "Point on Map" or to a "Latitude-Longitude."

- LOCTYP_ADDRESS: Navigated to an "Address" or "Contact."

- LOCTYP_HOME: Navigated to "Home."

- LOCTYP_POI: Navigated to a "Point of Interest."

- LOCTYP_undefined: No defined location.

- LOCTYP_FAVOURITE: Navigated to a "Favorite."

- LOCTYP_GPS: The current GPS location. If this is in a route stream, it is also the last known position. The current GPS position may be incorrect if there was no GPS coverage (in which case, the last known GPS location is stored).

■ **Location_CityName:** The city associated with the location.

■ **HouseNumber_Number:** The house number associated with the address.

There is no option to see if a location was visited, unless the Location_LocType is LOCTYP_GPS, in which case, the location was visited at some point in time. The relevant files and data identified include settings, favorite locations and searches, and recent destinations.

4.1   NavkitSettings.xml

The NavkitSettings.xml file contains the home locations and a range of settings.

■ **UP_HomeLocations:** This item stores the home locations. The TomTom application can store multiple numbered home locations. The location with the highest number is the current home location.

■ **TTPlusManager:** This item contains all the paid subscriptions activated in the TomTom application. Some of these subscriptions are for Mobile HD traffic, TomTom Places, Free POIs, Free Maps and Free Voices. The start and end times are stored with each subscription. The TTPlusManager data type has entries for the username, password, ConnectionData_LastValidTime, ConnectionData _LastConnectionTime and AccountInfo_DatelastUpdate. The times for ConnectionData_LastValidTime, ConnectionData _LastConnectionTime and AccountInfo_DatelastUpdate are off by one month and one day. Repeated observations indicated that the

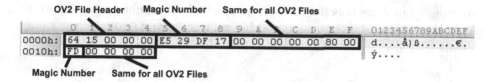

Figure 1. OV2 file header.

date on the TomTom servers is off by one month. The time is correct and is in Greenwich Mean Time (GMT).

- **LastDockedPositionX, LastDockedPositionY, LastDocked Time:** These three items reference the last docked location. Last-DockedPositionX and LastDockedPositionY contain the longitude and latitude of the last docked position in the location format. The time is stored differently from the other time records (i.e., minutes instead of seconds). Therefore, decoding requires the time to be multiplied by 60 to convert it to the time format used elsewhere in the application.

- **MapUpdateLastReminderDate,LastMapShareConnection Reminder, LMGDisplayDate, LastMapShareSubscription Reminder, LastTimeTempBTEnabled:** These items correspond to static dates and times. We were unable to alter the values.

- **UserTimeOffset:** This item stores the offset (in seconds) of the clock in the mobile device. For example, when the time offset is GMT +2 (summer time in The Netherlands), the value of the variable is 7,259. Dividing the value by 3,600 results in a value of approximately 2, which corresponds to the GMT offset.

- **ArrivalTime:** During testing, it was not possible to change the value of this item, which remained fixed at 86,401. We concluded that the value is not changed by the application.

- **LocalSearchService:** This item contains the local search history. A search term that is used multiple times is stored only once.

4.2   Favorites

The favorites are stored in the `Favorites.ov2` file. The OV2 file also appears in TomTom PNDs and the format is documented in the TomTom API [9]. Figure 1 shows the header of an OV2 file. The first five bytes are the OV2 file header. The next four bytes at offset `0x10`

are magic numbers specific to OV2 files, which are different for different
Android devices. The bytes located between 0x09 and 0x0F are the same
for all OV2 files.

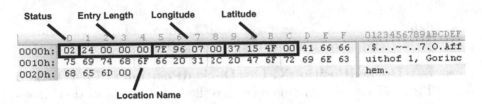

Figure 2.   OV2 Favorite entry.

Figure 2 shows an example Favorite entry. The first byte is a status
byte, which indicates that the entry is a current favorite. The next four
bytes denote the length of the entry (in this case, 0x35). The next eight
bytes hold the longitude and latitude of the location. The user string
is the last part on the entry, which is a null-terminated ASCII string.
Note that the home location is not stored as a favorite.

4.3   Benelux_XXXXXXXX.xml

The Benelux_XXXXXXXX.xml file contains a large number of relevant
fields. The XXXXXXXX in the Benelux filename is a number that is specific to a particular mobile device model. Each mobile device model is
assigned a number (not necessarily unique). For example, a Samsung
Galaxy S3 smartphone has the file Benelux_AF7DE92B.xml.

The most relevant portion of the Benelux_XXXXXXXX.xml file is the
data immediately preceding the final </string> tag. The XML items
in this file include: EngineRecents; AddressRecents; NeverAskedDe-
faultCountry; SafetyCameraWarnings; LastSelectedPoi; PoiSet; Route
Stream; LastSelectedSearchItem; LastKnownTrueGpsPosX; LastKnown
TrueGpsPosY; PDKAutoShutdown; PDKDisableiPodMenuIcon; Regu-
larRouteLocHome; RegularRouteLocWork; LastSelectedPoiData; PD-
KUseDefaultSettingsFromUserFile; TrafficOnMap; SoundVolumeHands-
Free; TrafficAutoUpdate; TrafficAutoReplan; TaiwanCenterAvailable;
CurrentTrafficRouteType; PoiWarnings; GeoFormat; CurrentSelected-
CountryIndex; TrafficUpdateFrequency; UserEnabledTraffic; PoicatHot
listCat; SupportASN; ValidPassword; PoicatHotListValidatedOnce; Poi
catHotlistHit; UserMarkerAvailable; TrafficWarnings; EnableBT.

The most relevant items from the forensic point of view are:

- **EngineRecents:** This item stores the recently visited locations in the location format. The locations include addresses, points of interest (POIs) and particular points on a map.

- **AddressRecents:** While EngineRecents stores all the locations, AddressRecents only stores the locations that are addresses.

- **RouteStream:** This item stores the departure location data, the destination location data and the departure time. If the device has a GPS lock, the departure location is the current GPS location. If not, the last known location is stored. The departure time is dependent on the clock of the device, not the GPS time. Therefore, if the time on the device is set incorrectly, the departure time is also incorrect.

- **LastSelectedPoi:** This item stores the last selected location (or POI) in the location format.

- **LastSelectedSearchItem:** The TomTom application has an option to perform a local search. The TomTom local search looks for the closest location of interest near the current location. For example, a user who wishes to find a retail store would enter the name of the store and TomTom would attempt to locate the closest stores using an Internet connection. In the local search screen, the last selected search item can be seen; this item is stored in LastSelectedSearchItem. The sub-data types are the same as for the EngineRecents data type.

- **RegularRouteLocHome/Work:** During the research, this item was observed not to store any data. However, the name suggests that it stores a regular route to help the user plan a trip. The item could, perhaps, be used by the user to see the amount of traffic on a home/work route.

- **LastKnownTrueGpsPosX/PosY:** These items store the last known GPS position. The GPS time is not stored.

- **LastSelectedPoiData:** This item stores the location of the last selected POI. An inconsistency regarding the stored data is that the GPS location must be halved in order to match the GPS location format used elsewhere in the application.

4.4 Voices

The TomTom Android program includes a VoiceProvidersDatabase that contains the locations of the available audio voice files. The audio voice files, which give directions to the user, are stored in an external micro SD card when available or in the internal storage of the device. If the user storage area is not large enough, the application will not work. The voice files and map chart material are downloaded and stored the first time that the program starts. The voices feature was not investigated further because no changes were observed between routes.

4.5   Times and Dates

The TomTom PND stores little time/date information with GPS coordinates. The most interesting temporal information in a TomTom PND is the triplog data, which contains the routes that were driven, along with their dates and times. It is essentially a breadcrumb trail along which the TomTom PND was driven. The TomTom NA does not contain a triplog; thus, this highly relevant information is not available.

The only TomTom NA location-specific temporal information that is available is found in the last docked locations time and the departure time. Unfortunately, these time/date items are set by the mobile device and could be incorrect. Also in the case of the departure time, if the data type is LOCTYP_GPS, it could be wrong if there was no GPS lock at that location. In short, limited time/date data is available, making it difficult to identify where a mobile device was at a certain point in time.

5.   TomTom PND versus TomTom NA

The TomTom Go 720 and TomTom Via 825 Live devices were chosen for comparison. The Go 720 is a first generation TomTom PND system. The relevant data is stored in the `mapsettings.cfg` file, which can be decoded by the TomTology program.

The Via 825 Live is a second generation TomTom PND. It is no longer possible to get a physical image of this device using a USB connection. Data extraction requires the chip to be removed or a proprietary non-destructive method to be used. The relevant data is stored in the `mapsettings.tlv` file, but other files also store data related to the data found in the first series of TomTom PNDs.

Table 1 shows the corresponding locations in TomTom PND and TomTom NA where user data of interest in forensic investigations is stored.

6.   Conclusions

The analysis of the Android TomTom NA on a Samsung Galaxy S3 smartphone provides important details about potential digital evidence. Files that contain location information for the device were identified by comparing filesystem changes between multiple physical captures.

Table 1. Corresponding TomTom PND and TomTom NA data locations.

Items	First Generation	Second Generation	Android Application
Triplogs	*Statdata* folder	*Statdata* folder	N/A
Home Location	mapsettings.cfg	userpatch.dat	NavkitSettings.xml
Favorites	mapsettings.cfg	Favorites.ov2	Favorites.ov2
Recent Destinations	mapsettings.cfg	mapsettings.tlv	Benelux file
Entered locations	mapsettings.cfg	mapsettings.tlv	Benelux file
Journeys	mapsettings.cfg	mapsettings.tlv	Benelux file with departure time
Last Docked	mapsettings.cfg	Userpatch.dat	NavkitSettings.xml with a timestamp
Bluetooth Coupled Devices	mapsettings.cfg	Settings.tlv	Handled by the Android OS
SIM Card Data	N/A	mobility.sim	Handled by the Android OS

Another important contribution is the comparison of the contents of files residing in a TomTom PND and a TomTom NA. A TomTom PND stores data in a binary format while the TomTom NA uses the XML format and the base64 encoding. The TomTom PND and TomTom NA record similar user favorites and search data, which enable digital forensic practitioners to determine where the devices have been.

Future research on the TomTom NA will focus on subscription services. Some of these services, including TomTom HD traffic and the services that provide information about speed cameras and danger zones, can provide detailed information about the geographical locations visited and routes taken, and may also reveal information about user actions (e.g., speeding). Future research will also focus on TomTom NA running on other smartphones models and on recovering deleted data.

References

[1] L. Aouad, T. Kechadi, J. Trentesaux and N. Le-Khac, An open framework for smartphone evidence acquisition, in *Advances in Digital Forensics VIII*, G. Peterson and S. Shenoi (Eds.), Springer, Heidelberg, Germany, pp. 159–166, 2012.

[2] L. Barkhuus and V. Polichar, Empowerment through seamfulness: Smartphones in everyday life, *Personal and Ubiquitous Computing*, vol. 15(6), pp. 629–639, 2011.

[3] Cellebrite, UFED Touch Ultimate, Petah Tikva, Israel (`www.celle brite.com/mobile-forensics/products/standalone/ufed-tou ch-ultimate`).

[4] comScore, comScore reports March 2013 U.S. smartphone subscriber market share, Reston, Virginia (`www.comscore.com/Insi ghts/Press_Releases/2013/5/comScore_Reports_March_2013_ US_Smartphone_Subscriber_Market_Share`), May 3, 2013.

[5] Forensic Navigation, TomTology2, Bromley, United Kingdom (`www. forensicnavigation.com/index.php/products/tomtology2`).

[6] P. Hannay, A methodology for the forensic acquisition of the Tom-Tom One Satellite Navigation System – A research in progress, presented at the *Fifth Australian Digital Forensics Conference*, 2007.

[7] J. Harkness, An Investigation of Mobile Phone Forensics, M.Sc. Thesis, School of Computer Science and Informatics, University College Dublin, Dublin, Ireland, 2011.

[8] B. Nutter, Pinpointing TomTom location records: A forensic analysis, *Digital Investigation*, vol. 5(1-2), pp. 10–18, 2008.

[9] TomTom, TomTom Navigator SDK (version 3.0, build 193), Amsterdam, The Netherlands (`www.tomtom.com/lib/doc/ttnavsdk3_ manual.pdf`), 2004.

[10] World Wide Web Consortium, Extensible Markup Language (XML), Massachusetts Institute of Technology, Cambridge, Massachusetts (`www.w3.org/XML`).

IV

FORENSIC TOOLS
AND TRAINING

Chapter 19

PERFORMANCE OF A LOGICAL, FIVE-PHASE, MULTITHREADED, BOOTABLE TRIAGE TOOL

Ibrahim Baggili, Andrew Marrington, and Yasser Jafar

Abstract   This paper describes a five-phase, multi-threaded bootable approach to digital forensic triage, which is implemented in a product called Forensics2020. The first phase collects metadata for every logical file on the hard drive of a computer system. The second phase collects EXIF camera data from each image found on the hard drive. The third phase analyzes and categorizes each file based on its header information. The fourth phase parses each executable file to provide a complete audit of the software applications on the system; a signature is generated for every executable file, which is later checked against a threat detection database. The fifth and final phase hashes each file and records its hash value. All five phases are performed in the background while the first responder interacts with the system. This paper assesses the forensic soundness of Forensics2020. The tool makes certain changes to a hard drive that are similar to those made by other bootable forensic examination environments, although the changes are greater in number. The paper also describes the lessons learned from developing Forensics2020, which can help guide the development of other forensic triage tools.

Keywords: Triage tool, bootable tool, forensic soundness, performance

1.   Introduction

Digital forensic triage is a topic of considerable interest to the digital forensics community. In the medical realm, three conditions must be satisfied for triage to occur [7]: (i) a scarcity of health resources; (ii) a triage officer must be able to assess the medical needs of each patient based on a brief examination; and (iii) the triage officer must be able to apply an algorithm or criteria to determine the treatment and treatment priority for each patient.

G. Peterson and S. Shenoi (Eds.): Advances in Digital Forensics X, IFIP AICT 433, pp. 279–295, 2014.
© IFIP International Federation for Information Processing 2014

The practice of medical triage arose from emergency situations in wartime. The earliest medical triage systems date back to the nineteenth century; many scholars attribute the first formal battlefield triage system to Baron Dominique-Jean Larrey, chief surgeon of Napoleon's Imperial Guard. Before medical triage came into existence, wounded soldiers were not treated effectively, sometimes not at all. Soldiers typically helped each other; there was no systematic approach for specialists to provide medical attention, creating a backlog of wounded soldiers.

The same situation frequently occurs when dealing with computer crimes. In the traditional digital forensic model, a computer system is seized and is typically transported to a laboratory where it is forensically imaged and analyzed. The vast majority of digital forensic practitioners state that they have huge case backlogs; often, the processing delays are as much as eight to twelve months [9]. The same problem is encountered with mobile devices [10]. Delays in the forensic laboratory translate to delays in criminal investigations and court proceedings, resulting in deleterious effects on the course of justice [4]. The digital forensic case backlogs have prompted research on systematic methodologies for improving the digital forensic process and, more specifically, digital forensic triage models and procedures.

2.   Related Work

A number of traditional models have been developed for digital forensic investigations [2, 3, 12, 15]. The traditional models involve a number of phases that focus on collecting evidence from a crime scene and processing the evidence in a laboratory environment [11]. These models have influenced the development of digital forensic triage models, primarily by emphasizing the idea of conducting an early inspection of a computer system at a crime scene before bringing it back to the laboratory.

Adelstein [1] has proposed the use of a mobile forensic platform to facilitate triage without requiring evidence to be brought back to the laboratory. Richards and Roussev [13] describe a a conceptually similar triage approach that they call "on-the-spot" forensics. Both approaches demonstrate that significant advantages can be gained during an investigation in terms of the reduction in time and the possibility of obtaining confessions from suspects when inspecting computer systems at the crime scene.

Rogers, *et al.* [14] have proposed a formal model for digital forensic triage. Their Cyber Forensics Field Triage Process Model (CFFTPM) incorporates an on-site field approach to digital forensic investigations. In particular, the model seeks to: (i) find usable evidence immediately;

(ii) identify the victims at acute risk; (iii) guide the ongoing investigation; (iv) identify the potential charges; and (v) accurately assess the offender's danger to society while preserving the integrity of the evidence for further examination and analysis. Much of the analysis can be performed on scene, where the investigator can generate user profiles, examine the home directory, file properties and registry, create a chronology and search for browser artifacts, email and instant messages [14]. However, one of the main drawbacks of CFFTPM is that it is highly manual and can only be performed by well-trained and experienced digital forensic investigators who can leverage a broad set of forensic tools.

Casey, *et al.* [4] propose a three-tiered approach to digital forensic examinations: (i) survey/triage forensic inspection, during which the potential sources of digital evidence are identified; (ii) preliminary forensic examination, during which relevant digital evidence is interpreted for individuals involved in the case (e.g., to assist in interviewing a suspect); and (iii) in-depth forensic examination, during which a full examination (typically, manual and time intensive) is performed to recover all the available digital evidence. The first two stages, triage and preliminary forensic examination, are intended to assist the investigation. The third stage is primarily intended to support the case going to trial [4]. Most of the well-known digital forensic tools support the third stage, although they may be used to support the other stages (especially the preliminary forensic examination stage).

3.   Forensics2020

The Forensics2020 tool described in this paper was developed as a result of an academia-industry partnership involving the first author and Cryptic Solutions (`www.cryptic.co.uk`). The tool was built after numerous meetings with digital forensic investigators in Ireland, the United Arab Emirates, the United Kingdom and the United States. During these meetings, law enforcement officers and corporate forensic investigators discussed the challenges they faced with existing tools and the lack of effective, easy-to-use digital forensic triage tools.

The law enforcement officers and corporate investigators were very interested in a digital forensic triage system that could deployed easily. It was highly desirable that the system could be operated by non-experts with minimal training (including first responders at crime scenes). Other important features included an automated system with minimal configuration and input, and the ability to view results while the system was processing evidence. Finally, it was deemed critical that the triage system operate in a forensically sound manner and always maintain the integrity of the evidence.

These recommendations were used as guidelines when designing and implementing the Forensics2020 tool. The CFFTPM was selected as the underlying framework due to its wide adoption by U.S. law enforcement agencies.

3.1   Software Design

The Forensics2020 triage tool was designed to serve as a bootable environment. A bootable environment is a controlled environment where the triage software runs in a known-safe operating system as opposed to running live in the uncontrolled environment of a native operating system. This enhances the trustworthiness of the results; the known-safe operating system is free from malware and anti-forensic software that may be present in the suspect's system. The bootable forensic examination environment approach is also common to many forensic live CD distributions (e.g., Helix3 Pro) and, thus, has an accepted basis.

However, there are two significant drawbacks to a bootable approach. First, items in memory could potentially be lost during the process of booting into the forensic triage environment. Second, if whole disk encryption is used, then triage will not be possible unless the encryption keys are known to the first responder. A live examination could address both these problems, but it could be subject to interference by malware and other untrusted software running on the suspect's computer system.

The Forensics2020 software is multi-phased and multi-threaded. The software is loaded from a bootable Windows Pre-installation Environment (PE) using a USB stick. The triage process is initiated after a password is entered. At this point, the first responder has the option to un-check a triage phase if it is not to be performed.

Forensics2020 has five major automated phases that proceed in sequence. The phases are illustrated in Figure 1 and their details are provided in Table 1. The order of the phases was chosen based on the time it typically takes for each phase to be completed – the first phase is the fastest and the last phase is the slowest (see Figure 5).

Since the Forensics2020 phases are threaded away from the user interface, the first responder can introduce other evidence via the interface and view it while the five triage phases complete in the background. At any time, the first responder can click on any part of the user interface and interact with the tool to view important evidentiary items such as registry keys, web browser history, and iPhone and Blackberry backup structures.

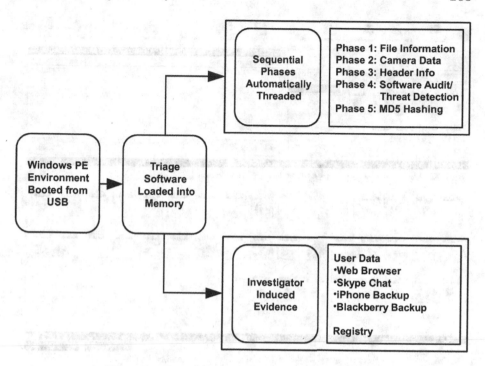

Figure 1.   High-level Forensics2020 triage process.

Table 1.   Forensics2020 phases.

Phase	Description
Phase I: File Information	Every file is logically collected from the hard drive along with its file metadata.
Phase II: Camera Data	Every photograph is analyzed for EXIF data.
Phase III: Header Information	Every file is analyzed and categorized based on its header, not on its extension.
Phase IV: Software Audit/ Threat Detection	The EXE files are parsed to provide a complete audit of all the software applications on the system. A proprietary algorithm is applied to each of the files to generate a signature. The signature is compared against a threat database if the user chooses to initiate this function.
Phase V: MD5 Hashing	Every file is hashed and the hash value is recorded. The hash values may be used to: (i) verify data integrity; and (ii) check against a hash value dataset that is relevant to the investigation.

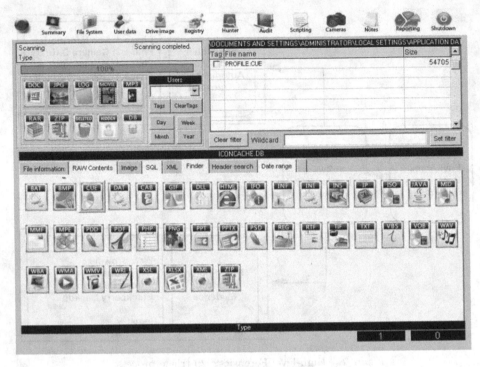

Figure 2.   Forensics2020 screen functionality.

3.2   Using Forensics2020

While Forensics2020 is operating, the first responder can interact with the user interface to see the results to that point and to request certain types of data. The first responder can search for file types based on their file extensions after Phase I is completed, and can search for file headers after Phase III is complete. The first responder can also filter searches based on files modified, accessed or created on specific dates or within specific time ranges, and can view files in raw format or in a "preview" mode (for supported file types). Figure 2 shows an example Forensics2020 screen that enables a first responder to search for specific types of files.

The first responder can also direct Forensics2020 to gather and view certain types of data from the filesystem. The data includes web browser history, Skype chat logs, iOS and Blackberry backup files, and other data relevant to the case. The first responder can also have the Windows registry mounted and search for particular keys that could reveal hardware devices that were connected to the system and software that was installed on the system.

4.   Experiments

We conducted five experiments to evaluate the efficacy of the Forensics2020 triage tool. The first experiment focused on testing the performance of Forensics2020 running on personal computers located in several university computer laboratories ($n = 57$). Four additional experiments were then conducted to validate the integrity of the hard drives and the files after Forensics2020 was loaded.

4.1   Experiment 1

The goal of this experiment was to test the Forensics2020 triage procedure on real computer systems that had been used for general purpose computing instead of computer systems or virtual machines (VMs) with traces of computer activity that were contrived specifically as an experimental dataset. The computers examined in the experiment were physical machines (not VMs) in laboratories that were made available to students for use in their classes, although the students may also have used the computers for personal reasons and for activities only peripherally related to their studies. Each computer may have had several "regular users" who consistently used the computer for their classwork, in addition to dozens of casual users who may have used the computer between classes for any purpose. A computer located in a shared computer laboratory typically has a different usage pattern compared with a computer located at an individual's home. Nevertheless, the computers used in the experiment were real computers with traces of real user activity. As such, they represented the most realistic dataset available for the experiment.

Overall, 26.33 TB of data was analyzed in the experiment; the average hard drive size was 473 GB. To assess the performance of Forensics2020, the tool was run on the test computers and the following times were recorded for each computer: (i) time taken for the tool to load into memory; and (ii) time taken for each of the five phases to complete.

- **Performance Results:** Figure 3 shows the average time (in seconds) for each of the five phases across the entire dataset. It is important to note that Phase II is faster than Phase I because the number of digital images triaged was significantly lower than the number of files found on the computer systems. Other interesting findings are:

  - Four computers generated errors during or after the scans.
  - Triage failed on one computer due to the condition of the hard drive (1.75% failure rate).

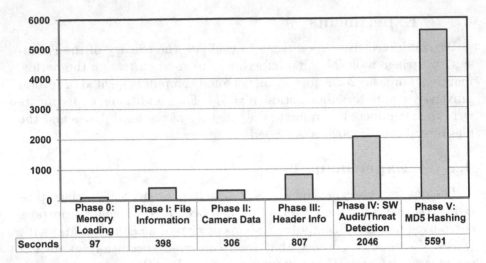

Seconds	Phase 0: Memory Loading	Phase I: File Information	Phase II: Camera Data	Phase III: Header Info	Phase IV: SW Audit/Threat Detection	Phase V: MD5 Hashing
	97	398	306	807	2046	5591

Figure 3. Average execution time of each phase across all 57 computers.

- Three failures (5.26% failure rate) were observed during Phase V (MD5 hashing).

- The average time taken to complete all five phases was 5,591 seconds (1 hour, 33 minutes and 11 seconds).

- The maximum time taken to complete all five phases was 10,356 seconds (2 hours, 52 minutes and 36 seconds).

- **User Data Results:** After all the computers were triaged, the results from every triage report were recorded and the data was analyzed accordingly. The following is a summary of the user data results for the 57 computers:

    - 260,101 software audit entries were detected on the 57 computers.

    - 40 software audit entries across the 57 computers were identified as possible viruses or malware (0.70 infections per computer).

    - On the average, 4,563 software audit entries were detected per computer.

    - Only one iPod backup was found.

    - 525 browsing history entries were detected for Google Chrome on the 57 computers (average of 9.21 entries per computer).

    - 351 browsing history entries were detected for Mozilla Firefox on the 57 computers (average of 6.15 entries per computer).

- 1,408 browsing history entries were detected for Internet Explorer on the 57 computers (average of 24.7 entries per computer).

- 3,475 Microsoft Word and Microsoft Excel files were found on the 57 computers (average of 60.96 Word/Excel files per computer).

- On the average, 14 camera models were detected per computer.

- As many as 44 camera models were detected on one of the 57 computers and 150 photo EXIF details were linked to the same computer.

- More than 2,340 photograph EXIF details were detected on the 57 computers.

4.2 Experiment 2

The goal of this experiment was to test if Forensics2020 modified the hard drive of a scanned computer.

- **Equipment:**

  - A Windows XP laptop with a 160 GB SATA hard drive.
  - A Logicube Forensic Dossier hardware imaging and verification device.
  - A Forensics2020 bootable USB stick.

- **Procedure:**

  1. The hard drive was extracted from the laptop and hashed using the Forensic Dossier device.

  2. The Forensics2020 USB stick was inserted into the laptop.

  3. The laptop was forced to boot from the Forensics2020 USB stick.

  4. Forensics2020 was left running until all the automated phases were completed upon which Forensics2020 was shut down.

  5. The hard drive was extracted and hashed again using the Forensic Dossier device.

  6. The hash values for the hard drive before and after running Forensics2020 were compared.

Table 2.   Experiment 2 results.

Stage	Hash
SHA-256 of the hard drive before running Forensics2020	D8C632E0 D922A8D9 6DCB17C1 3FE8A904 F821726E D405266D 736F0498 00885F3C
SHA-256 of the hard drive after running Forensics2020	D8C21317 E72B5577 0B40FA22 9B203744 FCE916AD 55017326 2B8f88E4 5824B4E6

- **Results:** Table 2 shows that different hash values were obtained for the hard drive before and after running Forensics2020. Additional experiments were required to investigate precisely when the changes occurred.

4.3   Experiment 3

The goal of this experiment was to investigate if the hash values changed after the Windows PE operating system was booted but before the laptop hard drive was mounted. The same equipment as in Experiment 2 was used.

- **Procedure:**

  1. The hard drive was extracted from the laptop and hashed using the Forensic Dossier device.
  2. The Forensics2020 USB stick was inserted into the laptop.
  3. The laptop was forced to boot from the Forensics2020 USB stick.
  4. Forensics2020 was shut down after the Windows PE operating system was loaded, but before the triage process was started (right before the program splash screen). Thus, the hard drive was not yet mounted when Forensics2020 was shut down.
  5. The hard drive was extracted and hashed again using the Forensic Dossier device.
  6. The hash values for the hard drive before and after running Forensics2020 were compared.

- **Results:** As shown in Table 3, the hash values for the hard drive did not change during the experiment; the integrity of the hard drive was maintained. This means that loading Forensics2020 into memory did not cause any hard drive writes. An additional experiment was required to determine if the hash values were changed after the hard drive was mounted.

Table 3. Experiment 3 results.

Stage	Hash
SHA-256 of the hard drive before running Forensics2020	55407B01 4F4847E0 66F25B87 FD24FBDC 73B4969B B94434E6 22CAFAE5 D72E2C17
SHA-256 of the hard drive after starting Forensics2020 and aborting before the program splash screen loaded	55407B01 4F4847E0 66F25B87 FD24FBDC 73B4969B B94434E6 22CAFAE5 D72E2C17

4.4   Experiment 4

The goal of this experiment was to determine if the hard drive retained its integrity after the Windows PE operating system was booted, after Forensics2020 was loaded into memory and after the laptop hard drive was mounted. The same equipment as in Experiment 2 was used.

- **Procedure:**

    1. The hard drive was extracted from the laptop and hashed using the Forensic Dossier device.
    2. The Forensics2020 USB stick was inserted into the laptop.
    3. The laptop was forced to boot from the Forensics2020 USB stick.
    4. Forensics2020 was shut down after the Windows PE operating system was loaded and after the triage process was started (right after the program splash screen). Thus, the hard drive was mounted when Forensics2020 was shut down.
    5. The hard drive was extracted and hashed again using the Forensic Dossier device.
    6. The hash values for the hard drive before and after running Forensics2020 were compared.

- **Results:** Table 4 shows the hash values for the hard drive before and after running Forensics2020. The results show that the hard drive was modified when it was mounted by the bootable Windows PE operating system. Therefore, it can be concluded that the changes were made to the hard drive as soon as it was mounted.

4.5   Experiment 5

In order to quantify the changes made by the Windows PE operating system mounting process, a differential analysis was performed on the

Table 4.   Experiment 4 results.

Stage	Hash
SHA-256 of the hard drive before running Forensics2020	55407B01 4F4847E0 66F25B87 FD24FBDC 73B4969B B94434E6 22CAFAE5 D72E2C17
SHA-256 of the hard drive after running Forensics2020, after the splash screen loaded and after the hard drive was mounted	783C9989 94F7A6A2 103C70DE C6A419ED C2B7B748 84F8B886 7AB31AB5 E2739F17

hard drive images taken before and after running Forensics2020. Differential analysis allows a forensic examiner to focus on the changes brought about as a result of the activity that takes place between the acquisition of an image A and the acquisition of an image B at a subsequent point in time [6].

■ **Equipment:**

- A Tableau T14 FireWire 800 IDE Bridge (write blocker).
- A Windows XP "suspect" laptop with a 40 GB IDE hard drive.
- A Windows 7 forensic workstation.
- A Forensics2020 bootable USB stick.
- AccessData FTK 1.71.
- AccessData FTK Imager 3.1.2.0.

Note that no images were acquired in the previous experiments. Instead, the hard drive was merely hashed before and after running Forensics2020. In this experiment, since differential forensic analysis had to be performed, it was necessary to acquire actual images of the "suspect" laptop for examination. Therefore, a write blocker was used instead of the Forensic Dossier device.

■ **Procedure:**

1. The hard drive was extracted from the "suspect" laptop.
2. An image of the "suspect" hard drive was acquired using FTK Imager, employing the hardware write blocker to prevent inadvertent writes.
3. The hard drive was replaced in the "suspect" laptop.
4. The Forensics2020 USB stick was inserted into the "suspect" laptop.

5. The "suspect" laptop was forced to boot from the Forensics2020 USB stick.

6. The system was shut down after the Windows PE operating system was loaded and after Forensics2020 was started (right after the program splash screen). Thus, the hard drive was mounted when Forensics2020 was shut down.

7. The hard drive was extracted from the "suspect" laptop.

8. An image of the "suspect" hard drive was acquired using FTK Imager, employing the hardware write blocker to prevent inadvertent writes.

9. The two image files were examined using AccessData FTK. Using the file filter, known "ignorable" files, OLE files and duplicate files were excluded. Duplicates in FTK are files that already existed when they were discovered – not the files that exist on both images; consequently, it was necessary to sort by whether the item was "primary" as well as to identify only the files that were unique to a particular image or different in each image. This procedure yielded a list of files/items recovered from unallocated space where there were differences in the contents of the two hard drive images.

■ **Results:** Consistent with the results of Experiments 3 and 4, the two image files had different hash values. Using the FTK file filter and sorting functionality, a differential analysis was performed on the two images. The following observations are significant:

– The $I30 file in each directory on the "suspect" hard drive was modified when the drive was mounted. $I30 is the NTFS directory index file that employs a B-tree data structure instead of a flat file structure; Windows constantly rebalances the B-tree structures and, thus, modifies the $I30 file. Interested readers are referred to [17] for a discussion of the forensic implications of $I30 files.

– The $LogFile was changed.

– The $MFT was changed.

– The *.log files in C:\Windows\System32\config were modified (to no significant extent).

– The deleted files corresponding to Symantec Anti-Virus were changed.

– Two deleted sets of Virtual PC *.vhd files were modified.

Table 5. Hard drive changes by bootable forensic examination environments.

Forensic Tool	Suspected Alteration	Altered File Hashes	Files Altered by Search
Helix3 Pro	Yes	Yes	$LogFile $MFT C:\WINDOWS\bootstat.dat
Kali	Yes	Yes	C:\$I30 $LogFile $MFT C:\WINDOWS\bootstat.dat
Knoppix	Yes	Yes	C:\$I30 $MFT C:\Documents And Settings\Administrator\Local Settings\$I30 C:\Program Files\Cisco Packet Tracer 5.3.1\sounds\simulationTab.wav
Forensics2020	Yes	Yes	1,667 different hash values

When considering the results of Experiment 5, it is important to note that many commonly-used Linux-based bootable forensic examination environments (e.g., Helix3 Pro and Backtrack) also perform mounts that modify filesystem metadata [16]. Therefore, the issues noted for Forensics2020 are not unique to the product or to the Windows PE operating system – they are problematic for other bootable forensic examination environments as well. Fathy, *et al.* [5] conducted an experiment similar to Experiment 5 for three bootable Linux-based forensic examination environments. Their results for Helix3 Pro, Kali and Knoppix are presented alongside the Forensics2020 results in Table 5. The Windows PE drive mounting process for Forensics2020 made the same sorts of changes as seen with Helix3 Pro, Kali and Knoppix, but in much greater quantities. However, the differential analysis revealed that Forensics2020 made no changes to the logical filesystem – the userspace files were not modified; only the filesystem metadata was changed. Whether or not this is acceptable from the perspective of forensic soundness is an open question.

5.   Conclusions

The experimental results demonstrate that Forensics2020 is an effective digital forensic triage tool. On the average, files on the hard drive can be enumerated within 398 seconds; the slowest phase, however, is MD5 hashing. The semi-automated and multi-phase implementation enables a first responder to interact with Forensics2020 while digital forensic processes are executing in the background, giving the first responder more control over the investigation. Like other bootable forensic examination environments, Forensics2020 makes certain changes to the hard drive. Differential analysis revealed that Forensics2020 made no changes to userspace files; only the filesystem metadata was modified. However, this result is, nevertheless, a concern from the perspective of forensic soundness.

Future efforts will concentrate on extensive testing of Forensics2020 in real-world investigations. Also, experiments will be undertaken to measure if an automated tool like Forensics2020 actually reduces the time spent on digital forensic investigations [8]. With respect to forensic soundness, a sector-by-sector comparison of the hard drive before and after the triage process will be conducted to provide better insights into the nature of the changes to digital evidence.

Finally, our experience developing and deploying Forensics2020 have resulted in two key lessons learned with regard to digital forensic triage. First, a multi-threaded, multi-stage approach that enables first responders to interact with the evidence while the system performs its forensic processing is a desirable feature that enhances performance and saves time. The second lesson is that the manner in which the hard drive is mounted by a bootable triage tool is crucial to perceptions of forensic soundness. It could be that small and predictable modifications of a suspect's hard drive would have to be accepted in order to facilitate triage using a bootable examination environment, but the nature and causes of the modifications must be thoroughly documented if the evidence recovered and analyzed by Forensics2020 is to have probative value in court proceedings.

Acknowledgement

The authors wish to acknowledge the collaboration with Cryptic Solutions, especially with David Shearmon, CEO of Cryptic Solutions; and also with David Duke, the developer of Forensics2020.

References

[1] F. Adelstein, MFP: The Mobile Forensics Platform, *International Journal of Digital Evidence*, vol. 2(1), 2003.

[2] N. Beebe and J. Clark, A hierarchical, objectives-based framework for the digital investigations process, *Digital Investigation*, vol. 2(2), pp. 147–167, 2005.

[3] B. Carrier and E. Spafford, Getting physical with the digital investigation process, *International Journal of Digital Evidence*, vol. 2(2), 2003.

[4] E. Casey, M. Ferraro and L. Nguyen, Investigation delayed is justice denied: Proposals for expediting forensic examinations of digital evidence, *Journal of Forensic Sciences*, vol. 54(6), pp. 1353–1364, 2009.

[5] A. Fathy, A. Marrington, F. Iqbal and I. Baggili, Testing the forensic soundness of forensic examination environments on bootable media, submitted for publication, 2014.

[6] S. Garfinkel, A. Nelson and J. Young, A general strategy for differential forensic analysis, *Digital Investigation*, vol. 9(S), pp. S50–S59, 2012.

[7] K. Iserson and J. Moskop, Triage in medicine, Part I: Concept, history and types, *Annals of Emergency Medicine*, vol. 49(3), pp. 275–281, 2007.

[8] J. James, A. Lopez-Fernandez and P. Gladyshev, Measuring accuracy of automated investigation tools and procedures in digital investigations, presented at the *Fifth International Conference on Digital Forensics and Cyber Crime*, 2013.

[9] D. Kennedy and D. Sun, How to triage computer evidence: Tackling Moore's law with less, *Evidence Technology Magazine*, vol. 8(2), 2010.

[10] R. Mislan, E. Casey and G. Kessler, The growing need for on-scene triage of mobile devices, *Digital Investigation*, vol. 3(3-4), pp. 112–124, 2010.

[11] M. Pollitt, An ad hoc review of digital forensic models, *Proceedings of the Second International Workshop on Systematic Approaches to Digital Forensic Engineering*, pp. 43–54, 2007.

[12] M. Reith, C. Carr and G. Gunsch, An examination of digital forensic models, *International Journal of Digital Evidence*, vol. 1(3), 2002.

[13] G. Richard III and V. Roussev, Digital forensics tools: The next generation, in *Digital Crime and Forensic Science in Cyberspace*, P. Kanellis, E. Kiountouzis, N. Kolokotronis and D. Martakos (Eds.), IGI Global, Hershey, Pennsylvania, pp. 76–91, 2006.

[14] M. Rogers, J. Goldman, R. Mislan, T. Wedge and S. Debrota, Computer Forensics Field Triage Process Model, *Proceedings of the Conference on Digital Forensics, Security and Law*, pp. 27–40, 2006.

[15] P. Stephenson, Modeling of post-incident root cause analysis, *International Journal of Digital Evidence*, vol. 2(2), 2003.

[16] M. Suhanov, Linux for Computer Investigators: Pitfalls of Mounting Filesystems (`www.forensicfocus.com/linux-forensics-pit falls-of-mounting-file-systems`), 2009.

[17] C. Tilbury, NTFS $I30 index attributes: Evidence of deleted and overwritten files, *SANS Digital Forensics and Incident Response* (`computer-forensics.sans.org/blog/2011/09/20/ntfs-i30-i ndex-attributes-evidence-of-deleted-and-overwritten-fil es`), September 20, 2011.

Chapter 20

TOWARDS FULLY AUTOMATED DIGITAL ALIBIS WITH SOCIAL INTERACTION

Stefanie Beyer, Martin Mulazzani, Sebastian Schrittwieser, Markus Huber, and Edgar Weippl

Abstract   Digital traces found on local hard drives as a result of online activities have become very valuable in reconstructing events in digital forensic investigations. This paper demonstrates that forged alibis can be created for online activities and social interactions. In particular, a novel, automated framework is presented that uses social interactions to create false digital alibis. The framework simulates user activity and supports communications via email as well as instant messaging using a chatbot. The framework is evaluated by extracting forensic artifacts and comparing them with the results obtained from a human user study.

Keywords: Digital evidence, automated alibis

1. Introduction

Digital forensic techniques are increasingly applied in criminal investigations due to the widespread involvement of computers, smartphones and other modern technologies in crimes. Traces such as MAC timestamps and operating system specific log files left on hard drives and information transmitted over network connections are often combined to produce a holistic reconstruction of events for specific times of interest [4, 16]. The resulting digital alibis are routinely presented and examined during investigations and in court proceedings.

This paper describes a framework that fully simulates user interactions and implements the automated creation of digital alibis with special focus on online social interactions such as writing email and sending chat messages. The framework is unique because it engages social in-

G. Peterson and S. Shenoi (Eds.): Advances in Digital Forensics X, IFIP AICT 433, pp. 297–307, 2014.

teractions that have been ignored in previous work. Additionally, the framework is highly configurable and is available under an open source license (github.com/mmulazzani/alibiFramework).

This paper evaluates the framework by comparing it with usage patterns of real world users, demonstrating that digital forensic analysis methods are not reliable if they are specifically targeted. The goal is to raise awareness in the digital forensics community that digital alibis can be forged and, consequently, it is important to always question the reliability of digital alibis.

2.   Background

Digital alibis have played an important role in numerous cases. In one case, Rodney Bradford was charged with armed robbery but was released because digital evidence demonstrated that he was actively using his Facebook account at the time of the crime [15]. His attorney noted that the digital evidence gave Bradford an "unbeatable alibi" [2]. In another case, a suspected murderer was acquitted because digital evidence revealed that he was working on his laptop when the murder took place [7, 17].

A digital forensic analyst is often confronted with multiple hard drives that have been imaged using hardware write blockers [3], and is asked specific questions about user actions that have been or have not been conducted on the associated computers [5]. Meanwhile, the widespread use of modern technologies and devices such as social networks [14] and smartphones [12, 13] dramatically increase the amount of digital traces that must be considered even in routine cases. The massive quantity of digital evidence and the accompanying case complexity render automated analysis crucial to extracting information of interest in a reasonable amount of time [10, 11].

Several researchers have focused on the creation of digital alibis [8, 9]. However, their alibi generators often use proprietary languages such as AutoIt (Windows) or Applescript (OS X) and are, therefore, specific to the underlying operating system (e.g., Windows [8, 9], OS X [7] or Android [1]). Our framework, on the other hand, is not so operating system specific because it is implemented in Python. Although the implementation was developed for Linux systems because no Linux-specific solutions existed, it is a simple matter to port it to other platforms. Additionally, the configuration parameters were set based on extensive studies of real world users, rendering the alibi generation approach statistically more difficult to detect and the persistently-stored evidence more realistic compared with other approaches.

While other alibi creation approaches attempt to hide their programs using innocuous file names or separate storage devices, our framework is designed to leave no obvious traces. Also, the framework does not employ a file wiper during the post processing phase to remove suspicious traces. The rationale is that a forensic analyst should not be able to determine if the digital evidence artifacts originated from the framework or from a human user. This is accomplished by instrumenting keyboard signals, mouse clicks and other events within the alibi creation framework.

3. Alibi Creation Framework

The alibi creation framework is intended to simulate user activity as realistically and as thoroughly as possible. To this end, it is necessary to simulate standard user activities such as browsing the web, communicating via email, chatting with instant messaging software and editing documents of various types. The concrete actions performed by the framework should be neither scripted nor predictable; they should be randomized, but still realistic and convincing to digital forensic investigators.

A variety of word lists and online sources such as Google Trends are used as inputs to capture a snapshot of current online interests while simultaneously incorporating specific user preferences. Many facets of computer usage are highly user dependent. For the alibi creation framework to be as realistic as possible, factors such as the social interaction partners for email and chatting, the language of communication and the time delays between actions and usual concurrent actions must be configured in advance. Social interactions, in particular, are vulnerable to traffic analysis because the content of the messages as well as the identities of the communicating parties are of interest. Also, the response times are dependent on message length, and must be considered carefully when simulating social interactions.

The proof-of-concept system was implemented on Ubuntu 12.04 LTS using Python. The core features of the framework were chosen in a similar manner as other approaches in the literature [7, 8].

The implementation has three main components: (i) scheduler; (ii) program manager; and (iii) social interaction component. The scheduler is responsible for the overall management; it controls startup and triggers the shutdown of all the involved programs. Also, it decides which actions to perform (both local and online) and when to perform them. The program manager runs and manages all applications, including the browser and the email and chat software. The social interaction

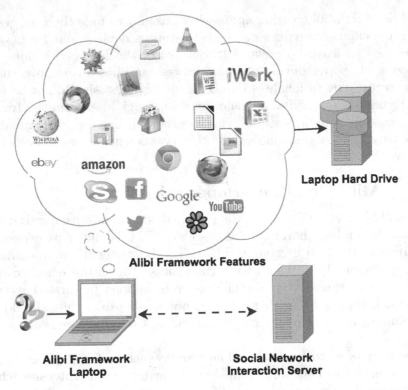

Figure 1. Conceptual view of the alibi creation framework.

component incorporates the email manager and a chatbot for instant messaging.

Figure 1 shows the main components of the alibi creation framework. The framework can launch and use local applications by sending key strokes and mouse clicks. It comes pre-configured for the use of several applications: Firefox, gedit, LibreOffice, Thunderbird, Skype and VLC. The Python libraries xautomation, skype4py and the chatbot implementation PyAIML are used for automation. Furthermore, splinter (based on Selenium) is used for the automation of Firefox. Thus, the implementation can browse the web, send and receive email, chat using Skype, open and edit documents (using LibreOffice and gedit) and launch programs such as music players and video players. The frequency and content of alibi events were derived from the forensic analysis of several typical office workstations at our university.

The framework can query Google and follow suggested links, tweet on Twitter and log into Facebook. Also, it can search for YouTube videos and browse websites with random mouse clicks and follow links. New email messages are drafted, received email messages are forwarded, and email responses are sent after reasonable delays. Additionally, it is possible to mark new email messages as read and to delete email messages. The action to be performed is chosen at random; not every email that is read is answered. The subject and content of email can be predefined and stored in lists. The answering of instant messages is supported with the help of a chatbot. Reasonable time delays are implemented based on the response message size and by using random delays. Chat templates are easily adapted via AIML [18]. When the timer of the scheduler expires, the chatbot says goodbye and shuts down. The editing of local documents is implemented by deleting a random amount of content or by randomly inserting predefined text that fits the content of the document. The use of LibreOffice is implemented by simulating key strokes and mouse clicks because no Python bindings for LibreOffice are available.

However, one post-processing step is necessary: Splinter has to use a separate Firefox profile and cannot work directly with the user profile. Therefore, during startup, `splinter` copies the user profile to `/tmp` and the user profile is overwritten at shutdown by moving it back. Depending on the user threat model, additional steps might be appropriate.

4. Evaluation

The implementation was evaluated by comparing its behavior with that of human users. Since the usage of a computer depends heavily on the person using it, the evaluation of the implementation focused on demonstrating that the default configuration is reasonable.

Nine human test subjects were asked to use a virtual machine for 30 minutes just like they would use their computers, and the results were compared with a single run of the framework. The test subjects were asked to browse the web, send email, chat, edit documents and to do anything they would normally do.

Sleuth Kit and Autopsy were subsequently applied to the virtual machine images to extract data in a forensic manner. Timestamps were extracted and the files containing user data of interest were inspected manually. Manual analysis was conducted on the browser history *places.sqlite* of Firefox, the local mailbox files of Thunderbird, and the chat history *main.db* of Skype to extract timestamps, message content, conversation partners and the time intervals between messages, email and website visits. Network forensics, namely the inspection of network traffic, would have been an alternative approach for evaluation. However, hard drive analysis allows unencrypted information as well as additional information such as local timestamps to be extracted; this motivated the use of

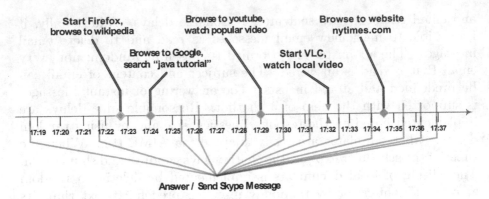

Figure 2. Example timeline of 20 minutes of framework activity.

the evaluation method. Various metrics were used to compare the framework behavior with that of real users during the 30 minute test period: number of visited websites, durations of website visits and numbers of chat messages sent and received.

Figure 2 shows an example timeline of 20 minutes of framework activity. The social interactions can be observed clearly. A total of twelve messages were sent by the social interaction component to various recipients, either as responses in ongoing conversations or as new messages to initiate conversations. The browser was directed to several websites and links were followed to simulate further browsing (not shown in the figure). The browsing activities accessed news sites such as nytimes.com and prominent news stories on the front page; and youtube.com and top videos from the "most popular" section based on random search queries. Local timestamps and history logs were written to disk in all cases. Furthermore, VLC was started and a local video from the hard drive was opened; this is reflected in the timestamps shown in Figure 2.

5. Test User Survey

Target websites and time patterns were extracted to capture the browsing behavior of the nine volunteers; the most popular websites visited were google.com, facebook.com and various Austrian news sites. On the other hand, the framework used a preconfigured list of websites and randomized Google queries. Nevertheless, four of the five most visited websites by the framework and the users matched. Table 1 shows three extracted time patterns. The test users did not receive any email as a result of the experimental setup, but they were asked to send email messages. On the average, one email message was sent per user. The maximum number of email messages sent by the users was three and the

Table 1. Website visit comparison.

	Framework	Users
Number of Websites	11	Min: 1; Max: 12; Avg: 9
Time on Website (Min)	8 sec	5 sec
Time on Website (Max)	2 min 16 sec	13 min 5 sec
Time on Website (Avg)	1 min 52 sec	2 min 50 sec

minimum was zero. The number of words in an email varied between six and 51, with an average of 21. The time between sending email varied between one minute and fifteen minutes.

Table 2. Observed chat behavior (min/max/avg).

	Framework	Users
Chat Messages Sent	22	(7/46/19)
Chat Messages Received	23	(15/35/21)
Chat Message Length	(1/18/8)	(1/23/4)
Response Time (sec)	(2/175/45)	(2/480/64)

Table 2 provides details about the observed chat behavior. Nearly all the test users conducted chat conversations. There were between seven and 46 outgoing messages and between fifteen and 35 incoming messages. The shortest message was one word long for each user. The maximum number of words in a chat message was 23. The chat message topics depended strongly on the test users; they included health, football and movies, as well as small talk. The response time for chat messages was at least two seconds and at most eight minutes. The average response time was about one minute and four seconds. The users edited or opened one document (.ods or .pdf) during the 30 minute timeframe, which was consistent with the actions of the framework.

6. Discussion

Table 3 compares the behavior of the alibi framework with that of the test subjects. The browsing behavior of the framework in terms of the number of websites visited is comparable to that of the test users. The time spent on each website is on the average shorter than the time spent by the test users, but this is a parameter that is easily changed in the framework (just like the number of websites to be visited). Some test users spent more than ten minutes at a site but, in general, the time spent by framework on websites generally matches the time spent by the

Table 3.   Overall comparison framework vs. survey users.

Feature	Framework	Users	
Websites Visited	11	Min: 1	Max: 12
Website Visit Time	1 min 52 sec	Min: 5 sec	Max: 2 min 50 sec
Most Visited Websites		Matching in 4/5 sites	
Email Messages (sent)	1	Min: 0	Max: 3
Email Messages (received)	2	Min: 0	Max: 0
Email Message Length (words)	6	Min: 6	Max: 51
Email Message Content		Matching in 1/4 topics	
Chat Messages (sent)	22	Min: 7	Max: 46
Chat Messages (received)	23	Min: 15	Max: 35
Chat Message Length (words)	Avg: 8	Min: 1	Max: 23
Response Time	Avg: 45 sec	Min: 2 sec	Max: 1 min 4 sec
Conversation Content		Matching in 2/5 topics	
Opened Documents	1	Min: 0	Max: 2
Document Types	.ods	.ods, .odt, .pdf	

test users. Four of the five most visited websites for the framework and the test users matched, which is a very good result because the websites visited by the framework were configured *a priori*. However, the actual sites visited by the test users depended strongly on user preferences; this feature will have to be adjusted in the framework. In summary, the framework adequately simulates web surfing activities, but it requires the implementation of a user-specific configuration feature.

With regard to chat conversations and the use of the social interaction server, the response time for chat messages matches the expected response time. The framework adequately models the behavior of test users in terms of the response time delays and the fact that not every message is answered.

7.   Limitations and Future Work

One limitation of the prototype is the lack of sophisticated contextual analysis of instant messages. While AIML can be used to generate genuine-looking conversations for short periods of time, a forensic analysis of the conversations would likely reveal the use of a chatbot. While this is definitely a problem in scenarios where the disk is analyzed forensically, the generated alibis would pass network forensic analysis because most protocols (e.g., Skype) implicitly encrypt messages. This limitation is more significant for unencrypted email conversations. Our future work will attempt to identify methods for creating better content-dependent responses.

Another limitation is adaptivity. To forge a digital alibi in a reliable manner, it is necessary to adapt the framework to user preferences. Currently, most of the framework parameters are configured manually and have to be adapted for each user. Ideally, the framework should be able to adapt the parameters automatically. This can be realized by collecting user-specific information from user data or by collecting it over a longer period during a learning phase. It would also be useful to compare long-term runs of the framework with real user data – 30 minutes is insufficient to cover all the use cases where digital alibis might be needed. Another future goal for the framework is supporting other operating systems and browsers.

An important point to note is that a user who has insufficient knowledge of the tools and the system could leave undesirable evidence. Therefore, it is essential to continuously update and refine the framework as operating systems and applications change. The current framework does not implement any obfuscation methods to hide its execution. Running the framework from external media as suggested in [6] could help strengthen the validity of a forged alibi.

8. Conclusions

The proof-of-concept alibi creation framework demonstrates that it is possible to forge digital alibis that adequately model real user behavior. The framework has the ability – if correctly configured – to simulate browsing, emailing, chatting and document editing behavior. The precise simulation that is obtained depends on the configurations that should, of course, be adapted to user preferences. This requires an intimate knowledge of user behavior and usage patterns. Our future research will focus on adding an automated configuration feature based on existing log files or learning user-specific behavior, with the goal of rendering the framework behavior more indistinguishable from normal human behavior, even after analysis by experienced forensic investigators.

References

[1] P. Albano, A. Castiglione, G. Cattaneo, G. De Maio and A. De Santis, On the construction of a false digital alibi on the Android OS, *Proceedings of the Third International Conference on Intelligent Networking and Collaborative Systems*, pp. 685–690, 2011.

[2] D. Beltrami, I'm innocent. Just check my status on Facebook, *New York Times*, November 11, 2009.

[3] D. Brezinski and T. Killalea, Guidelines for Evidence Collection and Archiving, RFC 3227, 2002.

[4] F. Buchholz and C. Falk, Design and implementation of Zeitline: A forensic timeline editor *Proceedings of the Fifth Digital Forensic Research Workshop*, 2005.

[5] B. Carrier, *File System Forensic Analysis*, Addison-Wesley, Upper Saddle River, New Jersey, 2005.

[6] A. Castiglione, G. Cattaneo, G. De Maio and A. De Santis, Automatic, selective and secure deletion of digital evidence, *Proceedings of the International Conference on Broadband and Wireless Computing, Communication and Applications*, pp. 392–398, 2011.

[7] A. Castiglione, G. Cattaneo, G. De Maio, A. De Santis, G. Costabile and M. Epifani, How to forge a digital alibi on Mac OS X, *Proceedings of the IFIP WG 8.4/8.9 International Cross Domain Conference and Workshop on Availability, Reliability and Security*, pp. 430–444, 2012.

[8] A. Castiglione, G. Cattaneo, G. De Maio, A. De Santis, G. Costabile and M. Epifani, The forensic analysis of a false digital alibi, *Proceedings of the Sixth International Conference on Innovative Mobile and Internet Services in Ubiquitous Computing*, pp. 114–121, 2012.

[9] A. De Santis, A. Castiglione, G. Cattaneo, G. De Maio and M. Ianulardo, Automated construction of a false digital alibi, *Proceedings of the IFIP WG 8.4/8.9 International Cross Domain Conference and Workshop on Availability, Reliability and Security*, pp. 359–373, 2011.

[10] S. Garfinkel, Digital forensics research: The next 10 years, *Digital Investigation*, vol. 7(S), pp. S64–S73, 2010.

[11] S. Garfinkel, Digital media triage with bulk data analysis and bulk_extractor, *Computers and Security*, vol. 32, pp. 56–72, 2012.

[12] A. Hoog, *Android Forensics: Investigation, Analysis and Mobile Security for Google Android*, Syngress, Waltham, Massachusetts, 2011.

[13] A. Hoog and K. Strzempka, *iPhone and iOS Forensics: Investigation, Analysis and Mobile Security for Apple iPhone, iPad and iOS Devices*, Syngress, Waltham, Massachusetts, 2011.

[14] M. Huber, M. Mulazzani, M. Leithner, S. Schrittwieser, G. Wondracek and E. Weippl, Social snapshots: Digital forensics for online social networks, *Proceedings of the Twenty-Seventh Annual Computer Security Applications Conference*, pp. 113–122, 2011.

[15] V. Juarez, Facebook status update provides alibi, *CNN*, November 13, 2009.

[16] J. Olsson and M. Boldt, Computer forensic timeline visualization tool, *Digital Investigation*, vol. 6(S), pp. S78–S87, 2009.

[17] R. Seifer, Garlasco, Alberto Stasi acquitted, *Xomba* (`richardse ifer.xomba.com/garlasco_alberto_stasi_acquitted`), December 13, 2004.

[18] R. Wallace, The Elements of AIML Style, A.L.I.C.E. AI Foundation, 2003.

Chapter 21

DATA CORPORA FOR DIGITAL FORENSICS EDUCATION AND RESEARCH

York Yannikos, Lukas Graner, Martin Steinebach, and Christian Winter

Abstract   Data corpora are very important for digital forensics education and research. Several corpora are available to academia; these range from small manually-created data sets of a few megabytes to many terabytes of real-world data. However, different corpora are suited to different forensic tasks. For example, real data corpora are often desirable for testing forensic tool properties such as effectiveness and efficiency, but these corpora typically lack the ground truth that is vital to performing proper evaluations. Synthetic data corpora can support tool development and testing, but only if the methodologies for generating the corpora guarantee data with realistic properties.

This paper presents an overview of the available digital forensic corpora and discusses the problems that may arise when working with specific corpora. The paper also describes a framework for generating synthetic corpora for education and research when suitable real-world data is not available.

Keywords: Forensic data corpora, synthetic disk images, model-based simulation

1.   Introduction

A digital forensic investigator must have a broad knowledge of forensic methodologies and experience with a wide range of tools. This includes multi-purpose forensic suites with advanced functionality and good usability as well as small tools for special tasks that may have moderate to low usability. Gaining expert-level skills in the operation of forensic tools requires a substantial amount of time. Additionally, advances in analysis methods, tools and technologies require continuous learning to maintain currency.

G. Peterson and S. Shenoi (Eds.): Advances in Digital Forensics X, IFIP AICT 433, pp. 309–325, 2014.

In digital forensics education, it is important to provide insights into specific technologies and how forensic methods must be applied to perform thorough and sound analyses. It is also very important to provide a rich learning environment where students can use forensic tools to rigorously analyze suitable test data.

The same is true in digital forensics research. New methodologies and new tools have to be tested against well-known data corpora. This provides a basis for comparing methodologies and tools so that the advantages and shortcomings can be identified. Forensic investigators can use the results of such evaluations to make informed decisions about the methodologies and tools that should be used for specific tasks. This helps increase the efficiency and the quality of forensic examinations while allowing objective evaluations by third parties.

The paper provides an overview of several real-world and synthetic data corpora that are available for digital forensics education and research. Also, it highlights the potential risks and problems encountered when using data corpora, along with the capabilities of existing tools that allow the generation of synthetic data corpora when real-world data is not available. Additionally, the paper describes a custom framework for synthetic data generation and evaluates the performance of the framework.

2.   Available Data Corpora

Several data corpora have been made available for public use. While some of the corpora are useful for digital forensics education and research, others are suited to very specific areas such as network forensics and forensic linguistics. This section presents an overview of the most relevant corpora.

2.1   Real Data Corpus

A few real-world data corpora are available to support digital forensics education and research. Garfinkel, *et al.* [7] have created the Real Data Corpus from used hard disks that were purchased from around the world. In a later work, Garfinkel [5] described the challenges and lessons learned while handling the Real Data Corpus, which by then had grown to more than 30 terabytes [5]. As of September 2013, the Real Data Corpus incorporated 1,289 hard disk images, 643 flash memory images and 98 optical discs. However, because this corpus was partly funded by the U.S. Government, access to the corpus requires the approval of an institutional review board in accordance with U.S. legislation. Additional information about the corpus and its access requirements are available at [6].

A smaller corpus, which includes specific scenarios created for educational purposes [25], can be downloaded without any restrictions. This smaller corpus contains:

- Three test disk images created especially for educational and testing purposes (e.g., filesystem analysis, file carving and handling encodings).

- Four realistic disk image sets created from USB memory sticks, a digital camera and a Windows XP computer.

- A set of almost 1,000,000 files, including 109,282 JPEG files.

- Five phone images from four different cell phone models.

- Mixed data corresponding to three fictional scenarios for educational purposes, including multiple network packet dumps and disk images.

Due to the variety of data it contains, the Real Data Corpus is a valuable resource for educators and researchers in the areas of multimedia forensics, mobile phone forensics and network forensics. To our knowledge, it is the largest publicly-available corpus in the area of digital forensics.

2.2 DARPA Intrusion Detection Data Sets

In 1998 and 1999, researchers at MIT Lincoln Laboratory [12, 13] created a simulation network in order to produce network traffic and audit logs for evaluating intrusion detection systems. The simulated infrastructure was attacked using well-known techniques as well as new techniques that were specially developed for the evaluation. In 2000, additional experiments were performed involving specific scenarios, including two DDoS attacks and an attack on a Windows NT system. The data sets for all three experiments are available at [11]; they include network traffic data in `tcpdump` format, audit logs and filesystem snapshots.

The methodologies employed in the 1998 and 1999 evaluations were criticized by McHugh [16]. McHugh states that the evaluation results miss important details and that portions of the evaluation procedures are unclear or inappropriate. Additionally, Garfinkel [4] points out that the data sets do not represent real-world traffic because they lack complexity and heterogeneity. Therefore, this corpus has limited use in network forensics research.

2.3   MemCorp Corpus

The MemCorp Corpus [22] contains memory images created from several virtual and physical machines. In particular, the corpus contains images extracted from 87 computer systems running various versions of Microsoft Windows; the images were extracted using common memory imaging tools.

The corpus includes the following images:

- 53 system memory images created from virtual machines.

- 23 system memory images created from physical machines with factory default configurations (i.e., with no additional software installed).

- 11 system memory images created from machines under specific scenarios (e.g., after malware was installed).

This corpus supports education and training efforts focused on memory analysis using tools such as the Volatile Framework [23]. However, as noted by the corpus creator [22], the corpus does not contain images created from real-world systems or images from operating systems other than Microsoft Windows, which reduces its applicability. The creator of the MemCorp Corpus provides access to the images upon request.

2.4   MORPH Corpus

Several corpora have been created in the area of face recognition [8]. Since a large corpus with facial images tagged with age information would be very useful for multimedia forensics, we have picked a sample corpus that could be a valuable resource for research (e.g., for detecting of illegal multimedia content like child pornography).

The MORPH Corpus [20] comprises 55,000 unique facial images of more than 13,000 individuals. The ages of the individuals range from 16 to 77 with a median age of 33. Four images on average were taken of each individual with an average time of 164 days between each image.

Facial images annotated with age information are useful for developing automated age detection systems. Currently, no reliable methods (i.e., with low error rates) exist for age identification. Steinebach, *et al.* [21] have employed face recognition techniques to identify known illegal multimedia content, but they did not consider age classification.

2.5   Enron Corpus

The Enron Corpus introduced in 2004 is a well-known corpus in the area of forensic linguistics [9]. In its raw form, the corpus contains

619,446 email messages from 158 executives of Enron Corporation; the email messages were seized during the investigation of the 2001 Enron scandal. After data cleansing, the corpus contains 200,399 messages. The Enron Corpus is one of the most referenced mass collections of real-world email data that is publicly available.

The corpus provides a valuable basis for research on email classification, an important area in forensic linguistics. Klimt and Yang [10] suggest using thread membership detection for email classification and provide the results of baseline experiments conducted with the Enron Corpus. Data sets from the Enron Corpus are available at [3].

2.6 Global Intelligence Files

In February 2012, WikiLeaks started publishing the Global Intelligence Files, a large corpus of email messages gathered from the intelligence company Stratfor. WikiLeaks claims to possess more than 5,000,000 email messages dated between July 2004 and December 2011. As of September 2013, almost 3,000,000 of these messages have been available for download by the public [24]. WikiLeaks continues to release new email messages from the corpus on an almost daily basis.

Like the Enron Corpus, the Global Intelligence Files would provide a valuable basis for research in forensic linguistics. However, we are not aware of any significant research conducted using the Global Intelligence Files.

2.7 Computer Forensic Reference Data Sets

The Computer Forensic Reference Data Sets maintained by NIST [19] is a small data corpus created for training and testing purposes. The data sets include test cases for file carving, system memory analysis and string search using different encodings.

The corpus contains the following data:

- One hacking case scenario.

- Two images for unicode string searches.

- Four images for filesystem analysis.

- One image for mobile device analysis.

- One image for system memory analysis.

- Two images for verifying the results of forensic imaging tools.

This corpus provides a small but valuable reference set for tool developers. It is also suitable for training in forensic analysis methods.

3.   Pitfalls of Data Corpora

Forensic corpora are very useful for education and research, but they have certain pitfalls.

- **Solution Specificity:** While a corpus is very valuable when developing methodologies and tools that solve research problems in digital forensics, it is difficult to find general solutions that are not somehow tailored to the corpus. Even when a solution is intended to work in general (with different corpora and in the real world), research and development efforts often slowly adapt the solution to the corpus over time, probably without even being noticed by the researchers. For example, the Enron Corpus is widely used by the forensics linguistics community as a single basis for research on email classification. It would be difficult to show that the research results based on this corpus apply to general email classification problems.

  This could also become an issue if, for instance, a general methodology or tool that solves a specific problem already exists, and another research group is working to enhance the solution. Using only one corpus during development increases the risk of crafting a solution that may be more effective and efficient than previous solutions, but only when used with that specific corpus.

- **Legal Issues:** The data in corpora such as Garfinkel's Real Data Corpus created from used hard disks bought from the secondary market may be subject to intellectual property and personal privacy laws. Even if the country that hosts the real-world corpus allows its use for research, legal restrictions could be imposed by a second country in which the research that uses the corpus is being conducted. The worst case is when local laws completely prohibit the use of the corpus.

- **Relevance:** Data corpora are often created as snapshots of a specific scenarios or environments. The data contained in corpora often loses its relevance as it ages. For example, network traffic from the 1990s is quite different from current network traffic – a fact that was pointed out for the DARPA Intrusion Detection Data Sets [4, 16]. Another example is a data corpus containing data extracted from mobile phones. Such a corpus must be updated very frequently with data from the latest devices if it is to be useful for mobile phone forensics.

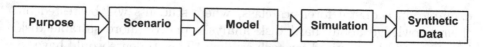

Figure 1. Generating synthetic data based on a real-world scenario.

■ **Transferability:** Many data corpora are created or taken from specific local environments. The email messages in the Enron Corpus are in English. While this corpus is valuable to forensic linguists in English-speaking countries, its value to researchers focused on other languages is debatable. Indeed, many important properties that are relevant to English and used for email classification may not be applicable to Arabic or Mandarin Chinese.

Likewise, corpora developed for testing forensic tools that analyze specific applications (e.g., instant messaging software and chat clients) may not be useful in other countries because of differences in jargon and communication patterns. Also, a corpus that mostly includes Facebook posts and IRC logs may not be of much value in a country where these services are not popular.

4. Synthetic Data Corpus Generation

Aside from methodologies for creating synthetic data corpora by manually reproducing real-world actions, little research has been done related to tool-supported synthetic data corpus generation. Moch and Freiling [17] have developed Forensig2, a tool that generates synthetic disk images using virtual machines. While the process for generating disk images has to be programmed in advance, the tool allows randomness to be introduced in order to create similar, but not identical, disk images. In a more recent work, Moch and Freiling [18] present the results of an evaluation of Forensig2 applied to student education scenarios.

A methodology for generating a synthetic data corpus for forensic accounting is proposed in [14] and evaluated in [15]. The authors demonstrate how to generate synthetic data containing fraudulent activities from smaller collections of real-world data. The data is then used for training and testing a fraud detection system.

5. Corpus Generation Process

This section describes the process for generating a synthetic data corpus using the model-based framework presented in [27].

Figure 1 presents the synthetic data generation process. The first step in generating a synthetic data corpus is to define the data use cases. For example, in a digital forensics class, where students will be tested on their knowledge about hard disk analysis, one or more suitable disk images would be required for each student. The students would have to search the disk images for traces of malware or recover multimedia data fragments using tools such as Foremost [1] and Sleuth Kit [2].

The disk images could be created in a reasonable amount of time manually or via scripting. However, if every student should receive different disk images for analysis, then significant effort may have to be expended to insert variations in the images. Also, if different tasks are assigned to different students (e.g., one student should recover JPEG files and another student should search for traces of a rootkit), more significant variations would have to be incorporated in the disk images.

The second step in the corpus generation process is to specify a real-world scenario in which the required kind of data is typically created. One example is a computer that is used by multiple individuals, who typically install and remove software, and download, copy, delete and overwrite files.

The third step is to create a model to match this scenario and serve as the basis of a simulation, which is the last step. A Markov chain consisting of states and state transitions can be created to model user behavior. The states correspond to the actions performed by the users and the transitions specify the actions that can be performed after the preceding actions.

5.1   Scenario Modeling using Markov Chains

Finite discrete-time Markov chains as described in [26] are used for synthetic data generation. One Markov chain is created for each type of subject whose actions are to be simulated. A subject corresponds to a user who performs actions on a hard disk such as software installations and file deletions. The states in the Markov chain correspond to the actions performed by the subject in the scenario.

In order to construct a suitable model, it is necessary to first define all the actions (states) that cause data to be created and deleted. The transitions between actions are then defined. Following this, the probability of each action is specified (state probability) along with the probability of each transition between two actions (transition probability); the probabilities are used during the Markov chain simulation to generate realistic data. The computation of feasible transition probabilities given state probabilities can involve some effort, but the process has been simplified in [28].

Next, the number of subjects who perform the actions are specified (e.g., number of individuals who share the computer). Finally, the details of each possible action are specified (e.g., what exactly happens during a download file action or a delete file action).

5.2   Model-Based Simulation

Having constructed a model of the desired real-world scenario, it is necessary to conduct a simulation based on the model. The number of actions to be performed by each user is specified and the simulation is then started. At the end of the simulation, the disk image contains synthetic data corresponding to the modeled real-world scenario.

5.3   Sample Scenario and Model

To demonstrate the synthetic data generation process, we consider a sample scenario. The purpose for generating the synthetic data is to test how different file carvers deal with fragmented data. The real-world scenario involves an individual who uses an USB memory stick to transfer large amounts of files, mainly photographs, between computers.

In the following, we define all the components in a model that would facilitate the creation of a synthetic disk image of a USB memory stick containing a large number of files, deleted files and file fragments. The resulting disk image would be used to test the ability of file carvers to reconstruct fragmented data.

- **States:** In the sample model, the following four actions are defined as Markov chain states:

  1. *Add Document File*: This action adds a document file (e.g., PDF or DOC) to the filesystem of the synthetic disk image. It is equivalent to copying a file from one hard disk to another using the Linux cp command.

  2. *Add Image File:* This action adds an image file (e.g., JPEG, PNG or GIF) to the filesystem. Again, it is equivalent to using the Linux cp command.

  3. *Write Fragmented Data:* This action takes a random image file, cuts it into multiple fragments and writes the fragments to the disk image, ignoring the filesystem. It is equivalent to using the Linux dd for each file fragment.

  4. *Delete File:* This action removes a random file from the filesystem. It is equivalent to using the Linux rm command.

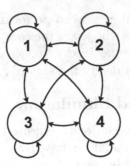

Figure 2.   Markov chain used to generate a synthetic disk image.

- **Transitions:** Next, the transitions between the actions are defined. Since the transitions are not really important in the scenario, the Markov chain is simply constructed as a complete digraph (Figure 2). The state numbers in the Markov chain correspond to the state numbers specified above.

- **State Probabilities:** Next, the probability π_i of each action (state) i to be performed during a Markov chain simulation is specified. We chose the following probabilities for the actions to ensure that a large number of files and file fragments are added to the synthetic disk image and only a maximum of about half of the added files are deleted:

$$\pi = (\pi_1, \ldots, \pi_4) = (0.2, 0.2, 0.4, 0.2).$$

- **State Transition Probabilities:** Finally, the feasible probabilities for the transitions between the actions are computed. The framework is designed to compute the transition probabilities automatically. One possible result is the simple set of transition probabilities specified in the matrix:

$$P = \begin{bmatrix} 0.2 & 0.2 & 0.4 & 0.2 \\ 0.2 & 0.2 & 0.4 & 0.2 \\ 0.2 & 0.2 & 0.4 & 0.2 \\ 0.2 & 0.2 & 0.4 & 0.2 \end{bmatrix}$$

where p_{ij} denotes the probability of a transition from action i to action j.

6.   Corpora Generation Framework

The framework developed for generating synthetic disk images is implemented in Java 1.7. It uses a modular design with a small set of core

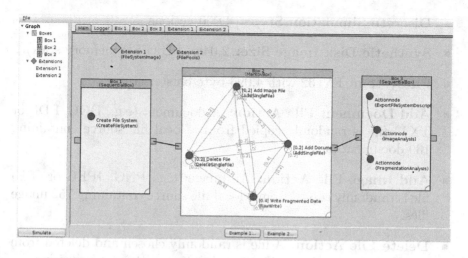

Figure 3. Screenshot of the model builder.

components, a graphical user interface (GUI) and modules that provide specific functionality. The GUI provides a model building interface that allows a model to be created quickly for a specific scenario using the actions available in the framework. Additionally, an image viewer is implemented to provide detailed views of the generated synthetic disk images.

New actions in the framework can be added by implementing a small number of interfaces that require minimal programming effort. Since the framework supports the specification and execution of an abstract synthetic data generation process, new actions can be implemented independently of a scenario for which a synthetic disk image is being created. For example, it is possible to work on a completely different scenario where financial data is to be created in an enterprise relationship management system. The corresponding actions that are relevant to creating the financial data can be implemented in a straightforward matter.

The screenshot in Figure 3 shows the model builder component of the framework. The Markov chain used for generating data corresponding to the sample scenario is shown in the center of the figure (green box).

7.   Framework Evaluation

This section evaluates the performance of the framework. The sample model described above is executed to simulate a computer user who performs write and delete actions on a USB memory stick. The evaluation setup is as follows:

- **Model:** Described in Section 5.3.

- **Discrete Simulation Steps:** 4,000 actions.

- **Synthetic Disk Image Size:** 2,048 MiB (USB memory stick).

- **Filesystem:** FAT32 with 4,096-byte cluster size.

- **Add Document File Action:** A document (e.g., DOC, PDF or TXT) file is randomly copied from a local file source containing 139 document files.

- **Add Image File Action:** An image (e.g., PNG, JPEG or GIF) file is randomly copied from a local file source containing 752 image files.

- **Delete File Action:** A file is randomly chosen and deleted from the filesystem of the synthetic disk image without overwriting.

- **Write Fragmented Data Action:** An image file is randomly chosen from the local file source containing 752 image files. The file is written to the filesystem of the synthetic disk image using a random number of fragments between 2 and 20, a random fragment size corresponding to a multiple of the filesystem cluster size and randomly-selected cluster-aligned locations for fragment insertion.

Twenty simulations of the model were executed using the setup. After each run, the time needed to completely generate the synthetic disk image was assessed, along with the amount of disk space used, number of files deleted, number of files still available in the filesystem and number of different file fragments written to the image.

Figure 4(a) shows the time required by framework to run each simulation. On the average, a simulation run was completed in 2 minutes and 21 seconds. Figure 4(b) presents an overview of the numbers of files that were allocated in and deleted from the synthetic disk images. Note that the allocated (created) files are shown in light gray while the deleted files are shown in dark gray; the average value is shown as a gray line. On the average, a disk image contained 792 allocated files and 803 deleted files, which are expected due to the probabilities chosen for the actions in the model.

Figure 5(a) shows the used disk space in the synthetic image corresponding to allocated files (light gray), deleted files (gray) and file fragments (dark gray). The used space differs considerably over the simulation runs because only the numbers of files to be written and deleted from the disk image were defined (individual file sizes were not specified). Since the files were chosen randomly during the simulation

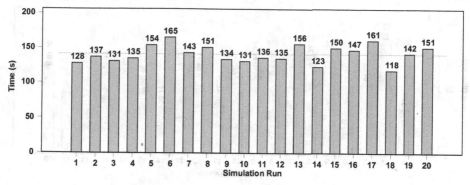

(a) Time required for each simulation run.

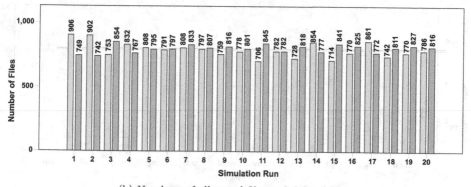

(b) Numbers of allocated files and deleted files.

Figure 4. Evaluation results for 20 simulation runs.

runs, the file sizes and, therefore, the disk space usage differ. On the average, 57% of the available disk space was used.

Figure 5(b) shows the average number of file fragments per file type over all 20 simulation runs. The writing of fragmented data used a dedicated file source containing only pictures; this explains the large numbers of JPEG and PNG fragments.

Figure 6 shows a screenshot of the image viewer provided by the framework. Information such as the data type, fragment size and filesystem status (allocated and deleted) is provided for each block.

8. Conclusions

The framework presented in this paper is well-suited to scenario-based model building and synthetic data generation. In particular, it provides a flexible and efficient approach for generating synthetic data corpora. The

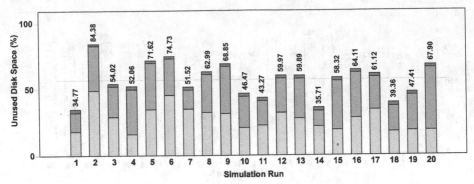

(a) Used disk space corresponding to allocated files, deleted files and file fragments.

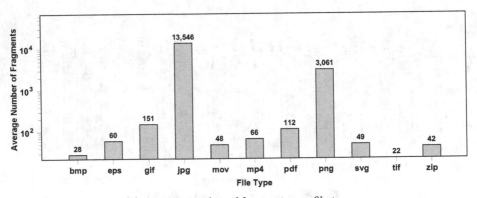

(b) Average number of fragments per file type.

Figure 5.   Evaluation results for 20 simulation runs.

experimental evaluation of creating a synthetic disk image for testing the fragment recovery performance of file carvers demonstrates the utility for the framework.

Unlike real-world corpora, synthetic corpora provide ground truth data that is very important in digital forensics education and research. This enables students as well as developers and testers to acquire detailed understanding of the capabilities and performance of digital forensic tools. The ability of the framework to generate synthetic corpora based on realistic scenarios can satisfy the need for test data in applications for which suitable real-world data corpora are not available. Moreover, the framework is generic enough to produce synthetic corpora for a variety of domains, including forensic accounting and network forensics.

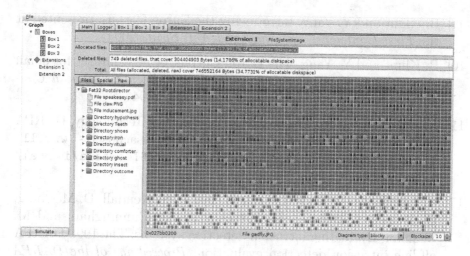

Figure 6. Screenshot of the image viewer.

Acknowledgement

This research was supported by the Center for Advanced Security Research Darmstadt (CASED).

References

[1] Air Force Office of Special Investigations, Foremost (`foremost.sourceforge.net`), 2001.

[2] B. Carrier, The Sleuth Kit (`www.sleuthkit.org/sleuthkit`), 2013.

[3] W. Cohen, Enron Email Dataset, School of Computer Science, Carnegie Mellon University, Pittsburgh, Pennsylvania (`www.cs.cmu.edu/~enron`), 2009.

[4] S. Garfinkel, Forensic corpora, a challenge for forensic research, unpublished manuscript, 2007.

[5] S. Garfinkel, Lessons learned writing digital forensics tools and managing a 30 TB digital evidence corpus, *Digital Investigation*, vol. 9(S), pp. S80–S89, 2012.

[6] S. Garfinkel, Digital Corpora (`digitalcorpora.org`), 2013.

[7] S. Garfinkel, P. Farrell, V. Roussev and G. Dinolt, Bringing science to digital forensics with standardized forensic corpora, *Digital Investigation*, vol. 6(S), pp. S2–S11, 2009.

[8] M. Grgic and K. Delac, Face Recognition Homepage, Zagreb, Croatia (`www.face-rec.org/databases`), 2013.

[9] B. Klimt and Y. Yang, Introducing the Enron Corpus, presented at the *First Conference on Email and Anti-Spam*, 2004.

[10] B. Klimt and Y. Yang, The Enron Corpus: A new dataset for email classification research, *Proceedings of the Fifteenth European Conference on Machine Learning*, pp. 217–226, 2004.

[11] Lincoln Laboratory, Massachusetts Institute of Technology, DARPA Intrusion Detection Data Sets, Lexington, Massachusetts (www.ll.mit.edu/mission/communications/cyber/CSTcorpora/idev al/data), 2013.

[12] R. Lippmann, D. Fried, I. Graf, J. Haines, K. Kendall, D. McClung, D. Weber, S. Webster, D. Wyschogrod, R. Cunningham and M. Zissman, Evaluating intrusion detection systems: The 1998 DARPA off-line intrusion detection evaluation, *Proceedings of the DARPA Information Survivability Conference and Exposition*, vol. 2, pp. 12–26, 2000.

[13] R. Lippmann, J. Haines, D. Fried, J. Korba and K. Das, The 1999 DARPA off-line intrusion detection evaluation, *Computer Networks*, vol. 34(4), pp. 579–595, 2000.

[14] E. Lundin, H. Kvarnstrom and E. Jonsson, A synthetic fraud data generation methodology, *Proceedings of the Fourth International Conference on Information and Communications Security*, pp. 265–277, 2002.

[15] E. Lundin Barse, H. Kvarnstrom and E. Jonsson, Synthesizing test data for fraud detection systems, *Proceedings of the Nineteenth Annual Computer Security Applications Conference*, pp. 384–394, 2003.

[16] J. McHugh, Testing intrusion detection systems: A critique of the 1998 and 1999 DARPA intrusion detection system evaluations as performed by Lincoln Laboratory, *ACM Transactions on Information and System Security*, vol. 3(4), pp. 262–294, 2000.

[17] C. Moch and F. Freiling, The Forensic Image Generator Generator (Forensig2), *Proceedings of the Fifth International Conference on IT Security Incident Management and IT Forensics*, pp. 78–93, 2009.

[18] C. Moch and F. Freiling, Evaluating the Forensic Image Generator Generator, *Proceedings of the Third International Conference on Digital Forensics and Cyber Crime*, pp. 238–252, 2011.

[19] National Institute of Standards and Technology, The CFReDS Project, Gaithersburg, Maryland (www.cfreds.nist.gov), 2013.

[20] K. Ricanek and T. Tesafaye, Morph: A longitudinal image database of normal adult age-progression, *Proceedings of the Seventh International Conference on Automatic Face and Gesture Recognition*, pp. 341–345, 2006.

[21] M. Steinebach, H. Liu and Y. Yannikos, FaceHash: Face detection and robust hashing, presented at the *Fifth International Conference on Digital Forensics and Cyber Crime*, 2013.

[22] T. Vidas, MemCorp: An open data corpus for memory analysis, *Proceedings of the Forty-Fourth Hawaii International Conference on System Sciences*, 2011.

[23] Volatilty, The Volatility Framework (`code.google.com/p/volatility`), 2014.

[24] WikiLeaks, The Global Intelligence Files (`wikileaks.org/the-gifiles.html`), 2013.

[25] K. Woods, C. Lee, S. Garfinkel, D. Dittrich, A. Russell and K. Kearton, Creating realistic corpora for security and forensic education, *Proceedings of the ADFSL Conference on Digital Forensics, Security and Law*, 2011.

[26] Y. Yannikos, F. Franke, C. Winter and M. Schneider, 3LSPG: Forensic tool evaluation by three layer stochastic process-based generation of data, *Proceedings of the Fourth International Conference on Computational Forensics*, pp. 200–211, 2010.

[27] Y. Yannikos and C. Winter, Model-based generation of synthetic disk images for digital forensic tool testing, *Proceedings of the Eighth International Conference on Availability, Reliability and Security*, pp. 498–505, 2013.

[28] Y. Yannikos, C. Winter and M. Schneider, Synthetic data creation for forensic tool testing: Improving performance of the 3LSPG Framework, *Proceedings of the Seventh International Conference on Availability, Reliability and Security*, pp. 613–619, 2012.

Chapter 22

EDUCATING THE NEXT GENERATION OF CYBERFORENSIC PROFESSIONALS

Mark Pollitt and Philip Craiger

Abstract   This paper provides a historical overview of the development of cyber-forensics as a scientific discipline, along with a description of the current state of training, educational programs, certification and accreditation. The paper traces the origins of cyberforensics, the acceptance of cyberforensics as forensic science and its recognition as a component of information security. It also discusses the development of professional certifications and standardized bodies of knowledge that have had a substantial impact on the discipline. Finally, it discusses the accreditation of cyberforensic educational programs, its linkage with the bodies of knowledge and its effect on cyberforensic educational programs.

Keywords: Digital forensics, education, certification, accreditation

1.   Introduction

Cyberforensics, also referred to as digital forensics, computer forensics and multimedia forensics, has a relatively short history. A new science, it has displayed rapid growth for several reasons, perhaps the most important of which is the world's increasing reliance on technology for computing and communications. The field changes rapidly due to advances in technology. The most illustrative example is the smartphone, which, unlike cellular phones of the past, is essentially a small, but powerful, personal computer. Although smartphones were introduced about a decade ago, a recent study has found that nearly 60% of American adults own a smartphone [18]. Other new technologies, such as wearable computers (e.g., Google Glass [10]) and life-enhancing technologies (e.g., driverless cars [16]) will drive the need for educated, trained and certified cyberforensic professionals. This paper explores where the dis-

G. Peterson and S. Shenoi (Eds.): Advances in Digital Forensics X, IFIP AICT 433, pp. 327–335, 2014.

cipline of cyberforensics has been, its current state and what the future
may hold.

The first question is: Is cyberforensics a scientific discipline? The
best way to answer this question is to observe how other sciences are
defined. We suggest the use of Thomas Kuhn's framework. In his book
The Structure of Scientific Revolutions [15], Kuhn says that "normal science" is defined by a common paradigm. The paradigm is a shared set
of theories, practices and models that are acknowledged by the community. The paradigm serves both a research purpose and an educational
purpose. The former allows scientists the luxury of relying on a foundation of acknowledged principles, freeing them from having to build a
foundation for every new research effort and having to re-articulate the
basis of every single element of research. It also serves an important
purpose in defining the things that a student must know in order to become a researcher or a practitioner. Ultimately, according to Kuhn, it is
the combination of shared models, educational experience and discipline-
specific language that define a mature science.

We posit that cyberforensics is a mature scientific discipline, notwith-
standing the fact that as technology changes, so must the discipline. To
support this argument, we offer brief histories of the practice of cyberforensics, the accreditation of cyberforensic laboratories and educational
programs, and the certification of cyberforensic practitioners. Note that
the term "accreditation" describes the process by which an external body
determines that a particular, unit, laboratory or educational program
meets the requirements of the education and/or practitioner communities, and "certification" is the attestation that an individual meets the
standards of a competent practitioner.

2.   Cyberforensics

It is difficult to identify the precise moment that the discipline of
cyberforensics started. Perhaps it was shortly after the very first digital computer was invented. But the term "computer forensics" did not
come into its own until the 1980s, when the Federal Bureau of Investigation (FBI) and the U.S. Internal Revenue Service (IRS) created small
teams of agents to conduct searches of mainframe computers in connection with criminal cases. By the early 1990s, personal computers
had become commonplace. Criminal investigators realized that computers were potentially a rich source of evidence. Local, state and federal
agencies launched programs to exploit this potential source of evidence.
The first training programs for what would be called "computer foren-

sic examiners" began at the Federal Law Enforcement Training Center (FLETC) in Glenco, Georgia [19].

During the mid 1990s, the explosion of the Internet facilitated many new computer-based crimes. In addition to computer and telecommunications fraud, child pornography became a law enforcement problem of unprecedented size. Online undercover operations, which sought to identify and prosecute subjects who were creating and exchanging child pornography, drove a massive need for cyberforensic examinations. Child pornography and all the other Internet-based crimes accelerated through the millennium and into the current era of global cloud computing [19].

Today, with the reality of ubiquitous mobile computing, cloud computing, social networks and other technologies, vast quantities of potential digital evidence are being produced at a phenomenal rate. The use of digital evidence in civil litigation has likewise exploded. Cyberforensic techniques and methodologies have become essential tools in information security and incident response. Cyberforensic examiners require broad and deep technical knowledge as well strong investigative skills.

3. Origins of Cyberforensics Training

A number of watershed events have steered the disorganized practice of forensics into a scientific discipline. Arguably, the creation of formal training and certification programs laid the first foundation for the discipline. In 1991, the International Association of Computer Investigative Specialists (IACIS) [11] was formed and it soon launched formal efforts to train law enforcement officers in conducting forensic examinations of computers. IACIS also created the first certification program for practitioners [19].

The establishment of formal law enforcement units to conduct digital forensic examinations also played a major role in the development of cyberforensics as a discipline. In 1992, the FBI created the Computer Analysis Response Team (CART) at the FBI Laboratory in Quantico, Virginia. This unit, along with similar units in the United States Secret Service (USSS) and the IRS would play important roles in the creation of stakeholder organizations that would develop standards for the nascent discipline. The FBI developed its own training unit and staff at the FBI Academy in Quantico, Virginia, while the USSS, IRS and others developed a robust training facility at FLETC in Glynco, Georgia [19].

In the late 1990s, commercial forensic tools became available. Vendors began to offer courses to train new users in the use of their tools and subsequently offered certifications such as EnCase Certified Examiner

(EnCE) [9] and Access Data Certified Examiner (ACE) [1]. Initially, these vendor certifications were the only certifications available outside of law enforcement agencies and other government organizations [19].

4.   Cyberforensic Functional Standards

In 1995, some 20 agencies from countries such as the United States, United Kingdom, France, Australia, The Netherlands and Sweden set up the International Organization on Computer Evidence (IOCE) [13]. This organization would go on to develop and promulgate the principles on which standards would be built. The IOCE Principles were developed from principles originally proposed by the Association of Chief Police Officers (ACPO) from the United Kingdom. While the ACPO principles were important, in and of themselves, it was the international consensus obtained by IOCE that was revolutionary. It marked the first time that disparate organizations publicly acknowledged a shared view of the forensic examination process. In 2000, the Group of Eight (G8) Subgroup on High Technology Crime voted to accept the IOCE Principles, thus gaining political recognition of the consensus view of the digital forensic community [19].

In 1998, the Scientific Working Group on Digital Evidence (SWGDE) [20] was established. The stated goal of this organization was to develop standards for the governance of digital forensics within the United States. SWGDE also sought to have digital forensics identified as a legitimate forensic laboratory discipline. SWGDE worked with the Association of Crime Laboratory Directors – Laboratory Accreditation Board (ASCLD-LAB) [4] to make digital evidence an accreditable discipline for crime laboratories. In 2003, ASCLD-LAB accredited the first digital evidence unit. As of 2013, ASCLD-LAB had accredited 73 digital evidence laboratories.

Meanwhile, the European forensic science community developed its own working group called the European Network of Forensic Science Institutes – Forensic Information Technology Working Group (ENFSI-FITWG) [7]. This group continues to provide a forum for training and standards development [19].

Near the end of the first decade of the 21st century, the United States Government established the National Initiative for Cybersecurity Education (NICE) [17]. This initiative sought to identify the knowledge, skills, experience and academic preparation needed for the cybersecurity workforce. The resulting NICE Framework (Version 1.0) identifies seven functional specialty areas. One of the areas is "Investigative Specialty," which has a sub-area dedicated to cyberforensics. In 2013 and 2014,

NICE utilized focus groups from the stakeholder communities to further develop the core definitions and duties associated with each specialty area and sub-area. The first author of this paper participated in this activity, and he can attest that the functional standards described above were relied upon heavily in the focus group deliberations. Version 2 of the NICE Framework, incorporating the work of the focus groups, is expected to be promulgated in 2014.

5.   Educational Program Accreditation

A number of organizations focusing on education, training and certification were established to ensure that practitioners would be knowledgeable in the principles and practice of cyberforensics. In 2006, the Technical Working Group on Education – Digital Evidence (TWGED-DE) was created by the National Institutes of Justice. This working group brought together academics (including the second author of this paper) and practitioners to develop a common understanding of the required knowledge and skills for digital forensic practitioners. TWGED-DE produced a document outlining the best practices for cyberforensics education and training [22]. This document has been the basis of much subsequent work in the discipline [8].

In 2008, the American Academy of Forensic Sciences (AAFS), the premier American professional organization for forensic sciences, established its Digital and Multimedia Sciences Section [3]. The section was formed with approximately 40 members. As of 2014, it had nearly 100 members.

Traditional forensic science education programs have existed for many years. However, as a result of the work done by TWGED-DE, AAFS created the Forensic Science Education Program Accreditation Commission (FEPAC) [8] in 2004. FEPAC focuses on the accreditation of digital forensic education programs. In 2012, FEPAC accredited its first master's program in digital evidence at Marshall University.

Recognizing the need for digital forensic practitioners in the U.S. Department of Defense, the Defense Cyber Crime Center (DC3) brought together a number of academics and practitioners to develop a certification and accreditation program for the Department of Defense called the Centers of Digital Forensics Academic Excellence (CDFAE) [5]. The standards, developed by consensus, drew on bodies of knowledge that were previously identified by other organizations, including ASCLD-LAB, TWGED-DE, FEPAC and the Digital Forensics Certification Board (DFCB) [6]. In 2013, CDFAE accredited its first two-year academic program [5].

In 2012, the Advanced Technology Education Program of the National Science Foundation (NSF-ATE) invested nearly $2 million in the Advanced Cyberforensics Education (ACE) Consortium [2] for the express purpose of developing cyberforensic education programs that meet the needs of government and industry. The authors of this paper are the Principal and Co-Principal Investigators, respectively, of the ACE effort. Key ACE initiatives are to develop and disseminate course curricula (including syllabi, course materials and laboratory exercises) and to conduct faculty training programs that will meet the educational accreditation standards of FEPAC and CDFAE. The goals of ACE are to: (i) ensure that faculty know and teach the core knowledge of the field; (ii) ensure that faculty teach courses that meet the needs of employers; (iii) ensure that academic institutions develop programs that are accreditable; (iv) prepare students for professional certifications; and (v) provide education and training opportunities for displaced professionals.

6.   Practitioner Certification

Similar to the development of standards and accreditations, the certification of cyberforensic practitioners grew organically. The first certification for professionals was likely created by the International Association of Computer Investigative Specialists (IACIS) in 1991. IACIS hosted *ab initio* training courses that were available only to sworn law enforcement professionals. Since training and certification predated the development of commercial digital forensic software, the courses focused heavily on understanding the operation of computers, operating systems, file systems and applications. Foundational tools such as hex editors were utilized in a methodological way to exploit the practitioner's understanding of the technology for forensic purposes [13, 19]. This instituted the paradigm of requiring professional certifications to cover a foundational set of knowledge, a forensic methodology and tool usage.

In the late 1990s, integrated commercial tools such as EnCase [9] and Forensic Toolkit [1] were sufficiently complex that practitioners required special training to utilize them effectively. Vendors thus began to offer training courses on the use of their tools; the courses were typically two to five days in length. While the vast majority of the training focused on using tools, some basic knowledge was covered to ensure that the participants had a common baseline. At the end of the training courses, the participants were offered the opportunity to take written and practical tests and be "certified" by the vendors. Formal training in these complex tools is necessary and important. Nevertheless, it is abundantly clear that a short tool-centered class does not provide the full range of knowledge and experience that defines a cyberforensic professional.

Over the past decade or so, a number of organizations in addition to IACIS have developed and fostered "professional certifications" that seek to recognize individuals who have broad foundational knowledge as well as adequate practical experience to demonstrate a professional level of competence in the cyberforensics field [19, 21]. Examples of these professional certifications are the Certified Computer Examiner (CCE) from the International Society of Forensic Computer Examiners (ISFCE) [14], Certified Forensic Computer Examiner (CFCE) from IACIS [11], Digital Forensics Certified Practitioner (DFCP) from DFCB [6] and Certified Cyber Forensics Professional (CCFP) from (ISC)^2 [12]. The authors of this paper were actively involved in developing some of these professional certifications and can vouch for the tremendous difficulty in developing such certifications. In 2014, the DC3 in conjunction with the CDFAE Accreditation Program [5] began to issue certifications to individual students who completed CDFAE-approved academic programs and passed written and practical tests.

While the certifications differ, they share a common set of requirements. All of them require demonstrated mastery of a core set of knowledge coupled with demonstrated skill and experience. Especially interesting is the fact that the core knowledge required by each of the certifications is remarkably similar. This should not be surprising because many of the individuals who contributed to the development of these certifications also helped set the functional and academic standards that were discussed previously.

7. Conclusions

Training, education, professional certifications and organizational accreditation have made substantial inroads in the cyberforensics field during the past decade. One might surmise that this is merely a "happy coincidence." However, we posit that, given the wide range of educators, practitioners, managers and government officials involved, the events described in this paper are evidence of the development of a paradigm that corresponds to the concept of "normal science" according to Kuhn [15]. Indeed, what has emerged is a common view of the fundamentals that form the basis of cyberforensics, an acknowledged set of processes that constitute the practice of cyberforensics, and an agreed set of norms that define the ethical conduct of cyberforensics.

The future is bright. The cyberforensics community is engaged in an active dialog involving government and industry, academics and prac-

titioners, investigators and forensic examiners, as well as certification
and accreditation bodies. This collaboration will enable standards to
evolve quickly in the dynamic world of technology. No doubt, there will
be bumps in the road. But the constant challenges and evolution that
characterize "normal science" will continue to strengthen cyberforensics
as a scientific discipline.

References

[1] AccessData, AccessData, Lindon, Utah (`www.accessdata.com`).

[2] Advanced Cyberforensics Education Consortium, Advanced Cyberforensics Education (ACE), Daytona State College, Daytona, Florida (`cyberace.org`).

[3] American Academy of Forensic Sciences, Digital and Multimedia Sciences, Colorado Springs, Colorado (`aafs.org/about/sections/digital-multimedia-sciences`).

[4] American Society of Crime Laboratory Directors/Laboratory Accreditation Board, Accredited Laboratory Index, Garner, North Carolina (`www.ascld-lab.org/accredited-laboratory-index`).

[5] Defense Cyber Crime Center, CDFAE, Linthicum, Maryland (`www.dc3.mil/cyber-training/cdfae`).

[6] Digital Forensics Certification Board, Digital Forensics Certification Board (DFCB) (`dfcb.org`).

[7] European Network of Forensic Science Institutes, Structure, Warsaw, Poland (`www.enfsi.eu/about-enfsi/structure`).

[8] Forensic Science Education Program Accreditation Commission, Forensic Science Education Program Accreditation Commission (FEPAC), Colorado Springs, Colorado (`fepac-edu.org`).

[9] Guidance Software, Guidance Software, Pasadena, California (`www.guidancesoftware.com`).

[10] M. Honan, I, Glasshole: My year with Google Glass, *Wired* (`www.wired.com/2013/12/glasshole`), December 30, 2013.

[11] International Association of Computer Investigative Specialists, About IACIS, Leesburg, Virginia (`www.iacis.com/about/overview`).

[12] International Information Systems Security Certification Consortium, (ISC)^2, Clearwater, Florida (`www.isc2.org//default.aspx`).

[13] International Organization on Computer Evidence, Guidelines for Best Practice in the Forensic Examination of Digital Technology (`www.ioce.org/fileadmin/user_upload/2002/ioce_bp_exam_digit_tech.html`).

[14] International Society of Forensic Computer Examiners, International Society of Forensic Computer Examiners (ISFCE), Brentwood, Tennessee (`www.isfce.com/index.html`).

[15] T. Kuhn, *The Structure of Scientific Revolutions*, University of Chicago Press, Chicago, Illinois, 1996.

[16] J. Markoff, Google cars drive themselves, in traffic, *New York Times*, October 9, 2010.

[17] National Institute of Standards and Technology, National Initiative for Cybersecurity Education (NICE), Gaithersburg, Maryland (`csrc.nist.gov/nice`).

[18] Pew Research Internet Project, Mobile Technology Fact Sheet, Pew Research Center, Washington, DC (www.pewinternet.org/fact-sheets/mobile-technology-fact-sheet), 2014.

[19] M. Pollitt, A history of digital forensics, in *Advances in Digital Forensics VI*, K. Chow and S. Shenoi (Eds.), Springer, Heidelberg, Germany, pp. 3–15, 2010.

[20] Scientific Working Group on Digital Evidence, Scientific Working Group on Digital Evidence (`www.swgde.org`).

[21] E. Tittel, Best computer forensics certifications for 2014, *Tom's IT Pro* (`www.tomsitpro.com/articles/computer-forensics-certifications,2-650.html`), November 15, 2013.

[22] West Virginia University Forensic Science Initiative, Technical Working Group for Education and Training in Digital Forensics, Morgantown, West Virginia (`www.ncjrs.gov/pdffiles1/nij/grants/219380.pdf`), 2007.

Printed in the United States
By Bookmasters